CW00385343

AppleRN Study Guide
Next Gen NCLEX-RN®

www.AppleRN.com

Prepared by

Dr. Anila Simon PhD, RN

This book is a supplement to the course conducted by AppleRN Classes.

To be fully effective, use the book in combination with the course.

To enroll in courses please visit our

website www.AppleRN.com

or contact any of our associates at

+1 651-615-5511 (USA)

+91 953-930-5316 (India)

(WhatsApp available on all numbers)

Copyright © 2023 AppleRN Classes

All rights reserved.

ISBN: 9798396568174

Index

Topic	Page	Topic	Page Number
Legal and Ethics	1	Eyes, Ears, and Nose	305
Infection Control & Infectious Diseases	13	Gastrointestinal System	319
Basic Safety and Comfort	34	Nutrition and Therapeutic Diets	349
Diagnostic Procedures & Care	50	GI Medications	354
Community Health Nursing	62	Endocrine System	360
Surgical Care	74	Endocrine Medications	382
NCLEX Specific Tubes and Care	81	Musculoskeletal System	388
Maternity Nursing	90	Musculoskeletal Medications	407
Pediatrics	127	Integumentary System	411
Maternity Medications	148	Hematological Concepts	425
ABG, Respiratory system	151	Oncology	437
Respiratory Medications	176	Immunology	466
Cardiovascular system	180	Hematology/Oncology Medications	472
Cardiac dysrhythmias - ECG	209	Psychosocial Concepts	483
Critical care special Topics	220	Psychosocial Medications	525
Pediatric Cardiovascular Disorders	234	Pharmacology Concepts	530
Cardiovascular Medications	243	Cultural Aspects	537
Neurology	249	Fluid and Electrolytes	540
Renal and Reproductive System	289	Evidence Based Practice	548
Renal and GU medications	303	Bioterrorism	549

Legal and Ethical Considerations

Advance directive

Overview

- Documents to communicate a client's wishes regarding end-of-life care; should the client become unable to do so.
- Two components- Living will (client's wishes) and durable medical power of attorney (a person designated to make decisions for the client, also called Health care proxy).

Nursing responsibility

- Give client information about advance directive.
- Inform and update heath care team about the status and contents of advance directive.
- Conflict? -Client's choice takes priority
- Document status of advance directive. Ensure that the advance directive is updated.

Advocacy

- Nurses' role in supporting clients by ensuring that they are properly informed, their rights are respected, they are receiving the proper level of care. Nurses must act as advocates even when they disagree with clients' decisions.
- Nurses are accountable for their actions even if they are carrying out a provider's prescription. It is the nurse's responsibility to question a provider's prescription if it could harm a client.
- Nurses must ensure that clients are informed of their rights. Do not direct or control client's decisions. Nurses may need to mediate on the client's behalf when changes need to be made in the plan of care.

- Situations in which nurses may need to advocate for clients or assist them to advocate for themselves include End-of-life decisions, Access to health care, Protection of client privacy, Informed consent, Substandard practice.

Privacy and Confidentiality

- Privacy is the patient's expectation to be treated with dignity and respect.
- Confidentiality is safeguarding patient information.
- Use only the minimum required information to take care of the patient.
- Do not tell unit clerk or a transporter about the actual diagnosis or prognosis of client. OK to tell them about safety precautions.
- The nurse is required to report an impaired coworker, a suspicious death, and abuse to appropriate authorities.
- The nurse is legally prohibited from sharing health information with client's employers or family members without the client's permission.

Ethical Dilemma

- A particular type of ethical problem: Situation in which a choice must be made between two equally undesirable actions.
- Nurses' role: identify such situation and refer to ethical principles to choose the right path of action.

Ethical principles

- **Confidentiality:** Privileged information should be kept private. Communications between the nurse and the patient should not be divulged to third parties.
- Justice: Treating every client equally regardless of gender, sexual orientation, religion, ethnicity, disease, or social standing
- **Autonomy** is freedom for a competent client to make decisions for oneself.
- **Accountability** is accepting responsibility for one's actions
- **Beneficence**: It is a nurse's responsibility to do good. Good care requires a holistic approach to patients, which includes attention to their beliefs, feelings, and wishes.

- **Nonmaleficence** means doing no harm.
  - It also relates to protecting clients who are unable to protect themselves due to their physical or mental condition (infants/children, dementia, sedated)
- **Fidelity** – faithful devotion to duty – the duty to keep one's promises or word: Keeping an appointment with a client is an example of fidelity. Nurses should keep commitments to others. Fidelity includes loyalty to agreements and responsibilities accepted as part of the practice of nursing.
- **Veracity:** Nurses should tell the truth and not intentionally deceive or mislead patients.

AMA: Against Medical Advice

- A competent client can refuse medical treatment and **leave against medical advice** (AMA).
- Inform the health care provider. Charge nurse can help.
- Explain the consequences to the client.
- Decides to leave the facility, even after explanation - Give AMA form (informed refusal) and allowed to go. Refuses to sign? still allowed to leave.
- OK to give discharge instructions, results, and prescriptions despite the client leaving AMA. Remove **IV catheter.** Document completely.

Incident Report

- Incident reports - records made of unexpected or unusual incidents that affected a client, employee, volunteer, or visitor in a health care facility.
- Completed by the person who identifies incident (within 24 hours of the incident). Include witnesses' names.
- Confidential and are not shared with the client. Not placed in records.
- However, a description of the incident itself should be documented factually in the client's record (including treatment)

Examples of Incident Reports

- Medication errors, Procedure/treatment errors
- Equipment-related injuries/errors, Needle stick injuries
- Client falls/injuries, Visitor/volunteer injuries. Threat made to client or staff
- Loss of property (dentures, jewelry, personal wheelchair)

Sentinel event

- Any unanticipated event in a health care setting that results in death or serious physical or psychological injury.
- All sentinel events should be reported.
- Collaboration/Multidisciplinary/Case Management
- Collaboration - discussion of client care issues -multiple problems.

- Multidisciplinary – across department

Case management - the coordination of care

- The goal - avoid fragmentation of care and control cost.
- Facilitating continuity of care. Utilization of resources.
- Limiting unnecessary costs and lengthy stays.
- Advocating for the client and family

Client Rights

Each client has the right to:

- Be informed about all aspects of care and take an active role in the decision-making process.
- Accept, refuse, or request modification to the plan of care.
- Receive care that is delivered by competent individuals who treat the client with respect.

Liability

- Tort- doing something harmful to others.
- Intentional tort – harming intentionally.
- Unintentional Tort - Negligence: The unintentional harm a client experiences because the nurse failed to act in a reasonable and prudent manner. A nurse fails /forgets to implement safety measures for a client.

Malpractice (professional negligence)

- Not reasonable at all (can be with negligence)
- A nurse administers a large dose of medication due to a calculation error.
- The client has a cardiac arrest and dies.

Common Negligent Acts

- Failure to assess and/or monitor, including making a nursing diagnosis.

- Failure to monitor in a timely fashion. Failure to use proper equipment to monitor the patient. Failure to document the monitoring.
- Failure to notify the health care provider of problems.
- Failure to follow orders. Failure to follow the six rights of medication administration. Failure to convey discharge instructions.
- Failure to ensure patient safety, especially for patients who have a history of falling, are heavily sedated, have disequilibrium problems, are frail, are mentally impaired, get up at night, and are uncooperative.
- Failure to follow policies and procedures. Failure to properly delegate and supervise.

Assault: The conduct of one person makes another person fearful and apprehensive

Battery

- Intentional and wrongful physical contact with a person that involves an injury or offensive contact. (Performing a procedure which client refuses - restraining a client and administering an injection against his wishes, giving medicines which are placebo).

False imprisonment: A person is confined or restrained against his will (confinement)

Informed Consent

Informed consent consists of three principles:

- 1. The **surgeon clearly explains** the current diagnosis, planned procedure along with risks and benefits, expected outcome, alternate treatment options, and prognosis if the procedure is not performed.
- 2. The client has indicated **their understanding** of the information.
- 3. The client is giving **voluntary**, legal consent to the procedure.

Special cases for Consent

- Interpreter should only provide literal translation of the words spoken by the HCP, not adding any personal advice/information.
- Lifesaving measures are needed?? – consent is not necessary (Good Samaritan law)
- If the need for an additional procedure is discovered during surgery, the client's family may give consent after speaking with the surgeon.

Adolescent can give consent (US)

- Emancipated adolescent: Independent - 16 years old and married, or serving U.S. army / living apart from parents and managing own money
- Adolescent with court decision granted as emancipated.
- Mature adolescent (in some cases): 14- 18 yrs. old can refuse/receive treatment for STI, family planning, alcohol and drugs abuse, blood donation and mental health care
- Who is a mentally or emotionally incompetent client? An individual who has been declared incompetent/ is unconscious/ is under the influence of chemical agents such as alcohol or drugs/ has chronic dementia or another mental deficiency that impairs thought processes and the ability to make decisions.

Delegation

- Nurses can only delegate tasks appropriate for the skill and education level of the health care provider who is receiving the assignment.
- RNs must delegate tasks so that they can complete higher level tasks that only RNs can perform.

RNs cannot delegate to LPNs or AP

- Nursing process (assessment {initial/critical}, planning, diagnosis)
- Client education – initial / clinical correlation /acute setting
- Tasks that require clinical judgment

- The nurse delegating a task remains legally responsible for the client's total care during the shift and may be held liable for delegating inappropriately.
- The registered nurse makes assignments according to staff members' experience, knowledge, and skill level.
- The more experienced – unstable patients
- New graduates/new nurse – stable patients
- The LPN should be assigned stable clients with expected outcomes.
- **Critical value:** A nurse or practitioner must personally take a laboratory critical value result and then initiate the appropriate steps for the needed interventions (no unit clerk or UAP)

Five Rights of Delegation

- Right task: What tasks should be delegated
- Right circumstance: Under what circumstances
- Right person: To whom (LPN? UAP?)
- Right direction/communication: What information should be communicated
- Right supervision/evaluation: How to supervise/evaluate

Conflicts

- When there is inter-staff disagreement, it is important to not have a public "show."
- Conflict with a physician? - Immediately leave and go to a private area.
- In managing the team, first find out (assess) the reason for a refusal to do a task. (If CNA refuses to do a task, ask for the reason first).
- Emphasize the common goal of working toward safe, quality client care.
- Defamation – damaging reputation of others by writing (libel) or verbally (slander)

Float Nurse

- To help with staffing. Float nurse should be given clients within the competency level of float nurse (acuity)

- Float nurse should inform supervisor if they are not competent/lack experience. A resource nurse will help float nurse in new unit.
- Nurses cannot "walk out" on patients when there is staffing issues – "charge of abandonment."

Quality/ Process/Performance improvement

- To improve client safety
- Every nurse is involved – common goal for effective client care outcome.
- Retrospective (past) and concurrent (same time) audits and peer reviews are part of QI
- Multidisciplinary collaboration / staff engagements are needed.

Nursing hand off

- Use accurate information.
- No vague statements.
- Routine care - is not necessary to report (bath, oral care)
- Give report at bedside (ideal)
- After shift, any information - shred

SBAR Communication Tool

- Situation, Background, Assessment, Recommendation
- Developed to increase handover quality.
- Increase patient safety.

All relevant information, organized in a logical fashion.

	Ask yourself	Example
S- Situation	Why am I calling doctor now? What made me pick up the phone?	Ms. Judy is having chest pain 7/10
B- Background	What was the context? What is the background?	She is the 70 years old female had knee replacement surgery yesterday
A- Assessment	What are the findings you can add? Lab/radiology/physical examination/clinical correlation	Her blood pressure is 150/90, saturation is 92 in room air and ECG shows Atrial fibrillation
R- Recommendation	What do you recommend?	I think she is having a cardiac event; I need you to come and see the client right now.

Bullying

- A bully uses their power to control/harm others.
- Verbal bullying is saying or writing mean things.
- Teasing, Name-calling, Inappropriate sexual comments, Threatening.
- Social bullying (Relational bullying) -hurting someone's reputation or relationships.
- Leaving someone out on purpose
- Telling other children not to be friends with someone
- Spreading rumors about someone, Embarrassing someone in public
- Physical bullying involves hurting a person's body or possessions.
- Hitting/kicking/pinching/Spitting, Tripping/pushing
- Taking or breaking someone's things, Making mean or rude hand gestures.

Victim Experiences:

- Depression and anxiety, increased feelings of sadness and loneliness
- Changes in sleep and eating patterns.
- Loss of interest in activities they used to enjoy.
- Health complaints

- Decreased academic achievement—GPA and standardized test scores—and school participation.
- They are more likely to miss, skip, or drop out of school.

Intimate partner violence (IPV) / Domestic violence

- Intimate partner violence (IPV) is abuse or aggression that occurs in a romantic relationship.
- "Intimate partner" refers to both current and former spouses and dating partners.
- IPV includes four types of behavior: Physical violence, Sexual violence, Stalking and Psychological

Community Resources

- Physical interventions include the care and treatment of any physical injuries.
- Services based on the unique needs and circumstances of victims and survivors and coordinated among community agencies and victim advocates.
- Shelter, hotlines, crisis intervention and counseling
- Housing programs - emergency shelter, transitional housing
- Legal help – protection orders

Electronic Health Record (EHR)

- Accurate, up-to-date, and complete information about patients at the point of care
- Quick and secure access to patient records, Privacy of data
- Helping providers more effectively diagnose patients, reduce medical errors, and provide safer care.
- Improving patient and provider interaction and communication
- Enabling safer, more reliable prescribing, promote legible, complete documentation.
- Accurate, streamlined coding and billing.

- Reducing costs through decreased paperwork, improved safety, reduced duplication of testing, and improved health.

Documentation Error

- Draw a straight line through the error.
- The nurse must initial and date it.
- Errors in charting on a paper chart should never be obliterated, recopied, or covered with correction fluid.
- The nurse should not leave blank lines on a chart or chart for anyone else.
- When entering nursing information on the client's chart, nurses should close the chart completely and sign off before leaving the client's room.

Mass casualty incident

- Goal - greatest good for the greatest number of casualties.
- Priority: airway, breathing, and circulation who are likely to survive.
- "Red," -client with a life-threatening injury who is likely to survive if receiving prompt treatment (<60 minutes). They go first.
- "Yellow," or second to go, can wait 1-2 hours without loss of life or limb.
- **"Green"** is considered the "walking wounded," who can wait indefinitely.
- "Black,": indicates the client is unlikely to survive given the severity of injuries, level of available care, or both. Last to go.

INFECTION CONTROL

Asepsis

- Medical asepsis – The use of precise practices to reduce the number, growth, and spread of micro-organisms ("clean technique"). It applies to administering oral medication, managing nasogastric tubes, providing personal hygiene, and performing many other common nursing tasks.
- Surgical asepsis – The use of precise practices to eliminate all micro-organisms from an object or area and prevent contamination ("sterile technique"). It applies to parenteral medication administration, insertion of urinary catheters, surgical procedures, sterile dressing changes, and many other common nursing procedures.

Latex Allergy

- Latex allergy is a reaction to certain proteins in latex rubber.
- **Highly** Associated food – **ABCK** – Avocado, Banana, Chestnut, Kiwi
- **Moderately** Associated food - ACCMPPT – Apple, Carrot, Celery, Melons, Papaya, Potato, Tomato
- Allergy - Can occur within minutes or hours later (depends on each case)
- Symptoms varies – rash/itching to respiratory distress.
- Prevention – use non latex products, wear a medical alert band.
- "Hypoallergenic" is Not equal to "latex-free."
- "Latex safe" zone for highly allergic workers - specially designated areas where only non-powdered latex and non-latex gloves and medical devices are used.
- The powder used in latex gloves – airborne- if inhaled by a latex allergic person – can cause symptoms.
- Have EpiPen available- epinephrine (adrenaline) auto-injector - IM.
- Other Clues in NCLEX questions: Balloons, elastic bands, rubber raincoats and rain boots, latex condoms, rubber bathmats, and rubber grips on toothbrushes, blood pressure cuffs, tourniquets, IV tubing, catheters, medication vial stopper.

- Latex allergies (for client and HC)

Hand Hygiene

Always use **hand hygiene**

- before and after every client contact,
- after removing gloves,
- after contact with body fluids,
- after contact with anything in clients' rooms
- after touching any contaminated items (whether or not gloves were worn)
- before putting gloves on and after taking them off.
- before eating, and after using the restroom.
- When hands are visibly soiled, wash them with soap and water.

Hand washing – Reminders

- Wash hands with soap and warm water. Rub hands together vigorously (15-20 seconds), and rinse under running water.
- Keep hands lower than the forearms so that water flows toward the fingertips.
- After washing, dry hands with a clean paper towel before turning off the faucet.
- The hands are dried, moving from the fingers to the forearms.
- Use a clean, dry paper towel to turn off the faucet.
- Alcohol-based hand sanitizer - Cover all surfaces until hands feel dry (about 20 sec). Surgical hand wash –antimicrobial soap- 2-6 minutes.

Health Care-Associated Infections (HAIs)

- Nosocomial/Hospital acquired.
- Client acquires while receiving care in a health care setting – UTI, Wound infection, C-Diff, MRSA, VRE
- Client and care giver education – Hand washing
- adequate fluids- prevents urinary stasis and skin break down.

- Ensure that pulmonary hygiene (turning, coughing, deep breathing, incentive spirometry). Cover cough

Standard Precautions

- Applies to all clients. Hand hygiene, Gloves
- Gown, Masks, eye protection, and face shields are required when care may cause splashing or spraying of body fluids.
- Proper disposal – contaminated linen in leak proof bags
- Sharp items- sharp container. Clean equipment as per policy

PPE: Personal Protective Equipment

- Donning PPE: GMEG: HW- Gown-Mask-Eye Protector-Gloves
- Removing PPE: GEGM: Gloves-Eye Protector-Gown-Mask – Handwash
- Front of the mask/respirator is contaminated – DO NOT TOUCH!
- Grasp ONLY bottom then top ties/elastics and remove.

Airborne precautions

- **MVS STD**: Measles, Varicella, SARS (severe acute respiratory syndrome) Smallpox, Tuberculosis, Disseminated herpes zoster.
- A private room.
- Health care team - Use an N95 mask.
- Negative pressure airflow exchange (6-12 per hour)
- Door should be closed. Use Ante room to enter and exit
- If splashing or spraying is a possibility, wear full face (eyes, nose, mouth) protection.
- Minimize patient movement. Patient wear surgical mask if going out of room: If skin lesions present - cover the affected areas.
- Ante-Room-enter: 1. Hand hygiene, 2. Gown, 3. N95 Respirator, 4. Goggles/face shield /combined, 5. Gloves. Enter the isolation room.
- Exit: Remove everything in isolation room doorway, except N95 (remove in anteroom)

Special Scenarios

SARS

- Caused by a coronavirus (2003)
- Virus spread by close personal contact, droplets/ airborne.
- CDC - standard, contact, droplet, and airborne precautions for SARS

Herpes Zoster

- Localized? cover lesions, use PPE
- Disseminated herpes zoster: standard precautions + airborne + contact precautions - until lesions are dry and crusted.

Droplet precautions

- A private room or a room with other clients with the same infectious disease, ensuring that each client has their own equipment.
- Surgical Masks for providers and visitors
- Surgical Mask for client when outside.
- Required in: **PPPP SS MM FRED**
- Streptococcal pharyngitis, Pneumonia (mycoplasma /meningococcal pneumonia), plague, pertussis.
- Scarlet fever (a streptococcus infection), Sepsis
- Meningitis, Mumps
- Flu, Rubella, Epiglotitis, Diphtheria

Plague

- Plague - affects animals and humans - bacterium Yersinia pestis
- **Bubonic plague** is the most common - infected flea bites a person/Y pestis enter through person's broken skin. It does not spread from person to person
- **Pneumonic plague** - spread from person to person through air
- First signs - fever, headache, weakness, and rapidly developing pneumonia with shortness of breath, chest pain, cough, and hemoptysis

- The pneumonia progresses for 2 to 4 days -respiratory failure and shock.
- Early treatment of pneumonic plague is essential. Antibiotics - within 24 hours of first symptoms.
- Antibiotic treatment for 7 days will protect people who have had direct, close contact with infected patients.
- Wearing a close-fitting surgical mask also protects against infection – droplet precautions
- Septicemic plague - Sepsis due to plague bacteria
- A plague vaccine is not currently available for use in the United States.

Contact precautions

- Protect visitors and caregivers when they are within 3 ft of the client against direct client and environmental contact infections
- A private room or a room with other clients with the same infection.
- Gloves and gowns worn by the caregivers and visitors.
- Disposal of infectious dressing material into a single, nonporous bag without touching the outside of the bag.
- C-Diff: Wash hands with soap and water. Disinfect bed and equipment with chlorine/bleach
- All surfaces within three feet of the bed are considered contaminated
- Requires in: **SHIVERS**: Staphylococcus (MRSA), Herpes simplex, Infected wounds, VRE, Enteric pathogens, RSV, Scabies
- Enteric pathogens- GRACE SS: Gardiasis, Rotavirus, A&E Hep, C-Diff, Echoli, Shigella, Salmonella
- Multy drug resistant???? – contact precaution

MRSA patient: Methicillin-resistant *Staphylococcus aureus* (MRSA)

- 2% Chlorhexidine (anti-microbial) - is better than plain water. Pre moistened cloths are better
- Visitors are ok – they need to wear gloves and gown. Need handwashing

- No need for facemask. Semiprivate room with same organism is ok
- Alcohol gel is ok for hand wash. Need X ray? Arrange for portable

Who is at risk for MRSA?

- Anyone can get MRSA – but keep these points in mind for your exam. Elderly, those who are Immunosuppressive, Long term antibiotic use, steroids use, long term Invasive tubes and lines (hemodialysis), ICU – ventilator clients, Chronic diseases – frequent flares and Nursing home residents

Central Venous Line – Special Note (CDC Recommendations)

- Better Site - subclavian (less infection) than jugular/ femoral site
- No subclavian for hemodialysis patients and patients with advanced kidney disease, to avoid subclavian vein stenosis.
- Use a fistula or graft if present. Use a CVC with the minimum number of ports or lumens essential for the management of the patient.
- When adherence to aseptic technique cannot be ensured -catheters inserted during a medical emergency- replace the catheter as soon as possible, i.e., within 48 hours
- No topical antibiotic ointment or creams on insertion sites (high chance for fungal infections and antimicrobial resistance). Might be used for dialysis catheters – case basis.
- Replace dressings used on short-term CVC sites every 2 days for gauze dressings, 7 days for transparent dressings (except Peads – case to case basis due to higher chances of displacement while changing)
- Gauze dressing Situations - diaphoresis, skin erosion, or bleeding

Sterile technique

- Prolonged exposure to airborne micro-organisms can make sterile items nonsterile.
- No coughing, sneezing, and talking directly over a sterile field. No sudden movements. Only sterile items may be in a sterile field.

- The outer wrappings and 1-inch edges of packaging that contains sterile items are not sterile. Discard any object that comes into contact with the 1-inch border. Touch sterile materials only with sterile gloves.
- Consider any object held below the waist or above the chest contaminated.
- Do not reach across or above a sterile field. Do not turn your back on a sterile field. Hold items to add to a sterile field at a minimum of six inches above the field. Keep all surfaces dry.
- Discard any sterile packages that are torn, punctured, or wet

Sepsis = SIRS + Infection

- SIRS- Systemic Inflammatory Response Syndrome (When any two of the following present)

  - Temperature >100.4 F (38 C) or <96.8 F (36 C)
  - Heart rate >90/min
  - Respiratory rate >20/min or pCO_2 <32 mm Hg (4.3 kPa)
  - White blood cells >12,000/mm^3 (12.0 × 10^9/L) or <4,000/mm^3 (4.0 × 10^9/L) or >10% bands

- Sepsis Management: Early fluid resuscitation & IV antibiotic therapy

INFECTIOUS DISEASES

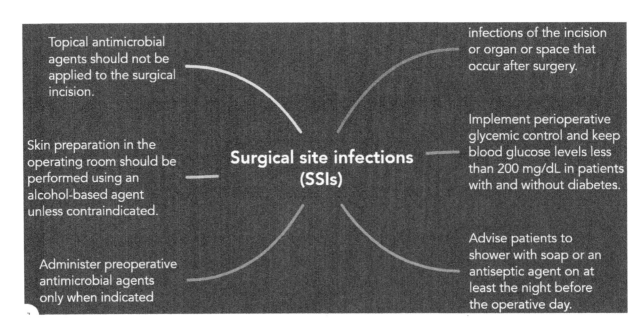

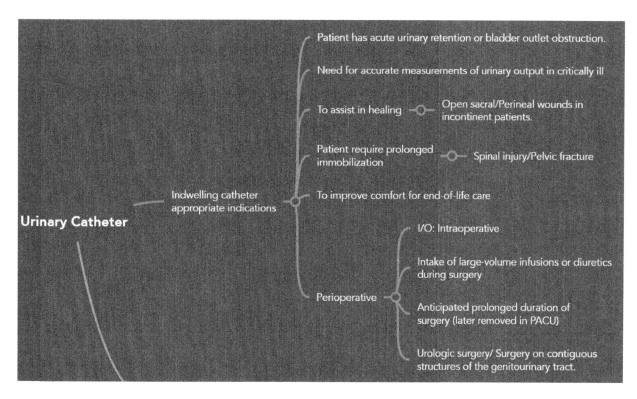

Urinary Catheter

Indwelling catheter appropriate indications
- Patient has acute urinary retention or bladder outlet obstruction.
- Need for accurate measurements of urinary output in critically ill
- To assist in healing — Open sacral/Perineal wounds in incontinent patients.
- Patient require prolonged immobilization — Spinal injury/Pelvic fracture
- To improve comfort for end-of-life care
- Perioperative
  - I/O: Intraoperative
  - Intake of large-volume infusions or diuretics during surgery
  - Anticipated prolonged duration of surgery (later removed in PACU)
  - Urologic surgery/ Surgery on contiguous structures of the genitourinary tract.

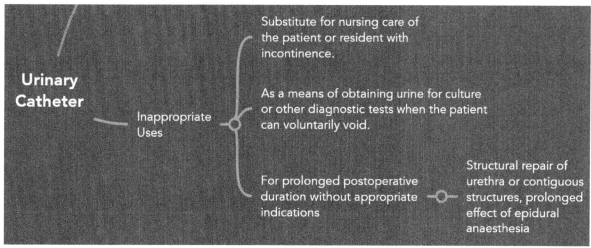

Urinary Catheter

Inappropriate Uses
- Substitute for nursing care of the patient or resident with incontinence.
- As a means of obtaining urine for culture or other diagnostic tests when the patient can voluntarily void.
- For prolonged postoperative duration without appropriate indications — Structural repair of urethra or contiguous structures, prolonged effect of epidural anaesthesia

Chickenpox (Varicella Zoster)

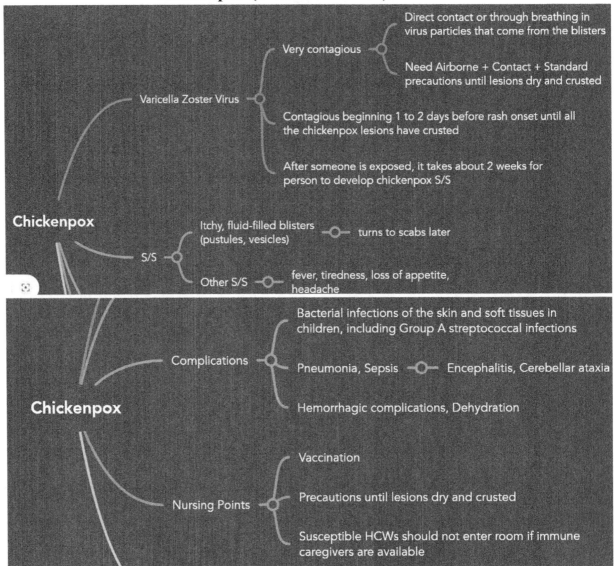

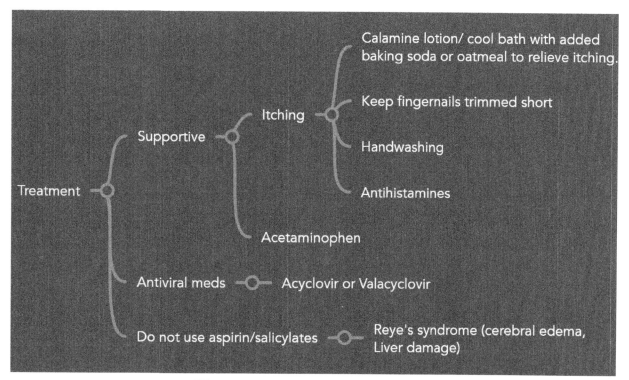

Herpes Zoster (Shingles)

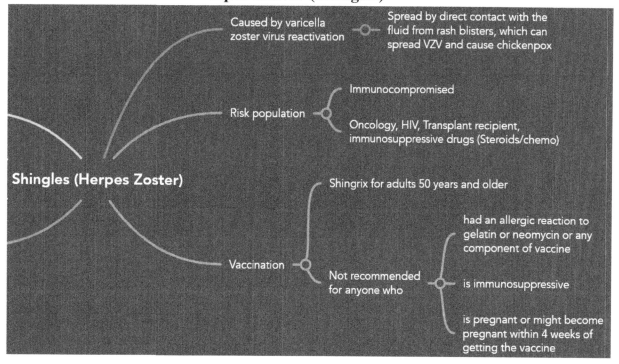

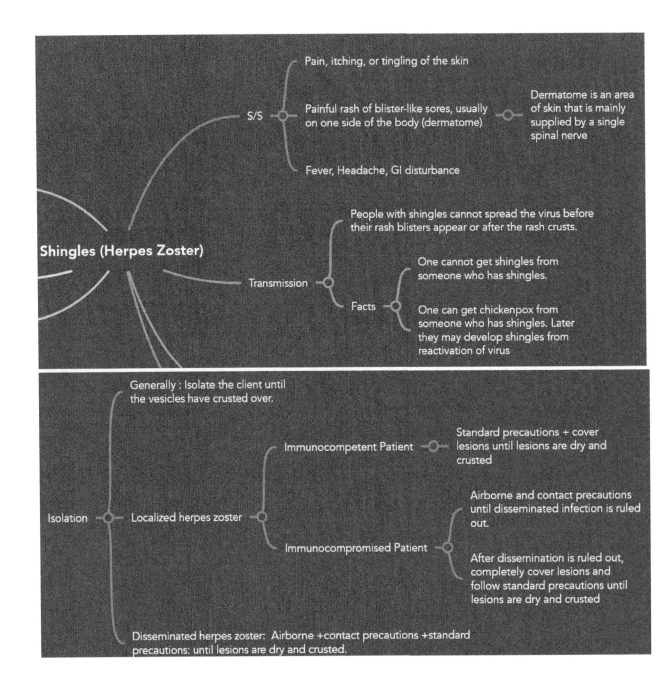

Shingles (Herpes Zoster)

S/S
- Pain, itching, or tingling of the skin
- Painful rash of blister-like sores, usually on one side of the body (dermatome) — Dermatome is an area of skin that is mainly supplied by a single spinal nerve
- Fever, Headache, GI disturbance

Transmission
- People with shingles cannot spread the virus before their rash blisters appear or after the rash crusts.
- **Facts**
  - One cannot get shingles from someone who has shingles.
  - One can get chickenpox from someone who has shingles. Later they may develop shingles from reactivation of virus

Isolation
- Generally : Isolate the client until the vesicles have crusted over.
- **Localized herpes zoster**
  - Immunocompetent Patient — Standard precautions + cover lesions until lesions are dry and crusted
  - Immunocompromised Patient
    - Airborne and contact precautions until disseminated infection is ruled out.
    - After dissemination is ruled out, completely cover lesions and follow standard precautions until lesions are dry and crusted
- Disseminated herpes zoster: Airborne +contact precautions +standard precautions: until lesions are dry and crusted.

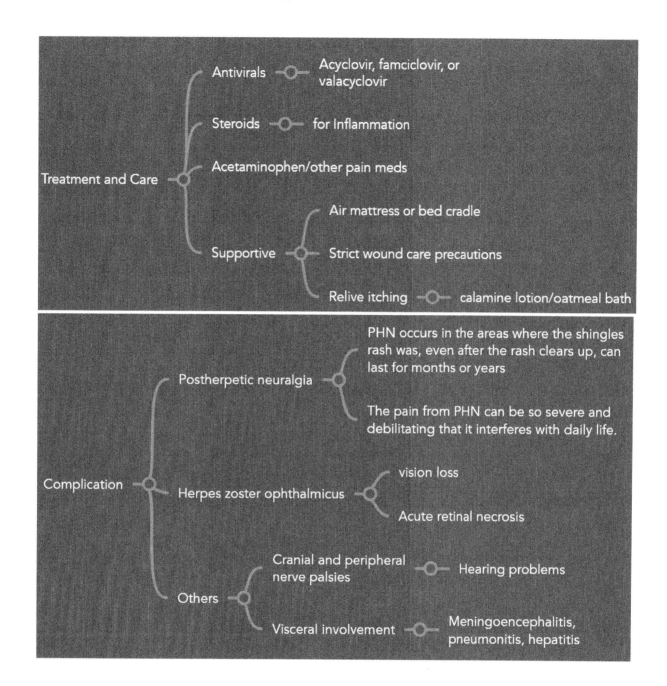

Treatment and Care
- Antivirals — Acyclovir, famciclovir, or valacyclovir
- Steroids — for Inflammation
- Acetaminophen/other pain meds
- Supportive
  - Air mattress or bed cradle
  - Strict wound care precautions
  - Relive itching — calamine lotion/oatmeal bath

Complication
- Postherpetic neuralgia
  - PHN occurs in the areas where the shingles rash was, even after the rash clears up, can last for months or years
  - The pain from PHN can be so severe and debilitating that it interferes with daily life.
- Herpes zoster ophthalmicus
  - vision loss
  - Acute retinal necrosis
- Others
  - Cranial and peripheral nerve palsies — Hearing problems
  - Visceral involvement — Meningoencephalitis, pneumonitis, hepatitis

Syphilis

- Sexually transmitted disease (STD) -Treponema pallidum bacterium
- Transmission – Sexual, mother-to fetus
- Stages: Primary, Secondary, Latent, Tertiary
- Primary: firm, round, small, & painless lesions – genital area/mouth
- Secondary: Skin rashes (palm/feet/torso), fever, sore throat, swollen lymph glands
- Latent phase – no symptoms (but relapse happens)
- Tertiary:
  - Neurosyphilis: Headaches, muscle weakness, paralysis, cognitive decline, dementia
  - Ocular syphilis: eye pain/vision changes/blindness.
  - Otosyphilis: Hearing loss/Tinnitus/Vertigo
- Treatment: Antibiotics: Penicillin

Congenital syphilis

- If pregnant mother gets syphilis: Miscarriage, Stillbirth, Prematurity, Low birth weight, or Death shortly after birth can happen.
- Babies born with CS may have
  - Deformed bones
  - Severe anemia, enlarged liver and spleen, Jaundice
  - Brain and nerve problems, like blindness or deafness
  - Meningitis, and Skin rashes.

Rubeola (Measles)

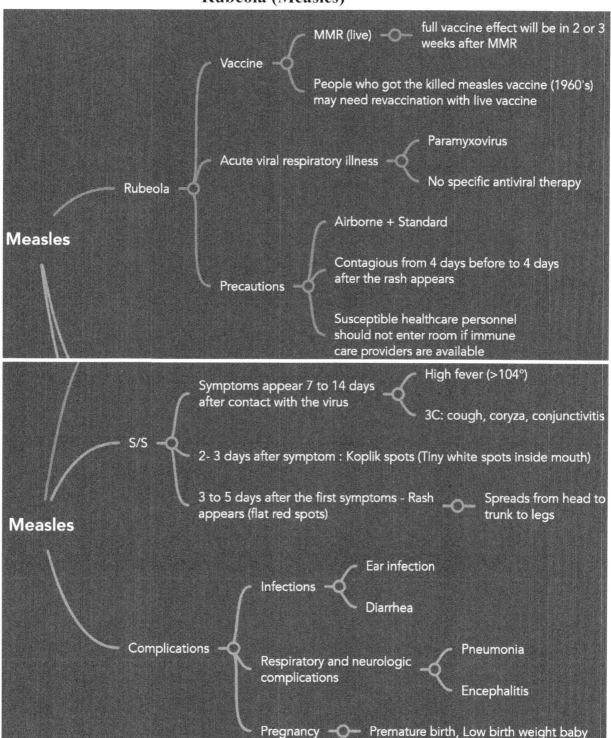

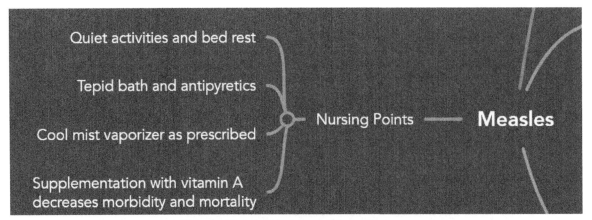

Rubella (German Measles)

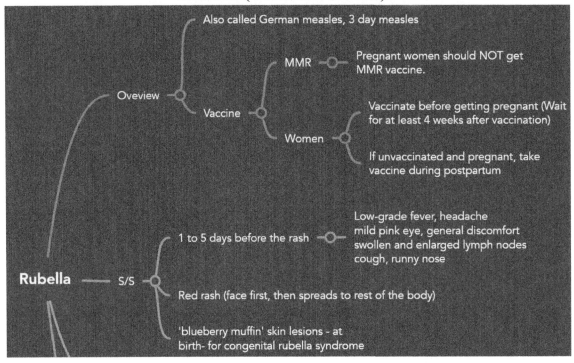

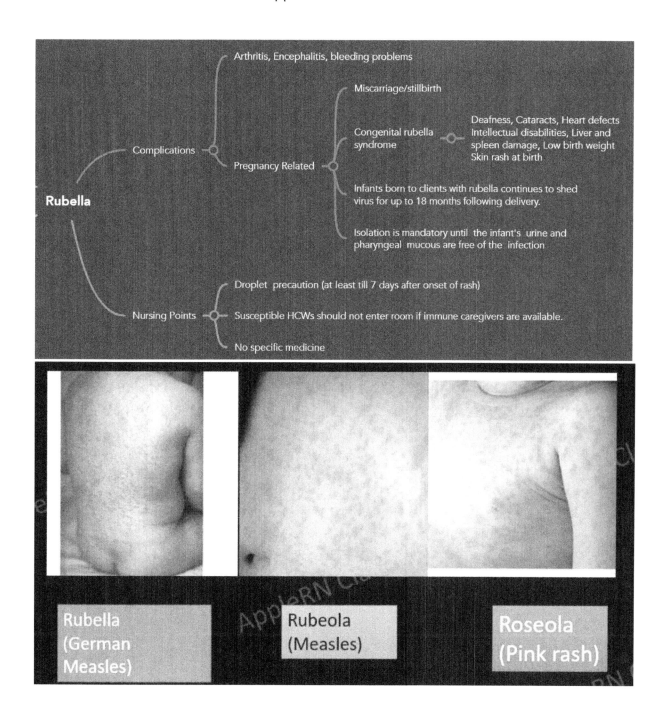

Rubella

Complications
- Arthritis, Encephalitis, bleeding problems
- Pregnancy Related
  - Miscarriage/stillbirth
  - Congenital rubella syndrome — Deafness, Cataracts, Heart defects, Intellectual disabilities, Liver and spleen damage, Low birth weight, Skin rash at birth
  - Infants born to clients with rubella continues to shed virus for up to 18 months following delivery.
  - Isolation is mandatory until the infant's urine and pharyngeal mucous are free of the infection

Nursing Points
- Droplet precaution (at least till 7 days after onset of rash)
- Susceptible HCWs should not enter room if immune caregivers are available.
- No specific medicine

Rubella (German Measles)

Rubeola (Measles)

Roseola (Pink rash)

Roseola (Exanthema Subitum/sixth disease, pseudorubella, exanthem criticum, three-day fever)

- Caused by Human herpesvirus 6B.
- The incubation period is 5 to 15 days.
- Affects babies and toddlers, causes a high temperature and a rash which is not usually itchy or uncomfortable.
- The child displays a high fever for 3 to 5 days but appears well.
- Most contagious when a child has a high temperature.
- Rash with presence of rose-colored macules that blanche (develop after fever), normally will fade and disappear within 2 days
- Interventions: Supportive home care

Mumps

- Paramyxovirus: Can spread by sharing water bottles or cups, kissing, practicing sports together, direct contact or droplet spread by coughing, sneezing, or talking.
- Starts with a few days of fever, headache, muscle aches, tiredness, and loss of appetite, then Parotid gland swelling, Jaw and ear pain with chewing
- Droplet precautions, Bed rest till parotid gland swelling subsides
- Heat and/or cold therapy to neck as prescribed.
- Avoid foods that require intense chewing (pain)
- Complications: Meningitis (look for s/s), encephalitis, orchitis, oophoritis, mastitis, pancreatitis, and deafness

MMR vaccine: Points to remember

- MMR is Live vaccine
- Contraindications: severe allergic reaction to a previous dose or vaccine component (gelatin, neomycin, eggs), Pregnancy, known immunodeficiency.
- The nurse should take a thorough history of the allergy to a previous MMR and report this to the physician.
- If it is the first MMR, the physician should be aware of the egg sensitivity before administering the vaccine

Pertussis (Whooping cough): 100-day cough

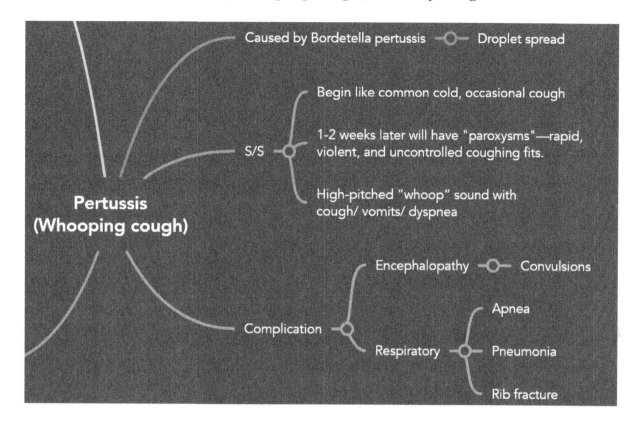

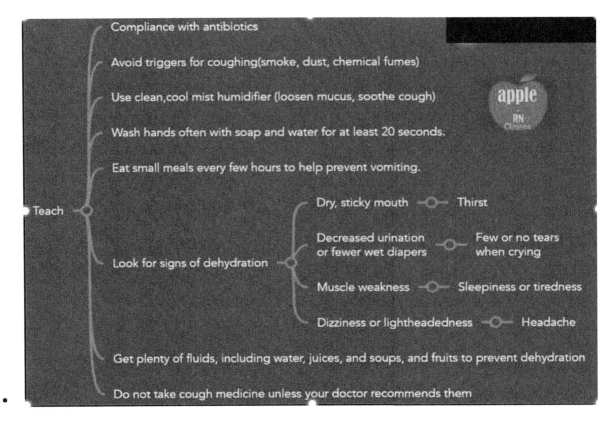

Teach
- Compliance with antibiotics
- Avoid triggers for coughing(smoke, dust, chemical fumes)
- Use clean,cool mist humidifier (loosen mucus, soothe cough)
- Wash hands often with soap and water for at least 20 seconds.
- Eat small meals every few hours to help prevent vomiting.
- Look for signs of dehydration
  - Dry, sticky mouth —○— Thirst
  - Decreased urination or fewer wet diapers —○— Few or no tears when crying
  - Muscle weakness —○— Sleepiness or tiredness
  - Dizziness or lightheadedness —○— Headache
- Get plenty of fluids, including water, juices, and soups, and fruits to prevent dehydration
- Do not take cough medicine unless your doctor recommends them

Whooping Cough Disease Progression

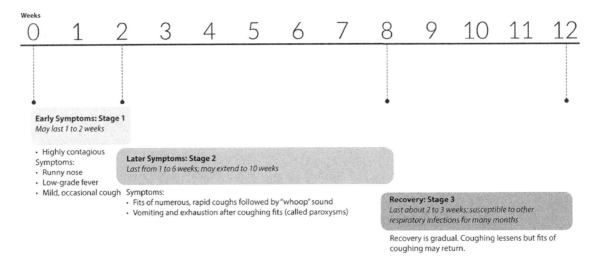

Weeks
0 1 2 3 4 5 6 7 8 9 10 11 12

Early Symptoms: Stage 1
May last 1 to 2 weeks

- Highly contagious
Symptoms:
- Runny nose
- Low-grade fever
- Mild, occasional cough

Later Symptoms: Stage 2
Last from 1 to 6 weeks; may extend to 10 weeks

Symptoms:
- Fits of numerous, rapid coughs followed by "whoop" sound
- Vomiting and exhaustion after coughing fits (called paroxysms)

Recovery: Stage 3
Last about 2 to 3 weeks; susceptible to other respiratory infections for many months

Recovery is gradual. Coughing lessens but fits of coughing may return.

cdc.gov/whoopingcough

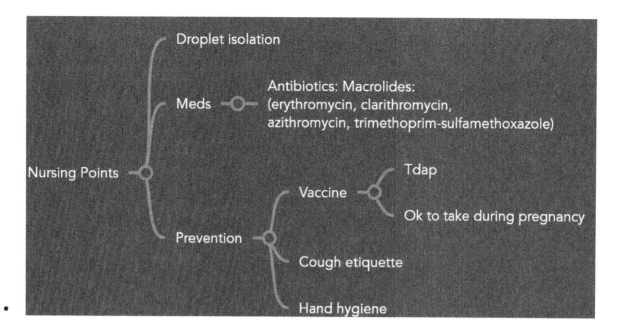

-

Diphtheria

- Caused by Corynebacterium diphtheriae toxin
- Transmission: Through respiratory droplets, direct contact with infected persons or from touching infected open sores or ulcers (cutaneous/skin)
- S/S: Dense, pseudo membrane of throat/nose; lymphadenitis; purulent nasal drainage, open sores if skin affected

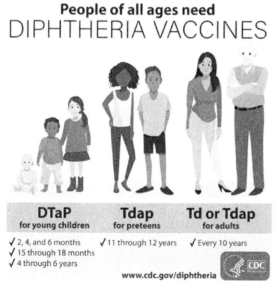

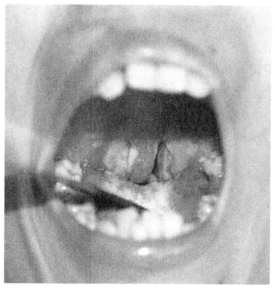

-

Isolation

- Cutaneous diphtheria: Contact + Standard
- Pharyngeal diphtheria: Droplet + Standard
- Administer diphtheria antitoxin
- Antibiotics: People with diphtheria are usually no longer able to infect others 48 hours after they begin taking antibiotics
- Provide suctioning, humidification, oxygen as prescribed
- If the toxin gets into the blood stream, it can cause Myocarditis, Polyneuropathy (nerve damage) and Kidney failure.

Scarlet fever

- Group- A Streptococcus: often live in the nose and throat
- incubation period: Approximately 2 through 5 days.
- Very contagious, Spread through respiratory droplets or direct contact; (Rarely through contaminated food)
- S/S: Very red, sore throat, Fever/chills, whitish coating / "Strawberry" tongue
- Skin Rash: Erythematous rash that blanches on pressure (Schultz-Charlton sign). Has a sandpaper feel.
- The rash usually persists for about one week and desquamation may follow.
- "Pastia's lines": Bright red skin in the creases of the underarm, elbow, and groin. Swollen glands in the neck
- Treatment: Penicillin or amoxicillin. Droplet precautions

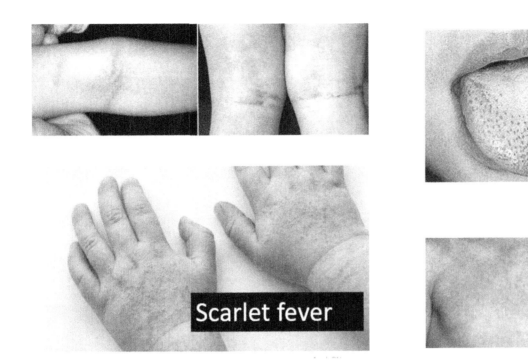

Scarlet fever

Erythema Infectiosum (Fifth Disease)

- Human parvovirus B19
  - Transmission through respiratory secretions/blood (pregnant mother to baby-babies usually do not have any problems.):
  - The communicability period is before the rash appears or symptoms begin.
- Assessment: Rash develops as erythema of face; maculopapular red spots symmetrically distributed on extremities. Intense fiery red edematous rash on the cheeks, slapped cheeks appearance. Painful and swollen joints
- Interventions
  - Droplet precaution
  - Supportive care: antipyretics, anti-inflammatories, analgesics

- Complications: Anemia

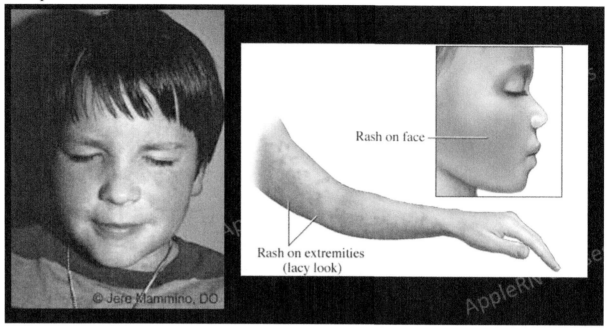

Infectious Mononucleosis

- Epstein-Barr virus: Transmission: Body fluids, Direct intimate contact
- Also called "the kissing disease" because it can spread through kissing
- Assessment: Fever; flu-like symptoms; lymphadenopathy; hepatosplenomegaly; discrete macular rash may appear over trunk
- Interventions: Standard precautions only. Bed rest, supportive care, Analgesics. Monitor closely for splenic rupture. Avoid contact sports

Rocky Mountain Spotted Fever

- Caused by Rickettsia rickettsii: Transmission: Bite of infected tick
- Start with fever, headache. GI disturbances and myalgia may also be present. Rash develops 2-4 days after fever.
- If not treated, it can progress to cerebral edema, pulmonary edema, ARDS, coma and multiorgan damage.
- Vascular damage leading to maculopapular or petechial rash, primarily on extremities – may lead to Severe Thrombocytopenia, necrosis and amputation If not addressed quickly

- Interventions
- Doxycycline is the recommended antibiotic treatment for RMSF in adults and children of all ages.
- Protective measures against tick bites
- Standard precautions only

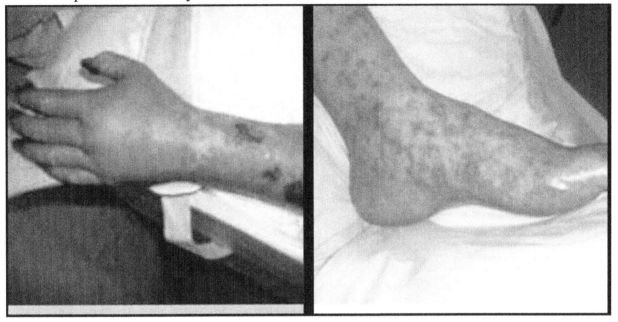

Client Teaching: Tick bite prevention and care

- Avoid forest areas. Use insect repellents
- Outdoors: wear clothing treated with 0.5% permethrin (an insecticide)
- Shower as soon as possible after spending time outdoors.
- Check for ticks daily. Ticks can hide under the armpits, behind the knees, in the hair, and in the groin.
- Tumble clothes in a dryer on high heat for 10 minutes to kill ticks.
- Never crush a live tick with your fingers.
- Do not use nail polish, petroleum jelly, or a hot match to make the tick detach.
- Dispose of a live tick by putting it in alcohol, placing it in a sealed bag/container, wrapping it tightly in tape, or flushing it down the toilet.
- Grasp the tick firmly and as close to the skin as possible.
- With a steady motion, pull the tick's body away from the skin.

- Do not be alarmed if the tick's mouthparts remain in the skin. If possible, take it out with tweezers.
- Cleanse the area by rubbing alcohol or soap and water.

Lyme Disease

- Ticks need to be attached for 36 to 48 hours before they can transmit Lyme disease bacteria *Borrelia burgdorferi*
- There is no evidence that Lyme disease is transmitted from person-to-person through touching, kissing, sex, breast feeding or blood transfusion
- Start treating patients without blood test: the antibodies will take several weeks to appear in blood sample.
- Once a patient tests positive, he or she will continue to test positive for months to years even when the bacteria are no longer present.

Signs and symptoms

- Early Signs: A characteristic skin rash, called erythema migrans ("bull's-eye")

  Fatigue, headache, Chills, and fever

  Muscle & joint pain, swollen lymph nodes

- Late Signs: Arthritis

- Nervous system symptoms: numbness, pain, nerve paralysis (facial palsy), meningitis, memory, sleep, and concentration difficulties
- Lyme carditis: Dysrhythmias

West Nile virus

- Mosquito-borne disease: spread to people by the bite of an infected mosquito.
- Infected birds – mosquito - human
- No vaccines. Mostly asymptomatic

- S/S: Fever, headache, body aches, joint pains, vomiting, diarrhea, or rash
- Treatment: Supportive
- Complications: Encephalitis, Meningitis, Neurological deficits (palsy, seizures)
- Prevention: use mosquito repellent, wear long-sleeved shirts and long pants
- Use permethrin to treat clothing and gear (such as boots, pants, socks, and tents) or buy permethrin-treated clothing and gear when outdoors

Tips for babies and children

- Always follow instructions when applying insect repellent to children.
- Do not use insect repellent on babies younger than 2 months old.
- Instead, dress child in clothing that covers arms and legs.
- Cover strollers and baby carriers with mosquito netting.
- Do not use products containing oil of lemon eucalyptus (ole) or para-menthane-diol (pmd) on children under 3 years old.
- If using sunscreen, apply sunscreen first and insect repellent second.
- Do not apply insect repellent to a child's hands, eyes, mouth, cuts, or irritated skin. Spray insect repellent onto adult hands and then apply to a child's face.

Ringworm

- Ringworm (tinea) is a common skin infection that is caused by a fungus.
- It is called "ringworm" because of a circular rash (shaped like a ring) that is usually red and itchy with raised edges.
- Ringworm on the feet – Tinea pedis (athlete's foot)
- Ringworm on groin, inner thighs, or buttocks (tinea cruris, jock itch)
- Ringworm on Scalp (tinea capitis)
- Ringworm on body – Tinea Corporis

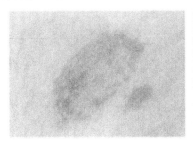  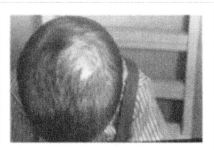

Ringworm on the back   **Ringworm on the arm**   **Ringworm on the scalp**

Health Education – Ringworm

- Keep skin clean and dry. Wear shoes that allow air to circulate freely around feet. Do not walk barefoot in areas like locker rooms or public showers.
- Clip fingernails and toenails short and keep them clean.
- Change socks and underwear at least once a day.
- Do not share clothing, towels, sheets, or other personal items with someone who has ringworm.
- Wash hands with soap and running water after playing with pets.
- Contact sports: shower immediately after match and keep all of sports gear and uniform clean.
- Do not share sports gear (helmet, etc.) with other players.

Fundamentals
Basic Safety and Comfort

Environmental Safety: Fire safety

- Turn off oxygen and appliances in vicinity of fire
- If fire occurs and client is on life support, maintain respiratory status manually with Ambu bag until client is moved
- PASS- Pull the Pin in handle, Aim the nozzle at the base of fire, Squeeze the level slowly, Sweep from side to side
- RACE – Rescue clients, Alarm, Contain/Confine, Evacuate/Extinguish
- Electrical safety. Use three-pronged electrical cords
- Any electrical equipment brought in by client or family must be inspected prior to use
- Check all electrical cords and outlets for exposed, frayed, damaged wires
- If client receives electrical shock, turn off electricity before touching client

Radiation safety

- Reduce exposure by limiting time spent near source, increase distance as much as possible, use shielding device.
- Never touch dislodged radiation implants
- Radiation exposure: Key aspects - time and distance.
- The greatest distance – better chance of survival
- Initially – all patients feel well. But bleeding may be internal

Disposal of infectious wastes

- Handle all infectious materials as hazard
- Dispose of all sharps immediately after use in closed, puncture-resistant, approved disposal container

Bomb Threat

- When a phone call is received: Extend the conversation as long as possible.
- Listen to distinguish background noises (music, voices, traffic, airplanes) and voice characteristics of the caller.
- Ask where and when the bomb is set to explode.
- Note whether the caller is familiar with the physical arrangement of the facility.
- Notify the appropriate authorities and personnel (police, administrator, director of nursing).
- Remain calm and alert and try not to alarm clients.

Special Population Safety

- Physiological changes in older client—increased risk of accidents (cognitive changes)

Children

- Keep children three feet away from anything that can get hot (space heater/ hot water/hot food on table-tablecloths/
- Prevent accidents (Install window guards/move chairs, cribs, and other furniture away from windows to prevent child crawling on top/ use straps for highchairs and swings/helmet for activities/life jacket for water activities)
- Keep materials locked up in a high place (cigar/matches/cleaning supplies/meds)

Fall risk precautions at hospital

- Orientation to room & call light. Call light within reach
- Bed in lowest position, Uncluttered room, Nonslip socks, or shoes
- Well-lit room, Belongings within reach, Bed alarm
- High fall risk signs, Room close to nurses' station
- Color-coded socks & wristbands

Morse Fall Scale

Item	Scale	
1. History of falling; immediate or within 3 months	No	0
	Yes	25
2. Secondary diagnosis	No	0
	Yes	15
3. Ambulatory aid		
Bed rest/nurse assist		0
Crutches/cane/walker		15
Furniture		30
4. IV/Heparin Lock	No	0
	Yes	20
5. Gait/Transferring		
Normal/bedrest/immobile		0
Weak		10
Impaired		20
6. Mental status		
Oriented to own ability		0
Forgets limitations		15

Sample Risk Level

Risk Level	MFS Score	Action
No Risk	0 - 24	Good Basic Nursing Care
Low Risk	25 - 50	Implement Standard Fall Prevention Interventions
High Risk	≥ 51	Implement High Risk Fall Prevention Interventions

Fall risk precautions at home

- Do Not leave the client alone, Bed in lowest position
- Uncluttered room, Nonslip socks, or shoes
- Assistive devices (walker), Well-lit room
- Belongings within reach, Remove all throw rugs
- Install grab bars in the bathroom

Falling Client

- Step slightly behind the client and place the arms under the axillae or around the client's waist
- Place your feet wide apart with knees bent -
- support, provides stability
- Place one foot behind the other and extend the front leg
- Let the client slide down to the floor

Concept Map for Fall

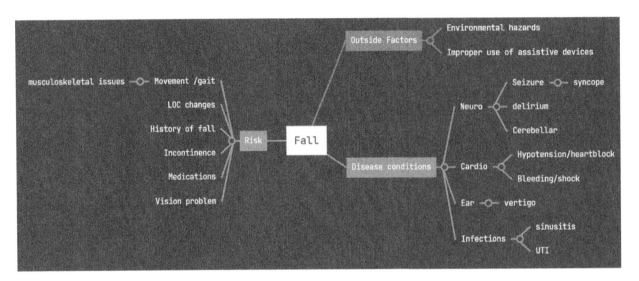

Catheter Associated Urinary Tract Infection (CAUTI)

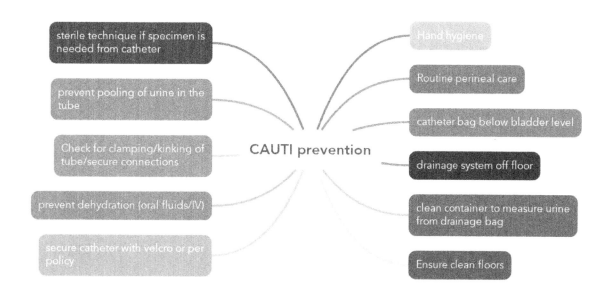

Sleep Hygiene

- "Sleep hygiene" refers to a series of healthy sleep habits that can improve your ability to fall asleep and stay asleep.
- Keep a consistent sleep schedule. Get up at the same time every day, even on weekends or during vacations.
- If did not fall asleep after 20 minutes, get out of bed. Do a quiet activity without a lot of light exposure. It is especially important to not get on electronics.
- Turn off electronic devices at least 30 minutes before bedtime.
- Limit exposure to bright light in the evenings.
- Keep bedroom quiet and relaxing.

Elderly and Pharmacology

- Drug use among older adults is high.
- Older patients are more sensitive to drugs/ more adverse drug reactions/ drug-drug interactions.

Concerns:

- Altered pharmacokinetics (due to organ/system degeneration/increase fat/reduced muscle & protein)
- Multiple and severe illnesses / Multiple-drug therapy
- Half-life increases – reduced hepatic and renal clearance
- Poor adherence
- Individualization of therapy for older adults is essential

Helpful Measures to Decrease Adverse Drug Reactions (ADRs)

- Taking a thorough drug history, including over-the-counter medications
- Initiating therapy with low doses/Using the simplest regimen possible
- Monitoring clinical responses/ plasma drug levels/ drug-drug interactions
- Periodically reviewing the need for continued drug therapy and discontinuing medications as appropriate
- Encouraging the patient to dispose of old medications
- Taking steps to promote adherence
- Avoiding drugs on the Beers list – List of drugs with a high likelihood of causing adverse effects in older adults

The American Geriatrics Society (AGS) Beers Criteria: Medications to be noted from Exam point of view

- Antispasmodics and skeletal muscle relaxants: Dicyclomine, Methocarbamol
- Anti-infective: Nitrofurantoin
- Cardiovascular: Antihypertensives, antiplatelets in high dose, digoxin
- Sedatives – Anti anxiety, Pain meds, antipsychotics
- Diabetic- Insulin, glyburide, Chlorpropamide
- Anticholinergics- cough meds/allergy meds
- Diphenhydramine, Meclizine, Promethazine, Chlorpheniramine, Atropin

Nonadherence

- Unintentional: Forgetfulness; failure to comprehend instructions, Inability to pay for medications, Use of complex regimens
- Intentional (75%): Patient's conviction that the drug was simply not needed in the dosage prescribed, Unpleasant side effects and expense

Nurses' role to promote medication adherence

- Recommending simplifying the regimen so that the number of drugs and doses per day are as small as possible
- Educating about the medications using clear, concise verbal and written instructions
- Helping to choose an appropriate dosage form (e.g., a liquid formulation if the patient has difficulty swallowing)
- Labeling drug containers clearly and avoiding containers that are difficult to open by patients with impaired dexterity
- Suggesting the use of a calendar, diary, or pill counter to record drug administration
- Asking the patient whether he or she has access to a pharmacy and can afford the medication
- Interpersonal/multidisciplinary collaboration - visiting healthcare professional
- Monitoring for therapeutic responses, adverse reactions, and plasma drug levels

Restraints

- Should be a last resort – always use alternatives
- Must have physician's prescription with specifics about type of restraint, time frame for use; must be renewed following agency policy
- The client situation, rather than the device, determines whether it is classified as a restraint.

- Prescribed orthopedic immobilizers and protective devices used temporarily are not restraints
- Should not interfere with any treatments or affect client's health care.
- Patient safety – never tie to side rails.
- Use a quick release tie to secure the restraint.
- Assess skin integrity and neurovascular status every 15- 30 minutes
- Remove restraints at least every 2 hours
- Geri chair –people with mobility issues to recline – OK. But if it is imposed for discipline or convenience and is restricting client movement– It is considered as a restraint

Actions to implement (instead of restraints)

- Orienting the client and family to the surroundings
- Explaining all procedures. Encouraging family and friends to stay
- Assigning confused or disoriented clients to a room near the nurses' station
- Providing appropriate stimuli to the client
- Maintaining toileting routines. Eliminating bothersome treatments
- Using relaxation techniques. Instituting an ambulation schedule

Restraints – Delegation

- Cannot be delegated: assessing a patient's behavior and level of orientation, determining the need for restraints, selecting the appropriate restraint type, performing the ongoing assessments required while a restraint is in place
- Can delegate: The re-application and routine checking of a restraint, Range of motion exercise

Pain: One major reason people seek health care

Nurses' role:

- Assess pain and communicate with health care team
- Ensure initiation of adequate pain relief measures.
- Evaluate effectiveness of interventions.

- Advocate for those in pain.
- Use both drug and nondrug therapies.

Criteria	Nonopioid	Opioid	Adjuvant
Addiction	No addiction	Can be present	Depends on drug
How to get	Can get OTC	Prescription	Prescription
Example	Aspirin, NSAID, Tylenol	Morphine, oxycodone, and codeine (can be combinations with non-opioid)	Corticosteroids Antidepressants Antiseizure drugs (Baclofen)
Side Effects	GI problems, renal insufficiency, and hypertension.	Constipation (long term), Urinary retention, Nausea/vomiting, Sedation – Fall Respiratory depression, Pruritus	Varies according to drug
Antidot	Sodium bicarbonate (aspirin). Acetylcysteine (Tylenol)	Nalaxone	

Wong-Baker FACES® Pain Rating Scale

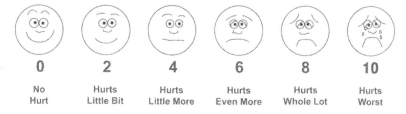

0	2	4	6	8	10
No Hurt	Hurts Little Bit	Hurts Little More	Hurts Even More	Hurts Whole Lot	Hurts Worst

-

- Wong Baker Faces: It is a self-assessment tool - must be understood by the patient, so they are able to choose the face that best illustrates the physical pain they are experiencing.
- It is not a tool to be used by a third person to assess the patient's pain if they are able to communicate.

Nondrug Therapy

- Massage
- Exercise
- TENS: Transcutaneous electrical nerve stimulation: Delivery of an electrical current through electrodes on the skin
- Acupuncture: Traditional Chinese medicine
- Heat or cold therapy – warm compress/ice packs
- Cognitive therapies – Distraction, Hypnosis, Relaxation

Community Health Promotion

- Chocking- First Aid
- Universal sign of choking—holding their neck with one or both hands.

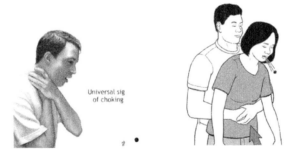

Universal sig of choking

1. Ask the person if they are choking. DO NOT perform first aid if the person is coughing forcefully and is able to speak. 2. If they are unable to speak, perform abdominal thrusts.

- Continue thrusts until the object is dislodged or the person loses consciousness. Call 911/emergency if needed

- For Infants (1 year or less): Place the infant stomach-down across your forearm and give five quick, forceful blows on the infant's back with heel of your hand.
- Place two fingers on the middle of the infant's breastbone and give five quick downward thrusts.

Physical activity Guideline

Adults

- At least 2 hours and 30 minutes (of moderate-intensity exercise, such as brisk walking or bicycling, every week. That is about 30 minutes a day, 5 days a week. (150 minutes per week)

Children

- Children and adolescents should get 1 hour of physical activity every day.
- Examples of sugary beverages: Regular soda, fruit drinks, sports drinks, energy drinks, sweetened waters, and coffee and tea beverages with added sugars.

Preconception care visit

- To take steps for healthy and safe pregnancy before a person gets pregnant
- Involves a complete review of both partners' medical history.
- Folic Acid recommended dose – 400 mcg per day

Poisons

- Accidental poisoning common in toddlers, preschoolers, young school-age children, so they must be protected
- Older adults with diminished eyesight, impaired memory may be at risk for accidental ingestion of poison
- Keep Poison Control Center phone number on phone or in view of phone

If poisoning occurs,

- Remove excess immediately,
- Identify type and amount, if possible,
- Call Poison Control,
- Induce vomiting only if instructed by Poison Control,
- Go to emergency room if instructed by Poison Control
- Call poison control center at 800.222.1222 right away - even if you are not completely sure.
- Store medicines up and away and out of the sight and reach of young children.
- Lock the Safety Cap

Metabolic Syndrome

- A cluster of progressive metabolic abnormalities – leads to insulin resistance, pro-inflammatory and pro-thrombotic state
- High chances of type 2 diabetes mellitus, cardiovascular disease, stroke, nonalcoholic fatty liver disease, cancers

Any three or more out of these five

- Increased waist circumference / BMI >30
- Elevated blood pressure (>135/85)
- Elevated triglycerides (≥150 mg/dL / on treatment)
- Decreased HDL
- Elevated fasting glucose ≥100 mg/dL

General Prevention

- Maintenance of healthy weight
- Built environment to promote healthy lifestyle choices and reduce sedentary time. Regular and sustained physical activity
- Limiting alcohol consumption. Stop smoking.
- Promote a Mediterranean and/or a low-carbohydrate diet, DASH diet, low-glycemic load diet, avoiding sugars, sweetened beverages, and starchy carbohydrates.

- Maintain healthy sleep patterns and regular stress management.

Childhood obesity

- Causes: Social and environmental factors (living situation), Eating, sleeping and physical activity patterns, genetics, disease conditions and medications
- Activity Recommendation
  - Kids 3-5 years: Should be physically active throughout the day
  - Kids 6 – 17 years: At least 60 minutes of moderate to vigorous physical activity every day
- Sleep Recommendation
  - Newborns need 14 to 17 hours of sleep per day (as they age, sleep hours decrease)
  - Teenagers need 8 to 10 hours of sleep per day

Weight Status Category	Percentile Range
Underweight	Less than the 5th percentile
Healthy Weight	5th percentile to less than the 85th percentile
Overweight	85th to less than the 95th percentile
Obesity	95th percentile or greater

Strategies the family can implement to reduce the risk of childhood obesity

- Avoid using food as a reward. Emphasize physical activity.
- Ensure a balanced diet is consumed.
- Teach children to select healthy foods and snacks.
- Avoid eating fast foods frequently. Avoid skipping meals.
- Model healthy behaviors

Breast milk storage

- After 4 days of refrigeration, the breast milk should be used or thrown away.
- Power outage: Freezers, if left unopened and full -will keep food safe for about 48 hours. The refrigerator will keep food cold for about 4 hours if it is

unopened. Frozen breast milk that has started to thaw but still contains ice crystals can be refrozen.

- If breast milk has completely thawed but still feels cold, put it in the refrigerator and use it within the next day or throw it away.

	STORAGE LOCATIONS AND TEMPERATURES		
TYPE OF BREAST MILK	**Countertop** 77°F (25°C) or colder *(room temperature)*	**Refrigerator** 40 °F (4°C)	**Freezer** 0°F (-18°C) or colder
Freshly Expressed or Pumped	Up to **4 Hours**	Up to **4 Days**	Within **6 months** is best Up to **12 months** is acceptable
Thawed, Previously Frozen	1–2 Hours	Up to **1 Day** *(24 hours)*	**NEVER** refreeze human milk after it has been thawed
Leftover from a Feeding *(baby did not finish the bottle)*	Use within **2 hours** after the baby is finished feeding		

Facts on Fluoride – Toothpaste

- Drinking fluoridated water keeps teeth strong and reduces cavities (also called tooth decay)
- Children should start using toothpaste with fluoride when they are 2 years old. For children younger than two, consult first with doctor /dentist
- Bottled water products labeled as de-ionized, purified, demineralized, or distilled have been treated in such a way that they contain no or only trace amounts of fluoride. Ok to use with infant formula if formula has enough fluoride
- Dental fluorosis is a condition that causes changes in the appearance of tooth enamel due to too much fluoride- white spots on the tooth surface.

Diagnostic Procedures and Care

Client Safety in Diagnostic Testing

- Knowledge of procedure, risk and benefits, pre- and post-care.
- Pregnancy? – radiation risk
- Informed consent - Sedation – No self-driving for clients
- Perform necessary lab studies pre procedure
- NPO? Hold Med. No anticoagulants
- Iodine based contrast – Hold Metformin 48 hrs. (risk for acidosis)
- Check for allergies. "Time out": Right procedure, Right client, Right site.

Contrast Dye- General Notes

- May be NPO – usually for 4-6 hrs.
- Assess for allergies – Shellfish, Iodine, contrast media
- May premedicate with Prednisone and Benadryl. Hypoallergic contrast available
- Intake output – give fluids post procedure (contraindication – HF, Renal disease)
- Baseline Lab- KFT? LFT? Ensure IV access (20 G)
- A warm flushed feeling, or salty, fishy, or metallic taste in mouth, possible nausea for 1-2 mts after injection is expected.

Radiographic Studies

- CT Scan: With contrast – (refer to previous slide). Need to lie still and flat

MRI:

- Remove all implants/metals/ jewelries/hearing aid/ dentures/ eyeglasses/hair clips/cloth with zippers, buckle or metal buttons, color contact lenses (which may have metal elements)

- Claustrophobia? / Loud noise (ear plugs)
- Weight limits
- Not safe in pregnancy
- Void before test (might take 40-90 mts for procedure)
- Functional MRI (fMRI) – to check specific brain region for activity- image taken while client performs/get stimuli
- No sedatives before procedure

Cerebral Angiogram

- To assess the blood flow to and within the brain (access through femoral/brachial)
- To identify aneurysms
- To define the vascularity of tumors (useful for surgical planning).
- It may also be used therapeutically to inject medications that treat blood clots or to administer chemotherapy.
- If the client is pregnant, a determination of the risks to the fetus versus the benefits.
- Refer general notes- NPO/contrast allergy /labs
- A mild sedative for relaxation may be administered prior to and during the procedure
- Void before test
- Mark peripheral pulse sites – for baseline
- Monitor vital signs/neuro status – pre/during/ post
- Post Procedure: Movements are restricted to seal the artery to prevent re-bleeding at the catheter site.
- Bedrest for 12 hours/ HOB flat /low fowlers as prescribed
- Sandbag /pressure dressing/ice bag at site
- Peripheral neurovascular monitoring
- If bleeding does occur, apply pressure over the artery and notify the provider.

PET Scan

- Positron Emission Tomography (to detect blood flow to brain and heart).
- Nuclear medicine- using a glucose-based tracer to see patterns of glucose and oxygen metabolism – areas with decreased metabolism- dysfunction (? dementia/tumor/Parkinson's/head injury/seizure, MS)
- Radiation is short lived increase fluids to clear it through kidneys
- Assess for a history of diabetes mellitus: To avoid hyperglycemia or hypoglycemia before and after this procedure

Electroencephalography (EEG)

- To identify and determine seizure activity/ sleep disorders/ behavioral (? autism) changes.
- Wash client's hair prior to the procedure and eliminate all oils, gels, and sprays
- No stimulants/sedatives/antidepressants/antiseizure meds 24-48 hrs. before test (no need to be NPO)
- Instruct the client to be sleep-deprived because this provides cranial stress, increasing the possibility of abnormal electrical activity.
- Increased electrical activity may be stimulated with exposure to bright flashing lights or hyperventilate for 3 to 4 minutes.

Lumbar Puncture

- L3 and L4: Cannon ball position/sitting up
- Local anesthesia
- Prep skin with antiseptic (no chlorhexidine – as its neurotoxic and should not be in contact with CSF)
- Empty bladder before procedure
- CSF leakage – spinal headache
- Encourage the client to lie flat in bed. Provide fluids for hydration
- Prepare the client for an epidural blood patch to seal off the hole in the dura if the headache persists.

Myelography

- LP- inject dye /air – to visualize the subarachnoid space (to check for Spinal cord compression/ Herniated disk / Bone displacement/ Lesions)
- Pre procedure: NPO 4-6 hrs.
- Table tilt – to allow dye to reach different levels
- Post procedure – Position depends on air/dye
  - o Water-based dye (Metazamide) - elevate head of bed semi fowlers
  - o Oil-based (Pantopaque) – prone position/ head of bed flat / 15 degree
  - o Air - keep head lower than trunk
- Increase fluid intake to flush out dye

Cerebrospinal Fluid: CSF

- Specimen – immediately send to lab - Hematologic analysis within one hour
- Room temperature is preferred. No need to refrigerate – flu and meningitis virus will die in freezing temperature.
- If the CSF is to be scanned for xanthochromia (? blood), Protect sample from light. Place specimen bag inside a brown envelope
- Do not use the pneumatic tube delivery system.
- CSF is normally clear. Cloudy - Infection

Normal CSF:

- No RBC
- Protein= (15 to 45 mg/dL)
- Glucose = (45 to 74 mg/dL)
- White blood cells (0 to 8 cells/mm3)
- Halo sign – when CSF mixed with blood- yellow ring

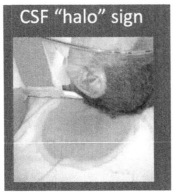

CSF "halo" sign

Holter monitoring

- Instruct client to resume normal activities, maintain diary of activities, no shower or swim with electrodes.

Echocardiography

- To evaluate structural, functional changes in heart
- TEE (Trans esophageal)- Consent, NPO, IV-line, endoscopy general care

Exercise testing (stress test)

- Client to wear non-constrictive & comfortable clothing, supportive shoes
- Consent, NPO for few hours, no caffeine, alcohol, smoking
- Check for medications – hold bradycardic meds (need to check how HR increases)
- Pharmacology stress test – meds to increase HR (dobutamine/adenosine)
- EKG: Cardiac dysrhythmias

Central venous pressure (CVP)

- Pressure of right heart filling (no left heart)
- Catheter tip at SVC at juncture with RA
- Measure CVP with client supine, HOB at 45 degrees
- Zero point of transducer should be at level of right atrium (Lt mid axillary line, 4 ICS)
- Normal CVP value = 2 to 8 mm Hg
- High CVP- Hypervolemia, CHF (crackles, JVD, edema, Hepatomegaly, Taut skin turgor)
- Low CVP – Hypovolemia (poor skin turgor, dry mucous membrane)
- No coughing/sneezing-/straining – increase intra thoracic pressure – increase CVP – false reading

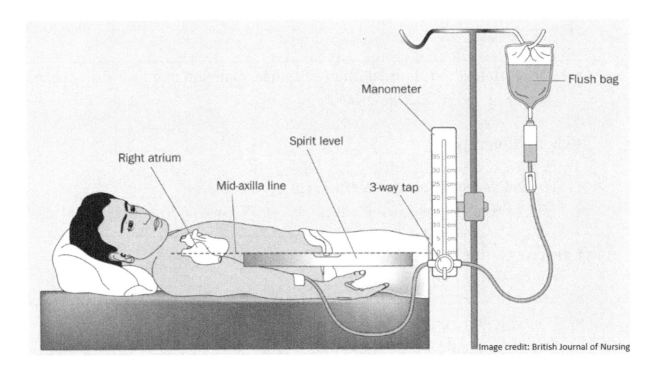

Image credit: British Journal of Nursing

A Multigated Acquisition (MUGA) scan

- Nuclear Imaging test to determine Cardiac function - Ventricular Ejection Fraction. Resting MUGA/ Stress MUGA
- Uses a radioactive tracer- attaches to RBC (tagged)
- The test is called "multi-gated" because a gamma camera takes pictures at specific times during each heartbeat.
- Consent, IV, NPO for at least 3 hrs.
- Wear comfortable clothing and shoes. After scan – PO fluids
- Precautions to avoid radioactive contamination are needed for 24 hours after a MUGA scan (Avoid pregnant staff)

Percutaneous transluminal coronary angiography Angioplasty (PTCA)

- Balloon catheter
- Pre procedural: NPO, Hold anticoagulants, lab /x ray studies, consent, void
- Post procedure: Neuro assessment - distal pulses, CNS changes, Vital signs Q 15 mts (per protocol), Monitor site: bleeding, pain, swelling.
- Maintain bed rest with limb straight for 6 to 8 hours
- Report chest pain (MI?), Back/thigh/groin pain (retroperitoneal bleed?)

- Coronary artery stents
- Acute thrombosis major concern post-procedure: client placed on antiplatelet therapy for several months following procedure

Gastrointestinal Procedures

General Concerns

- NPO/ Bowel prep
- Watch for Fluid and Electrolyte disturbances

Endoscopy - General points

- Avoid red/orange/purple liquids (?? Bleeding)
- Watch for bowel perforation/obstruction
- Moderate sedation- safety precautions (Vitals/gag reflex/ no driving)
- Post Sore throat – use lozenges, saline gargles (after gag reflex returns)

Computed Tomography (CT)

- NPO for 4-6 hr., With or without contrast
- With contrast - Allergy

Abdominal Ultrasound

- Restrict food and fluids 4-8 hrs. prior to test
- Eat fat free meal on evening prior to ultrasound
- (For pelvic and renal US- need full bladder)

Esophagogastroduodenoscopy

- NPO, Consent (moderate sedation)
- Position – Left lateral during procedure (aspiration risk)
- Hold anticoagulants
- Post- gas pains/burping of air

Barium Studies

- Contrast – Barium / Meglumine (Gastrografin)
- Aspiration risk? – Barium is better.
- Perforation suspected? – Gastografin is better
- Upper GI tract study (barium swallow). Lower GI tract study (barium enema)
- NPO after midnight before day of test. Administer laxative
- Post Procedure – Increase PO fluid intake.
- Lower GI tract study (barium enema): Low-residue diet 1 to 2 days prior to procedure

Colonoscopy

- Hold anticoagulants
- No red/orange/purple liquids PO Day before test
- NPO after midnight, Bowel prep – Golytely
- Lateral position/ sims position
- Endoscopy General points

Presence of Colon polyp – Risk for Colorectal cancer

- Obtain Individual and family history
- Regular screening for polyps and cancer
  - o Flexible sigmoidoscopy every 5 years
  - o Colonoscopy every 10 years
  - o Double-contrast barium enema study every 5 years
  - o CT colonography every 5 years

ERCP/MRCP (Hepatobiliary system)

- ERCP: Endoscopic Retrograde Cholangiopancreatography
- NPO 6 to 8 hours
- Position changed during procedure- to allow flexible endoscope to advance
- Allergy for ERCP dye
- Endoscopy General points

MRCP: Magnetic Resonance Cholangiopancreatography

- Uses MRI – pacemaker/pregnancy – contraindicated

Liver Biopsy

- Review coagulation profile (pre)
- Client may be supine/left lateral during procedure
- Instruct client to exhale breath and hold for at least 10 seconds while the needle is inserted.
- Post Position – Lay on right side with pillow under coastal area (no coughing/straining)
- Rest and avoid heavy lifting minimum 24 hrs.
- No aspirin, NSAID, anticoagulants * 2 weeks

Guaiac fecal occult blood test

- Ask if red meat or vitamin C supplements taken over last three days

- Medication - aspirin, anticoagulants, iron, ibuprofen, and corticosteroids.
- Collect the fecal samples from two different areas of the specimen
- If the test paper turns blue: It's a positive guaiac result – blood present.

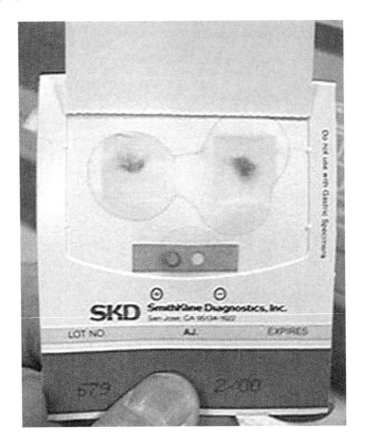

Paracentesis

Pre procedure:

- Have client void, measure abdominal girth,
- Measure weight, baseline vital signs
- Fowler's position/upright

Post procedure:

- Vital signs, Measure abdominal girth, weight
- Dry sterile dressing to site

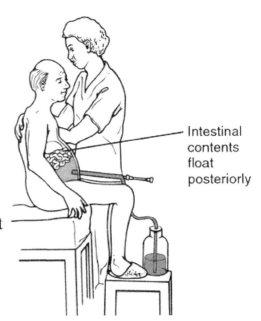

Intestinal contents float posteriorly

- Monitor for hypovolemia, electrolyte loss, mental status changes, encephalopathy
- Monitor for hematuria - educate client to report urine that is pink, red, bloody

Musculoskeletal System

Arthroscopy and Arthrocentesis

- Arthroscopy – using endoscope and visualization, might also collect tissue samples (biopsy)
- Arthrocentesis - Aspiration of synovial fluid (to diagnose/infection) / to give medicine
- Post: Instruct client to rest joint 8 to 24 hours
- Elevate and use Ice (12-24 hrs.) to reduce swelling
- Elastic compression bandage (2-4 days)
- Notify physician if fever or swelling of joint develops -? Bleeding? Infection

Arthrography (X ray with dye)

- Assess client for allergies to iodine, shellfish
- Instruct client that joint may be edematous, tender for 1 to 2 days post procedure. Treat with ice packs, analgesics

Bone Densitometry

- X ray to measure bone density. No special preparation needed, Noninvasive

Bone Scan

- Gallium scan – radioisotope (very minimal amount)
- NPO (few hours - if needed), Consent
- Isotope may be given 24-72 hrs. before test – to concentrate on bone tissue
- Void - A full bladder can distort the bones of the pelvis, also need to take out excess isotope that did not concentrated in bone

- Flush toilet three times after voiding (to avoid radioactive substance)
- Laxative may be given. Increase PO fluids.

Renal Procedures

Urine culture and sensitivity

- Clean perineal area, Collect midstream sample in sterile container
- urine is positive for leukoesterase and nitrites –? UTI

Voiding Cystourethrogram

- X ray taken when client is voiding. Provide privacy

KUB – X ray of Kidney, Ureters and Bladder (? stone)

- Intravenous pyelography/urography – IV radiopaque dye
- Pre: Consent, KFT, NPO, laxative and enema for better visualization
- Post – increase PO fluids, I/O

24 hr. /12 hr. urine collection

- Client to void at the beginning of the collection period and discards this urine sample because this urine has been stored in the bladder for an undetermined length of time.
- All urine thereafter is saved preferably in an iced or refrigerated container.
- The client is asked to void at the finish time, and this sample is the last specimen added to the collection.
- Straining the urine is contraindicated for timed urine collections.
- The container is labeled, placed on fresh ice, and sent to the laboratory immediately after the 12/ 24-hour urine collection has ended.

Renal angiography:

- Preparation and nursing care same as femoral approach for coronary angiography

Cystoscopy

- Flexible fiber-optic scope inserted through the urethra to urinary bladder.
- The client is in the lithotomy position (leg cramps may occur after procedure)
- Monitor for urinary retention, bleeding, and infection

Kidney Biopsy

- Pre- Consent, vitals, NPO, hold anticoagulants
- Post: Place client in supine position, bed rest for 8 hours
- Increase fluid intake. Report any decrease in urine output / burning on urination

Respiratory System

Sputum specimen

- Obtain early morning sterile specimen from suctioning, expectoration after respiratory treatment
- Always collect specimen prior to antibiotic therapy
- If culture prescribed, transport to laboratory immediately

Bronchoscopy

- Direct visual examination of larynx, trachea, bronchi with fiberoptic bronchoscope. Refer to endoscopy general care

VQ Scan

- Nuclear lung scan after inhaling a mixture of air, oxygen, radioactive gas.
- Deep breath and hold – images taken
- Report chest pain and shortness of breath (PE)

Pulmonary Function Test

- Lung capacity assessment
- Client to avoid eating heavy meal or smoking prior to test
- Hold medications which might sedate

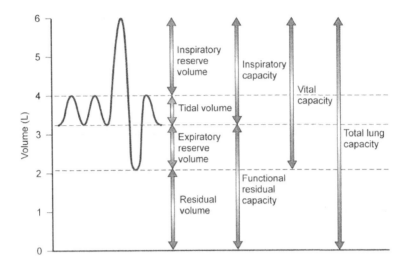

Thoracentesis

- Removal of fluid or air from pleural space via trans thoracic aspiration

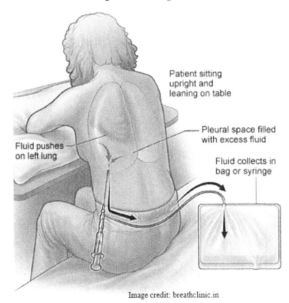

Image credit: breathclinic.in

- If client cannot sit up for procedure, place lying in bed toward unaffected side with head of bed elevated
- Stay still – Instruct
  - o not to cough

- o no deep breath
- o do not move during procedure

  (Unless told by doctor)

- Post procedure: Monitor respiratory status, Monitor for signs of pneumothorax, air embolism, pulmonary edema

Community Health Nursing

- It is a broad field that allows nurses to practice in a wide variety of setting
- Health and welfare of clients across the lifespan
- Diverse populations (school/prison/clinics/telehealth/nursing home/special needs...etc.)
- Main Goal: Protecting, promoting, preserving, and maintaining health, as well as preventing disease.
- Health Education – major component of community nursing

Community Health Education Plan

- Identify population-specific learning needs
- Identify barriers to learning (age/language/illness)
- Design the educational program (content/delivery/evaluation)
- Implement the education program (minimal distractions, favorable to interaction, learner comfort, readability).
- Evaluate effectiveness.

Health promotion and disease Prevention

- Three levels of prevention – primary, secondary, and tertiary
- Helps people to change their lifestyles in order to move toward a state of optimal health (physical and psychosocial).
- Preventive services
  - o Preventive health education and counseling
  - o Immunizations
  - o Other actions to prevent a potential disease or disability.

Primary prevention

- Prevention of the initial occurrence of disease or injury
- Nutrition education
- Family planning and sex education
- Smoking cessation education

- Communicable disease education
- Education about health and hygiene issues to specific groups (day care workers, restaurant workers)
- Safety education (seat belt use, helmet use)
- Prenatal classes
- Providing immunizations
- Advocating for access to health care
- Healthy environments

Secondary Prevention

- Health screening for diseases
- Cancer (breast, cervical, testicular, prostate, colorectal)
- Diabetes mellitus, Hypertension, Hypercholesterolemia
- Sensory impairments
- Tuberculosis
- Lead exposure
- Genetic disorders/metabolic deficiencies in newborns

Tertiary Prevention

- Maximization of recovery after an injury or illness (rehabilitation)
- Nutrition counseling
- Exercise rehabilitation, Exercise for individual hypertensive clients
- Case management (chronic illness, mental illness)
- Physical and occupational therapy
- Support groups

School Nurse

Primary

- Educating about dental health
- Teaching heart healthy ideas (nutrition, exercise, not smoking)
- Discussing safety (seat belts, bicycle helmets, stranger safety)

- Administering immunizations
- Advocating for safe playground equipment

Secondary

- Performing tuberculin skin tests, routine checks for pediculosis
- Screening for lead exposure
- Identifying students at risk for suicide or self-harm
- Performing vision and hearing screenings
- Checking heights and weights

Tertiary

- Teaching about allergic triggers for students with asthma
- Administering medications to treat chronic conditions (asthma, diabetes, seizure disorders)
- Teaching Monitoring blood glucose and Diabetes Diet

Environmental Risks

- Toxins: Lead, pesticides, mercury, solvents, asbestos.
- Air pollution: Carbon monoxide, lead, aerosols, nitrogen dioxide, sulfur dioxide, and tobacco smoke.
- Water pollution: Wastes, erosion after mining or timbering, and run-off from chemicals added to the soil.

Roles for Nurses in environmental Health

- Facilitate public participation to prevent risky behaviors
- Perform individual and population risk assessments.
- Implement risk communication with community
- Conduct epidemiological investigations.
- Participate in policy development.

Assessment of Environmental Health: "I PREPARE"

- I = Investigate potential exposures
- P = Present work (exposures, use of personal protective equipment)
- R = Residence (age of home, heating, recent remodeling, chemical storage, water)
- E = Environmental concerns (air, water, soil, industries in neighborhood, waste site nearby)
- P = Past work (exposures, farm work, military, volunteer, seasonal, length of work)
- A = Activities (hobbies, activities, gardening, fishing, hunting, soldering, melting, burning)
- R = Referrals and resources (Environmental Protection Agency, poison control)
- E = Educate (risk reduction, prevention, follow-up)

Health Problems of Migrant Workers

- Dental disease (less access to services)
- Tuberculosis (Poor and unsanitary working and housing conditions)
- Chronic conditions (Exposure to environmental pesticides)
- Stress, anxiety, and other mental health concerns
- Iron deficiency anemia (nutrition), Lack of prenatal care (Inability to afford care)
- Higher infant mortality rates (Inability to afford care/ transportation)
- Language barriers and cultural aspects of health care

Strategies for Migrant Health Care

Primary Prevention: Educate regarding measures to reduce exposure to pesticides. Teach regarding accident prevention measures. Provide prenatal care. › Mobilize preventive services (dental, immunizations).

Secondary Prevention: Screen for pesticide exposure, skin cancer, chronic preventable diseases. Screen for communicable diseases

Tertiary Prevention: Treat for symptoms of pesticide exposure. Mobilize primary care and emergency services.

Surgical Care

Preop Care

Assessment of risk factors is one of the major aspects of preoperative care.

- Infection (risk of sepsis)
- Anemia (malnutrition, oxygenation, healing impact)
- Hypovolemia from dehydration or blood loss (circulatory compromise)
- Electrolyte imbalance through inadequate diet or disease process (dysrhythmias)
- Age (older adults are at greater risk because of decreased liver and kidney function due to age, and the use of multiple prescribed medications)
- Pregnancy (fetal risk with anesthesia)
- Respiratory disease (COPD, pneumonia, asthma)
- Cardiovascular disease (cerebrovascular accident, heart failure, myocardial infarction, hypertension, dysrhythmias)
- Diabetes mellitus (decreased intestinal motility, altered blood glucose levels, delayed healing)
- Liver disease (altered medication metabolism and increased risk for bleeding)
- Kidney disease (altered elimination and medication excretion)
- Endocrine disorders (hypo/hyperthyroidism, Addison's disease, Cushing's syndrome)
- Immune system disorders (allergies, immunocompromised)
- Coagulation defect (increased risk of bleeding)
- Malnutrition (delayed healing)
- Obesity (pulmonary complications due to hypoventilation, impact on anesthesia, elimination, and wound healing)
- Certain medications (antihypertensives, anticoagulants, NSAIDs, tricyclic antidepressants, herbal medications, over-the-counter medications)
- Substance use (tobacco, alcohol)
- Family history (malignant hyperthermia)
- Allergies (latex, anesthetic agents)

Perioperative Care

- Obtaining informed consent/ ensuring consent has been taken
- Nutrition: NPO as prescribed
- Avoid cigarette smoking for 24 hr. preop
- Stop herbal meds /hold anticoagulants– risk of bleeding
- Elimination: Void immediately before surgery
- Bowel prep if needed (laxative, enema)
- Surgical site: Hair should be clipped with electric clippers or chemical depilatory to prevent traumatizing the skin and increasing the risk for infection.
- Preoperative checklist – labs, latex allergy

Pre op check

- Give Preoperative medications: Sedative? Fall risk- client in bed with side rails up
- Prophylactic antibiotics are administered 1 hr. prior to surgical incision.
- Client already on Beta-blocker? Give a dose prior to surgery to prevent a cardiac event and mortality.
- Hormonal meds are usually continued.
- Cover the client with lightweight cotton blanket heated in a warmer to prevent hypothermia.
- Hypothermia increases the chance for surgical wound infections, alters metabolism of medication and causes coagulation problems and cardiac dysrhythmias.

Preoperative Client Teaching

- Postoperative pain control techniques (medications, immobilization, patient-controlled analgesia, pumps, splinting)
- Invasive devices (drains, catheters, IV lines)
- Demonstration and importance of range-of-motion exercises and early ambulation. (Sequential compression device/elastic stockings)

- Psychological aspects (believes/feelings/support system)
- Language barriers/communication

Explanation of procedure

- Toddler: Immediately prior to surgery, give a brief and simple explanation
- Preschoolers: give a brief and simple explanation, play therapy
- School age: Age appropriate but complete explanation, use pictures, dolls, and videos.
- Adolescents: Privacy is extremely important. Clear explanation.
- Adults: complete information

Anesthesia notes

- General Anesthesia: Loss of sensation, loss of consciousness, amnesia, respiratory and CV support needed. Use IV and Inhalation agents
- Regional Anesthesia: - Nerve blocks (bupivacaine), spinal and epidural block
- IV regional (local) anesthesia (Bier block) - Tourniquet pain may occur
- Local Anesthesia: Lidocaine – loss of sensation locally. No LOC changes.
- Monitored Anesthesia Care - MAC (Conscious sedation) - Lower dose IV sedatives/opioids – but no inhalation. Patient is responsive. But amnesia can be present.

Immediate postoperative stage

- Assess, monitor airway – adequate ventilation? secretions? respirations? signs of respiratory distress?
- Assess for symmetry of breath sounds and chest wall movement. Absent breath sounds on the left (ET tube migrated to right bronchus? / Pneumothorax?)
- Snoring or stridor (a high pitch crowing type sound) – upper airway obstruction
- Assess / monitor for bleeding, surgical site, drains, wound, return of bowel sounds

- Neuro - Orient to environment
- Shivering? Apply warm blankets and prescribed oxygen
- Assess/ monitor for - hypocalcemia, hyperglycemia, acidosis / alkalosis

Post-operative Notes

- Semi/low Fowler's position - unless contraindicated
- If comatose/ semi-comatose, position on side with oral airway in place
- Turn client to side-lying position if vomiting occurs
- Do not put pillows under knees or elevate the knee gatch on the bed (decreases venous return).
- Expect client to void in 6 to 8 hours postoperatively
- Assess and re- assess pain
- Reinforce wound with sterile dressing PRN; notify physician if bleeding
- Maintain NPO status until gag reflex and peristalsis return

Transcutaneous Electrical Nerve Stimulation (TENS)

- The TENS unit consists of a battery-operated transmitter, lead wires, and electrodes
- The electrodes are placed directly over or near the site of pain.
- Hair or skin preparations should be removed before attaching the electrodes.
- Unlike with opioids, pain relief is achieved without drowsiness

Common Complications

- Hypoxia, Pneumonia, Atelectasis:
- Prevention: Suction/ Cough and deep breath/ Incentive Spirometry/ frequent Reposition. Ambulate early and regularly.
- Hemorrhage and Shock – Stop bleed, give O2, blood and fluids, monitor, position
- Pulmonary Embolism, DVT: Assess leg(s) for swelling, inflammation, pain, tenderness, cyanosis. Elevate extremity 30 degrees without pressure in popliteal space. SCD, TEDS. Passive range of motion every 2 hours/ Ambulate as soon as possible

Malignant hyperthermia

- Genetic disorder -Always check for family history.
- Reaction to combination of anesthetic agents (the muscle relaxant succinylcholine and inhalation agents such as halothanes) - Result in uncontrolled skeletal muscle contractions & hyperthermia
- Hyper metabolic condition - muscle rigidity, hyperthermia, and damage to CNS
- Tachycardia is a first manifestation - can quickly lead to a potentially fatal hyperthermia.
- An elevated temperature is a late manifestation – rising 1° to 2° C (2° to 4° F) every 5 min.
- Other signs: Dysrhythmias, muscle rigidity, hypotension, tachypnea, skin mottling, cyanosis, and protein in urine.
- Terminate surgery
- ›› Dantrolene (Dantrium) is a muscle relaxant to treat the condition
- ›› 100% oxygen, ABG, IV saline, Cooling blanket, ice to axillae, groin, neck, and head, iced lavage

Urinary Retention

- Involuntary accumulation of urine in bladder
- Assessment: Inability to void, lower abdominal pain, distended bladder, hypertension, tympany sound on percussion of bladder

Interventions

- Strict intake and output, Assess for distended bladder
- Encourage ambulation, Provide privacy for voiding
- Pour warm water over perineum, run water for client to hear to promote voiding. Catheterize as prescribed

Constipation

- Abdominal distention, absence of bowel movements, anorexia, headache, nausea

Interventions

- Encourage fluid intake up to 3000 mL/day unless contraindicated
- Encourage early ambulation
- Encourage consumption of high-fiber foods unless contraindicated
- Administer stool softeners and laxatives as prescribed

Paralytic Ileus: No peristalsis: Interventions

- Maintain NPO status until bowel sounds return
- Strict intake and output
- Maintain patency of nasogastric tube if in place
- Encourage ambulation
- Administer IV fluids, parenteral nutrition, medications as prescribed

Wound Infection

- Infection caused by poor aseptic technique or contaminated wound before surgical exploration; occurs 3 to 6 days postoperatively
- Assessment: Fever, chills, warm, tender, painful, inflamed incision site, elevated white blood cell count
- Monitor temperature, vital signs, Monitor incision site for signs of infection
- Maintain patency of drains, assessing drainage, Change dressings as prescribed
- Administer antibiotics as prescribed

Wound Dehiscence/Evisceration

- Separation of wound edges from suture line
- Assessment: Increased drainage, open wound edges, appearance of underlying tissue through wound
- Place in low Fowler's position, with knees bent, if abdominal incision
- Cover wound with sterile normal saline dressing, Notify physician
- Administer antiemetics if abdominal incision to prevent vomiting, strain on incision
- Instruct client to splint abdominal incision when coughing

Ambulatory Surgery

- General criteria for client discharge
- Alert and oriented, has voided, has no respiratory distress
- Ambulates, swallows, coughs
- Experiencing minimal pain, bleeding, has no vomiting
- Has someone to take home; physician has signed release
- Discharge teaching: Performed prior to procedure taking place, Both verbal and written instructions in primary language

NCLEX Specific Tubes and Nursing Care

Nasogastric Tubes

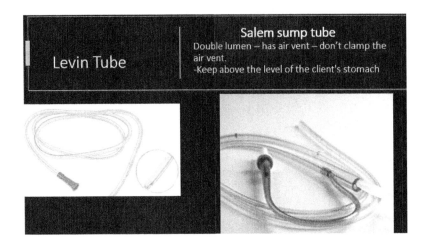

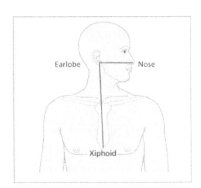

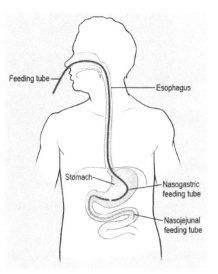

Purpose

- Decrease risk of aspiration
- Decompress stomach after abdominal surgery
- Provide enteral feedings

Intubation procedures

- Place client in high Fowler's position
- Measure tube from tip of nose to earlobe to xiphoid process to determine length of insertion
- Lubricate tube with water-soluble jelly
- Instruct client to bend head forward
- Insert tube into nostril, advance backward
- Have client take sips of water, advancing tube while he or she swallows
- When in place, tape appropriately

Placement

- GI Aspirates: pH below 5 will indicate correct placement.
- Respiratory secretions are almost always alkaline, with a pH = 6 or more

- The gold standard for nasogastric/enteric feeding tube placement is radiographic confirmation with a chest x-ray.

Irrigation

- Irrigation should be performed every 4 hours as prescribed
- Assess placement of tube prior to irrigation
- Gently instill 30 to 50 mL of water or NS, according to agency policy, with irrigation syringe
- Pull back syringe plunger to withdraw fluid to check patency; repeat if tube remains sluggish

Removal of nasogastric tube

- Client should take deep breath and hold; breath-holding minimizes the risk of aspirating spilled gastric contents
- Remove tube slowly, while coiling on hand

Intubated patient – NG tube feed- prevent aspiration

- Assessment – residual, abd distention, pain, bowel sounds, bowel movement, tube placement
- HOB 30, suction, ET tube cuff – inflated (25 cm H20)
- No bolus feeds – high risk of aspiration
- No oversedation

Gastrointestinal Tubes

- Types of tubes
- Nasogastric: Nose to stomach
- Nasoduodenal: Nose to duodenum or jejunum
- Nasojejunal: Nose to jejunum
- Gastrostomy: Stomach - PEG tube
- Jejunostomy: Jejunum

- Types of Feed: Bolus, continuous, cyclical

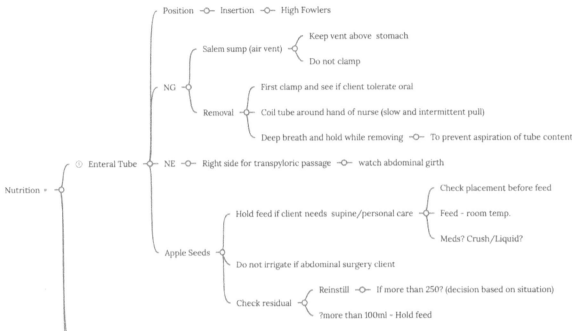

Percutaneous endoscopic gastrostomy (PEG) tube

- The tube's tract begins to mature in 1-2 weeks
- But can take up to 4-6 weeks to fully mature
- Tube dislodgement – the tract will start to close immediately - notify Dr.
- If tube dislodgment happened in less than 7 days of insertion – might need new surgical or endoscopic replacement
- If old tube – reinsertion may be attempted by experienced dr. (foley cath/PEG- but careful to avoid going into peritoneal cavity – sepsis)

Common causes for obstruction of enteral feeding tube

- The tube is not flushed frequently enough
- Meds not crushed or diluted as required
- Use of a thick feeding formula
- Use of small-bore feeding tube

Intervention in case of enteral tube obstruction

- First attempt: dislodge the clogged contents by using a large-barrel syringe to flush and aspirate warm water.
- Second: use a digestive enzyme solution: commercial de-clogging kits contain prefilled syringes of enzymatic solution

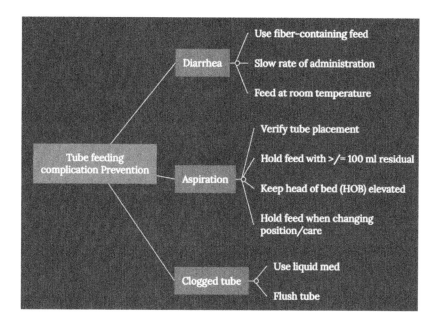

Colostomy irrigation

Respiratory Tubes

Tracheostomy

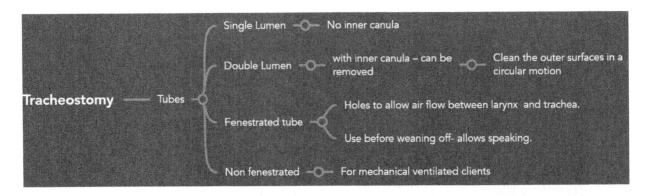

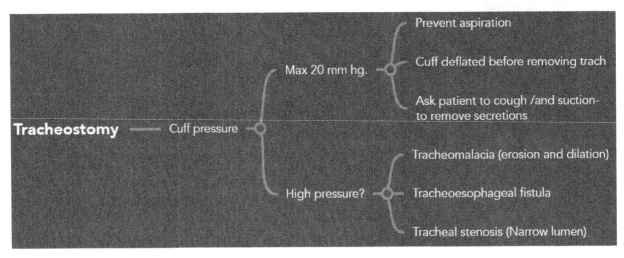

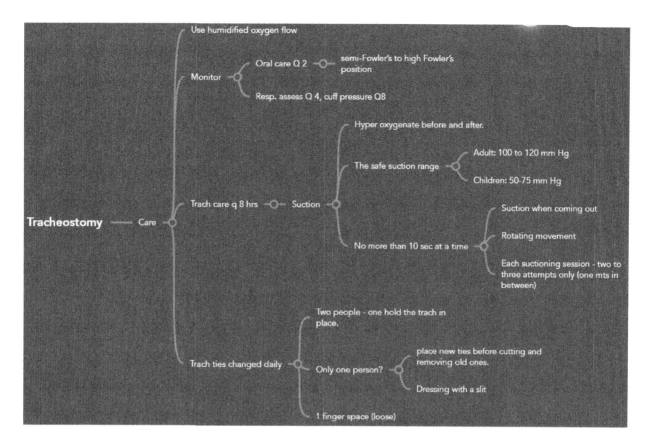

- Ties: one finger breath (not too tight)
- Ambu bag and spare Trach kit: Always at bedside

Accidental dislodgement of the tube

- Complete healing of the stoma typically takes approximately 1 week.
- 1. Pull on the retention sutures (tighten the sides) to keep the tracheostomy opening open
- 2. Keep the stoma open by inserting a curved hemostat
- 3. If worsen - Apply a sterile occlusive dressing over the stoma and ventilate with AMBU over the nose and mouth

On discharge

- Ask patients to have two spare trach tubes all the time with them – one of same size, another with smaller size (to use in emergency)

Chest Tube

To remove air and fluids from pleural space

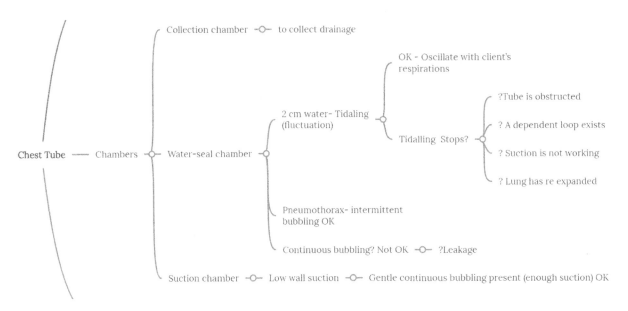

- The water seal chamber prevents air from re-entering the client's pleural space. Intermittent bubbling in this chamber may be noted and indicates air leaving the pleural space (ok)
- Continuous and vigorous bubbling indicates air leak in the drainage system or the presence of a pneumothorax.
- Air leak?
  - Check all of the connections.
  - Notify provider if an air leak is noted, and if prescribed, gently apply a padded clamp to determine the location of the air leak. Remove the clamp immediately following assessment.
  - Chest tubes are clamped only when ordered by the provider in specific circumstances, such as in the case of an air leak
  - Three-sided dressing for open pneumothorax

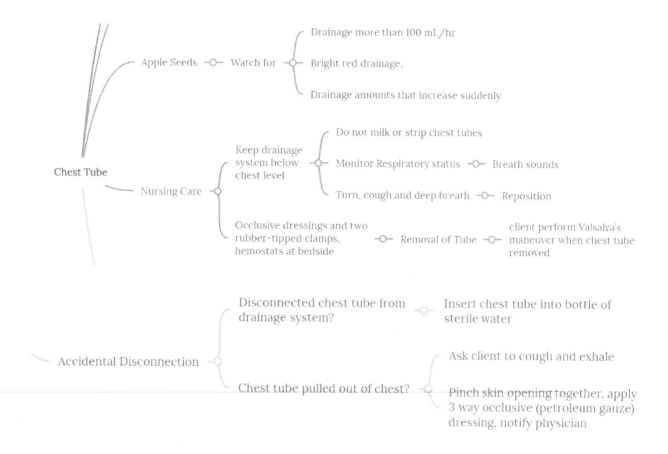

Urinary and Renal Tubes

- Types of urinary catheters
  - Urinary catheter, ureteral tubes, nephrostomy tubes
- Routine urinary catheter care:
  - Maintain collection bag below level of bladder, use clean container to empty urine
- Ureteral and nephrostomy tubes
  - Never clamp tube; maintain patency
  - Monitor strict intake and output
  - Irrigate only with physician's prescriptions, using strict aseptic technique (5 ml max)

Wound drainage

- Measure and record every shift
- JP drain and Hemovac- Maintain pressure after emptying the bulb
- Penrose drain – dressing changes
- T-Tube – bile drainage
    - Keep T-tube below level of surgical wound
    - Up to 500 ml expected first 24 hrs.
    - About 200 ml in 2-3 days
    - D/C home? - Clamping schedule- before and after meal

Maternity Nursing

Physiological Maternal Changes

- Cardiovascular system: Pulse may increase (10 beats/min), Blood pressure may decrease in second trimester.
- Respiratory system: Oxygen consumption increases by 15% to 20%
- GI: Nausea, Vomiting, Constipation, Hemorrhoids
- Renal system: Frequency of urination increases in first and third trimesters
- Endocrine system: BMR rises, Body weight increases
- Reproductive system: Uterus enlarges, Cervix changes
    - Leukorrhea is normal – white /milky discharge PV – due to hormonal changes (if foul smelling/itching/burning – need to report)
- Skeletal system: Center of gravity changes – Lordosis
- Integumentary Changes: Vascular Spider nevi – due to lot of estrogen in pregnancy; Chloasma, Linea nigra and Striae

Weight gain during pregnancy

- Total Recommended: 25 to 35 lb.
- Underweight woman: total 28 to 40 lb.
- overweight women: 15 to 25 lb.
- 1st trimester: up to 2 kg (4.4 lb.) depends on pre pregnancy wight/symptoms
- 2nd and 3rd Trimester -: 0.4 kg (1 lb.) per week - depends on pre-pregnancy weight
- Ok to do exercise – Yoga/swimming/walking.
- Avoid contact sports/falls

Pica

- Abnormal, compulsive craving for and consumption of substances (not nutritionally valuable or edible)
- Ice, cornstarch, chalk, clay, dirt, and paper.
- Associated with iron deficiency anemia. So, monitor the Hb and HCT

Laboratory Tests

- Blood type and Rh factor – RH negative mother? Rho(D) immune globulin (RhoGAM) within 72 hours of birth of first baby
- With every other pregnancy, RhoGAM at 28th week and within 72 hours of birth of baby
- Tuberculin skin test - Positive? Need chest x-ray to rule out active disease
- In pregnant client, x-ray cannot be performed until after 20th week of gestation
- Urine: Glucose – ??Diabetes; Protein – Pre-Eclampsia
    - Nitrates and WBC – Infection
    - pH may be decreased, and specific gravity may be increased (vomiting)
- Blood: HCG levels (human chorionic gonadotropin)
- Ultrasonography – mother - no supine position – low venous return
    - Outlines, identifies fetal and maternal structures (amniotic fluid level)
    - Assists in confirming gestational age and estimated date of confinement
- Chorionic villus sampling (High Risk)
    - Assessment of a portion of the developing placenta (chorionic villi), which is aspirated through a thin sterile catheter or syringe. (10-12 weeks)
    - Detects genetic abnormalities by sampling chorionic villus tissue at eighth to twelfth week of gestation.
- Kick counts (fetal movement counting) (at least 10 kicks/2 hr.)

Amniocentesis

- Aspiration of amniotic fluid – 13-14 week onwards
- Used to determine genetic disorders, metabolic defects, fetal lung maturity
- Risks: maternal hemorrhage, infection, abruptio placentae, premature rupture of membranes
- AFP / can be measured/ Fetal lung tests ratio can be obtained

Post Procedure

- Administer RhO(D) immune globulin (RhOGAM) to the client if she is Rh-negative
- Advise the client to report to her provider if she experiences fever, chills, leakage of fluid, or bleeding from the insertion site, decreased fetal movement, vaginal bleeding, or uterine contractions after the procedure.
- Encourage the client to drink plenty of liquids and rest for the 24-hr. post procedure.
- Alpha-fetoprotein (AFP) can be measured from the amniotic fluid
    - High levels of AFP - neural tube defects, such as anencephaly (incomplete development of fetal skull and brain), spina bifida (open spine), or omphalocele (abdominal wall defect). Can also be in normal multifetal pregnancies.
    - Low levels of AFP - chromosomal disorders (Down syndrome) or gestational trophoblastic disease (hydatidiform mole).
- Fetal lung tests
    - Lecithin/sphingomyelin (L/S) ratio – a 2:1 ratio indicating fetal lung maturity (2.5:1 or 3:1 for a client who has diabetes mellitus).
    - Presence of phosphatidylglycerol (PG) – absence of PG is associated with respiratory distress
- Fern test: microscopic slide test to determine presence of amniotic fluid leakage
- Nitrazine test: Determines presence of amniotic fluid in vaginal secretions; shades of blue indicate that membranes probably ruptured
- Quad marker screening – a blood test that ascertains information about the likelihood of fetal birth defects.
    - It does not diagnose the actual defect.
    - Checks HCG, AFP, Estriol, Inhibin – all proteins from fetus and placenta
- Sustained fetal tachycardia (>160/min for >10 minutes) is a concerning finding that requires further follow-up

Nonstress test (Positive –reactive - is normal)

- Performed to assess placental function and oxygenation (usually in 3rd trimester)
- Assesses fetal well-being – FHR vs Fetal movement = minimum for 20 mts
- Normal- Increased FHR with FM
- The NST is reactive (normal) when 2 or more FHR accelerations of at least fifteen beats/min (each with a duration of at least 15 seconds) occur in a 20-minute period of test
- (Wait at least for 40 mts if no FHR acceleration, before saying its abnormal)
- Outpatient clinic, external monitor

CST: Contraction Stress Test

- Contraction stress test (positive is abnormal)
- Performed to assess placental function, oxygenation and baby tolerate labor?
- FHR vs Contractions – Nipple stimulation/ oxytocin (OCT)
- Normal - No late deceleration, no variable deceleration
- Early deceleration is ok- due to head compression to maternal pelvis
- Assesses fetal ability to tolerate labor, fetal well-being
- Do not perform CST with preterm labor risk/placenta previa

Early Decelerations

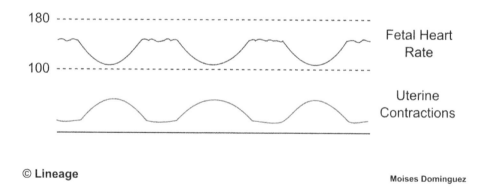

© Lineage

Moises Dominguez

- Variable deceleration – may be due to cord compression, cord prolapse, uterine tachysystole (fast contractions), chorioamnionitis, placenta abruption, nuchal cord, PROM with fetal distress, maternal pushing during labor

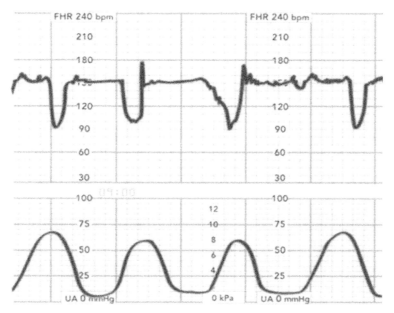

- Late: Due to decreased cardiac output from mother / decreased blood to the placenta. Common causes are maternal dehydration, anemia, hypoxia, hypotension from epidural analgesia, uterine tachysystole, and placental abruption.

Fetal Monitoring

External fetal monitoring

- Noninvasive; performed using transducer or Doppler

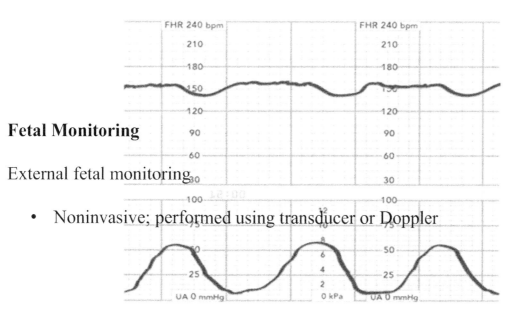

- Transducer, fastened with belt, should be placed on side of mother where fetal back is located (find using Leopold's maneuvers)

Internal fetal monitoring

- Invasive; requires rupturing of membranes.
- Attachment of electrode to presenting part of fetus; mother must be dilated 2 to 3 cm to perform this procedure
- Contra indication- Closed cervix, Placenta previa, STD (Sexually Transmitted Diseases), Breach position, AIDS, Hep B

Fetal Assessment Biophysical profile (BPP)

Check 5 things and score 0 or 2- by doctor with help of ultrasound

1. Fetal heart rate/NST
2. Fetal breathing movements
3. Fetal body movements
4. Fetal muscle tone
5. Amount of amniotic fluid

   Score 8-10 = Reassuring = good 6 - Equivocal (suspicious). Need another BPP within the next 12–24 hours,4 or less – Non reassuring – may need immediate attention/delivery

Gestational Age Assessments

- Nägele's rule: To estimate date of confinement, delivery date: subtract 3 months from the first day of the last menstrual period, add 7 days, and adjust the year
- McDonald's Method – Fundal height – correlate with GA until third trimester. Consistency (same person, same measurement) is important

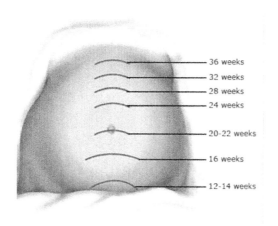

GTPAL acronym

- Gravidity – number of pregnancies.
  - Nulligravida – a woman who has never been pregnant
  - Primigravida – a woman in her first pregnancy
  - Multigravida – a woman who has had two or more pregnancies

GTPAL	
G- Gravida	Number of pregnancies
T - Term	Deliveries (37 weeks and after)
P- Preterm	Deliveries (20 weeks to 37 weeks)
A – Abortion	Pregnancy ended before 20 weeks
L – Living	Number of currently alive children

TORCH: Malformations, fetal death

- Toxoplasmosis: uncooked meals/soil contaminated vegetables, cat liter
- Other infection (? Hepatitis): poor hand washing, blood, and body fluids contamination
- Rubella: Droplet spread – rubella virus
- Cytomegalovirus: droplet, body fluids (including tears, saliva, breast milk). Hand washing.
- Herpes Simplex: STI

Presumptive signs

- (subjective): changes that the woman experiences that make her think that she may be pregnant.
- Amenorrhea
- Fatigue, Nausea, and vomiting
- Urinary frequency
- Breast changes – darkened areolae, Montgomery's glands around breast
- Quickening – slight fluttering movements of the fetus felt by a woman, usually between 16 to 20 weeks of gestation – primi might take longer to feel it
- Uterine enlargement

Probable signs

- Probable signs (objective): changes that make the examiner suspect a woman is pregnant (primarily related to physical changes of the uterus).
- Abdominal enlargement related to changes in uterine size, shape, and position
- Braxton Hicks contractions – false contractions; painless, irregular, and usually relieved by walking
- Positive pregnancy test, Fetal outline felt by examiner
- Hegar's sign: Softening and thinning of lower uterine segment at about sixth week of gestation
- Goodell's sign: Softening of cervix, beginning at second month of gestation
- Chadwick's sign: bluish coloration of mucous membranes of cervix, vagina, vulva at about sixth week of gestation
- Ballottement: Rebounding of fetus against examiner's fingers on palpation

Pregnancy Positive Signs

- Fetal heart rate: 120 to 160 per mt.
- Active fetal movement
- Outline of fetus on x-ray or ultrasonogram

Common Discomforts of Pregnancy

Urinary Frequency

Measure to avoid UTI

- Encourage the client to wipe the perineal area from front to back after voiding.
- Avoid bubble baths, Wear cotton underpants; avoid tight-fitting pants.
- Consume plenty of water (8 glasses per day). Avoid urinary stasis

Nausea and vomiting

- Eat crackers or dry toast 30 min to 1 hr. before rising in the morning to relieve discomfort.
- Small frequent meals, High Protein Snacks
- Instruct the client to avoid having an empty stomach and ingesting spicy, greasy, or gas-forming foods.
- Encourage the client to drink fluids between meals.
- Consume foods high in vitamin B6 (e.g., nuts, seeds, legumes)

Heartburn: Eat small frequent meals, Not allow the stomach to get too empty or too full, sit up for 30 min after meals, check with her provider prior to using any over-the-counter antacids.

Fatigue: May occur during the first and third trimesters – frequent rest periods

Backaches: Exercise regularly, perform pelvic tilt exercises (alternately arching and straightening the back). Use proper body mechanics by using the legs to lift rather than the back. Use the side-lying position.

Constipation:

- The client is encouraged to drink plenty of fluids, eat a diet high in fiber, and exercise regularly.
- Bulk-forming fiber supplements: Psyllium, methylcellulose, wheat dextrin

- Hemorrhoids
- A warm sitz bath and application of topical ointments will help relieve discomfort.

Medications

- NSAIDs must be avoided during pregnancy
- Especially during the third trimester due to the risk of causing premature closure of the ductus arteriosus in the fetus.
- Tylenol is a safe alternative for mild fever and pain.
- ACE/ARB Should be avoided- Fetal cardiac and renal problems.
- No Live vaccines. Tdap (Tetanus, diphtheria, and pertussis) is OK to give (pertussis immunity to baby)
- Live Vaccines: Viral: measles, mumps, rubella, vaccinia, varicella, zoster, yellow fever, rotavirus, intranasal influenza
    - Bacterial: oral typhoid
    - Other: BCG, Oral polio (Not used in some countries)

Warning Signs of pregnancy

- Gush of fluid from the vagina (rupture of amniotic fluid) prior to 37 weeks of gestation
- Vaginal bleeding (placental problems such as abruption or previa)
- Abdominal pain (premature labor, abruptio placentae, or ectopic pregnancy)
- Changes in fetal activity (decreased fetal movement may indicate fetal distress)
- Persistent vomiting (hyperemesis gravidarum)
- Severe headaches, edema, epigastric pain - (gestational hypertension)
- Elevated temperature (infection)
- Dysuria (urinary tract infection)

Adolescent pregnancy

Major concerns

- Poor nutritional status: Normal weight gain during pregnancy – 25-35 lb.
- Emotional and behavioral difficulties, Lack of social support systems
- Increased risk of stillbirth, Low–birth-weight infants, Fetal mortality

Travel Plans in pregnancy

- Healthy client – domestic travel ok till 36 weeks
- Need to let HCP know. Have all medical records ready
- Wear elastic compression stockings. Avoid dehydration – to prevent clots
- Seat belt – should not compress uterus- across thighs/hips- ok

High Risk Antenatal

General Points

Routine health screening

- Avoid travelling to areas affected by Zika virus (causes developmental dysfunction to babies)
- No alcohol (of any kind/amount)- It freely crosses placenta
- Diet – balanced diet:
- Avoid unpasteurized milk products/raw meat/unwashed fruits and vegetables
- Avoid deli meat/hot dogs (unless heated steaming hot)
- Avoid fish high in mercury (shark, swordfish, king mackerel, tilefish)
- Folic Acid 400-800 mcg daily when planning for pregnancy- to avoid neural tube defects. Green leafy vegetables, fortified grain (cereals, pasta, bread)
- Liver is high in folate (but also high in vit A- which may not be good in pregnancy)

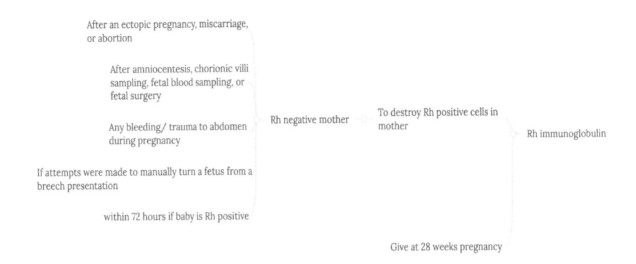

Ectopic Pregnancy

- Abnormal implantation of a fertilized ovum outside of the uterine cavity.
- Usually in the fallopian tube, which can result in a tubal rupture causing a fatal hemorrhage.
- Unilateral stabbing pain and tenderness in the lower-abdominal quadrant.
- Referred shoulder pain due to blood in the peritoneal cavity irritating the diaphragm or phrenic nerve after tubal rupture.

Nursing Actions

- Monitor client for hypovolemic shock - Dizziness, hypotension, tachycardia, lightheadedness
- Replace fluids and maintain electrolyte balance (to avoid shock)
- Provide client education and psychological support.
- RhoGAM if needed

Hyperemesis gravidarum

- Excessive nausea and vomiting past 12 weeks and results in a 5% weight loss, electrolyte imbalance, and ketosis

Nursing Care

- Monitor the client's I&O. (urine sp. gravity – increases if dehydration-ketone may be present due to fat breakdown with starvation)
- Give IV fluids, Assess skin turgor and mucous membranes.
- Monitor the client's vital signs (hypotension, tachycardia)
- Monitor the client's weight.
- Have the client remain NPO for 24 to 48 hr./ Meds/easily digestible food

Diabetes Mellitus

- Screen: 24th- 28th week of gestation
- Can be treated by diet alone; some may need insulin
- 2 and 3rd trimester – maternal insulin needs increase (placental hormones – increases insulin resistance)
- Fetus produces own insulin and pulls glucose from mother – mother at risk for hypoglycemia
- Risk for polyhydramnios, eclampsia, dystocia, infections (yeast)
- Newborn infant of diabetic mother at risk for hypoglycemia, hyperbilirubinemia, respiratory distress syndrome, hypocalcemia, congenital anomalies

Assessment

- Signs similar to those of diabetes mellitus in nonpregnant women (polyuria, polydipsia, polyphagia)
- Monitor the client's blood glucose. Monitor the fetus.? Insulin?

Client education

- Diet and Exercise, Insulin
- Metformin may be given (pregnancy cat B – no increased risk for fetus as per new research) – Best practice: take the medication before breakfast and before dinner
- hypo/hyper signs; Perform kick counts.

- Post partum – High risk for hemorrhage

Gestational Trophoblastic Disease

- Hydatidiform Mole - Molar Pregnancy
- Swollen, fluid-filled - grape-like clusters.
- No fetus in utero.
- Hyperemesis gravidarum- due to elevated hCG levels
- Symptoms of preeclampsia may be present
- Rapid uterine growth more than expected - over proliferation of cells
- Nursing Actions: Measure fundal height, assess vaginal bleeding and discharge, RhO(D) immune globulin (RhoGAM) to the client who is Rh-negative

Preterm Labor

- Occurs after 20th week, but before 37th week of gestation.
- Risk Factors – H/O preterm delivery or cervical surgery (cone biopsy), mother age (<17 or >35), current infection (dental/UTI), substance abuse, malnutrition
- Contractions - 10 minutes or less, last 30 seconds or longer, persist. (Patient c/o low back pain/pelvic pressure or heaviness/abdominal cramps)
- Assessment: Rupture of amniotic membranes

Interventions

- Maintain left lateral position, Monitor fetal status.
- Betamethasone to hasten surfactant production.
- Administer tocolytics (to stop contractions) -Ritodrine, Turbutaline, Mag sulphate, Nifedipine, Indomethacin
- Tocolytics – Contraindications: Active vaginal bleeding, dilation of the cervix greater than 6 cm, chorioamnionitis, greater than 34 weeks of gestation, and acute fetal distress.
- Betamethasone: Adverse effects: pulmonary edema & hyperglycemia
- Indomethacin: Adverse effects: PP hemorrhage, blood-tinged sputum

- Magnesium sulfate toxicity: -BLURP (Decreased Blood pressure, Level of consciousness, urine output, respiration, patellar reflex)

Client Education

- Immediate Actions - suspected premature labor (home)
- 1. Empty Bladder
- 2. Left Lying Position
- 3. Drink 3-4 cups of water
- 4.Palpate abdomen to assess contraction, ten mts apart or closer- contact doc
- 5. Rest for thirty mts and slowly resume activity if symptoms disappear. If symptoms persist up to 1 hr., contact doc

Premature Rupture of Membranes (PROM)

- Rupture of the amniotic sac before onset of true labor, regardless of length of gestation
- Assessment: Nitrazine test and Fern test positive
- Presence of pool of fluid near cervix, client statement of leaking fluid
- Nitrazine test – ask about recent sexual intercourse as semen is alkaline (false positive)

Interventions

- May remain in hospital or at home on bed rest /activity limitations
- NO PV (unless absolute necessary, sterile technique), check temp Q 2hrs, hydration

If home

- Pelvic rest (no PV, no sexual activity)
- Avoid breast stimulation – can cause uterine contraction
- Monitor temperature; report temperature of 100° F immediately
- Administer antibiotics to mother as prescribed

Placenta Previa

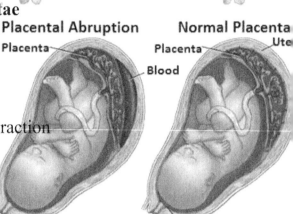

- Improperly implanted placenta
- Sudden onset of painless and bright red
- Vaginal bleeding (? shock- IV, Blood,
- Meds-steroids/betamethasone)
- Mother - side-lying position
- C-section
- ? fetal distress -oxygen
- No bleeding? OK to be home: Need pelvic rest (no PV, No sexual activity)

Abruptio Placentae

- Premature separation of the placenta
- Findings
  - Dark red, painful vaginal bleeding
  - Uterine rigidity / frequent uterine contraction
- Risk - Gestational HTN, Fall/accidents
- Bed rest; oxygen, IV, Blood, Meds-steroids
- Assess FHR pattern – delivery ASAP

Placentae accrete

- The placenta – deep into uterine wall- myometrium (normal implantation is in the endometrium).
- Placentae accrete is suspected if placenta has not been delivered within 30 minutes of the infant's delivery.
- Life-threatening hemorrhage and retained placental fragments
- Type and crossmatch (blood transfusion)
- Two large bore IV site

Supine Hypotensive Syndrome

- Vena Cava Syndrome– weight of uterus presses on vena cava- reduced cardiac return - hypotension

- Assessment: Faintness, lightheadedness, vertigo, hypotension, fetal distress
- Interventions: Position client in lateral recumbent position to shift weight of fetus off inferior vena cava
- Monitor maternal and fetal vital signs

HIV/AIDS

- Routine laboratory testing in the early prenatal period.
- No invasive procedures, such as amniocentesis, episiotomy, internal fetal monitors, vacuum extraction, and forceps
- No oxytocin induction – To avoid strong uterine contractions and vaginal tear
- Baby- No injections and blood testing -until the first bath
- Instruct the client not to breastfeed
- If mother immunocompromised- isolation
- Antiviral prophylaxis (retrovir -Zidovudine)
- Administer retrovir at 14 weeks of gestation, throughout the pregnancy, and before the onset of labor or cesarean birth.
- Administer retrovir to the infant at delivery and for 6 weeks following birth

Group B, Streptococcus ß-Hemolytic

- GBS - bacterial infection that can be passed to a fetus during labor and delivery.
- Positive GBS – PROM, preterm labor, and delivery, chorioamnionitis, infections of the urinary tract, and maternal sepsis.
- Vaginal and rectal cultures are performed at 36 to 37 weeks of gestation.
- Administer intrapartum antibiotic prophylaxis (Penicillin)
  - Client who delivered previous infant with GBS infection, has GBS bacteriuria during current pregnancy / GBS-positive screening during current pregnancy / unknown GBS status who is delivering at less than 37 weeks of gestation/ has maternal fever of 38° C (100.4° F)/ Rupture of membranes for 18 hr. or longer

Bleeding in Pregnancy

- Abortion: Pregnancy that ends before 20th week of gestation, spontaneously or electively: fetal weight less than 500 g.
- Spontaneous vaginal bleeding; passage of clots or tissue through vagina; low uterine cramping or contractions
- Interventions: Count perineal pads to evaluate blood loss, save expelled tissues and clots, educate client, family regarding dilation and curettage (D&C) as prescribed

SPONTANEOUS ABORTION (MISCARRIAGE) ASSESSMENT				
Type	Cramps	Bleeding	Tissue Passed	Cervical Opening
› Threatened	› With or without slight cramps	› Spotting to moderate	› None	› Closed
› Inevitable	› Moderate	› Mild to severe	› None	› Dilated with membranes or tissue bulging at cervix
› Incomplete	› Severe	› Continuous and severe	› Partial fetal tissue or placenta	› Dilated with tissue in cervical canal or passage of tissue
› Complete	› Mild	› Minimal	› Complete expulsion of uterine contents	› Closed with no tissue in cervical canal
› Missed	› None	› Brownish discharge	› None, prolonged retention of tissue	› Closed
› Septic	› Varies	› Malodorous discharge	› Varies	› Usually dilated
› Recurrent	› Varies	› Varies	› Yes	› Usually dilated

SUMMARY OF CAUSES OF BLEEDING DURING PREGNANCY		
Time	Complication	Signs and symptoms
› First trimester	› Spontaneous abortion	› Vaginal bleeding, uterine cramping, and partial or complete expulsion of products of conception
	› Ectopic pregnancy	› Abrupt unilateral lower-quadrant abdominal pain with or without vaginal bleeding
› Second trimester	› Gestational trophoblastic disease	› Uterine size increasing abnormally fast, abnormally high levels of hCG, nausea and increased emesis, no fetus present on ultrasound, and scant or profuse dark brown or red vaginal bleeding
› Third trimester	› Placenta previa	› Painless vaginal bleeding
	› Abruptio placenta	› Vaginal bleeding, sharp abdominal pain, and tender rigid uterus

Source: ATI Nursing Education

Oligohydramnios

- Low amniotic fluid volume (normal 800 ml to 1200 ml)
- Amnioinfusion – infusing isotonic saline to add volume-though intra uterine pressure catheter- transvaginal
- Monitor for over fluid - (uterine tone >20 mm hg)
- Decreased fundal height, irregular contour of abdomen

Major complications

- Pulmonary hypoplasia - due to the lack of normal alveolar distension by amniotic fluid- baby might need resuscitation.
- Umbilical cord compression -Monitor for variable decelerations

Anemia

- Increased fetal iron requirement in second trimester.
- Predisposes client to postpartum infection
- Assessment: Fatigue, headache, pallor, tachycardia, hemoglobin level lower than 10 mg/dL, hematocrit level lower than 30 g/dL
- Monitor hemoglobin and hematocrit levels every 2 weeks
- Instruct client to take iron and folic acid supplements
- Iron rich food: Meat, dried fruits
- Ferrous sulfate (325 mg) iron supplements twice daily
    - Take on an empty stomach/ with Vit C food
    - Increase roughage and fluid intake in diet – prevent constipation.
- Iron dextran: Used in the treatment of iron-deficiency anemia when oral iron supplements cannot be tolerated by the client who is pregnant.

Gestational Hypertension (GH)

- New HTN - after 20 weeks of gestation
- BP- 140/90 mm Hg or greater recorded at least twice, 4 to 6 hr apart, and within a 1-week period, after the 20th week of pregnancy

- Risk - placental abruption, kidney failure, hepatic rupture, preterm birth, and fetal and maternal death.

Predisposing conditions

- Chronic conditions, such as renal disease, hypertension, diabetes mellitus
- Primigravida (younger than 19 years or older than 40 years of age)

Preeclampsia

- Preeclampsia is a condition that occurs in pregnancy in which hypertension and proteinuria develop after 20 weeks of gestation in a client who previously had neither condition.
- Can be safely managed at home (frequent maternal and fetal evaluation needed)
- Preeclampsia with severe features: Severe hypertension, 160/110 mm Hg; massive, generalized edema; weight gain; proteinuria 3+ to 4+; oliguria; visual disturbances; headache; epigastric pain, HELLP (hemolysis, elevated liver enzymes, low platelets)
- Patient might c/o epigastric /RUQ pain (liver), Nausea, vomiting, malaise (don't ignore). Eclampsia: Characterized by generalized seizures

Magnesium sulfate

- Medication of choice for prophylaxis or treatment to lower blood pressure and depress the CNS.

Nursing Considerations

- Need IV pump
- Inform the client that she may initially feel flushed, hot, and sedated with the magnesium sulfate bolus.
- Monitor the client's BP, PR, RR, and deep-tendon reflexes.
- Monitor level of consciousness, urinary output (indwelling urinary catheter for accuracy),

- Monitor for presence of headache, visual disturbances, epigastric pain
- Monitor uterine contractions, FHR, and activity.
- Place the client on fluid restriction of 100 to 125 mL/hr and maintain a urinary output of 30 mL/hr or greater.
- Therapeutic magnesium level: 4-7 mEq/L
- Monitor the client for signs of magnesium sulfate toxicity.
- BLURP: decreased blood pressure; decreased level of consciousness decreased urinary output; respiratory depression; depressed or absent patellar reflex
- Cardiac dysrhythmias (Telemetry)
- Contraindications for Magnesium: Acute fetal distress, Vaginal bleeding, and Cervical dilation greater than 6 cm
- If magnesium toxicity is suspected:
  - Immediately discontinue infusion.
  - Administer antidote calcium gluconate.
  - Prepare for actions to prevent respiratory or cardiac arrest.

Interventions

- GH: Close monitoring of blood pressure, renal, I/O, Frequent rest periods, antihypertensives
- Preeclampsia
  - Monitor neurological status, DTR (? seizure), Monitor for HELLP
  - No added salt diet, with increase in dietary protein and carbohydrates
- Severe preeclampsia
  - Administer magnesium sulfate as prescribed? signs of magnesium toxicity, including BLURP. Always keep calcium gluconate at bedside
  - Gestational week 37? - term? – prepare for delivery
- Eclampsia
  - Provide care as with any seizure; monitor fetal heart rate and contractions. Administer magnesium sulfate as prescribed
  - Emergency - Prepare for delivery of fetus

Discharge instructions with GH

- Bed rest, side-lying position. Promote diversional activities.
- Avoid foods that are high in sodium (may not completely restrict sodium – possibility of Hypovolemia and fetal distress)
- Have a high protein diet. No alcohol and limited caffeine. Be adequately hydrated.
- Maintain a dark quiet environment to avoid stimuli that may precipitate a seizure.
- Maintain a patent airway in the event of a seizure.
- Administer antihypertensive medications

Labor and Birth

Labor

- Lightening: Fetus descends into pelvis about 2 weeks before delivery
- Leopold maneuvers – abdominal palpation of fetus
- Braxton-Hicks contractions increase
- True labor
  - Contractions increase in duration and intensity
  - Cervical dilation, effacement is progressive
- False labor
  - Labor does not produce dilation, effacement, or descent
  - Contractions are irregular, without progression
  - Walking has no effect on contractions; often relieves false labor

CHARACTERISTICS OF TRUE VS. FALSE LABOR (BRAXTON HICKS CONTRACTIONS) TRUE LABOR LEADS TO CERVICAL DILATION AND EFFACEMENT	
True Labor	False Labor
› Contractions	› Contractions
» May begin irregularly, but become regular in frequency	» Painless, irregular frequency, and intermittent
» Stronger, last longer, and are more frequent	» Decrease in frequency, duration, and intensity with walking or position changes
» Felt in lower back, radiating to abdomen	» Felt in lower back or abdomen above umbilicus
» Walking can increase contraction intensity	» Often stop with sleep or comfort measures such as oral hydration or emptying of the bladder
» Continue despite comfort measures	
› Cervix (assessed by vaginal exam)	› Cervix (assessed by vaginal exam)
» Progressive change in dilation and effacement	» No significant change in dilation or effacement
» Moves to anterior position	» Often remains in posterior position
» Bloody show	» No significant bloody show
› Fetus	› Fetus
» Presenting part engages in pelvis	» Presenting part is not engaged in pelvis

Source: ATI Nursing Education

Bishop score

- Bishop score is a system for the assessment and rating of cervical favorability and readiness for induction of labor
- A higher Bishop score- better chances of vaginal birth
- For nulliparous women, a score ≥8 usually indicates that induction will be successful

Cervix	Bishop score			
	0	1	2	3
Consistency	Firm	Medium	Soft	—
Position	Posterior	Mid-position	Anterior	—
Dilation	0 cm	1-2 cm	3-4 cm	≥5 cm
Effacement	0%-30%	40%-50%	60%-70%	≥80%
Station	−3	−2	−1, 0	+1, +2

Stages of labor		
Stage		Definition
1	Latent	0-5 cm cervical dilation
	Active	6-10 cm cervical dilation (breathing techniques, don't push till 10 cm) Transition – last 9-10 cm
2		10 cm (complete) cervical dilation to birth (ok to push)
3		Birth of baby to expulsion of placenta
4		1-4 hours after birth, maternal physiologic readjustment (post partum begins)

Assessment during Labor (initial)

- BP, PR, RR - q 1 hr, Temp – Q 2 hr
- Contractions q 30 mts (q15 mts – high risk)
- Watch for Uterine tachysystole – More than twelve contractions in 20 mts
- Ice chips and clear liquids – prevent dehydration
- Position comfortably (Lithotomy- stage 2). Relaxation Techniques

Assessment during Labor (later)

- BP, PR, RR, FHR - q 5 -15 mts. Contraction – continuous
- Uterine fundus tone
- Episiotomy: document degree (1,2,3,4)
- (1- virginal mucosal wall   2-muscle and facia 3. Anal sphincter 4. Rectal lumen)
- Monitor FHR -? Any decelerations??

Pain management

- Nonpharmacological: Position changes, Hydrotherapy, Breathing techniques & Relaxation
- Pharmacological: - Should be minimal risk.

- Lumbar Epidural block
    - Contraindicated – hypotension, infection at epidural site, coagulopathy (HELLP- bleeding leads to spinal cord compression)
    - Monitor urinary output (retention) Monitor BP (maternal hypotension)
    - Maternal hypotension after an epidural anesthesia: "STOP"
    - 1. Stop oxytocin if infusing.
    - 2. Turn the client on the left side.
    - 3. Oxygen - Administer oxygen.
    - 4. Push IV fluids - If hypovolemia is present
- Pudendal nerve block
    - Local anesthesia (Lidocane) to pudendal nerve areas (perineal area)
    - Help to relieve perineal pressure (no effect on contraction)
    - works quickly, better in later stages of delivery
- A note on oxytocin
    - To induce contractions (goal: one contraction every 2-3 minutes)
    - Give with IV pump – high alert medication
    - Need continuous FHR monitoring
    - Adverse: Uterine tachysystole (>5 contractions in 10 mts) – reduces placental blood flow – Action: decrease /stop oxytocin
- Systemic analgesia in L&D
    - All systemic drugs cross placental barrier
    - Given at peak of contraction- blood flow to baby is minimum at this time – so medicine effect reach baby slower
    - Two major drugs used: Butorphanol tartrate (Stadol) Nalbuphine hydrochloride (Nubain).
    - Maximum three doses: have ceiling effect: won't be effective after 3 doses
    - Do not use for mothers with opioid abuse history
    - Best is for mothers with 2-4 hours more to deliver. Imminent birth is a relative contraindication – (baby do not get enough time in utero to recover from dose)
- Parameters for safer administration
    - Stable maternal vital signs

- Fetus with heart rate of 110-160 beats/min
- Well-established labor contractions
- Cervix dilated to at least 4-5 cm in primipara and 4 cm in multipara

Dystocia

- Difficult labor that is prolonged or more painful
- May occur because of problems caused by uterine contractions, fetus, or bone and tissues of maternal pelvis, Diabetic mothers – large baby
  - Assessment: Fetal distress, Lack of progress in labor
- Interventions
  - Assess fetal heart rate (FHR); monitor for distress
  - Monitor uterine contractions
  - Assess for prolapse of cord after rupture of membranes

Fetal Positions

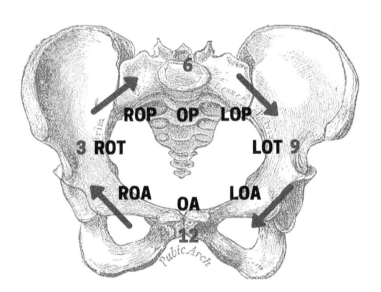

- ROA and LOA are most optimal (better) for delivery
- ROP and LOP:
  - mother have more back pain (back labor)

- most common malposition
  - Apply counterpressure to the client's sacrum during contractions - alleviate back pain
  - Firm, continuous pressure is applied with a nurse's closed fist, heel of the hand, or other firm object like a back massager.
- ROT or LOT – Dystocia – might need manual rotation of baby during labor
- Breech Position
  - Fetal feet or buttocks presenting first in the maternal pelvis
  - No back pains
  - Complications
    - Ineffective dilation of the cervix - dystocia
    - Increased risk of umbilical cord prolapses.

Shoulder Dystocia (SD)

- Baby's shoulders get stuck during labor.
- "Turtle sign": baby head retracts back
- Do not pull-on baby, No fundal pressure (suprapubic ok)
- No forceps/vacuum recommended
- Complications:
  - Fetal asphyxia – if >5 mts delay
  - Brachial plexus injuries for baby (Erb-Duchenne paralysis)
  - postpartum hemorrhage and third- and fourth-degree perineal tears
- Management of SD HELPERR
- H: call for Help
- E: evaluate for Episiotomy
- L: legs (McRoberts' maneuver) - hyperflexing the mother's legs tightly to her abdomen to straighten sacrum
- P: give suprapubic pressure
- E: Enter: maneuvers (internal rotation)
- R: Remove the posterior arm
- R: Roll the patient to hands and knees (all-fours position)

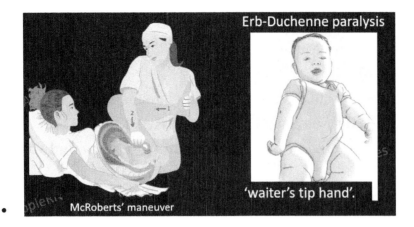

- McRoberts' maneuver

Erb-Duchenne paralysis 'waiter's tip hand'.

Prolapsed Cord

- Umbilical cord displaced between presenting part and amnion or protrudes through cervix, causing compression, compromising fetal circulation
- Assessment: Visible umbilical cord, Irregular and slow FHR (deceleration) especially abrupt after rupture of membrane

Interventions

- Relieve cord pressure immediately, call for help.
- Turn mother side to side or elevate her hips (knee - chest) to shift fetal presenting part toward her diaphragm
- Elevate fetal presenting part lying on cord by applying finger pressure with sterile gloved hand
- Do not attempt to push cord into uterus
- Monitor FHR and for signs of hypoxia, Administer oxygen to mother as prescribed
- Prepare for emergency cesarean birth as prescribed

Amniotomy

- Amniotomy = artificial rupture of membranes (AROM)
- After procedure – mother in upright position to facilitate drainage of fluid
- Note amniotic fluid color, amount, and odor.
- Yellowish-green fluid: meconium in utero

- Strong, foul odor: infection
- Complications: Prolapsed cord, Fetal bradycardia (cord compression.), Infection – monitor temp every 2 hrs.

Rupture of Uterus

- Complete or incomplete separation of uterine tissue as result of tear in wall of uterus from stress of labor
- Risk – with a precipitous labor – 3 hours or less
- Assessment: Fetus palpated outside uterus (complete rupture)

Interventions

- ? signs of shock: oxygen, IVF, blood products as prescribed
- Cesarean section / hysterotomy /hysterectomy
- Provide emotional support for client, partner, family

Vaginal birth after cesarean (VBAC)

- Risk- uterine rupture – Monitor for Non -reassuring fetal heart pattern (i.e., variable, or late decelerations, bradycardia).
- Maternal manifestations: change in uterine shape, severe abdominal pain, and cessation of uterine contractions.
- Signs of hemorrhage and hypovolemic shock
- If forceps/vacuum: Traction is used only during contractions.
    - Do not apply additional fundal pressure (uterine rupture)

Amniotic Fluid Embolism

- Escape of amniotic fluid into maternal circulation; debris containing amniotic fluid deposits in pulmonary arterioles, usually fatal to mother
- Assessment: Abrupt onset of respiratory distress, chest pain; cyanosis; seizures; heart failure, pulmonary edema; fetal bradycardia, distress
- Interventions:
    - Institute emergency measures to maintain life
    - Administer oxygen 8 to 10 L/min; prepare for intubation, mechanical ventilation

Fetal Distress

- FHR lower than 120 or more than 160 beats/min, Meconium-stained amniotic fluid
- Fetal hyperactivity, Progressive decrease in baseline variability
- Severe variable decelerations, late decelerations

Interventions

- Place mother in lateral position; elevate legs
- oxygen at 8 to 10 L/min via face mask as prescribed
- Discontinue oxytocin (Pitocin) if infusing as prescribed
- Monitor maternal and fetal vital signs
- Prepare for emergency cesarean section as prescribed

Intrauterine fetal demise

- Also called still birth
- Perinatal bereavement process
- Help bathe and dress the infant
- Provide privacy
- Encourage to view and hold the body before discharge to the funeral home
- Encourage family members to name the infant,
- Obtain handprints and footprints of baby
- Cut a lock of the infant's hair for keepsake
- Photograph the infant - if parents prefer
- Notify organ procurement organization as per policy

Adoption

- Emotional and psychosocial responses
- Encourage birth mother to create memories
- Hold newborn closely, Take pictures
- Name the baby, give chance to say goodbye to baby
- Nurse- avoid negative phrases (e.g.: give baby away)

Post Partum Care

Post Partum Period

- Starts immediately after delivery; around sixth week following delivery.
- Involution: Rapid decrease in size of uterus as it returns to pre pregnant state; fundal height decreases one fingerbreadth (1 cm) per day.
- (Fundus second day – at umbilicus. Day 10 – uterus in pelvis)
- Boggy uterus (soft and relaxed) – risk for hemorrhage
- Afterpains are normal
- First 48 hrs. of post-partum are greater risk for CV patients
- PP diuresis – 2 to 3 L more output first day- considered normal
- Full bladder – increased risk for bleeding

Lochia

- Discharge from uterus; consists of blood from vessels of placental site and debris
  - Rubra (red) occurs from delivery to day three
  - Serosa (brownish pink) occurs from days 4 to 10
  - Alba (white) occurs from days 10 to 14
- Amount can increase by exertion or breast feeding.
- Comfort: Ice to perineum: twenty mts on 10 mts off for first 24 hrs. Sitz bath prn
- Abnormal Lochia
  - Excessive - Saturation of a perineal pad in 15 min or less or pooling of blood under the client's buttocks – is critically serious- Possibly a cervical or vaginal tear.
  - Numerous large clots/Perineal pad saturating fast (15 mts – 1 hr) essential to report to HCP
  - Foul odor - suggestive of infection (endometritis)
  - Persistent lochia rubra beyond day 3 - Retained placental fragments.
- Continued flow of lochia serosa or alba beyond the normal length of time may indicate endometritis, especially if it is accompanied by fever, pain, or abdominal tenderness.

General Points

- Hyperthermia is common in first 24 hours. Bradycardia common in first week
- RHO(D) immune globulin (RhoGAM)
- Facilitate bonding with newborn
- Perineal discomfort: Occurs as result of delivery

Episiotomy:

- Educate client to perform perineal care after voiding
- Encourage use of analgesic spray, analgesics PO as prescribed

- REEDA scale for assessment of episiotomy healing: Redness, Edema, Ecchymosis, Discharge, Approximation (REEDA) scale: (score 0-3 for each item. The higher the score - the more problem)

Focused postpartum assessment

- B – Breasts
- U – Uterus (fundal height, placement, consistency)
- B – Bowel and GI function
- B – Bladder function
- L – Lochia (color, odor, consistency, and amount [COCA])
- E – Episiotomy/ Emotional Status
- H – Homan's sign – to detect DVT
- Vital signs, to include pain assessment
- Teaching needs

Warning Signs to Report

- Bleeding – bright red/large clots
- Temp > 100.4 F, Chills, Excessive Pain, Red/Warm breast
- Red episiotomy, Foul smelling lochia, Urinary retention
- Calf pain/tenderness/swelling

Phases of maternal role attainment

Dependent: taking-in phase	Dependent-independent: taking-hold phase	Interdependent: letting-go phase
First 24 to 48 hours	Begins on day 2 or 3; up to 10 days to several weeks	Focus on family as a unit
Focus is on meeting personal needs	Focus on baby care and improving care-giving competency	Resumption of role (intimate partner, individual)
Rely on others for assistance	Want to take charge but need acceptance from others	
Excited, talkative; need to review birth experience with others	Want to learn and practice	

Postpartum depression is more serious than baby blues.

BABY BLUES

- Very common
- Usually starts 2-3 days after birth
- May experience feelings of worry, unhappiness and fatigue
- Usually gets better on its own within 2 weeks

POSTPARTUM DEPRESSION

- Usually starts 1-3 weeks after birth
- Interferes with ability to do daily life activities
- Intense symptoms of sadness, anxiety, and hopelessness
- May include loss of interest in activities, withdrawing from friends and family, or thoughts of hurting self or baby
- Can occur up to a year after birth
- Usually requires treatment

Breast-feeding

- Assess LATCH: Latch achieved by infant, Audible swallowing, Type of nipple (Flat/inverted), Comfort of mother, Help given to mother during nursing

- Cracked nipples: Expose nipples to air 10 to 20 minutes after feeding; rotate position of newborn for each feeding

Proper breastfeeding position.

- Lips sealed completely around areola.
- Baby position- Nose close to breast,

Lips sealed completely around areola,

lower lip turned outward, baby's chin touching mother's breast

- Feed for 15-20 mts each side, Feed "on demand"/ 2-3 hourly

Breast Engorgement

- May occur on the third or fifth postpartum day,
- Apply cold compresses 15 min on and 45 min off.
- Breast-feed frequently; apply ice packs between feedings.
- Fresh, cold cabbage leaves can be placed inside the supporting bra.
- Apply warm packs just before feeding if needed to increase milk flow and promote the letdown reflex.
- Reverse pressure softening: Displaces the fluid from the nipple momentarily, to help the infant latch on when the nipples and areolas are swollen from engorgement - place the fingers and thumb around the base of the nipple on the areola and push back toward the ribs.
- Mild analgesics may be taken for pain and discomfort of breast engorgement.

Hematoma

- Localized collection of blood into tissues of reproductive tract after delivery
- Assessment: Sensitive, bulging mass in perineal area, discolored skin, Potential for development of shock

Interventions

- Monitor vital signs, presence of abnormal pain, intake and output, signs of infection
- Place ice packs at hematoma site as prescribed
- Administer analgesics / Administer blood products as prescribed
- Prepare client for incision and evacuation of hematoma if necessary

Hemorrhage

- Bleeding of 500 mL or more following delivery.
- Can be caused by uterine atony- inability of the uterine muscle to contract adequately after birth
- Assessment: First 24 hours, early hemorrhage; after first 24 hours, late hemorrhage
- PPH med: Methylergonovine – cause vasoconstriction - Do not give if Mother's BP is high. Misoprostol – OK for HTN mother for PPH
- Special note on Misoprostol: Not used prenatal- as it is teratogenic (congenital defects). However, it can be used for medicated abortion and for cervical ripening for procedures, and to induce labor. This is also used to prevent gastric ulcer in patients using long term NSAID.

Interventions for signs of hemorrhage or shock

- Massage fundus, but no over massage, Vitals (5-15mts), pad count, labs (H/H)
- Prepare for administration of oxytocin (Pitocin) and/or blood transfusions if prescribed

Infection

- Any infectious process of reproductive organs that occurs within 28 days of delivery or abortion

Assessment

- Chills, Anorexia, Pelvic discomfort, or pain
- Vaginal discharge, Elevated WBC count, Fever
- Risk Factors: a history of previous infections, excessive number of vaginal examinations, cesarean births, prolonged rupture of the membranes, prolonged labor, trauma, and retained placental fragments.

Interventions

- Monitor vital signs every 2 to 4 hours
- Provide comfort measures, including position changes, providing warmth
- Isolate newborn from mother only if mother can infect baby
- Provide high-calorie, high-protein diet; fluid intake of 3000 to 4000 mL/day
- Encourage frequent voiding; monitor intake and output
- Administer antibiotics as prescribed, following obtaining cultures

Mastitis

- Inflammation of breast as result of infection, usually occurring in breast-feeding mothers, 2 to 3 weeks after delivery
- Assessment: Localized heat and edema, Pain, Fever, Complaints of flu-like symptoms

Interventions

- Instruct mother in good hand washing and breast hygiene techniques
- Promote comfort, Maintain lactation in breast-feeding mothers
- Encourage manual expression of milk or use of breast pump every 4 hours
- Encourage use of supportive bra, to be worn at all times
- Administer analgesics, antibiotics, as prescribed

Pediatrics

Newborn Care

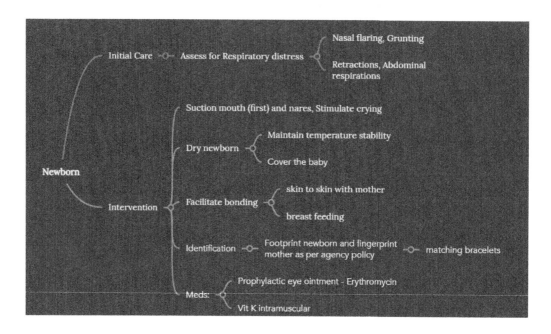

Apgar Score System

- Apgar score at 1 minute and 5 minutes (for all babies). 5-minute intervals thereafter until 20 minutes for infants with a score less than 7
  - Scores: 8 to 10: No intervention
  - 4 to 7: Gently stimulate; rub infant's back; oxygen
  - 0 to 3: Infant requires resuscitation

SCORE	0	1	2
Heart rate	› Absent	› Less than 100	› Greater than 100
Respiratory rate	› Absent	› Slow, weak cry	› Good cry
Muscle tone	› Flaccid	› Some flexion	› Well-flexed
Reflex irritability	› None	› Grimace	› Cry
Color	› Blue, pale	› Pink body, cyanotic hands and feet (acrocyanosis)	› Completely pink

Source: ATI Nursing Education

Newborn Assessment

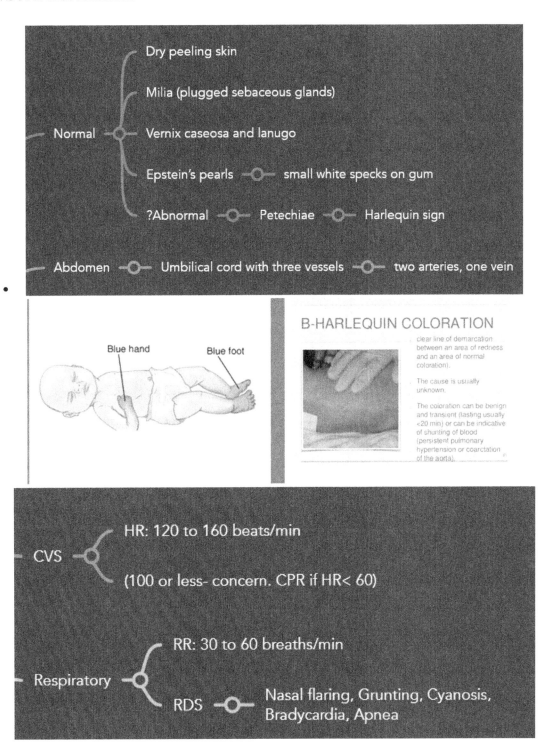

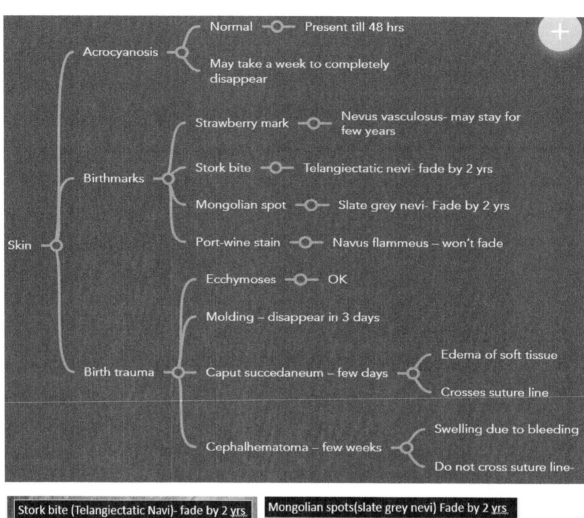

Acrocyanosis
- Normal — Present till 48 hrs
- May take a week to completely disappear

Birthmarks
- Strawberry mark — Nevus vasculosus- may stay for few years
- Stork bite — Telangiectatic nevi- fade by 2 yrs
- Mongolian spot — Slate grey nevi- Fade by 2 yrs
- Port-wine stain — Navus flammeus – won't fade

Skin

Birth trauma
- Ecchymoses — OK
- Molding – disappear in 3 days
- Caput succedaneum – few days
  - Edema of soft tissue
  - Crosses suture line
- Cephalhematoma – few weeks
  - Swelling due to bleeding
  - Do not cross suture line-

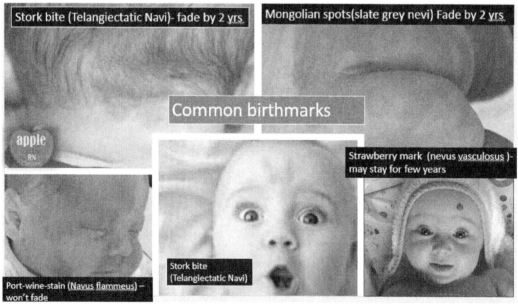

Stork bite (Telangiectatic Navi)- fade by 2 yrs

Mongolian spots(slate grey nevi) Fade by 2 yrs

Common birthmarks

Strawberry mark (nevus vasculosus)- may stay for few years

Stork bite (Telangiectatic Navi)

Port-wine-stain (Navus flammeus) – won't fade

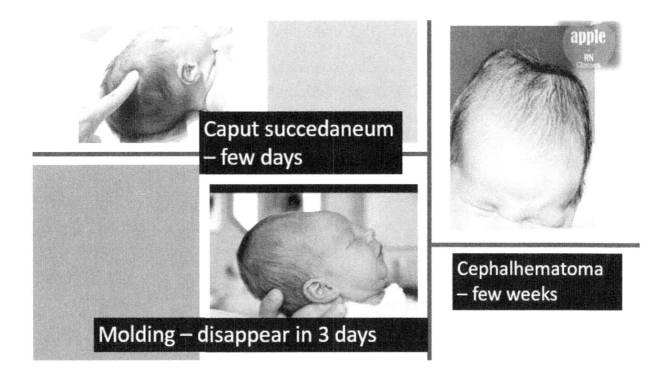

Caput succedaneum – few days

Cephalhematoma – few weeks

Molding – disappear in 3 days

•

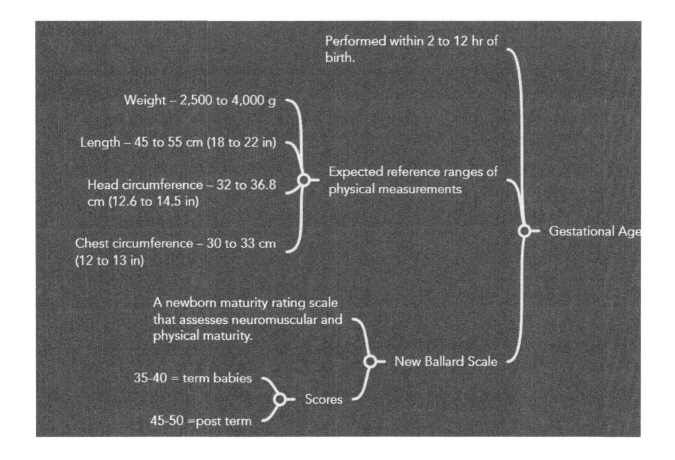

Performed within 2 to 12 hr of birth.

Weight – 2,500 to 4,000 g

Length – 45 to 55 cm (18 to 22 in)

Head circumference – 32 to 36.8 cm (12.6 to 14.5 in)

Chest circumference – 30 to 33 cm (12 to 13 in)

Expected reference ranges of physical measurements

Gestational Age

A newborn maturity rating scale that assesses neuromuscular and physical maturity.

35-40 = term babies

45-50 =post term

Scores

New Ballard Scale

Cord Care

- Before discharge, the cord clamp is removed.
- Keep cord dry, top of the diaper folded underneath it.
- Sponge baths until cord falls off (10 to 14 days after birth) (Tub bathing and submersion after)
- Cord infection: cord is moist and red, has a foul odor, or has purulent drainage - Notify the provider immediately

Teaching

Infant abduction

- Nurse's role is protection of newborn from abduction
- Maintain security measures (e.g., locked units) as per agency policy
- Check visitors for identification as per agency policy
- If locked door alarm goes off, respond quickly as per agency policy

Circumcision:

- Teach mother to clean penis after each voiding by squeezing warm water over penis (no soap/alcohol)
- Do not remove the yellow exudate which may be present for 2-3 days (part of healing process)
- Plastibell- suture around the penis- will fall off itself
- OK to use petroleum jelly gauze
- Uncircumcised newborn: Instruct mother not to pull back on foreskin

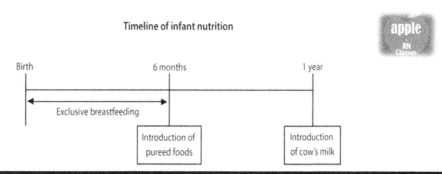

Stool color of breast-fed baby – Yellow/seedy.   Bottle - brownish
Weight loss upto 6% - OK in first few days. More than 7% - need evaluation
Up to 1 year- Avoid : Egg whites and wheat products - allergy.
Avoid honey

SUGGESTED INTRODUCTION OF FOODS	
Birth to 4 Months	› Breast milk (until 6 months) or formula (at 4 months)
4 to 6 Months	› Iron-fortified rice cereal
6 to 8 Months	› Vegetables, fruits
8 to 10 Months	› Strained meats, fish, poultry
9 to 12 Months	› Table foods (cooked, chopped, and unseasoned)
12 Months	› Cow's milk, eggs, cheese

Source: ATI Nursing Education

Preterm Infant

- Thin skin with visible blood vessels, minimal subcutaneous fat; jaundiced, weak reflexes, lanugo
- Undescended testes in boys, narrow labia in girls
- Interventions: Vital signs: Prevent Cold Stress, Oxygen
- Monitor I/O, electrolytes, daily weight
- Handle newborn carefully, changing position Q 1 to 2 hr.
- Avoid exposure to infections

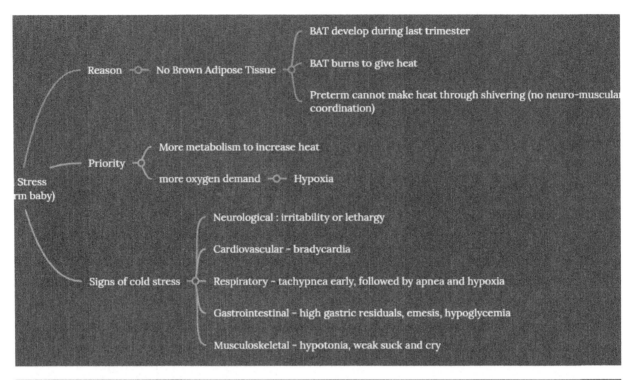

Cold Stress (Preterm baby)

Reason — No Brown Adipose Tissue
- BAT develop during last trimester
- BAT burns to give heat
- Preterm cannot make heat through shivering (no neuro-muscular coordination)

Priority
- More metabolism to increase heat
- more oxygen demand — Hypoxia

Signs of cold stress
- Neurological : irritability or lethargy
- Cardiovascular - bradycardia
- Respiratory - tachypnea early, followed by apnea and hypoxia
- Gastrointestinal - high gastric residuals, emesis, hypoglycemia
- Musculoskeletal - hypotonia, weak suck and cry

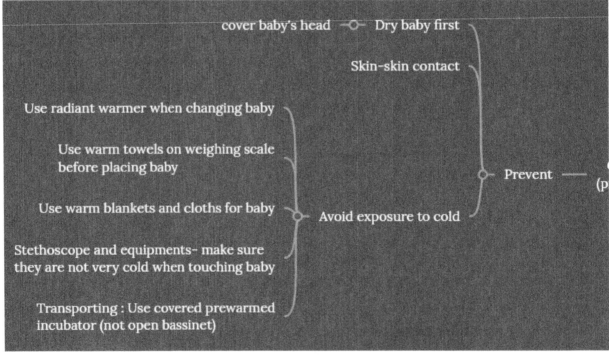

cover baby's head — Dry baby first

Skin-skin contact

Use radiant warmer when changing baby

Use warm towels on weighing scale before placing baby

Use warm blankets and cloths for baby

Stethoscope and equipments- make sure they are not very cold when touching baby

Transporting : Use covered prewarmed incubator (not open bassinet)

Avoid exposure to cold

Prevent — (p

Post-term Newborn

- Born after 42 weeks of gestation
- Hypoglycemia; parchment-like skin without lanugo; long fingernails, more scalp hair; long, thin body due to loss of fat and muscle in extremities; meconium staining.
- Interventions: Provide normal newborn care, Monitor for meconium aspiration, hypoglycemia,

Physiological jaundice

- Also known as normal or milk jaundice
- Occurs after first 24 hours (in full-term), first 48 hours (premature neonates
- Benign resulting from normal newborn physiology of increased bilirubin production due to the shortened lifespan and breakdown of fetal RBCs and liver immaturity.
- Not associated with any other abnormality – Feed the baby

Pathological jaundice

- Occurs in the first 24 hours; may be caused by early hemolysis of red blood cells.
- Associated with other diseases, or with anemia and hepatosplenomegaly
- Phototherapy can be used

Hyperbilirubinemia

- Maintain well-hydrated status
- Administer early, frequent feedings as prescribed
- Expose as much of newborn's skin as possible, except for shielding eyes and genital area
- Remove shields, patches at least once per shift and assess eyes for infection or irritation
- Monitor skin temperature frequently
- Assess for dehydration. Increase fluid intake as prescribed
- Educate parents that stools and urine may be green

- Remove Q 4hrs, Reposition newborn Q2 hours
- Provide stimulation to newborn
- Turn off the phototherapy lights before drawing blood for testing.
- Avoid applying lotions or ointments to the skin because they absorb heat and can cause burns

The Addicted Newborn

- Addicting drugs: Heroin, Methadone, Cocaine
- Some withdrawal symptoms: start within 24 hours after birth.
- Neonatal Abstinence Syndrome- can be 48–72 hours after birth
- Addicted mom? – methadone given to mom during pregnancy and breastfeeding to reduce opioid craving and withdrawal
- Clinical manifestations of withdrawal in infants: irritability, jitteriness, high-pitched cry, Yawning, stuffy nose, or sneezing
- Increased sweating, diarrhea, vomiting, poor feeding, dehydration
- Monitor vital signs – Respiratory & Cardiac
- Hold newborn firm and close to body during feeding and when giving care
- Swaddle infant, gentle rocking is ok
- Provide small, frequent feedings
- Monitor intake and output, give IV
- Reduce environmental stimulation
- Provide emotional support for mother

Fetal Alcohol Syndrome

- Due to maternal alcohol use during pregnancy
- Both physical and mental retardation

FETAL ALCOHOL SYNDROME

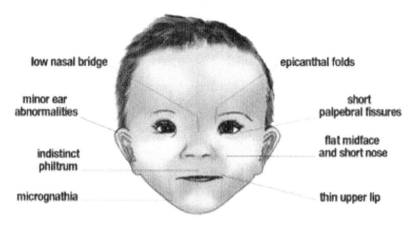

low nasal bridge

minor ear
abnormalities

indistinct
philtrum

micrognathia

epicanthal folds

short
palpebral fissures

flat midface
and short nose

thin upper lip

Image credit: The National Institutes of
Health

- Monitor for respiratory distress
- Position on side to facilitate secretion drainage
- Suction PRN, Assess suck and swallow reflexes, small feedings
- Monitor I/O, weight, head circumference
- Decrease environmental stimuli

Meconium Aspiration Syndrome

- Aspiration can occur in utero or with first breath
- Assessment: Signs of respiratory distress, Yellow-stained nails, skin, umbilical cord
- Interventions: Suctioning immediately after head is delivered

TORCH Syndrome

- TORCH: toxoplasmosis; other viruses; rubella; cytomegalovirus; herpes
- General symptoms for infections: fever; tachypnea; apnea; tachycardia; poor feeding; decreased muscle tone; lethargy; irritability.
- Mother with rubella – Baby should be isolated until the infant's urine and pharyngeal mucous are free of the infection
- Hep B mother: Ok to breastfeed baby (unless nipples are bleeding/Hep B immunoglobulin prophylaxis not given)

- Oral candidiasis of baby: which non-removable patches on oral mucosa, palate, and tongue of baby (might bleed/painful) – baby having difficulty sucking

Down Syndrome/Trisomy 21

- Flat facial profile
- Upward slant to the eyes
- Small ears, protruding tongue, Hypotonia
- Single transverse crease across palm of the hand
- Trisomy 18 (Edwards syndrome) – cardiac defects/musculoskeletal deformity – Discuss end of life care
- Trisomy 13 (Patau syndrome) also results in early death.

Exstrophy of the bladder

- Congenital disorder – need surgical repair
- Bladder exposed externally
- Pre-op- Place a protective film of plastic (Saran wrap) over the exposed bladder. It keeps the tissue moist and prevents infection.

Newborn of mother with AIDS

- No immediate invasive procedures: No circumcision
- The newborn can room with mother.
- Administer zidovudine (AZT) as prescribed for first 6 weeks of life
- Monitor for early signs of immune deficiency
- Instruct mother on follow-up care for newborn
- Vaccine: No Live Vaccine till HIV status confirmed, Give all other.
- Newborn test - p24 Antigen

Newborn of Diabetic Mother

- Neonate born to insulin-dependent mother or gestational diabetic mother
- May lead to development of congenital anomalies, hypoglycemia, hyperbilirubinemia, increased metabolic demand for fetus leading to hypoxemia, polycythemia, and respiratory distress syndrome.

Assessment

- LGA: Large for gestational age newborn, edema in face and cheeks
- Signs of respiratory distress, including tachypnea, grunting, retractions, cyanosis, and nasal flaring
- Signs of hypoglycemia, including twitching, jitteriness, lethargy, seizures; hyperbilirubinemia
- The normal S. glucose – term newborn at day one is 40-60 mg/dL
- From Day 2 normal 50- 90 mg/dl
- Obtain daily weight
- Feed infant soon after birth with glucose in water, breast milk, or formula as prescribed, Administer glucose IV as prescribed

Cleft lip and palate

- Baby unable to create suction and pull milk or formula from the nipple.
- At risk for aspiration and inadequate nutrition

Feeding cleft lip baby

- Hold upright position: aspiration risk
- Tilt the bottle to fill nipple. Point it down and away from the cleft.
- Use special bottles and nipples: Free flow of formula
- Use a squeezable bottle - Press to get more feed to baby
- Burp more often
- Feed slowly: over 20–30 minutes
- Feed frequently: every 3–4 hours

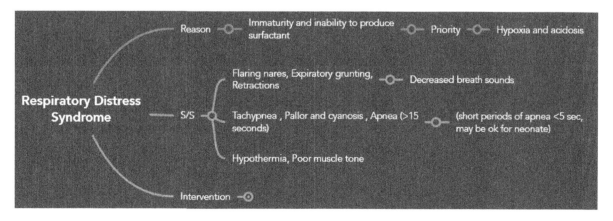

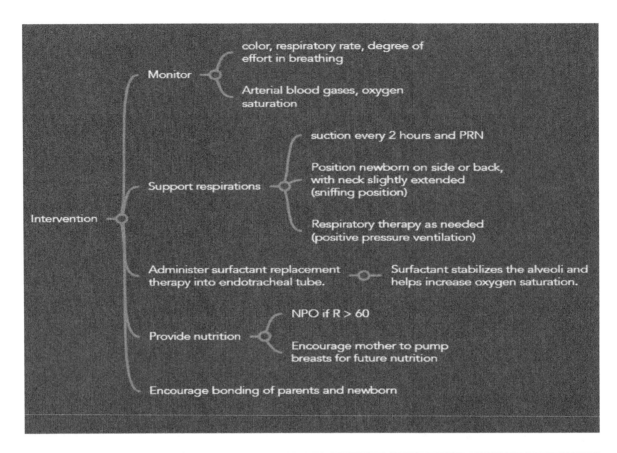

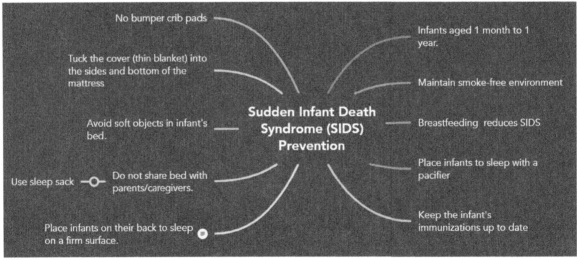

- To Prevent SIDS: No pillow; No soft toys; No bumper pads

Epistaxis

1. Calm the child
2. Position child to sit up and lean forward
3. Apply pressure to nose (10 minutes), if still bleeding insert cotton balls to nostrils
4. Apply ice to nasal bridge
5. Contact HCP

Actions to take if child is uncooperative

- Engage both the child and parent.
- Be firm and direct about expected behavior.
- Complete the assessment as quickly as possible.
- Use a calm voice.
- Reduce environmental stimuli.
- Limit the people in the room

Childhood Obesity

- Strategies the family can implement to reduce the risk of childhood obesity
- Avoid using food as a reward.
- Emphasize physical activity.
- Ensure a balanced diet is consumed.
- Teach children to select healthy foods and snacks.
- Avoid eating fast foods frequently.
- Avoid skipping meals.
- Model healthy behaviors

Growth and Development

Infants

- The infant's posterior fontanel closes by 2 to 3 months & anterior fontanel closes by 12 to 18 months of age.
- Exclusive breast feeding is preferred for 6 months. Solid food is appropriate around 6 months.
- Avoid cows' milk and honey till 1 year
- Erikson: trust vs. mistrust
- Hold infant frequently, give stimulation, Pacifier if NPO
- Separation anxiety develops between 4 and 8 months of age

AGE	GROSS MOTOR SKILLS	FINE MOTOR SKILLS
1 month	› Demonstrates head lag	› Has a grasp reflex
2 months	› Lifts head off mattress	› Holds hands in an open position
3 months	› Raises head and shoulders off mattress	› No longer has a grasp reflex › Keeps hands loosely open
4 months	› Rolls from back to side	› Places objects in mouth
5 months	› Rolls from front to back	› Uses palmar grasp dominantly
6 months	› Rolls from back to front	› Holds bottle
7 months	› Bears full weight on feet	› Moves objects from hand to hand
8 months	› Sits unsupported	› Begins using pincer grasp
9 months	› Pulls to a standing position	› Has a crude pincer grasp
10 months	› Changes from prone to sitting position	› Grasps rattle by its handle
11 months	› Walks while holding on to something	› Can place objects into a container
12 months	› Sits down from a standing position without assistance	› Tries to build a two-block tower without success

Source: ATI nursing education

- Respond in a calm and soothing voice, be responsive to cries.
- Parents should remove gyms and mobiles by 4 months because injury can occur from choking or strangulation.

Car Seats:

- Infants in a car seat should face the rear of the vehicle until age 2 or until they reach the maximum height and weight for the seat.
- Infants should have car seats with five-point harness systems.

0-2	2-7	4-12	8-adult
Rear-facing car seat	Forward-facing car seat	Booster seat	Seatbelt

Toddlers (1 to 3 Years)

- Independence: toddlers attempt to do everything for themselves.
- Erikson's stage: Autonomy vs Shame and doubt – Allow choices /self-feeding / putting on own cloths, play therapy, learn, and use toddler's own words for common items
- Prepare toddler for procedure just before- no long waits
- Explain in simple terms, repeat if needed, allow to handle equipment's
- Egocentric: only from their point of view, Gender identity by age 3
- Separation anxiety continues, Regressive behavior, ok to hold comfort objects of their own (blankets/soft toys)
- Temper tantrums: Provide consistent, age-appropriate expectations

Appropriate play activities

- Filling and emptying containers, Playing with blocks
- Looking at books, playing with push and pull toys, Tossing a ball

AGE	GROSS MOTOR SKILLS	FINE MOTOR SKILLS
15 months	› Walks without help. Creeps up stairs.	› Uses cup well. Builds tower of two blocks.
18 months	› Assumes standing position. Jumps in place with both feet.	› Manages spoon without rotation. Turns pages in book two or three at a time.
2 years	› Walks up and down stairs.	› Builds a tower with six or seven blocks.
2.5 years	› Jumps with both feet. Stands on one foot momentarily.	› Draws circles. Has good hand-finger coordination.

Source: ATI nursing education

Preschoolers (3 to 6 Years)

- 3 yr. old: Ride a tricycle, jump off bottom step, Stand on one foot for a few seconds
- 4 yr. old: Skip and hop on one foot, Throw ball overhead
- 5 yr. old: Jump rope, Walk backward with heel to toe,
- Move up and down stairs easily
- Erikson's: Initiative vs. Guilt
- Preschoolers feel good about themselves for mastering skills, such as dressing and feeding that allow independence.
- Favorite toys and play help ease fears, allow time to respond,
- Pretend play is healthy.

Age-Appropriate Activities

- Playing ball, Putting puzzles together.
- Riding tricycles.
- Pretend and dress-up activities, cooking, and housekeeping toys.
- Musical toys, Painting, drawing, and coloring.
- Looking at illustrated books.

School-Age Children (6 to 12 Years)

- Erikson's: industry vs. inferiority (developing social, physical, and learning skills)
- Peers and teachers have great influence.
- Changes related to puberty begin to appear.
- More emphasis on privacy.
- Prefer the company of same-gender companions.
- Competitive and cooperative play predominates.
- Play board, video, and number games.
- Play hopscotch, Jump rope, Ride bicycles, team sports
- Build models, crafts, hobbies, read books
- Encourage independence, give choices, explain all procedures using body diagrams and outlines, set limits

Adolescents (12 to 20 Years)

- Erikson's: Identity vs. role confusion
- Physical development and changes- fear of body harm/pain
- Allow own cloths, explain all procedures, explore feelings, allow favorite food if ok, provide privacy
- Adolescents often feel invincible to bad outcomes of risky behaviors
- Peer relationships develop as a support system.
- Screening for scoliosis- a lateral curvature of the spine- is essential, especially for girls.
- Eating disorders

Age-Appropriate Activities

- Nonviolent video games, music, movies, Sports, social events, Caring for a pet, Career-training programs, Reading

Young Adults (20 to 35 Years)

- Erikson's: intimacy vs. isolation
- Risk for alterations in health from:
    - Substance use disorders

- o Periodontal disease due to poor oral hygiene
- o Unplanned pregnancies – a source of high stress
- o Sexually transmitted infections (STIs), Infertility
- o Work-related injuries or exposures
- o Violent death and injury

Middle Adults (35 to 65 years)

- Erikson's: Generativity vs. stagnation
- At risk for
  - o Obesity, Type 2 diabetes mellitus
  - o Cardiovascular disease, Cancer
  - o Substance use disorders (alcoholism)
  - o Psychosocial stressors

Older Adults (65 Years and Older)

- Erikson's: integrity vs. despair.
- Chronic disorders, CV disorders, mobility disorders, Mental health issues.

Nursing Points:

- Safety precautions, Fall Precautions
- Examine risk factors, Identify support systems.
- Refer clients to educational/community/support resources
- Use behavior-change strategies (clients' readiness, goals, acceptable intervention), Promote healthy lifestyle behaviors

General Healthy Lifestyle Behaviors

- Use stress management strategies.
- Get adequate sleep and rest.
- Eat a nutritious diet. Avoid saturated fats.
- Participate in regular physical activity most days.
- While outdoors, wear protective clothing, use sunscreen, and avoid sun exposure between 10 a.m. and 4 p.m.
- Wear safety gear (bike helmets, knee, and elbow pads)

- Avoid tobacco products, alcohol, and illegal drugs.
- Safer Sex- contraception
- Seek medical care, when necessary, get routine screenings, and perform recommended
- Self-examinations (breast, testicular).

Failure to Thrive (FTT)

- FTT: When a child has a low weight/height ratio: Weight less than 80% of ideal for age
- Can be due to inadequate caloric intake, inadequate absorption of calories, or excess caloric expenditure (malignancy, Cardiac condition)

Risk factors for FTT

- Young parent age, Unplanned or unwanted pregnancy
- Lower levels of parental education, Single-parent home
- Social isolation, Chronic life stresses/anxiety in the home
- Substance abuse, Domestic violence and/or parental history of child abuse
- Poverty, food insecurity
- Parents who have a negative perception of the child, Disordered feeding techniques (negative attitude to food, no proper mealtime, prolonged bottle feed)

Management

- Correct the cause (disease).
- Referral for resources
- Observation of feeding is very important: Observation of the child while being fed may provide information related to the cause of inadequate dietary intake, including disturbances in feeding behavior and psychosocial factors.
- Health education and behavioral counselling for parents

Lead poisoning

- Lead poisoning still occurs in the United States, although not as often as in previous decades.
- A common source of exposure is lead-based paints found in houses built before 1978, when such paint was banned. • Active renovations can significantly increase the amount of lead released into the home environment
- Blood lead level (BLL) screenings are recommended at ages 1 and 2, and up to age 6 if not previously tested. (≥5 mcg/dL)
- Lead poisoning is most threatening to the kidneys and neurological system.
- Dangerous in young children due to immature development of the brain and nervous system.
- Neurocognitive: Hyperactivity and impulsiveness; reading difficulties, and visual-motor issues.
- Extremely elevated BLLs can lead to permanent cognitive impairment, seizures, blindness, or even death.

www.AppleRN.com

Maternity Medications

Name	Action	Side Effect	Nursing Role
oxytocin (Pitocin)	Uterine stimulants increase the strength, frequency, and length of uterine contractions	Uterine rupture	Preassess risk factors, such as multiple deliveries. »Monitor the length, strength, and duration of contractions. » Have magnesium sulfate on standby if needed for relaxation of myometrium. Continuously monitor blood pressure and pulse rate, uterine hyperstimulation. Use infusion pump, report fetal distress. •If uterine hyperstimulation or non-reassuring FHR occurs, **stop medication immediately, turn client to side, infuse IV normal saline, administer oxygen via face mask ; notify physician**
dinoprostone (Cervidil),	To promote cervical ripening and to stimulate uterine contractions.	Diarrhea; nausea, vomiting; fever; chills; flushing; dysrhythmias; bronchoconstriction; peripheral vasoconstriction	•Should not be given to clients with significant cardiovascular disease or history of asthma, pulmonary disease, Before administration, have woman void, then maintain supine or side-lying position for 30 to 40 minutes after administration.
methylergonovine (Methergine)	serious postpartum hemorrhage	Hypertensive crisis	Monitor for manifestations of hypertensive crisis (headache, nausea, vomiting, increased blood pressure). Methergine is for use only after, and not during labor. Do not administer before delivery of placenta
Tocolytic Medications			
terbutaline sulfate, nifedipine, indomethacin	uterine smooth muscle relaxation.	Tachycardia, palpitations, chest pain, Tremors, anxiety, headache	Given subcutaneous. Monitor FHR, uterine contractions, pulse, blood pressure, respiratory rate, lung sounds, and daily weights. Limit fluid intake to 1,500 to 2,400 mL/24 hr. Med contraindicated for greater than 34 weeks gestation, Fetal distress, eclampsia, vaginal bleeding
Opioid Analgesics			

www.AppleRN.com

Name	Action	Side Effect	Nursing Role
meperidine hydrochloride (Demerol), butorphanol (Stadol), nalbuphine (Nubain)	decrease the perception of pain without the loss of consciousness.	Dry mouth, Nausea and vomiting, Tachycardia, hypotension, decreased fetal heart rate (FHR) variability, Neonatal depression	Provide ice chips, Administer antiemetic, Have nalaxone available at delivery (for neonatal depression), Monitor vital signs and fetal heart rate, safety (sedation)

www.AppleRN.com

Name	Action	Side Effect	Nursing Role
Magnesium Sulfate			
Magnesium Sulphate	•Central nervous system depressant and anticonvulsant; also causes smooth muscle relaxation, thus decreasing blood pressure, Helps stop preterm labor, prevents and controls seizures in preeclamptic and eclamptic clients	•Respiratory depression, depressed deep tendon reflexes, hypotension, decreased urinary output—symptoms of magnesium toxicity	•Calcium gluconate is antidote. Monitor for signs of magnesium toxicity Monitor vital signs, especially respirations, every 30 to 60 minutes Administer IV infusion via infusion pump or monitoring device Monitor deep tendon reflexes hourly Do not administer if client's patellar reflex absent or respiratory rate below 16 breaths/min, as prescribed Monitor hourly intake and output; and report hourly output less than 30 mL
Betamethasone			
Betamethasone	Corticosteroid; increases production of surfactant	•Immunosuppressive to mother	•Monitor maternal vital signs; monitor mother for signs of infection; monitor maternal white blood cell count
Eye Prophylaxis for the Neonate			
Erythromycin (0.5% Ilotycin) and tetracycline (1%)	•Bacteriostatic and bactericidal ointments and/or eye drops . Prevent infection by Neisseria gonorrhoeae and Chlamydia trachomatis		•Cleanse neonate's eyes before instilling drops or ointment; instill within 1 hour after delivery
Vitamin K (AquaMEPHYTON)			
Vit. K	•Vitamin K necessary to help production of active prothrombin; newborns are deficient in vitamin K for first 5 to 8 days of life because of lack of intestinal flora necessary to absorb vitamin K	Hyperbilirubinemia in newborn	•Administer in vastus lateralis muscle early in neonatal period. •Monitor for bruising, signs of bleeding

Respiratory System

Arterial Blood Gas (ABG)

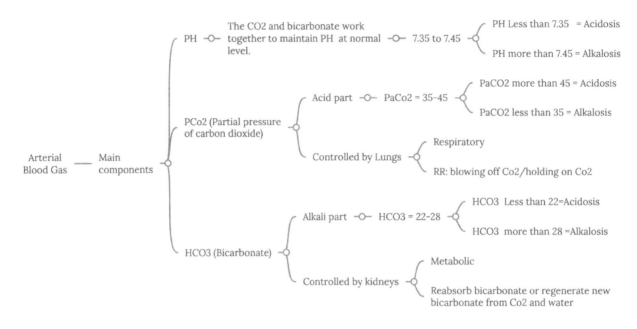

Arterial Blood Gas — Main components

- PH — The CO2 and bicarbonate work together to maintain PH at normal level. — 7.35 to 7.45
  - PH Less than 7.35 = Acidosis
  - PH more than 7.45 = Alkalosis

- PCo2 (Partial pressure of carbon dioxide)
  - Acid part — PaCo2 = 35-45
    - PaCO2 more than 45 = Acidosis
    - PaCO2 less than 35 = Alkalosis
  - Controlled by Lungs
    - Respiratory
    - RR: blowing off Co2/holding on Co2

- HCO3 (Bicarbonate)
  - Alkali part — HCO3 = 22-28
    - HCO3 Less than 22 = Acidosis
    - HCO3 more than 28 = Alkalosis
  - Controlled by kidneys
    - Metabolic
    - Reabsorb bicarbonate or regenerate new bicarbonate from Co2 and water

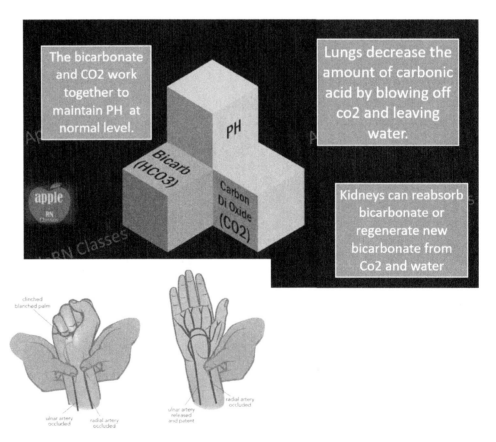

The bicarbonate and CO2 work together to maintain PH at normal level.

Lungs decrease the amount of carbonic acid by blowing off co2 and leaving water.

Kidneys can reabsorb bicarbonate or regenerate new bicarbonate from Co2 and water

- Normal values
    - PH value = 7.35 to 7.45
    - HCO3 = 22-28
    - PaCo2 = 35-45

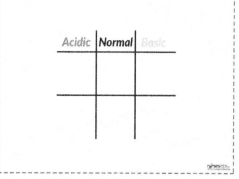

- PH Less than 7.35   = Acidosis, PH more than 7.45 = Alkalosis
- HCO3 Less than 22 = Acidosis, HCO3 more than 28 = Alkalosis
- PaCO2 more than 45 = Acidosis, PaCO2 less than 35 = Alkalosis

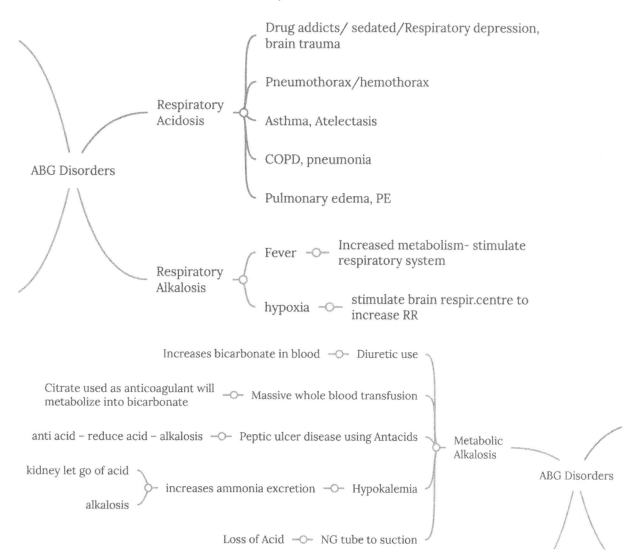

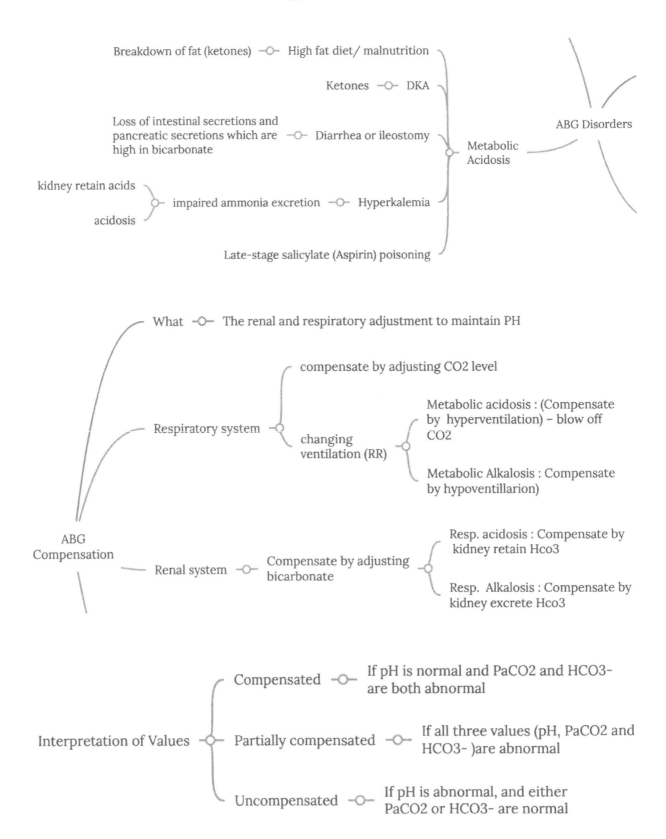

Breakdown of fat (ketones) —○— High fat diet/ malnutrition

Ketones —○— DKA

Loss of intestinal secretions and pancreatic secretions which are —○— Diarrhea or ileostomy high in bicarbonate

Metabolic Acidosis

ABG Disorders

kidney retain acids
acidosis —○— impaired ammonia excretion —○— Hyperkalemia

Late-stage salicylate (Aspirin) poisoning

What —○— The renal and respiratory adjustment to maintain PH

compensate by adjusting CO2 level

Respiratory system —○— changing ventilation (RR)

Metabolic acidosis : (Compensate by hyperventilation) – blow off CO2

Metabolic Alkalosis : Compensate by hypoventillarion)

ABG Compensation

Renal system —○— Compensate by adjusting bicarbonate

Resp. acidosis : Compensate by kidney retain Hco3

Resp. Alkalosis : Compensate by kidney excrete Hco3

Compensated —○— If pH is normal and PaCO2 and HCO3- are both abnormal

Interpretation of Values —○— Partially compensated —○— If all three values (pH, PaCO2 and HCO3-)are abnormal

Uncompensated —○— If pH is abnormal, and either PaCO2 or HCO3- are normal

Respiratory System Disorders

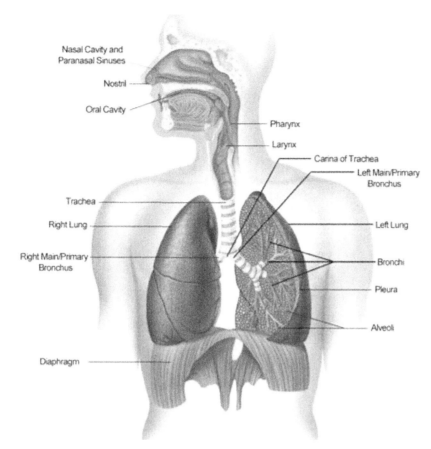

-

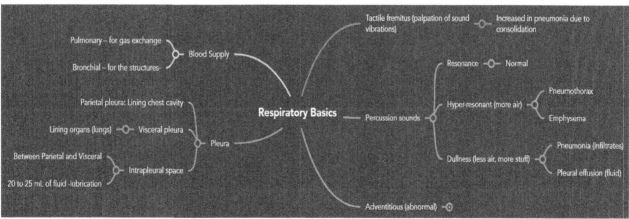

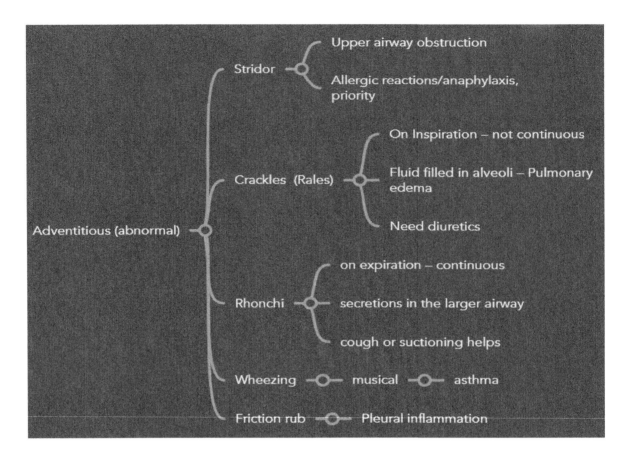

Labs

ABG

- Sputum –Do Rinse mouth first- avoid contamination
- AFB –Acid Fast Bacilli- TB? – 3 days, early morning- negative pressure room

Skin test – PPD

- Positive Indicate exposure to TB (not active disease)
- Read result in 48 to 72 hrs.

Pulse oximetry

- SpO2- 95 % or above in room air, COPD- 88% ok
- Remove nail polish, artificial nails to be removed.
- PFT – Pulmonary Function Test

Oxygen administration

Type	How much	Concentration
Nasal Canula	1-6 L/M	24- 44 %
Face mask with O2 reservoir	6 – 10 L/M	40 – 90%
Venturi mask	Deliver oxygen in precise concentration	24%, 28%, 35%, 40%
Nonrebreather mask (Hudson)	10 -15 L/M (Adjust O2 flow to keep mask inflated during inhalation)	95 -100%

Hypoxia Manifestations

EARLY FINDINGS	LATE FINDINGS
› Tachypnea	› Confusion and stupor
› Tachycardia	› Cyanotic skin and mucous membranes
› Restlessness	› Bradypnea
› Pale skin and mucous membranes	› Bradycardia
› Elevated blood pressure	› Hypotension
› Symptoms of respiratory distress (use of accessory muscles, nasal flaring, tracheal tugging, and adventitious lung sounds)	› Cardiac dysrhythmias

Source: ATI nursing education

Acute Respiratory Disorders

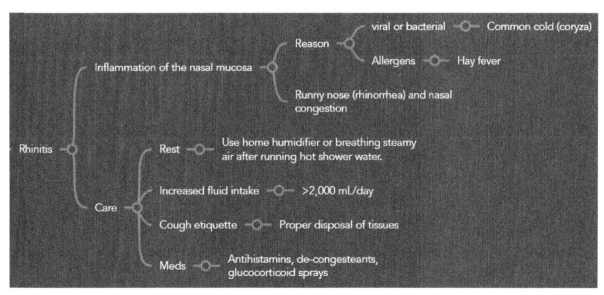

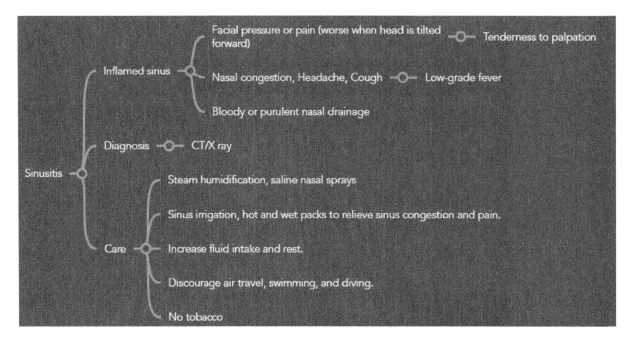

Influenza

- Highly contagious acute viral infection: Droplet precautions
- H1N1 ("swine flu") and H5N1 ("avian flu").
- Preventable by vaccine – Ok to take even if h/o egg allergy
- S/S: Severe headache, muscle aches, Fatigue, weakness, Hypoxia, Severe diarrhea, and cough (avian flu)
- Human parainfluenza viruses – contact and droplet precautions - No vaccine, supportive care

Nursing Care:

- Airborne /contact precautions for hospitalized with pandemic flu Provide saline gargles. Monitor hydration/ intake and output, Fluids
- Monitor respiratory status (complications).
- Antiviral med: reduce severity of symptoms:
- Oseltamivir (pill/liquid), Zanamivir (inhale), Peramivir (single dose IV), Baloxavir (single dose pill)

Pneumonia

- Inflammatory process: produces excess fluid.
- Cause - infectious organisms or aspiration

- Risk Factor - Immobility
- Types: Community-acquired and Health care-associated
- Community-acquired pneumonia (CAP) is the most common type and often occurs as a complication of influenza.
- Health care-associated pneumonia (HAP) has a higher mortality rate and is more likely to be resistant to antibiotics.
    - VAP – Ventilator associated Pneumonia: purulent sputum, positive sputum culture, leukocytosis (12,000 mm3), fever, and infiltrates on chest x-ray.

Laboratory Tests

- Sputum culture and sensitivity
- Obtain specimen before starting antibiotic therapy (suction for specimen if needed).
- CBC – Elevated WBC count (may not be present in older adult clients)
- ABGs – Hypoxemia (decreased PaO2 less than 80 mm Hg)
- Blood culture – To rule out organisms in the blood
- Serum electrolytes – To identify causes of dehydration
- Bacterial or viral (X ray infiltrates/consolidation)
- Clinical Manifestations: Fever, chills, chest pain, SOB, cough, crackle (mucus filled alveoli), wheezes
- Management
    - Meds -Antibiotics, analgesics, Steroids, bronchodilators.
    - Oxygen, nutrition, fluids
    - Chest physiotherapy, huff cough to remove secretions
    - Position with good lung down (gravity help to increase blood flow to the good lung, which can oxygenate more blood)
- At home: OK to use mist humidifier / warm bath / Prevention in hospitalized patients – measures
    - Infection control, avoid crowded areas
    - Aspiration precautions- Fowler's position

o Early ambulation / Turn, Cough and deep breath, Incentive spirometry
o Nutrition, Fluids, Immunization

Complications of pneumonia

- Atelectasis
    o Risk of hypoxemia. (SOB)
    o The client has diminished, or absent breath sounds over the affected area. A chest x-ray shows an area of density.
- Bacteremia (sepsis)
    o If pathogens enter the bloodstream from the infection in the lungs.
- Acute Respiratory Distress Syndrome (ARDS)
    o Hypoxemia persists despite oxygen therapy (Also called Refractory Hypoxemia – due pulmonary edema)
    o The client's dyspnea worsens as bilateral pulmonary edema develops that is non cardiac related.
    o A chest x-ray shows an area of density with a "ground glass" look
    o ABG findings: High CO_2 levels (>50) and low PaO_2 (<60)

Pneumonia Vaccine

- To prevent pneumococcal disease caused by pneumococcal bacteria (about 90 kinds of bacteria are known)
- Pneumococcal conjugate vaccines (PCV13, PCV15, and PCV20)
- Pneumococcal polysaccharide vaccine (PPSV23)
- Besides pneumonia, pneumococcal bacteria can also cause: Ear infections, Sinus infections, Meningitis, Bacteremia (bloodstream infection)

NAME	PCV13	PCV15/20	PPSV23
Age	All children younger than 2 years old People 2 through 18 years old with certain medical conditions.	Adults 65 years or older Adults 19 through 64 years old with certain medical conditions or risk factors	All adults 65 years or older Children 2 - 18 years old with certain medical conditions As a second dose for adults 19 years or older who got PCV15
Frequency of dose	4 doses of PCV13, at ages 2, 4, 6, and 12–15 months. Afterwards- if any medical condition – single dose	Single dose (may need later dose of PPSV23 if high risk)	Most people need only one dose of PPSV23 High-risk groups – revaccination is recommended Revaccination time : 5 years from first dose

Pneumonic plague

- By Yersinia pestis- spread from person to person through air
- Droplet precautions
- First signs - fever, headache, weakness, and rapidly developing pneumonia with shortness of breath, chest pain, cough, and hemoptysis
- The pneumonia progresses for 2 to 4 days -respiratory failure and shock.
- Early treatment of pneumonic plague is essential. Antibiotics - within 24 hours of the first symptoms. Antibiotic treatment for 7 days will protect people who have had direct, close contact with infected patients.
- A plague vaccine is not currently available for use in the United States.

Epiglottitis and (Croup / Laryngo-tracheo-bronchitis)

- Inflammation and swelling of epiglottis (bacterial)
- Croup is characterized by a "seal-like barking" cough (mostly viral)
- Flu- fever, sore throat, dysphagia, dysphonia
- Tripod position (sit upright leaning on arms, chin thrust out, mouth open).
- Droplet precautions (mask). Don't exam the throat – spasm!!!
- Endotracheal tube (ET) & tracheostomy set at bedside.
- Management includes NPO, IV fluids, Antipyretics, antibiotics
- Hib Vaccine can reduce the incidence

Chronic Obstructive Pulmonary Disease (COPD)

Health Promotion and Disease Prevention

- Smoking cessation, Avoid exposure to secondhand smoke, Protection from occupational hazards (mask, proper ventilation), Vaccines (flu, pneumonia)

COPD – ASTHMA

- Chronic inflammation of airway leading to intermittent obstruction
- Spasm of bronchial smooth muscle with airway edema.
- Mucosal edema, Bronchoconstriction, Excessive mucus production.
- Pulmonary function tests (PFTs) are the most accurate tests for diagnosing asthma and its severity.
- Watch for triggers

Triggers

- Environmental factors, - changes in temperature (especially warm to cold) and humidity, Air pollutants, Strong odors (perfume)
- Allergens (grass, tree, and weed pollens, mold, feathers, dust, roaches, animal dander)
- Foods treated with sulfites: Example: Baked goods, Jams, Canned vegetables, Pickled foods, Potato chips (patient might have wheezing, chest tightness and cough)
- Stress and emotional distress

Nursing Care

- High- Fowlers, Oxygen, IV, Rest, meds, vaccine, Teaching
- ABG, Tele (dysrhythmias), PFT monitoring
- Medications: Steroids, Bronchodilators, Anticholinergics
- Two inhaled medications? keep 5 minutes between medications

Tiotropium (Spiriva)

- A long-acting, 24-hour, anticholinergic, capsule-inhaler system (HandiHaler)

- Do not swallow tablet, Button on the inhaler must be pushed when using.

MDI: Metered Dose Inhaler

1. Sit straight
2. Shake the MDI
3. Exhale
4. Keep MDI close (2 fingers) to open mouth (if no spacer) – and press – breath in simultaneously
5. Hold breath for 10 sec
6. Exhale

Dry Powder Inhaler

- Contain dry powder – do not shake before use (MDI – shake)
- Do not Tilt – powder may fall
- Inspiration – deep and rapid (MDI – deep and slow)
- No spacer- no need for coordinating with inhalation as its rapid dispersion
- Most of them has dose counter
- Rinse mouth afterwards

Dry Powder Inhaler Use

1. Remove mouthpiece cap
2. Engage the lever for medicine to be available
3. Exhale completely
4. Close lips tightly around the mouthpiece
5. Breath in deeply
6. Hold breath for 10 seconds
7. Rinse mouth with water

Status asthmaticus

- This is a life-threatening episode of airway obstruction that is often unresponsive to common treatment.

- It involves extreme wheezing, labored breathing, use of accessory muscles, distended neck veins, and creates a risk for cardiac and/or respiratory arrest.
- Nursing Actions
- Prepare for emergency intubation.
- As prescribed, administer oxygen, bronchodilators, epinephrine, and initiate systemic steroid therapy.

COPD – Emphysema

- Progressive destruction of alveoli due to chronic inflammation – decreased surface area for gas exchange- lose of elasticity of lung tissue- airway collapse
- Primary cause – smoking
- CXR – Hyperinflated lung, Heart small or normal
- "Pink puffer" – barrel chest + pursed lip + accessory muscle breathing+ underweight.
- Persistent tachycardia- inadequate oxygen
- Wheezing, diminished breath sounds
- Hyper resonance on percussion due to "trapped air"
- Difficulty with exhalation due to obstructed airway and mucus
- Pursed Lip Breathing:
  - o Instruct the client to: Form the mouth as if preparing to whistle.
  - o Take a breath in through the nose and out through the lips/mouth.
  - o Do not puff the cheeks.
  - o Take breaths deep and slow.
- The low-pressure "huff" cough: for COPD patients to remove secretions.
  - o Position upright (lung expansion)
  - o Deeply inhale and, while leaning forward, force the breath out gently using the abdominal muscles while making a "ha" sound (huff cough).
  - o Repeat two more times (e.g., "ha, ha, ha") – keeps airways open while moving secretions up and out of the lungs.

COPD- Bronchitis

- Chronic airway inflammation with chronic productive cough lasting at least 3 months in 2 years
- "Blue bloater": - Bluish-red skin (cyanosis + Polycythemia), Obesity
- CXR – Congested lung, Heart enlarged
- Chronic productive cough- thick mucus- foul smelling, Celia disappears – Ineffective airway clearance, Frequent pulmonary infection, Dyspnea, Increased AP diameter

Nursing Care

- Ideal weight- nutritious food/ Meds, Oxygen, Avoid irritants, Immunizations
- Mucolytic Agents: These agents help thin secretions making it easier for the client to expel. Ex: Acetylcysteine (Mucomyst). Expectorant – guaifenesin
- Avoid OTC cough suppressants: Impair the secretion clearance
- Position - high-Fowler's is 90°
- Encourage effective coughing, / suction/ deep breathing /IS
- Administer breathing treatments/ medications / oxygen as prescribed.
- Monitor for skin breakdown around the nose and mouth from the oxygen device.
- Promote adequate nutrition- soft, high-calorie foods
- CO2 Narcosis (tolerance with high levels of CO2)
- Oxygen use complications – Fire Hazard, Oxygen Toxicity (rare), Infection (constant moist O2- bacterial growth)

Cor Pulmonale (complication of COPD)

- Air trapping, airway collapse, and stiff alveoli lead to Increased pulmonary pressures.
- Right side heart failure- Increased workload for heart
- Blood flow through the lung tissue is difficult. Enlargement and thickening of RA, RV
- Signs
    - Low oxygenation levels, Cyanotic lips

- o Enlarged and tender liver
- o Distended neck veins and Dependent edema
- Nursing care
  - o Monitor respiratory status and administer oxygen
  - o Monitor heart rate and rhythm.
  - o Meds, IV fluids

COPD- Care after Discharge

- Referrals to assistance programs, such as food delivery services, home care services such as portable oxygen.

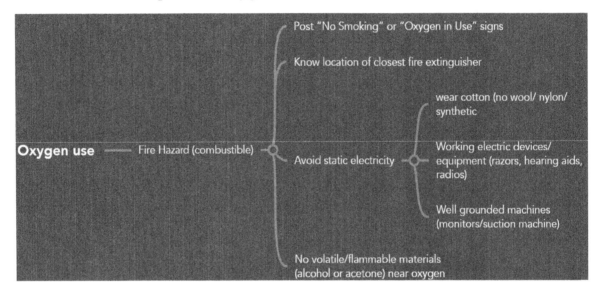

Client Education

- High-calorie foods to promote energy. Encourage rest periods as needed.
- Promote hand hygiene to prevent infection.
- Reinforce the importance of taking medications as prescribed.
- Promote smoking cessation if the client is a smoker. Encourage immunizations
- Clients should use oxygen as prescribed. Inform other caregivers not to smoke around the oxygen due to flammability.
- Provide support to the client and family

Legionnaire's Disease

- Form of pneumonia caused by Legionella pneumophila which grows and multiplies in a building water system (Steam/hot tubs)
  - o Assessment: 1 to 2 days of prodromal symptoms followed by high fever, dyspnea, vomiting, diarrhea, confusion, elevated WBC count
- Interventions
  - o Administer antibiotics as prescribed
  - o Supportive care, including respiratory support, nutritional support, fluid, and electrolyte management

Pneumothorax, Hemothorax

- Pneumothorax - air or gas in the pleural space - lung collapse
- Hemothorax - blood in the pleural space
- Tension pneumothorax - air enters the pleural space during inspiration and is not able to exit upon expiration.
- The trapped air causes pressure on the heart and the lung leading to a decrease in cardiac output.

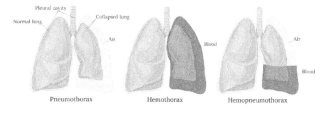

Pneumothorax, Hemothorax and Hemopneumothorax

Signs

- Dyspnea (first sign), crepitus
- Tracheal deviation towards unaffected side
- Diminished breath sound in affected side- late sign
- Unequal chest expansion (reduced on affected side)

Management

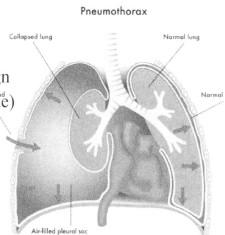

- Vitals, oxygen, chest tube care, nutrition
- Prevent infection, respiratory failure
- Meds- analgesics, antibiotics

Pleural Effusion

- Collection of fluid in pleural space
- Assessment: Sharp pleuritic pain; increases with inspiration, Dry, nonproductive cough, decreased breath sounds over affected area
- Chest x-ray shows pleural effusion, mediastinal shift
- Interventions: Identify, treat underlying cause. Place client in high Fowler's position, Encourage coughing, deep breathing, Surgery

Cystic Fibrosis (genetic/exocrine)

- Multisystem- thick mucus
- Steatorrhea, Sweat test – more NaCl
- Newborn- meconium ileus –first sign
- (Immunoreactive trypsinogen test)
- Affects – bronchioles – infection
- Small intestine – unable to absorb fats and protein
- Retarded growth and puberty
- Pancreatic and bile duct – clogged-digestion and absorption issues
- Diet - High calorie, high protien, high-fat, high-salt diet.
- Management – respiratory hygiene (vest vibrator, chest physiotherapy), avoid infection, supportive care

Tuberculosis (TB)

- Highly communicable disease caused by Mycobacterium tuberculosis
- Improper, noncompliant use of treatment programs
- Risk factors: Alcoholism; drinking unpasteurized milk from infected cow; younger and older clients; clients who are homeless and from lower socioeconomic group; crowded living conditions; intravenous drug user; malnutrition
- Transmission: Airborne route by droplet infection

- After infected individual has received TB medication for 2 to 3 weeks, risk of transmission reduced greatly

Tuberculosis: **Clinical manifestations**

- Fatigue; lethargy; anorexia; weight loss; low-grade fever; chills; night sweats; persistent cough with production of blood-tinged sputum; tight chest
- Chest assessment: Chest x-ray not definitive, but presence of multinodular infiltrates with calcification in upper lobes suggests TB
- Sputum cultures: Acid-fast smear identifies M. tuberculosis, confirming diagnosis
    - After medications started, sputum samples obtained to gauge effectiveness of therapy
- Hospitalized client
    - Respiratory isolation in negative-pressure room, Airborne isolation
    - If client needs to leave room, wears surgical mask
- Client education
    - Follow medication regimen, follow up care
    - Adequate nutrition, well-balanced diet
    - Family members should be tested for TB.
    - Cough etiquette

Mantoux test:

- False positives- Need chest x-ray to see active TB infection.
- Give in area not heavily pigmented, clear of hairy areas or lesions
- Teach importance of returning within 48 to 72 hr.
- Advise client not to scratch site, avoid washing site
- TB QuantiFERON blood test – measure a person's immune reactivity to Mycobacterium tuberculosis.
    - Test cannot differentiate latent tuberculosis (carrier state) from active tuberculosis disease.
    - Best For: Persons who have received BCG; Persons from groups that historically have poor rates of return for TST reading.
- No risk factors - 15

- An induration of 5 mm is considered a positive test for immuno-compromised clients.
  - Ex: HIV Patients, oncology pts, long term corticosteroid (> than six weeks), Organ transplant recipients
- A positive Mantoux test indicates that the client has developed an immune response to TB – NOT a confirmation of active disease
- An induration (palpable, raised, hardened area) of 10 mm or greater in diameter indicates a positive skin test.

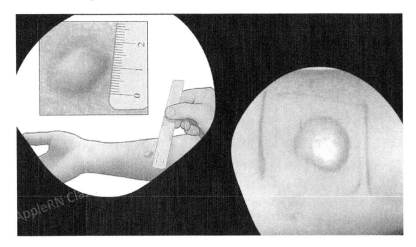

- Ten mm or more is considered to be within positive range for:
  - Recent arrivals (less than five years) from high-prevalence countries
  - Injectable drug users
  - Residents and employees of high-risk congregate settings (e.g., prisons, nursing homes, hospitals, homeless shelters, etc.)
  - Mycobacteriology lab personnel
  - Persons with clinical conditions that place them at high risk (e.g., diabetes, leukemia, end-stage renal disease, chronic malabsorption syndromes, low body weight, etc.)
  - Children less than four years of age, or children and adolescents exposed to adults in high-risk categories
  - Infants, children, and adolescents exposed to adults in high-risk categories

TB Medications

- Combination therapy – 6 to 12 months
- Hepatotoxic: Advise the client to report yellowing of the skin, pain or swelling of joints, loss of appetite, or malaise immediately.
- Antibiotic property
- Isoniazid (Nydrazid): (INH)
    - This medication should be taken on an empty stomach.
    - Monitor for hepatotoxicity and neurotoxicity, such as tingling of the hands and feet.
    - Vitamin B6 (pyridoxine) is used to prevent neurotoxicity from isoniazid.
- Rifampin (Rifadin)
    - Inform the client that urine and other secretions will be orange.
    - Inform the client this medication may interfere with the efficacy of oral contraceptives.
- Pyrazinamide
    - Take with a glass of water
- Ethambutol: suppress RNA synthesis
    - Optic neuritis: Can affect vision- need eye check up
- Streptomycin
    - Nephrotoxic and ototoxic
    - Report oliguria, KFT, tinnitus
    - Drink lots of fluids

Pulmonary Embolism

- Risk Factors
    - Immobility, DVT, Oral contraceptive use and estrogen therapy
    - Pregnancy, Platelet problems, Tobacco use
    - Heart failure or chronic atrial fibrillation
    - Autoimmune hemolytic anemia (sickle cell)
    - Long bone fractures, surgery

- A pulmonary embolism (PE) occurs when a substance (solid, gaseous, or liquid) enters venous circulation and forms a blockage in the pulmonary vasculature.
- Health Promotion and Disease Prevention
    - Promote smoking cessation.
    - Maintain appropriate weight for height and body frame, a healthy diet and physical activity.
    - Prevent deep-vein thrombosis (DVT)

Signs and symptoms

- Subjective Data
    - Anxiety, Feelings of impending doom
    - Pressure in chest, Pain upon inspiration and chest wall tenderness
    - Dyspnea and air hunger
- Objective Data
    - Adventitious breath sounds (crackles) and cough
    - Pleurisy, Pleural friction rub, Pleural effusion (fluid in the lungs)
    - Tachycardia, Tachypnea
    - Hypotension, Heart murmur in S3 and S4
    - Diaphoresis, Decreased oxygen saturation levels
    - Low-grade fever, low SaO2, cyanosis

Management

- Diagnostics
    - CT scan, Ventilation-perfusion (V/Q) scan
    - D- Dimer: (0.43 to 2.33 mcg/mL).
- Nursing care
    - Oxygen therapy, Semi-Fowler's, IV access, Vitals
    - Provide emotional support and comfort
    - Monitor changes in LOC and mental status
- Medications – watch for bleeding
- Anticoagulants – prevent clots from getting bigger
- Thrombolytic – dissolve clots

o Assess contraindication - active bleeding, peptic ulcer disease, history of stroke, recent trauma

Discharge education

- Smoking cessation
- Avoid immobility. Increase physical activity: Get up at least once in every hour
- Wear compression stockings. Avoid crossing his legs. Drink lots of water (refer to DVT prevention)
- Bleeding precautions: No ASA
- Food on warfarin: Advise the client to monitor intake of foods high in vitamin K (green, leafy vegetables) if taking warfarin.
  o Vitamin K can reduce the anticoagulant effects of warfarin.
- Advise the client to adhere to a schedule for monitoring PT and INR, follow instructions regarding medication dosage adjustments (for clients on warfarin), and adhere to weekly blood draws.

Mechanical ventilation

Function

- To deliver high concentrations of oxygen into the lungs.
- To help get rid of carbon dioxide.
- To decrease the amount of energy a patient uses on breathing so their body can concentrate on fighting infection or recovering.
- To breathe for a person who is not breathing because of injury to the nervous system, like the brain or spinal cord, or who has very weak muscles.
- To breathe for a patient who is unconscious because of a severe infection, buildup of toxins, or drug overdose.

Non-invasive

CPAP

- CPAP – Continuous Positive Airway Pressure (3 to 12 mm H2O)
- Positive airway pressure during inspiration and expiration

- Mainly for mild-moderate Sleep Apnea
- Patient should take spontaneous breath

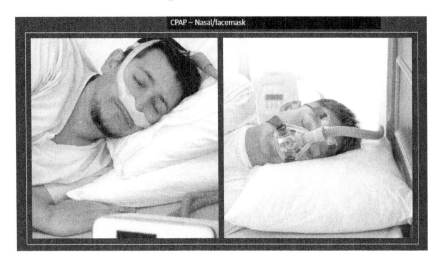

BiPAP – Bilevel Positive Airway Pressure (5 to 25 mm H2O)

- Inspiratory positive airway pressure (IPAP) and expiratory positive airway pressure (EPAP)
- Positive airway pressure during inspiration. But provides just enough pressure during expiration to keep airway open.
- OSA, Neuromuscular respiratory issues, COPD hypoxia, Chest wall deformity issues, heart failure, asthma, pulmonary edema

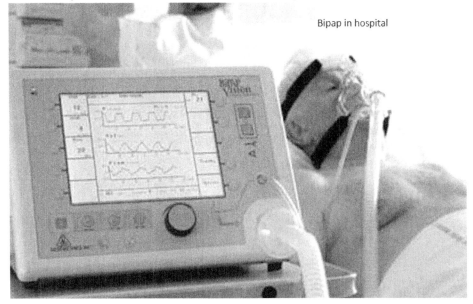

Bipap in hospital

Contraindications to NIPPV

- The need for intubation, Encephalopathy or altered mental status
- Hemodynamic instability
- Facial trauma or facial defects, Airway obstruction secondary to a mass
- Anticipated need for prolonged mechanical ventilation
- Gastrointestinal bleeding
- Patient wish

Invasive

- ET tube connected to ventilator
- The ventilator pushes a mixture of air and oxygen into the patient's lungs to get oxygen into the body.
- The ventilator can also hold a constant amount of low pressure, called positive end-expiratory pressure (PEEP), in order to prevent alveoli collapse
- The endotracheal tube allows to remove mucous/suction
- Different settings (modes): Volume of air/ Pressure /rate/ Flow/ Oxygen level

Modes of ventilation

Controlled

- Amount of air (tidal volume) and rate are preset to ventilator
- Clients cannot initiate a breath (100% controlled by ventilator)

Pressure Support Ventilation (PSV)

- All breaths are patient-triggered - the ventilator has no backup rate

Assist-control (Continues Modulated Ventilator- CMV)

- Amount of air and rate are preset to ventilator
- If client takes breath, ventilator gives the preset volume of air, but allows the client to control rate of breath (but won't allow to go below the minimum RR set for ventilator)

- Problem?? Hyperventilation/respiratory alkalosis if client's RR increases

Synchronized intermittent mechanical ventilation (SIMV)

- Similar to Assist control (preset tidal volume and rate)
- But let client takes breath and volume if they can initiate. And if RR goes above preset rate, no assistance is given to tidal volume – depend solely on lung compliance and patient effort.
- Ventilator will adjust the delivery of its breaths with the patient's efforts

Alarms

- There are three types of ventilator alarms: volume, pressure, and apnea alarms.
- Volume (low pressure) alarms indicate a low exhaled volume due to a disconnection, cuff leak, and/or tube displacement.
- Pressure (high pressure) alarms indicate excess secretions, client biting the tubing, kinks in the tubing, client coughing, pulmonary edema, bronchospasm, and/or pneumothorax.
- Apnea alarms indicate that the ventilator does not detect spontaneous respiration in a preset time period.

Respiratory Medications

Bronchodilators (inhalers)

Albuterol (Proventil, Ventolin):

- Bronchodilatation
- Provide rapid relief of acute symptoms and prevent exercise induced asthma.
- Watch the client for tremors and tachycardia. Short acting
- Prevention of asthma episode (exercise-induced) • Inhaled, short-acting one is used for prevention of asthma Episode

Asthma Medications

- Anticholinergic medications, such as ipratropium (Atrovent)
- It decreases pulmonary secretions.
- Advise clients to rinse the mouth after inhalation to decrease unpleasant taste.
- Observe the client for dry mouth.
- Hard candies, more fluids can be given to patients.
- Salmeterol primarily used for asthma attack prevention in long term.
- Not used to abort an asthma attack and not at the onset of an attack.
- It is long acting

Tiotropium (Spiriva)

- A long-acting, 24-hour, anticholinergic, inhaled medication used to control chronic obstructive pulmonary disease (COPD).
- It is administered most commonly using a capsule-inhaler system called the HandiHaler
- The capsule should not be swallowed and that the button on the inhaler must be pushed to allow for medication dispersion

Steroid Medications

- Steroids- To relieve inflammation
- Example: fluticasone (Flovent) and prednisone (Deltasone)

Client Education

- Encourage the client to drink plenty of fluids to promote hydration.
- Encourage the client to take prednisone with food.
- Decreased immune function, weight gain, fluid retention, risk of bleeding, hyperglycemia, reduced ht(growth) in children
- Encourage client to avoid persons with respiratory infections.
- Use good mouth care. Rinse mouth after use (prevent infection)
- Monitor the client's throat and mouth for aphthous lesions (canker sores).
- Do not stop the use of this type of medication suddenly.
- Bone loss: Take vit D
- When a client is prescribed an inhaled albuterol and an inhaled glucocorticoid, advise the client to inhale the albuterol before inhaling the glucocorticoid.
- Albuterol promotes bronchodilation and enhances absorption of the glucocorticoid.
- If two inhaled medications are prescribed, instruct clients to wait at least 5 min between medications

Xanthine: Theophylline (Theo-24)

- Narrow therapeutic range. (5 to 15 mcg/mL).
- Mild toxicity: GI distress and restlessness.
- Severe toxicity: Tachycardia, dysrhythmias, and seizures.
- If manifestations occur, stop the medication.
- Activated charcoal is used to decrease absorption
- Lidocaine is used to treat dysrhythmias
- Diazepam is used to control seizures.
- Caffeine can increase theophylline levels.
- Avoid Cola, coffee, and chocolate which contain xanthine
- Phenobarbital and phenytoin decrease theophylline levels.

Antitussives

- Opioids: Codeine suppresses cough through its action on the central nervous system.
- for chronic nonproductive cough.

Safety precautions

- GI distress- take with food
- Non-opioid: dextromethorphan (found in many different products for cough, such as Robitussin), benzonatate (Tessalon), diphenhydramine (Benadryl)
- Mild nausea, dizziness, and sedation may occur.

Expectorants

- Guaifenesin (Mucinex): allow clients to decrease chest congestion by coughing out secretions.
- GI upset: Take with food if GI upset occurs.
- Drowsiness, dizziness: Do not take prior to driving or activities if these reactions occur.
- Allergic reaction (rash): Stop taking guaifenesin and obtain medical care if rash or other symptoms of allergy occur.
- Increase intake of fluids: thin secretions

Mucolytics

- Acetylcysteine (Mucomyst, Acetadote)
- Mucolytics enhance the flow of secretions in the respiratory passages.
- S/E; Aspiration and bronchospasm when administered orally
- Advise clients that acetylcysteine has an odor that smells like rotten eggs.
- Mucolytics are used in clients who have cystic fibrosis.
- Acetylcysteine is the antidote for acetaminophen poisoning.
- Should not be used in clients at risk for GI hemorrhage.

Decongestants

- Ex: phenylephrine: To treat allergic or non-allergic rhinitis by relieving nasal stuffiness. S/E: Vasoconstriction: Avoid in CAD
- Rebound congestion secondary to prolonged use of topical agents
- Advise clients to use for short-term therapy, no more than 3 to 5 days.
- Taper use and discontinue medication using one nostril at a time.

Cardiovascular System

Overview

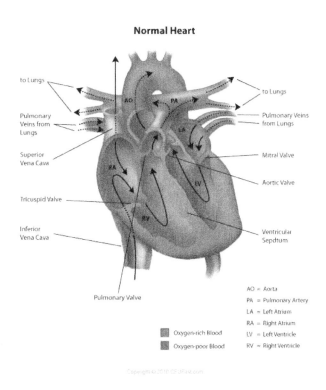

Normal Heart

to Lungs
to Lungs
Pulmonary Veins from Lungs
Pulmonary Veins from Lungs
Superior Vena Cava
Mitral Valve
Aortic Valve
Tricuspid Valve
Inferior Vena Cava
Ventricular Sepdtum
Pulmonary Valve

Oxygen-rich Blood
Oxygen-poor Blood

AO = Aorta
PA = Pulmonary Artery
LA = Left Atrium
RA = Right Atrium
LV = Left Ventricle
RV = Right Ventricle

Heart Sounds

- S1- Lub- Closure of the mitral and tricuspid valves the beginning of ventricular systole (contraction)
- S2- Dub- Closure of the aortic and pulmonic valves the beginning of ventricular diastole (relaxation)
- S3 sound (ventricular gallop) Due to rapid ventricular filling can be an expected finding in children and young adults. Use the bell of the stethoscope.
- S4 sound reflects a strong atrial contraction, can be an expected finding in older and athletic adults and children. Use the bell of the stethoscope.

<u>5 AREAS FOR LISTENING TO THE HEART</u>

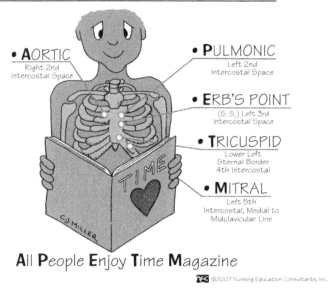

- **AORTIC** Right 2nd Intercostal Space
- **PULMONIC** Left 2nd Intercostal Space
- **ERB'S POINT** (S₂ S₂) Left 3rd Intercostal Space
- **TRICUSPID** Lower Left Sternal Border 4th Intercostal
- **MITRAL** Left 5th Intercostal, Medial to Midclavicular Line

All **P**eople **E**njoy **T**ime **M**agazine

©2007 Nursing Education Consultants, Inc.

- Assess the peripheral vascular system for bruits
- Carotid arteries – over the carotid pulses
- Abdominal aorta – just below the xiphoid process
- Renal arteries – midclavicular lines above the umbilicus on the abdomen
- Iliac arteries – midclavicular lines below the umbilicus on the abdomen
- Femoral arteries – over the femoral pulses
- Pulse Pressure: Narrow = hypovolemia shock

Measuring Orthostatic Blood Pressure

- 1. Have the patient lie down for 5 minutes.
- 2. Measure blood pressure and pulse rate.
- 3. Have the patient stand.
- 4. Repeat blood pressure and pulse rate measurements after standing 1 and 3 minutes.
- A drop in BP of ≥20 mm Hg, or in diastolic BP of ≥10 mm Hg, or experiencing lightheadedness or dizziness is considered abnormal.
- Other Symptoms: nausea, dizziness, lightheadedness, tachycardia, pallor, and reports of seeing spots

TEST	EXPECTED REFERENCE RANGE	PURPOSE
Cholesterol (total)	› Less than 200 mg/dL	› Screening for heart disease
HDL	› Females – 35 to 80 mg/dL › Males – 35 to 65 mg/dL	› "Good" cholesterol produced by the liver
LDL	› Less than 130 mg/dL	› "Bad" cholesterol can be up to 70% of total cholesterol
Triglycerides	› Males – 40 to 160 mg/dL › Females – 35 to 135 mg/dL › Older adults (over age 65) – 55 to 220 mg/dL	› Evaluating for atherosclerosis

Source: ATI nursing education

Angina

- Chest pain resulting from myocardial ischemia
- Patterns of angina
  - Stable/ Exertional angina: occurs with activities that involve exertion, exercise, emotional stress
  - Unstable: Unpredictable
  - Prinzmetal (variant) Angina – Arterial Spasm (cold weather/stress/smoking/substance abuse) often awaking client from sleep.
- Assessment
  - Mild or moderate pain, may radiate to shoulders, arms, jaw, neck, back, usually lasts less than 5 minutes, relieved by rest and/or nitroglycerin; dyspnea; pallor; diaphoresis
  - ECG changes (inverted T wave, ST depression, or may be normal)
  - Stress test causes chest pain or changes in ECG
  - Cardiac enzyme levels can be normal. Confirmation- Cardiac catheterization

Chest Pain Initial Care

- Assess airway, breathing, and circulation (ABCs), Position upright
- Apply oxygen, if hypoxic
- Obtain baseline vital signs, heart, and lung sounds
- Obtain a 12-lead electrocardiogram (ECG)

- Insert 2-3 large-bore IV catheters
- Assess pain – OLDCART, Medicate for pain: morphine/ nitroglycerin (Sildenafil + Nitro –severe hypotension)
- Initiate continuous electrocardiogram (ECG) monitoring
- Obtain blood work (e.g., cardiac markers, serum electrolytes)
- Obtain portable chest x-ray
- Assess for contraindications to antiplatelet and anticoagulant therapy
- Administer aspirin unless contraindicated

Angina Interventions

- Assess pain, Bed rest
- Administer oxygen, nitroglycerin as prescribed – S/E: headache
- Assess ECG strip
- Instruct client about diet, weight management, exercise, lifestyle changes following acute episode
- Surgical procedures: Same as for coronary artery disease

Myocardial Infarction

- Myocardial tissue abruptly, severely deprived of oxygen, leading to necrosis and infarction; develops over several hours
- Location of MI
    - LAD: Left anterior descending artery: Anterior or septal MI
    - Circumflex artery: Posterior or lateral wall MI
    - Right coronary artery: Inferior wall MI
- Risk factors- Modifiable vs Non modifiable
    - Atherosclerosis; coronary artery disease; elevated cholesterol levels; smoking; hypertension; obesity; inactivity; impaired glucose tolerance; stress
- Diagnostic studies – ECG, cardiac enzyme
- Interventions, acute stage: Same as Chest Pain Initial Care
- Interventions following acute episode
    - Bed rest; range-of-motion exercises as prescribed
    - Activity progression as tolerated

- Monitor for complications
  - Dysrhythmias; heart failure; pulmonary edema; cardiogenic shock; thrombophlebitis; pericarditis
  - Papillary Muscle Rupture – new murmur
- Cardiac rehabilitation
  - Arrange for client to begin prior to discharge, Teaching
  - Bleeding precautions – soft toothbrush, electric razor, avoid trauma or injury, Medic alert identification.

CARDIAC ENZYME	EXPECTED REFERENCE RANGE	ELEVATED LEVELS FIRST DETECTABLE FOLLOWING MYOCARDIAL INJURY	EXPECTED DURATION OF ELEVATED LEVELS
Creatine kinase MB isoenzyme (CK-MB) – more sensitive to myocardium	0% of total CK (30 to 170 units/L)	4 to 6 hr	3 days
Troponin T	Less than 0.2 ng/L	3 to 5 hr	14 to 21 days
Troponin I	Less than 0.03 ng/L	3 hr	7 to 10 days
Myoglobin	Less than 90 mcg/L	2 hr	24 hr

Source: ATI nursing education

Heart Failure

- Inability of heart to maintain adequate circulation to meet metabolic needs of body
- Classification: Acute, chronic
- Types of heart failure
  - Right ventricular: RV reduced capacity to pump into pulmonary circulation – back up in rest of body
  - left ventricular: LV reduced capacity to pump into systemic circulation- back up in lungs
- Compensatory mechanisms: To restore cardiac output:
  - increased heart rate, improved stroke volume, arterial vasoconstriction, sodium and water retention, myocardial hypertrophy
- Assessment
  - Right-sided failure: JVD, dependent edema, ascites, nausea, hepatosplenomegaly

- o Left-sided failure: orthopnea, cough, adventitious breath sounds, tachycardia, dyspnea on exertion, S3
- Pulmonary edema presents as – acute restlessness, anxiety, crackles, pallor, dyspnea, orthopnea, pink frothy sputum, diaphoresis
- BNP: B-type natriuretic peptides: Made and released by ventricles in response to stretching
  - o Causes natriuresis (excretion of sodium in the urine)
  - o Stretching of the ventricles - increased blood volume (fluid overload) - heart failure.
  - o Elevation of BNP >100 pg/mL helps to distinguish cardiac from respiratory causes of dyspnea.

- Assessment of Jugular Venous Distention (JVD)

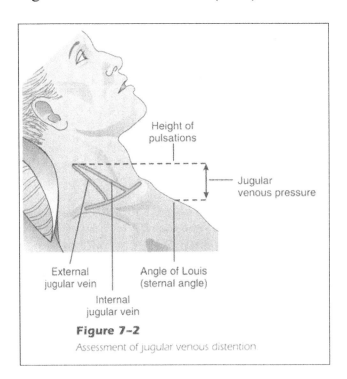

Figure 7-2

Assessment of jugular venous distention

- Head of the bed at a 30- to 45-degree
- Normal is 3cm. Above 3 cm – Increased JVP

Management

- Place client in high Fowler's position
- Rest period between activities, Calm environment
- Administer oxygen as prescribed (N/C)
- Better gas exchange, decrease workload, Suction PRN
- Monitor vital signs frequently: watch for hypotension, orthostatic hypo
- Strict intake and output, Fluid restriction, Daily weight
- Medications
  - Administer diuretics as prescribed: Monitor Electrolytes (K levels)
  - Vasodilators: Nitro- reduce preload
  - ACE inhibitors/ARB- Reduce afterload
  - Beta blocker- Reduce workload, improve contractions
  - Administer morphine sulfate: Watch for sedation, respiratory depression
  - Administer digitalis as prescribed: Improve contractility (hold HR<60)

Teaching

- Instruct client about modifiable risk factors
- Instruct client in proper administration of medication regimen
- Instruct client to avoid over-the-counter medications
- Instruct client to eat a low-sodium, low-fat, low-cholesterol diet
- Instruct client to balance activity level
- Daily weight – report 3 lb a day or 5 lb a week increase

Coronary Artery Disease

- Narrowing or obstruction of one or more coronary arteries as result of atherosclerosis

Assessment

- May be asymptomatic – atypical chest pain – especially in women
- Chest pain, Palpitations, Dyspnea, Syncope, Cough, Excessive fatigue

Diagnostic studies

- ECG shows ST depression or inverted T wave.
- Cardiac catheterization provides definitive diagnosis.
- Blood lipid levels may be elevated

Interventions

- Educate client about diagnostic tests
- Educate client about modifiable risk factors
- Diet: Instruct client to eat low-calorie, low-sodium, low-cholesterol, low-fat diet, with increase in dietary fiber
- Instruct client about importance of regular exercise

Surgical procedures

- PTCA - Percutaneous transluminal coronary angioplasty - Ballooning
- Laser angioplasty, Atherectomy, Vascular stent
- Coronary artery bypass graft (CABG)
- Coronary Artery Bypass Grafts
- Performed to bypass an obstruction in one or more of the coronary arteries.
- Minimally invasive direct coronary artery bypass (MIDCAB) – incision between ribs- painful

Pre-procedure

- Informed consent form.
- Diagnostics: chest x-ray, ECG, and laboratory reports

- Preoperative medications as prescribed.
- Anxiolytics, such as lorazepam (Ativan) and diazepam (Valium)
- Prophylactic antibiotics
- Anticholinergics, such as scopolamine, to reduce secretions
- Provide safe transport of the client to the OR.
- Monitor HR, Rhythm, vitals
- Educate patient and family – post op tubes, IS, cough and deep breath, splint incision, pacemaker

Medications

- Medications frequently discontinued for CABG
- Diuretics 2 to 3 days before surgery
- Aspirin and other anticoagulants 1 week before surgery
- Medications often continued for CABG
- Potassium supplements
- Scheduled antidysrhythmic, such as amiodarone
- Scheduled antihypertensives, such as metoprolol -a beta-blocker, and diltiazem - a calcium-channel blocker
- Insulin (clients who have diabetes mellitus and are insulin-dependent usually receive half the regular insulin dose)

Post op Care

- Maintain patent airway and adequate ventilation.
- Monitor RR, breath sounds, ventilator settings, Chest tube, Suction as needed.
- Splint the incision while deep breathing and coughing.
- Dangle and turn the client from side to side as tolerated within 2 hr following extubating.
- Assist the client to a chair within 24 hr.
- Ambulate the client 25 to 100 ft by post operative day #1
- Continually monitor client's heart rate and rhythm. Treat dysrhythmias per protocol.
- Multidisciplinary team

- Maintain an adequate circulating blood volume.
  - Hypotension - graft collapse.
  - Hypertension - bleeding from grafts and sutures.
- Monitor the client's level of consciousness.
- Assess neurological status every 30 to 60 min until the client awakens from anesthesia, then Q2 0r q4
- Prevent and monitor for infection: Hand hygiene, asepsis, antibiotics, blood tests, incision, vital signs
- Prevent pulmonary complications- atelectasis, pneumonia, and pulmonary edema – suction, turn and reposition, cough and deep breath, IS, monitor breath sounds, ABG, SaO2

Client Education

- Monitor and report manifestations of infection such as fever, incisional drainage, and redness.
- Instruct the client to treat angina. S/L Nitro
- Diabetes Client - monitor blood glucose levels.
- Heart-healthy diet (low fat, low cholesterol, high fiber, low salt).
- Smoking cessation.
- Encourage physical activity - cardiac rehabilitation
- Discuss home environment and social supports.

Complications CABG

- Fluid and Electrolyte Imbalances
- Cardiac Dysrhythmias
- Decreased cardiac output: can result from dysrhythmias, cardiac tamponade, hypovolemia, left ventricular failure, or MI.
- Hypothermia: can cause vasoconstriction, metabolic acidosis, and hypertension.
  - Monitor temperature, and provide warming measures, such as warm blankets and heat lamps.
- Monitor blood pressure. Administer vasodilators if prescribed.
- Assure the client that shivering is common following surgery.

Inflammatory Diseases of the Heart

Pericarditis

- Inflammation of the pericardium
  - Commonly follows a respiratory infection
  - Can be due to a myocardial infarction (Dressler's syndrome)
- Grating pain, aggravated by breathing
- Pain worsens when in supine position, relieved by leaning forward
- Position client in high Fowler's position, upright, leaning forward
- Monitor for signs of cardiac tamponade

Nursing Care

- Auscultate heart sounds (listen for murmur), breath sounds (friction rub).
- Review ABGs, SaO2, ECG and chest x-ray results. Oxygen as needed
- Monitor vital signs (watch for fever), Cardiac tamponade, heart failure.
- Obtain throat cultures to identify bacteria - antibiotic therapy.
- Administer antibiotics and antipyretics as prescribed.
- Pain assessment – Pain med. Encourage bed rest.
- Provide emotional support to the client and family, encourage the verbalization of feelings regarding the illness.

Myocarditis

- Inflammation of the myocardium: Can be due to a viral, fungal, or bacterial infection, can be a result of pericarditis
- Assessment: Fever; pericardial friction rub; murmur
- Interventions: Administer analgesics, salicylates, nonsteroidal anti-inflammatory drugs, antibiotics, digoxin as prescribed

Endocarditis

- Inflammation of inner lining of heart and valves by bacteria (staph aureus- acute, or strep viridians- chronic)
- Assessment:
  - Fever; positive blood culture

- o New heart murmur
- o Petechiae, Splinter hemorrhages in nail beds.
- o Osler's nodes – painful nodes on fingers and toes
- o Janeway's lesions (irregular, erythematous, flat, painless macules on the palms, soles)
- o Roth's spots – retinal lesion surrounded by bleeding

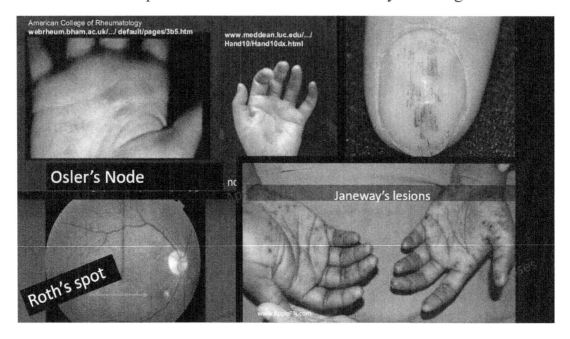

- • Endocarditis: Interventions:
    - o Prevent venous stasis- periods of rest and activity.
    - o Maintain anti embolic stockings as prescribed
    - o IV therapy – antibiotics (6 weeks)
    - o Monitor cardiovascular status
    - o Monitor for signs of emboli throughout body as the bacterial vegetations over the valves can break off and embolize to various organs- lead to stroke, MI, PE, ischemia to extremity etc.

Client Education

- • Encourage the client to
    - o Take rest periods as needed.
    - o Wash hands to prevent infection.
    - o Avoid crowded areas to reduce the risk of infection.

- o Participate in smoking cessation (if the client is a smoker).
- Educate the client about the importance of taking medications as prescribed.
- Ask the client to demonstrate the administration of intravenous antibiotics and management before discharge.
- Educate the client and family about the illness and encourage them to express their feelings.
- Home infusion therapy and management
- Notify that they can have repeated episodes of endocarditis: Report – fever, anorexia, malaise (might be due to recurrence of the disease)
- Gentle, thorough oral care (vigorous brushing can lead bacteria to enter blood through gum)
- Need prophylactic antibiotics before invasive procedures
- To prevent infectious endocarditis antibiotic prophylaxis before dental work is recommended for: -
  - o Clients who have prosthetic heart valves.
  - o Clients with prior history of infective endocarditis
  - o Clients with congenital heart defects
  - o Clients with structural valvular heart disease (not acquired/ age related)
  - o Transplanted hearts

Cardiogenic Shock

- Failure of heart to pump adequately – reduced cardiac output & perfusion
- Assessment: Hypotension, Oliguria, Poor peripheral pulses, Tachypnea, Tachycardia, Disorientation, confusion

Interventions

- Administer morphine sulfate, diuretics, nitrates to decrease heart workload – help heart to work more effectively
- Inotrops - stimulate and increase the force of contraction of the heart muscle
- Administer oxygen; prepare for intubation and mechanical ventilation as prescribed

- Monitor vital signs, arterial blood gases, strict intake and output, arterial pressures as prescribed

Cardiac Tamponade

- Pericardial effusion: occurs when space between parietal and visceral layers of pericardium fill with fluid

Assessment

- Pulsus paradoxus (variance of 10 mm Hg or more in systolic blood pressure between expiration and inspiration).
- Beck's Triad (Low arterial blood pressure, distended neck veins, and distant, muffled heart sounds)

Interventions

- Place client in critical care unit as prescribed
- Administer IV fluids as prescribed (to increase cardiac output)
- Prepare client for pericardiocentesis (position)
  - o Supine with the head of the bed raised to an angle of 45 to 60 degrees. This places the heart in proximity to the chest wall for easier insertion of the needle into the pericardial sac.
- Monitor for recurrence of tamponade following pericardiocentesis

Valvular Heart Disease

- Occurs when heart valves are stenosed (cannot fully open) or insufficient or regurgitant (cannot close completely)
- Asymptomatic until late in the progression – Echocardiogram

Repair procedures

- Balloon valvuloplasty; mitral angioplasty
- Commissurotomy (relieve stenosis on leaflets), Valvotomy

Valve replacement procedures

- Prosthetic valves can be mechanical or tissue.

- Mechanical valves last longer but require anticoagulation.
- Tissue valves last 10 to 15 years.
- The aortic valve must be replaced by a mechanical (prosthetic) valve because of the velocity of the blood flow through the valve.
- A tissue or biologic valve would not withstand the force.

Risk Factors

- Hypertension, Rheumatic fever (mitral stenosis and insufficiency)
- Infective endocarditis, Congenital malformations
- Marfan syndrome (connective tissue disorder that affects the heart and other areas of the body - genetic)
- In older adult client's causes are: - degenerative calcification, papillary muscle dysfunction, infective endocarditis

Signs and Symptoms: Refer to table. usually asymptomatic until late

- Murmurs (due to turbulent blood flow) are usually present.
- C/O Fatigue is a concern =? Decreased cardiac output
- Left-sided valve – backflow into Left Atrium? LHF
- Right side valve – backflow into Right Atrium? RHF

MITRAL STENOSIS	MITRAL INSUFFICIENCY	AORTIC STENOSIS	AORTIC INSUFFICIENCY
› Diastolic murmur	› Systolic murmur	› Systolic murmur	› Diastolic murmur
› Atrial fibrillation	› S_3 and/or S_4 sounds	› S_3 and/or S_4 sounds	› S_3 sounds
› Palpitations	› Atrial fibrillation	› Angina	› Sinus tachycardia
› Jugular venous distention	› Palpitations	› Syncope	› Palpitations
› Pitting edema	› Jugular venous distention	› Decreased SVR	› Angina
› Hemoptysis	› Pitting edema	› Narrowed pulse pressure	› Widened pulse pressure
› Cough	› Crackles in lungs		
› Dysphagia	› Possible diminished lung sounds		
› Hoarseness			

TRICUSPID STENOSIS	TRICUSPID INSUFFICIENCY	PULMONIC STENOSIS	PULMONIC INSUFFICIENCY
› Diastolic murmur	› Systolic murmur	› Systolic murmur	› Diastolic murmur
› Atrial dysrhythmias	› Supraventricular tachycardia	› Angina	› Possible split S_2
› Decreased cardiac output	› Conduction delays	› Syncope	
	› "Fluttering" neck vein sensations	› Cyanosis	

Source: ATI nursing education

General interventions

- Administer prescribed treatment for heart failure as prescribed
- Administer oxygen/ IV fluids/ diuretics, digoxin as prescribed
- Provide low-sodium diet as prescribed
- Administer antibiotics as prescribed
- Teaching: Better to avoid dental procedures for 6 months after valve replacements
- A clicking sound – heard for prosthetic valve

Cardiomyopathy

- Subacute or chronic disorder of heart muscle
- Dilated cardiomyopathy: (most common): All four chambers enlarged
  - Heart ejects less than 40% of blood in left ventricle; followed by decreased contractility
  - Reduced cardiac output leads to heart failure
- Hypertrophic cardiomyopathy:

- o Characterized by massive ventricular hypertrophy (thickening)
- o Increased pulmonary and venous pressure – reduces CO
- Restrictive cardiomyopathy
  - o Characterized by restriction of filling of ventricles (stiff)
  - o Rigid walls – do not stretch - HF
- Manifestations
  - o Fatigue, weakness, orthostatic hypotension (fall risk)
  - o Heart failure (LHF -dilated type, RHF- restrictive type
  - o Dysrhythmias (heart block), Angina (hypertrophic type)
  - o S3 gallop
  - o Cardiomegaly (enlarged heart), severe with dilated type
  - o BNP – elevated (100-400 pg/mL)
- Treatment – Heart failure
  - o Treatment symptomatic, similar to care of heart failure (dilated and restrictive cardiomyopathy),
  - o Similar to care of MI (hypertrophic cardiomyopathy)

Vascular Disorders

- Venous thrombosis: inflammatory process
- Phlebitis: Vein inflammation associated with invasive procedures, such as IV lines
- Deep vein thrombophlebitis: More serious than superficial thrombophlebitis because of risk for pulmonary embolism
  - o Elevate affected extremity above level of heart –to prevent further swelling
  - o Rest when acute DVT, but once treatment begins, move as soon as possible to prevent recurrence
  - o Avoid using knee gatch or pillow under knees
  - o Do not massage extremity

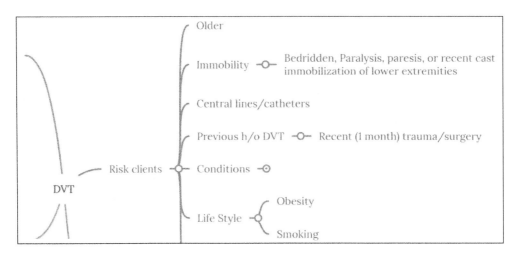

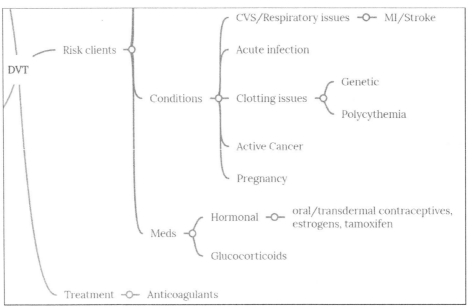

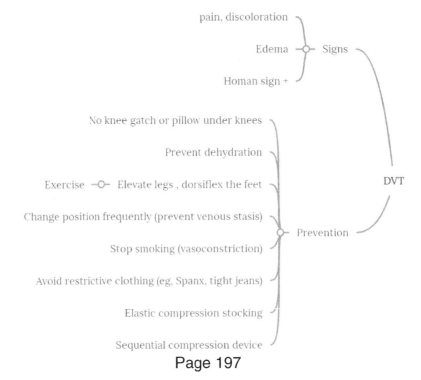

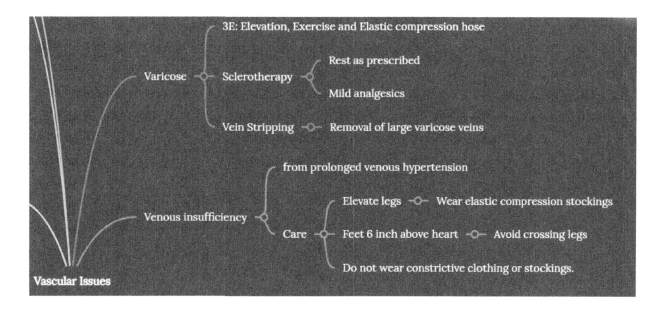

Arterial Disorders

- Assess pain (intermittent claudication)
- Monitor extremities for color, motion, sensation, pulses
- Assess for signs of ulcer formation
- Assist client in developing individualized exercise program
- Instruct client to avoid extreme cold temperatures, constrictive clothing on extremities, crossing legs
- Instruct client never to apply direct heat to extremities
- Instruct client to avoid smoking, caffeine

Raynaud's disease

- Vasospasm of arterioles, arteries of upper and lower extremities
- Assess for blanching of extremity, followed by cyanosis; reddened tissue when vasospasm is relieved; numbness, tingling, cold temperature of affected extremity part
- Attacks are triggered by exposure to cold, nicotine, caffeine, trauma to the fingertips, and stress.

Interventions

- Monitor pulses (diminished or absent peripheral pulses))
- Administer vasodilators as prescribed

- Instruct client to avoid precipitating factors such as cold and stress
- No smoking, instruct client to avoid injuries to hands, fingers
- Advice pt to keep hands warm
- Wear gloves when outdoors, or handling cold food

Buerger's disease (thromboangitis obliterans)

- Occlusive disease of median and small arteries and veins
- Assess for ischemic pain in digits while at rest; aching pain that is more severe at night; cool, numb, or tingling sensation; cool and reddened extremities in dependent position

Interventions:

- Instruct client to stop smoking, Monitor pulses
- Instruct client to avoid injury to upper and lower extremities
- Administer vasodilators as prescribed

Cellulitis

- Cellulitis is characterized by an edematous rash from subcutaneous tissue inflammation.
- The nurse should elevate the extremity to promote lymphatic drainage of edema

Arterial Vs. Venous Disorder

Assessment	Arterial Disease	Venous Disease
Color	Pale	Rudy /cyanotic
Edema	None or minimal	Usually, present
Nails	Thick/brittle	Normal
Pain	Worse with elevation and exercise, claudication, Rest pain (awaken at night)	Better with elevation, Homan's sign, Dull/heavy
Pulse	Decreased/Weak/Absent	Normal
Temperature	Cool	Warm
Ulcer	Dry and Necrotic	Moist

Aortic Aneurysm

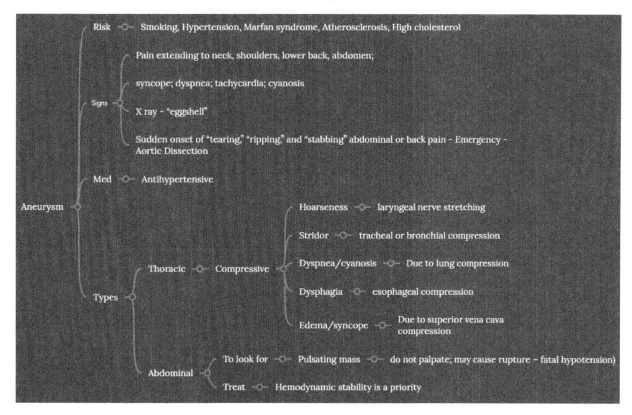

Abdominal aortic aneurysm (AAA)

- Most common, related to atherosclerosis
- Constant gnawing feeling in abdomen; flank or back pain
- Pulsating abdominal mass (do not palpate; may cause rupture – fatal hypotension)
- Bruit, Elevated blood pressure (unless in cardiac tamponade or rupture of aneurysm)

Surgical resection or excision of aneurysm

- Repair- femoral percutaneous placement of a stent graft (endovascular aneurysm repair) Or an open surgical incision of the aneurysm with synthetic graft placement.
- Following repair of an abdominal aortic aneurysm, hemodynamic stability is a priority.
- Prolonged hypotension can lead to graft thrombosis.
- A falling blood pressure and rising pulse rate can also signify graft leakage.

Postoperative interventions

- Vital signs and peripheral pulses distal to graft site
- Limit elevation of HOB to 45 degrees
- Strict intake and output
- Assess incisional site for bleeding, signs of infection
- Instruct client not to lift objects heavier than 15 to 20 lb for 6 to 12 weeks
- Instruct client to avoid strenuous activities

Hypertension

- Increased blood pressure described on more than one reading of over 140/90 mm Hg
- Primary or essential hypertension: No known cause for increased BP
- Secondary hypertension: Occurs as result of other disorders or conditions
- Assessment: May be asymptomatic; headache; dizziness; chest pain; flushed face; visual disturbances; epistaxis
- Chronic hypertension can result in ventricular hypertrophy

- Pre-hypertension – systolic 120 to 139 mm Hg; diastolic 80 to 89 mm Hg
- Stage I hypertension – systolic 140 to 159 mm Hg / diastolic 90 to 99 mm Hg
- Stage II hypertension – systolic greater than or equal to 160 mm Hg/ diastolic greater than or equal to 100 mm Hg
- Mean arterial pressure (MAP)= average pressure within the arterial system – normal= >60. MAP = (SBP + 2 DP)/3
- The goal of treatment is to maintain a blood pressure of 130/85 mm Hg or less and control other CVD risk factors.

Interventions

- Obtain BP readings in both arms, sitting and standing
- Determine family history of hypertension
- Obtain weight, Assess renal function as prescribed
- Nonpharmacological interventions
  - Instruct client in weight reduction, exercise, relaxation techniques/avoid smoking /low sodium diet
- Stepped-care approach: Administer medications and re-evaluate
- Modifiable/Non modifiable risk factors: Identify and manage them

Client education

- Instruct client about diet management- DASH diet

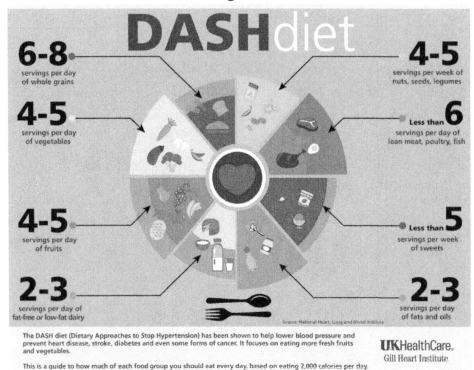

- Medications and side effects to report to physician
- Reading labels on foods to assess for sodium
- How to monitor and take blood pressure
- Cheese: No String cheese/Singles/ Feta / Blue cheese
- Moderate amount of Cheddar, Mozzarella, Ricotta, Swiss, Cottage, Cream cheese is OK.
- Hypertensive Crisis
  - o Any clinical condition requiring immediate reduction in BP
  - o Acute and life-threatening condition
- Assessment
  - o Diastolic pressure higher than 120 mm Hg.
  - o Headache; confusion; changes in neurological status; Blurred vision, dizziness, and disorientation
  - o Tachycardia; tachypnea; dyspnea; cyanosis; Seizures, Epistaxis
- Interventions
  - o Maintain patent airway

- o Administer antihypertensives as prescribed (IV): nitroprusside, nicardipine, labetalol hydrochloride
- o Monitor vital signs, BP every 5 minutes
- o Assess neurological status such as pupils, LOC, muscle strength, to monitor for cerebrovascular change.
- o Maintain emergency medications
- o Have resuscitation equipment readily available
- o Bed rest with HOB at 45 degrees
- o Strict intake and output

Pacemakers

- Temporary or permanent device
- Provides electrical stimulation
- Maintains heart rate when client's intrinsic pacemaker fails to provide perfusing rhythm
- Settings: Synchronous or demand
  - o Paces only if client's intrinsic rate falls below set pacemaker rate
- Asynchronous or fixed rate
  - o Paces at preset rate, regardless of client's intrinsic rate
- Spikes
  - o When pacing stimulus delivered to heart, straight vertical line on ECG strip or monitor
- Temporary pacemakers
  - o Noninvasive temporary pacing; transvenous invasive temporary pacing
  - o Permanent pacemakers
  - o Pulse generator internal, surgically implanted in subcutaneous pocket under clavicle or abdominal wall
  - o Function can be checked by pacemaker interrogator or programmer in office or from home using telephone transmitter device

Post procedure nursing care:

- Monitor EKG, monitor Pacemaker site – bleeding, infection

- Infection of a pacemaker incision site can travel down the lead wires to the heart, causing myocarditis and/or endocarditis. Infection may disrupt pacemaker function, resulting in failure to sense or pace
- Signs and symptoms of pacemaker malfunction (e.g., dizziness) should be assessed immediately.
- Arm and shoulder restriction, Sling, Dressing clean and dry
- No MRI, Identification card all the time
- Do not place a cell phone in a pocket located directly over the pacemaker. Also, when talking on the cell phone, hold it to the ear on the opposite side of the pacemaker's implantation site
- Avoid anti-theft detectors in store entryways

Failure to Capture

- Failure to capture means that the ventricles fail to response to the pacemaker impulse. On an EKG tracing, the pacemaker spike will appear, but it will not be followed by a QRS complex.

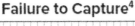

Failure to Capture[4]

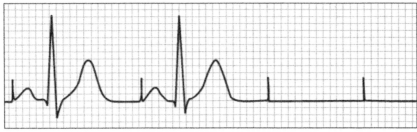

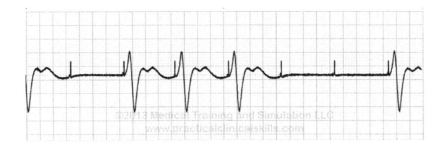

Cardioversion and Defibrillation

- Do TEE to identify the clot.
- Clients with Afibrillation for unknown duration must receive adequate anticoagulation for 4 to 6 weeks prior to cardioversion therapy to prevent dislodgement of thrombi into the bloodstream.
- Digoxin is held for 48 hr prior to elective cardioversion
- Explain the procedure to the client, ensure consent.
- Administer oxygen.
- Document pre procedure and post procedure rhythm.
- Have emergency equipment available.

- Complications
    - Embolism: Cardioversion can dislodge blood clots, potentially causing PE, MI, CVA. Provide therapeutic anticoagulation for clients who have dysrhythmias
    - Decreased cardiac output and heart failure: Cardioversion may damage heart tissue and impair heart function.
        - Monitor the client for signs of decreased cardiac output (hypotension, syncope, tachycardia, LOC changes, activity intolerance) and heart failure
        - Provide medications to increase output (inotropic agents) and to decrease cardiac workload (Digoxin, Dopamine, Dobutamine, milrinone)

Cardioversion	Defibrillation
Direct countershock to the heart **synchronized to the QRS complex.** Requires activation of the synchronizer button	Direct countershock to the heart, **unsynchronized.**
Elective treatment of atrial dysrhythmias, SVT and VT with a pulse.	For VF or pulseless ventricular tachycardia
converts undesirable rhythm to stable rhythm	Defibrillation stops all electrical activity of the heart, then restarts
Can lead to ventricular fibrillation if defibrillator discharges on T wave	Allows the SA node to take over and re-establish a perfusing rhythm
Cardioversion usually begins with 50 to 100 joules.	360 joules.

www.AppleRN.com

S-ICD: Subcutaneous implantable cardioverter-defibrillator

- Components
    - Pulse generator: implanted near the left mid-axillary line
    - A subcutaneous lead: consisting of sensing electrodes and a shocking coil which is tunneled 1 to 2 cm to the left of the mid-sternal line.
- Output
    - Delivers 80-J transthoracic shocks and 30 s of post-shock pacing.
- Battery life
    - The S-ICD has a lithium battery with a projected life of 5 years

Implantable Cardioverter-Defibrillator (ICD)

- ICD (via subclavian to endocardium)
- Sensor will Check for VT or VF
- Gives shock - 25 joules or less (directly to heart muscle)
- Will repeat shock if unsuccessful.
- Instruct patient

- o basic functions of ICD and report issues
- o to take pulse
- o to avoid strenuous activity or contact sports
- o to report any signs of infection or feelings of faintness, nausea, and vomiting

Renin Angiotensin Mechanism

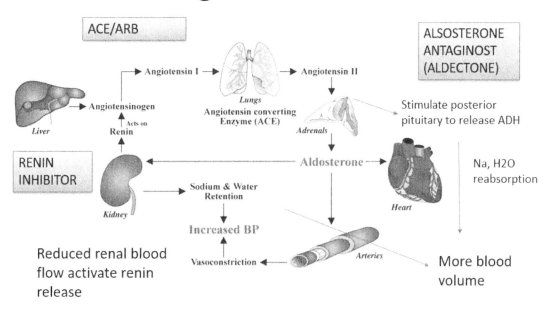

Cardiac dysrhythmias

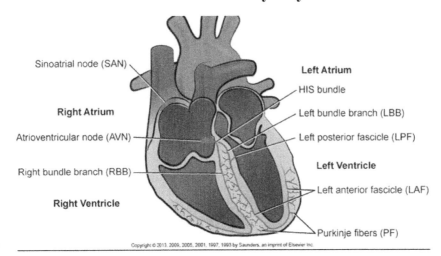

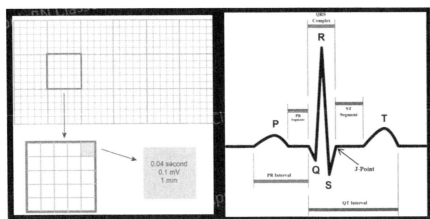

- P wave - Atrial depolarization (squeeze/contract/systole)
- Q- Septum depolarization – starts ventricles
- R – ventricular Depolarization (main mass)
- S- ventricular Depolarization -Last part
- T – ventricular Repolarization (relax/diastole)
- PQ – Time taken to reach from SA node to AV node
- Heart Rate:
    o SA node = 60 to 100 beats/min
    o AV node = 40 to 60 beats/min
    o Ventricles (Purkinje fibers) = 15 to 40 beats/min

Electrode Placement for ECG

- V1 - Fourth intercostal space on the right sternum

  V2 - Fourth intercostal space at the left sternum – Tricuspid

  V3 - Midway between placement of V2 and V4

  V4 - Fifth intercostal space at the midclavicular line – Mitral

  V5 - Anterior axillary line on the same horizontal level as V4

V6 - Mid-axillary line on the same horizontal level as V4 and V5

- RA (Right Arm) - Anywhere between the right shoulder and right elbow
  - » RL (Right Leg) - Anywhere below the right torso and above the right ankle
  - » LA (Left Arm) - Anywhere between the left shoulder and the left elbow
  - » LL (Left Leg) - Anywhere below the left torso and above the left ankle
- Steps: V2 (tricuspid 4th ICS), V1 (Right side), V4 (5 ICS), V3 (in between V2 and V4), V6 (axilla), V5 (in between V4 and V6)
- Normal Numbers
  - o PR interval = 0.12 -0.20 seconds (3 -5 small blocks)
  - o QT interval = 0.36 – 0.44 seconds (9-11 small blocks)
- First and most important ▪ ASSESS YOUR PATIENT!! Any symptoms of Decreased cardiac output????

Normal Sinus Rhythm

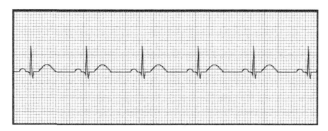

- Originates from SA node - 60 to 100 beats/min
- Finding Heart Rate (Regular)
  - o Count the blocks (big blocks) between R and R
  - o HR = 300/ number of blocks
- Finding Heart Rate (Irregular rhythm)
  - o Count the number of R waves in a six second strip and multiply by 10.
  - o 30 large squares = 6 seconds

Sinus bradycardia

- Rates less than 60 beats/min

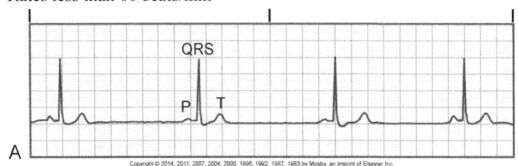

Copyright © 2014, 2011, 2007, 2004, 2000, 1996, 1992, 1987, 1983 by Mosby, an imprint of Elsevier Inc.

- Attempt to determine cause (Chronic cocaine use)
- If medication (digoxin/lol) is suspected cause, hold, notify physician
- Athletic hearts – bradycardia - normal
- Symptomatic bradycardia: A symptomatic bradycardia exists clinically when three criteria are present
  - o 1. The heart rate is slow
  - o 2. The patient has symptoms
  - o 3. The symptoms are due to the slow heart rate.
- Meds: Atropine sulfate (max 3 mg) / Dopamine / epinephrine
- Atropine: 0.5 mg IV. This may be repeated every 3 to 5 minutes up to 3mg / 6 doses.
- Epinephrine 2 to 10 µg/min, Dopamine 2 to 20 µg/kg per minute

Sinus tachycardia

- Atrial and ventricular rates more than one hundred beats/min

Sinus Tachycardia

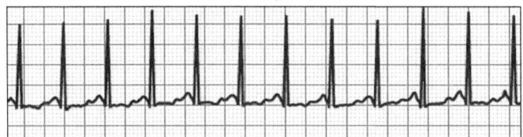

- Assess patient – Are they symptomatic? Are they stable?
- Oxygen? Monitor blood pressure and heart rate
- Start IV if not already established

- Notify MD
  - Look for the cause of the tachycardia and treat it
  - Fever – give acetaminophen or ibuprofen
  - Stimulants – stop use (caffeine, OTC meds, herbs, illicit drugs, pain)
  - Anxiety – give reassurance or ant-anxiety medication
  - Sepsis, Anemia, Hypotension, MI, Heart Failure, Hypoxia

Atrial fibrillation

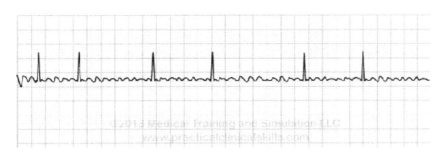

- No definitive P wave can be observed, Always Irregular
- Hypoxia, HTN, CAD, CHF
- Administer oxygen and anticoagulants, prepare for cardioversion

Atrial Flutter

- Rate varies; usually regular; saw-toothed
- Common: In Valve disorder (mitral), Cardiomyopathy/ Ischemia, COPD
- Cardioversion – treatment of choice
- Antiarrhythmics such as procainamide to convert the flutter
- Slow the ventricular rate by using diltiazem, verapamil, digitalis, or beta blocker
- Heparin to reduce incidence of thrombus formation

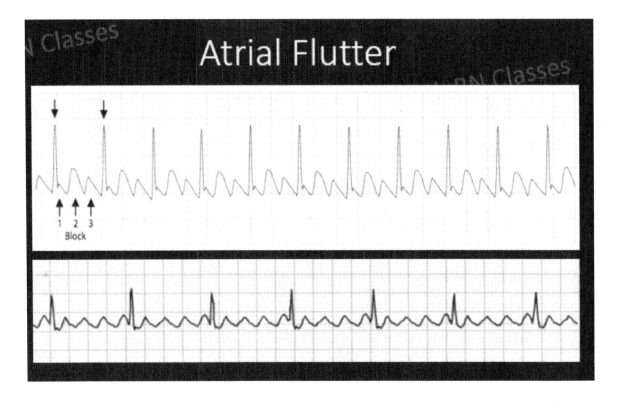

Supraventricular Tachycardia (>150 bpm)

- Causes: Stimulants • Hypoxia • Stress or over-exertion • Hypokalemia • Atherosclerotic heart disease
- Some types of SVT may run in families, such as Wolff-Parkinson-White syndrome – additional electrical pathway between Atrium and Ventricles (in addition to AV node)

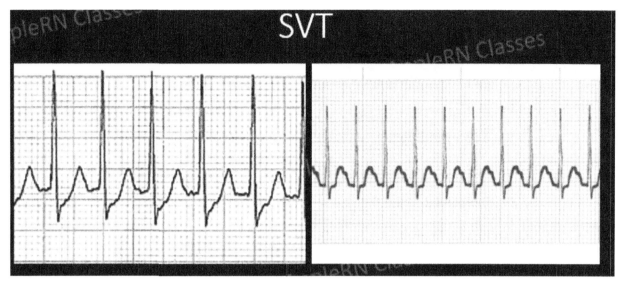

- Treatment: Vagal maneuvers
- Gagging, Coughing, holding breath and bearing down (Valsalva maneuver).
- Immersing face in ice-cold water (diving reflex).
- Drug – Adenosine – Give rapidly (1-2 sec) + rapid saline flush (short half-life – 10 sec)
- Cardioversion

Premature ventricular contractions (PVCs)

- PVC is not a rhythm- ectopic beat that arises from an irritable site in the ventricles.
- PVCs appear in many different patterns and shapes, but are always wide and bizarre compared to a "normal" beat
- If every other beat PVC – Bigeminy. PVC every third beat – trigeminy
- PVC every fourth beat – quadrigeminy
- PVCs can be associated with stimulants (e.g., caffeine), medications (e.g., digoxin), heart diseases, electrolyte imbalances (e.g.: hypokalemia), hypoxia, and emotional stress.
- Isolated PVC is OK. Give oxygen

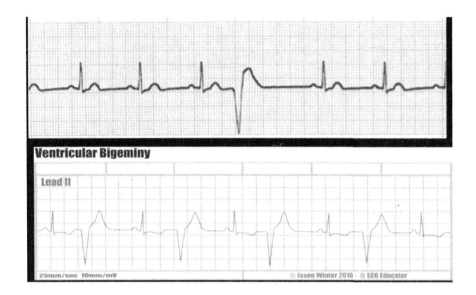

Ventricular Bigeminy

Lead II

25mm/sec 10mm/mV   © Jason Winter 2016 - © ECG Educator

- Notify physician if complaints of chest pain or ventricular tachycardia occur.
- Medication -Lidocaine

Ventricular tachycardia

- Repetitive firing of irritable ventricular ectopic focus at rate of 140 to 250

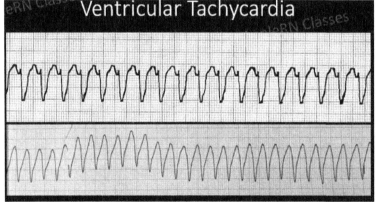

Ventricular Tachycardia

beats/min
- Client may be stable or unstable. No pulse? Begin CPR, Defib.
- If pulse present and client stable – Cardiovert, start meds
- Meds: Amiodarone and lidocaine (Xylocaine), antiarrhythmics (procainamide, sotalol)

- Torsades de pointes – A form of ventricular tachycardia (with twists) –

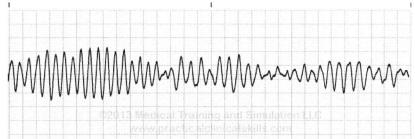

- Associated with hypomagnesemia and hypokalemic clients. QT – prolong

Ventricular Fibrillation

- Chaotic rapid rhythm; ventricles quiver
- Defibrillate immediately as prescribed, initiate CPR

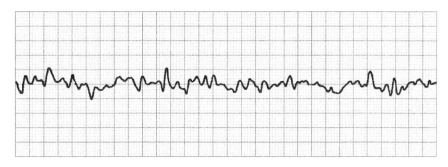

Sinus Pause/Block

- Caused by a malfunctioning sinus node

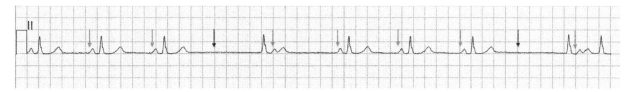

- May be seen in Sick sinus syndrome (SSS): Sick sinus syndrome (SSS) is a general term for a group of disorders caused by a malfunctioning sinus node – missed beats

Artifacts

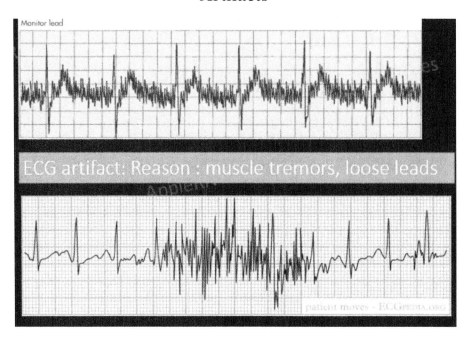

Pulseless Electrical Activity

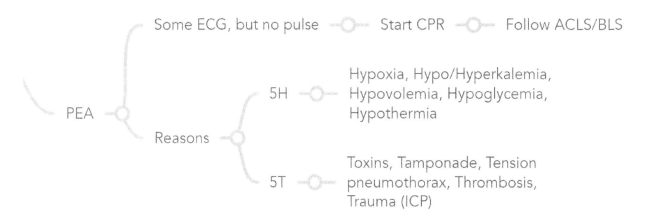

Atrioventricular Blocks

- Always assess for decreased cardiac output and treat cause
- Four types:
  o First-degree block

o Second-degree block, Mobitz type I Wenckebach

o Second-degree block, Mobitz type II

o Third-degree block (complete)

Heart Block: First degree

- A delay of impulse from SA node to reach AV node. PR interval >.20 sec (3 to 5 small blocks) But same PR interval for each beat.

First-Degree AV Block

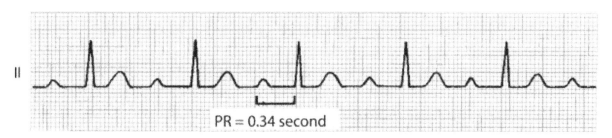

PR = 0.34 second

- Can be due to meds such as digoxin.
- No specific treatment- watch for worsening to second or third degree

Second Degree

- Can be due to MI/Meds (digoxin, beta blocker)/cardiac surgery
- Second Degree AV Block – Type I (Wenckebach) (Mobitz I)

Second Degree AV Block Mobitz Type I (wenckebach)

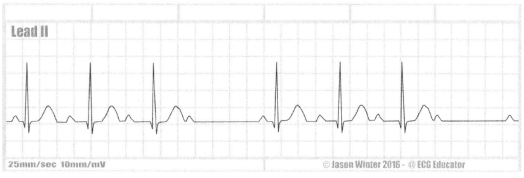

Lead II

25mm/sec 10mm/mV   © Jason Winter 2016 - @ ECG Educator

- Progressive prolongation of the PR interval, then one dropped QRS
- Watch for progression into complete heart block
- S/S – bradycardia symptoms – give atropine to increase HR

- May need temporary pacemaker if med not working

Second Degree AV Block – Type II

- The PR interval does not lengthen before a dropped beat.

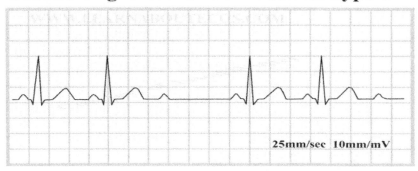

Second Degree AV Block - Mobitz Type 2

25mm/sec 10mm/mV

- Due to BBB. Seen in – MI, CAD, RHD, Drug toxicity.
- Might need pacemakers

Third Degree/complete

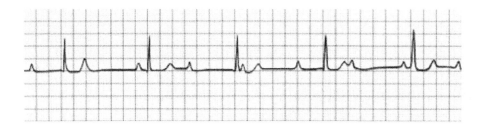

- Complete absence of conduction between atria and ventricles
- Nursing priority: assess the patient for possible causes
- monitor blood pressure, pulse, and other vital signs.
- Assess for syncope, palpitations, or shortness of breath.
- Hypotension may occur due to a low ventricular rate.
- For patient safety, lie your patient down to prevent syncope and potential falls.

Critical Care Special Topics

When to stop A Stress test (NCLEX POINTS)

- BP changes (SBP drops more than 10; Hypertensive crisis 250/115)
- ECG changes (arrythmia) / Chest pain/angina
- S/S decreased perfusion - Neuro (dizziness, ataxia); cyanosis, pallor
- Fatigue, shortness of breath, leg cramps, wheezing, or claudication
- Patient desire to stop
- Technical issues

Result

Expectation	Normal/Negative	Positive	Equivocal
Bruce protocol, complete 3 stages, remain on treadmill for 9 mts	BP and HR increases as per protocol.	ST changes Angina.	uncertain
100% of Maximum Predicted Heart Rate (220 minus age) reached. *Acceptable* : Minimum of 85% of maximum predicted rate	No ECG changes. No complaints from client (no chest pain/decreased perfusion)	BP and HR does not change as normal expectation	(Meds/other diseases / technical issues)

Ventricular Assistive Device

- This is an alternative to heart transplantation for patients with advanced heart failure.
- It is a form of mechanical circulatory support device (MCSD)
- An LVAD is the most common type of MCSD.
- LVAD is a battery-operated mechanical pump that's surgically implanted into the patient's chest to support heart function and blood flow.
- Today, over 15,000 U.S. patients have an MCSD

Types:

- Right ventricular assist device (RVAD)
  - RVAD helps pump blood from the right ventricle to the pulmonary artery
  - Used for short term purposes. Patients must stay in the hospital
- Biventricular assist device (BIVAD)
  - Used if both ventricles need support
- Left Ventricular Assistive Device (LVAD)
  - The LVAD is the most common type of VAD
  - It works by unloading the left ventricle and pumping blood to the aorta.

Parts:

- An inflow Canula: draws blood from the left ventricle into the pump.
- An outflow cannula carries blood from the pump to the ascending aorta
- Pump: located at the apex of left ventricle: two types: Pulsatile (durability issues) or continuous (Mostly used)
- Driveline: To send signals from controller: It is the connecting wire.
- System controller: Regulates power, monitors LVAD performance, and collects data on system operation (alarms)
- Power source: Batteries or AC current Continuous flow pump: These are designed to unload the heart throughout the cardiac cycle using a central rotor (motor)
  - The rotor continuously propels blood, providing continuous blood flow into systemic circulation.
  - This may result in a weak, irregular, or nonpalpable pulse due to the continuous forward flow from the VAD
-

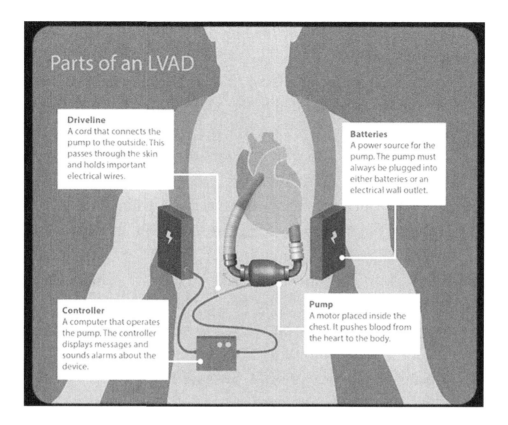

Image credit: JAMA

- The pump speeds.
  - This is a fixed number, set by the VAD team, which directly measures how fast the rotor of the pump spins.
  - The speed is determined by hemodynamic and echocardiographic measurements and is set in revolutions per minute (RPMs).
  - The only parameter on the LVAD that can be adjusted is the RPMs, which are determined and adjusted by a member of the VAD team
- The pump flow is an approximation of the blood flow through the LVAD, estimated based on pump speed and power.
  - The pump flow is patient's cardiac output in liters per minute (L/min)
- The pump power is a measure of voltage and current power consumption of the pump.
  - A gradual increase in power may be a sign of thrombus inside the LVAD

- Pulsatility index (PI): In systole the blood flow in pump increases. Diastole it decreases.
    - PI helps to make an average of blood flow for every 15 seconds.
    - The PI is inversely related to the amount of assistance provided by the LVAD.
    - A high PI indicates more native ventricular filling and less pump support.
    - A lower PI value indicates less ventricular filling due to less circulating blood volume or an obstruction in the LVAD, meaning the patient requires more pump support
- Suction events: Low PIs can lead to "suction events," which means the left ventricle is underfilled and is being "sucked" into the LVAD.
- Management: Give IV fluids (but a VAD team should be contacted)
- The VAD team may decrease the RPMs, to reduce the speed of the device.
- LVADs depend on adequate preload. So, avoid dehydration, overdiuresis, bleeding etc. leading to hypovolemia

Alarms:

- Pump failure alarm: Due to driveline disconnection, electrical failure, or connector malfunction.
    - Assess the connection from the driveline, controller, and power source
- Low battery alarm: Connect the LVAD to either battery or AC power
- Controller failure alarm: Change controller
    - Patients should have a spare controller with them that's already programmed

Major complications

- Hypotension
    - Due to infection, gastrointestinal bleeding, and dehydration.
    - Nursing consideration: Pulse many are not palpated in Continuous flow LVADs.
    - Might need doppler / arterial line to obtain BP measurements

- o MAPs should be maintained between 70- and 80-mm Hg and shouldn't exceed 90 mm Hg to ensure appropriate perfusion and to prevent retrograde flow.
- Infection
  - o Can be related to devise issues, endocarditis, bacteremia, or non-device-related infections such as urinary tract infections, respiratory tract infections, cholecystitis, and Clostridium difficile infection.
  - o Nursing Consideration: Monitor for infection – sepsis
  - o Secure driveline by an anchoring device
  - o Sterile technique should always be used when performing LVAD site care
  - o Initial dressing changes are usually done daily, then decrease in frequency to every other day or weekly
  - o If a driveline infection is suspected, the dressing changes are increased too daily.
  - o Patient education: Report erythema, purulent drainage, fever
- GI bleed: Neurologic events. Patients with an LVAD are at increased risk for ischemic and hemorrhagic strokes: So, will need anticoagulants: watch for GI bleed
  - o VAD also affects the intestinal perfusion - changes in GI system – leading to bleeding
  - o Treatment: Fluids and blood products, fresh frozen plasma, Vit K
  - o Risk: thrombosis and other thrombotic events
- Dysrhythmia: Management of atrial dysrhythmias in patients with an LVAD is similar to patients without an LVAD
  - o Most patients with an LVAD have an implantable cardioverter-defibrillator (ICD).
  - o CPR for patient with LVAD: Follow ACLS protocol – watch for bleeding. Call the VAD coordinators.

Hemodynamics Monitoring

- The goal of hemodynamic monitoring is to maintain adequate tissue perfusion
- Used in: Surgery (CABG), shock, fluid status, medical issues (Kidney failure/burn/Trauma), ARDS
- Monitoring: invasive and non-invasive methods.
- Non-invasive methods:
    - Routine blood pressure monitoring, capillary refill, Pulse rate
    - Measuring jugular venous distention provides an estimate of intravascular volume.
    - Jugular venous distention occurs when central venous pressure is elevated.
    - Observe the highest point of pulsation in the internal jugular vein.
    - Any fullness in the vein extending >3 cm above the sternal angle is considered elevated jugular venous pressure.
- Invasive modalities
    - Pulmonary artery pressure monitoring: measure pressures in the pulmonary artery and the left side of the heart (as its impossible to measure the left heart pressure directly at bedside)
    - Right atrial pressure monitoring: Also known as central venous pressure monitoring or CVP, is used to estimate central venous blood/fluid volume and right heart function
    - Arterial pressure monitoring: most accurate method of monitoring blood pressure

Pulmonary Artery Pressure Monitoring

- Pulmonary artery catheter (PAC)
- Introduced in 1970: Drs. Swan and Ganz
- Reflects left ventricular function
- Pulmonary artery catheters provide direct measures of cardiac output.

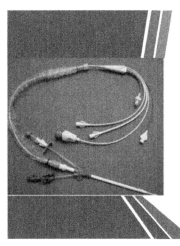

Black lines on catheter – 10 cm each

Balloon port is Red

Yellow Port = Distal port = PA port = the one which goes all the way to the end of the catheter.

Blue port = CVP port. OK to infuse IV fluids, and obtain venous blood samples.

White / Clear = Medications infusion

Others – to connect to cable/transducer/thermistor (to check temperature)

Pressure bag

- A pressure bag placed around the flush solution that's maintained at 300 mm Hg of pressure
- The pressurized flush system delivers 3 to 5 mL of solution per hour through the catheter to prevent clotting and backflow of blood into the pressure monitoring system

Pulmonary artery catheter

- Inserted by physicians via the subclavian, internal jugular, or femoral vein.
- Inserted with balloon deflated: Inflation is then selected to "float" catheter into PA: Using the balloon as a "raft" that follows right ventricular blood flow, floating the catheter into the pulmonary artery (like sail on a sailboat).
- Level the transducer at the phlebostatic axis before readings and with all position changes: If placed low – high reading.: Called "Zero reference" - This eliminates the effect of atmospheric pressure on the fluid-filled monitoring system (like your BP monitor placed on axillary level)

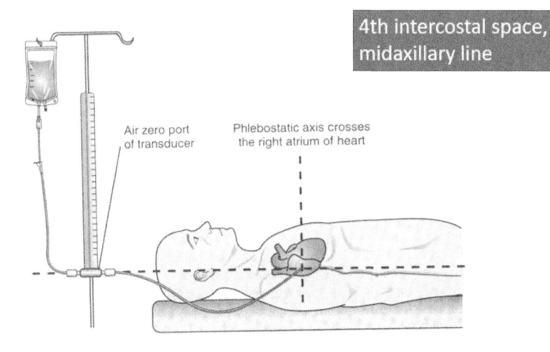

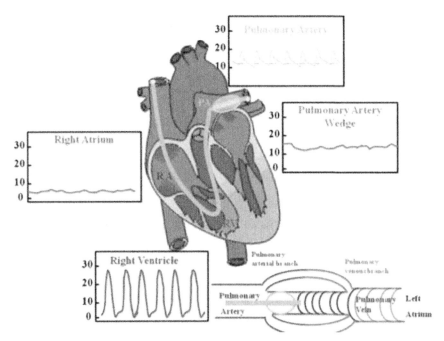

Why wave forms are different?

- Each area (RA, RV, PA, PAW) pressures gives different waveforms.
- It's important to monitor the changing waveforms as the PAC threads through the heart.

- If appropriate waveform is not present in the monitor – it indicates that the PAC is coiling up – rather than travelling through heart – to reach PA
- If RA waveform is continuously present – then it's stuck in RA – so, deflate balloon and pull back – and then inflate and monitor again for the waveform to change.

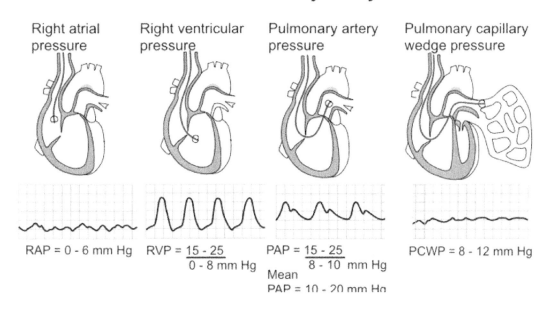

Flotation of the Pulmonary Artery Catheter

Right atrial pressure | Right ventricular pressure | Pulmonary artery pressure | Pulmonary capillary wedge pressure

RAP = 0 - 6 mm Hg

$$RVP = \frac{15 - 25}{0 - 8} \text{ mm Hg}$$

$$PAP = \frac{15 - 25}{8 - 10} \text{ mm Hg}$$

Mean PAP = 10 - 20 mm Hg

PCWP = 8 - 12 mm Hg

Nurses Role

- Consent, Position (supine/Trendelenburg)
- Know the waveforms
- If malposition – reposition the client or ask the client to cough, as these actions may correct the position of the catheter tip.
- If checking PAWP: The balloon should be inflated for only 10-15 seconds (coz you are blocking PA) and then allowed to deflate passively.
- Inflate with 1.5 mls of air: - to prevent balloon rupture
- A balloon that is inflated for a long period may cause PA rupture or damage.
- Always Lock the balloon port to prevent the balloon from being accidentally inflated.
- Chest x-ray: performed to document placement and rule out complications such as pneumothorax

- Monitor for complications –Dysrhythmias, Pneumothorax or hemothorax, Infection, Air embolus, Thromboembolism, PA rupture
- Measure and record catheter length once it has been placed in proper position.
- PAWP Elevated with fluid excess, HF, Pulmonary HTN. Decreased with hypovolemia

Critical care concepts

Shock

- Hypovolemic shock occurs when blood volume decreases (Hemorrhage, fluid loss, fluid shift)

Treatment goals:

- 1. Prevent further fluid loss
- 2. Give isotonic IV fluid to restore fluid volume
- 3. Give vasoactive medications - norepinephrine, dopamine
- These meds cause vasoconstriction and improved heart contractibility/output.
- Don't stop suddenly- its effects end quickly. It should be tapered slowly.
- Ventilator Associated Pneumonia

Things to Remember	To prevent VAP (Pneumonia more than 48 hrs. after intubation)
Infection Control	Handwashing, Monitor Vitals signs, Wean as soon as possible
Aspiration Control	Semi fowlers Position, HOB elevate to 30 - 45, ET tube with cuff, NPO, Minimize sedation, No stomach distention, Continuous tube feeding isa better choice than bolus feeding.
Hygiene	Oral care with antiseptics (chlorhexidine) Suction only as required (too much aggressive suction – more irritation and worsen pneumonia)
Others	Natural acidity of stomach acid is important in killing bacteria. So no need for routine PPI if patient is not at risk for developing stress ulcer.

Drop in oxygen saturation ON Ventilator – what to look for

- 1. Assess the client to determine the cause of hypoventilation
- 2. Tube Placement: Auscultating lung sounds is the first step and quickest intervention to confirm proper tube placement.
- 3: Look for complications – pneumothorax
- 4.Mucus plug – ventilator high pressure alarm will sound – need suction

Rapid response team

- To provide immediate attention to unstable clients in noncritical care units
- Usually consists of a respiratory therapist, a critical care nurse, and a physician or advanced practice registered nurse.
- When to activate rapid response:
  - o Any provider worried about the client's condition OR
  - o An acute change in any of the following:
    - Heart rate <40 or >130/min
    - Systolic blood pressure <90 mm Hg
    - Respiratory rate <8 or >28/min

- Oxygen saturation <90 despite oxygen
- Urine output <50 mL/4 hr
- Level of consciousness

Defibrillator pad placement

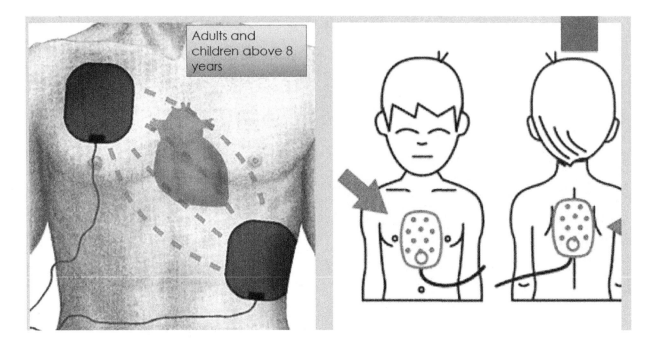

Tooth Avuls

- It is an emergency situation in dentistry (for permanent tooth)
- Avulsion - complete displacement of a tooth from its socket in alveolar bone after a trauma

Management at Home

- Keep patient calm
- Find the tooth and pick it up by the crown (the white part). Avoid touching the root.
- If the tooth is dirty, wash it briefly (10 seconds) under cold running water and replant / reposition it.
- Bite on a handkerchief to hold it in position.
- Seek emergency dental treatment immediately.

Storage of tooth (if cannot replant immediately)

- Place the tooth in a suitable storage medium:
- A glass of milk (has nutrients, pH better) or Hanks balanced storage medium is better choice.
- Other options are Saline and Patient's own Saliva.
- Water – not a good choice
- The tooth can also be transported to hospital/dentist office in the mouth, keeping it between the molars and the inside of the cheek (beware of swallowing)
- At dentist: Suture gingival laceration, splint for 2 weeks, then root canal. May also need antibiotics and tetanus injection
- Teaching afterwards:
  - Avoid participation in contact sports.
  - Soft food for up to 2 weeks.
  - Brush teeth with a soft toothbrush after each meal.
  - Use a chlorhexidine (0.1 %) mouth rinse twice a day for 1 week.
  - Follow up for root canal, X rays

Capnography

- It is the measurement of carbon dioxide in a patient's exhaled breath over time.
- Carbon dioxide (CO_2) absorbs infrared radiation.
- When the patient exhales, a beam of infrared light is passed over the gas sample on a sensor.
- The CO_2 levels are then displayed on the detector
- The presence or lack of CO_2 is inversely indicated by the amount of light that passes through the sensor.
- High CO_2 levels are indicated by low infrared, whereas low CO_2 levels result in high amounts of light.

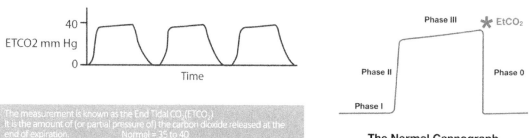

The measurement is known as the End Tidal CO_2 ($ETCO_2$). It is the amount of (or partial pressure of) the carbon dioxide released at the end of expiration. Normal = 35 to 40

The Normal Capnograph

Indication

- Any respiratory distress condition (asthma, COPD etc.)
- Ventilated patients: hypercapnia
- Gives early warning signs of hypoventilation or airway obstruction (before HR or BP changes)
- Monitor during anesthesia
- Identify reduced perfusion – warning signs of shock
- Evaluate success of CPR

Phases of Capnograph

- Phase I (inspiratory baseline) reflects inspired gas, which is normally devoid of carbon dioxide.
- Phase II (expiratory upstroke) is the transition between ventilatory dead space_ which does not participate in gas exchange_ and alveolar gas from the respiratory bronchioles and alveoli.
- Phase III is the alveolar plateau (the amount in alveoli)
- Phase 0 is the inspiratory downstroke, the beginning of the next inspiration.

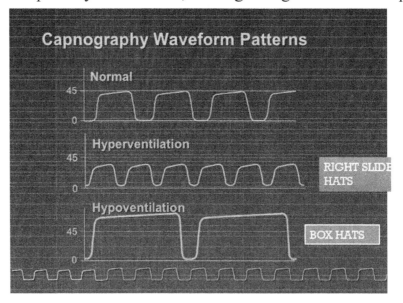

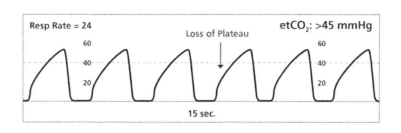

Bronchoconstriction – SHARK FIN
(asthma, pneumonia, COPD)

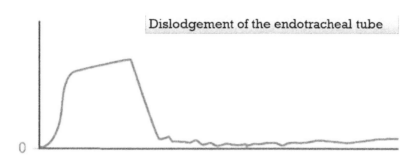

Dislodgement of the endotracheal tube

Modified CPR

- Notes to remember - CPR in Pregnancy
- 1. Mother supine – vena cava compression – reduced cardiac output
- 2. Displace the uterus to the client's left side. Put a rolled towel or wedge under right hip
- 3. Perform chest compressions slightly higher on the sternum. Don't compress baby
- 4. Immediate cesarean delivery should be anticipated

Pediatric considerations: Cardiovascular System

Congestive Heart Failure (CHF) (Pediatrics)

- Educate parents: diagnosis, administration of medications
- Administer meds 1 to 2 hours after feedings: Mark calendar
- Do not mix medication with foods, fluid.
- Give water after digoxin elixir to prevent tooth decay.

- If dose is missed and more than 4 hours has elapsed, withhold dose, and give next dose at prescribed time; if less than 4 hours, then administer dose
- If child vomits, do not administer replacement dose. If more than two consecutive doses missed, notify physician
- Withhold Digoxin
- If pulse is less than 90/min in an infant
- If pulse is less than 70/min in children

Defects with Increased Pulmonary Blood Flow

- Intra cardiac communications along septum or abnormal connection between great arteries, allowing blood to flow from higher pressure on left side of heart to lower pressure on right side of heart

Atrial septal defect (ASD)

- Infant may be asymptomatic or may develop CHF,
- Left to right shunt, dyspnea, fatigue, poor growth, soft systolic murmur
- Diagnosed by echo, can be visualized by heart cath
- Need surgery to close the defect

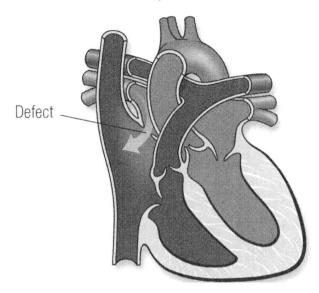

Atrial Septal Defect
source: AHA

Defect

Ventricular septal defect (VSD)

- Signs, symptoms of CHF commonly present:
- Respiratory distress and head bobbing
- Left to right shunt, dyspnea, fatigue,
- Poor growth, palpable thrill,
- Murmur at Left sternal boarder

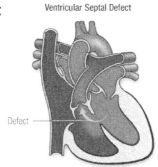

Ventricular Septal Defect

Defect

Source: AHA

Atrioventricular canal defect

- ASD +VSD+ Valve leaflet issues
- Infant usually has mild to moderate CHF; cyanosis increases with crying

Patent ductus arteriosus

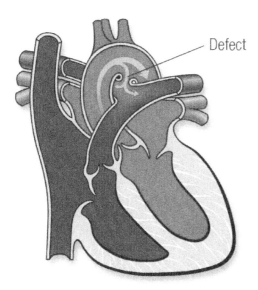

Patent Ductus Arteriosus

Defect

- Normal fetal circulation conduit between the pulmonary artery and the aorta fails to close.
- Widened pulse pressure, bounding pulses present, "machine hum" murmur
- Meds: Indomethacin or Ibuprofen
o Indoethacin affects blood flow to organs and so may lead to complications such as renal failure.

Source: AHA

Obstructive Defects

- Blood exiting the heart meets area of anatomic narrowing (stenosis), causing obstruction of blood flow
- Infants, children exhibit signs of CHF

Aortic stenosis

- A narrowing of the aortic valve
- Infants: Faint pulse, Hypotension, Tachycardia, Poor feeding tolerance
- Children: Intolerance to exercise, Dizziness, Chest pain, Ejection murmur, signs of exercise intolerance, chest pain, dizziness when standing for long periods

Pulmonic stenosis

- Narrowing of the pulmonary valve or pulmonary artery that results in obstruction of blood flow from the ventricles
- Systolic ejection murmur, Cardiomegaly, HF
- Newborns with severe narrowing are cyanotic

Coarctation of aorta

- Narrowing of the lumen of the aorta, that results in obstruction of blood flow from the ventricle
- BP higher, bounding pulses in upper extremities versus lower and weak or absent pulses in lower extremities versus upper extremities, as well as cool lower extremities

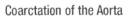

Coarctation of the Aorta

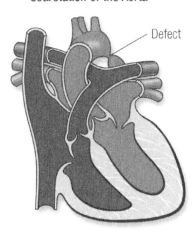

Source: AHA

- Signs of CHF may occur in infants

Other signs: -

- Elevated blood pressure in the arms
- Bounding pulses in the upper extremities
- Decreased blood pressure in the lower extremities (difference of 20 mm between upper and lower extremities)
- Cool skin of lower extremities
- Weak or absent femoral pulses
- Heart failure in infants
- Dizziness, headaches, fainting, or nosebleeds in older children

Defects with Decreased Pulmonary Blood Flow

- Obstructed pulmonary blood flow and anatomic defect between right and left sides of heart
- Pressure on right side of heart increases, exceeding pressure on left side of heart; allows unoxygenated blood to enter systemic circulation

Tricuspid atresia

- A complete closure of the tricuspid valve that results in mixed blood flow.
- An atrial septal opening need to be present to allow blood to enter the left atrium.
- Infants – cyanosis, dyspnea, tachycardia
- Older children – hypoxemia, clubbing of fingers

Tetralogy of Fallot

- Four defects that result in mixed blood flow
  - o Pulmonary stenosis
  - o Ventricular septal defect
  - o Overriding aorta

o Right ventricular hypertrophy

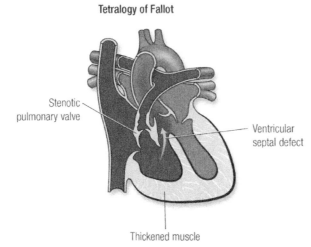

Tetralogy of Fallot

Stenotic pulmonary valve

Ventricular septal defect

Thickened muscle

Source: AHA

- Infants have acute episodes of cyanosis (hyper cyanotic spells, blue spells, tetralogy [TET] spells) during periods of crying, feeding, defecating. Knee chest position is recommended.
- Children present with squatting, clubbing of fingers, poor growth.
- Infants with TOF will normally maintain oxygen saturations of 65%-85% until the defect is surgically corrected.
- Children can develop polycythemia (RBC)as a compensatory mechanism due to prolonged tissue hypoxia. Polycythemia will increase blood viscosity, placing an infant at risk for stroke or thromboembolism

Mixed Defects

- Truncus arteriosus- failure of septum formation, resulting in a single vessel that comes off of the ventricles
- Characteristic murmur
- moderate to severe CHF,
- variable cyanosis, poor growth, activity intolerance

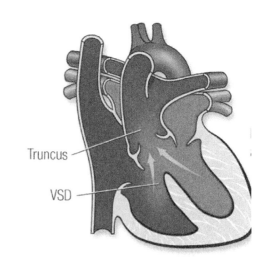

Truncus

VSD

Interventions: Cardiovascular Defects

- Monitor for signs of defect, Vital signs closely

- Respiratory status for symptoms of respiratory distress
- Auscultate lungs for presence of crackles, rhonchi, wheezes
- Position in Reverse Trendelenburg's if respiratory effort increases
- Administer humidified oxygen, Provide endotracheal tube, ventilator care as prescribed
- Monitor for hyper cyanotic spells, Assess for signs of CHF
- Assess peripheral pulses, Maintain strict fluid restriction
- Monitor intake, output, Obtain daily weight
- Provide high-calorie diet, Administer medications as prescribed
- Keep child as stress-free as possible, Child should have maximal rest
- Prepare child, parents for cardiac catheterization, if appropriate

Cardiac Surgery: Postoperative interventions

- Monitor vital signs, Maintain aseptic technique
- Monitor for signs of sepsis, including diaphoresis, lethargy, fever, altered level of consciousness
- Monitor all lines, tubes, catheters as appropriate
- Assess for discomfort, pain; medicate as prescribed
- Encourage periods of rest
- If bleeding occurs at a catheterization site in the groin, the nurse should apply direct pressure approximately 2.5 cm (1") above the insertion site.

Postoperative home care

- Omit outside play for 2 to 3 weeks
- Avoid strenuous activities and activities where child could fall for 2 to 4 weeks, No organized physical education for 2 months
- Avoid crowds for 2 weeks, maintain normal childhood routines and discipline
- No-added-salt (NAS) diet as prescribed
- Maintain clean, dry incision
- Avoid immunizations, invasive procedures, dental care for 2 months
- Stress importance of dental care, after waiting period, every 6 months

- If signs of infection, respiratory difficulty, changes in normal behavior occur, notify physician

Rheumatic Fever

- Inflammatory, autoimmune disease that affects connective tissues of heart, joints, subcutaneous tissues, blood vessels of central nervous system.
- Presents 2 to 6 weeks after untreated or partially treated group A beta-hemolytic streptococcal infection of upper respiratory tract
- Assessment: Fever, inflamed joints/ nodules present, erythema marginatum, carditis (Aschoff bodies)

Laboratory Tests

- Throat culture for GABHS
- Serum antistreptolysin-O (ASO) titer – elevated or rising titer, most reliable diagnostic test
- C-reactive protein (CRP) – elevated in response to an inflammatory reaction
- Erythrocyte sedimentation rate – elevated in response to an inflammatory reaction

Intervention

- Administer massage, heat, and cold therapies for joint pain
- Bed rest during febrile phase, Limit physical exercise in child with carditis
- Administer salicylates, anti-inflammatory agents as prescribed
- Sydenham chorea- neurological disorder –seizure - from GABHS infection – seizure precautions
- Instruct parents about follow-up care, need for prophylactic antibiotic therapy prior to dental care and invasive procedures

Kawasaki Disease

- Mucocutaneous lymph node syndrome/Acute systemic vasculitis
- Acute systemic inflammatory disease - unknown cause

- Cardiac involvement most serious complication (MI)

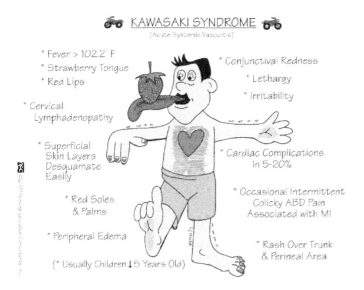

KAWASAKI SYNDROME
(Acute Systemic Vasculitis)

* Fever > 102.2° F
* Strawberry Tongue
* Red Lips
* Cervical Lymphadenopathy
* Superficial Skin Layers Desquamate Easily
* Red Soles & Palms
* Peripheral Edema
(* Usually Children ↓ 5 Years Old)

* Conjunctival Redness
* Lethargy
* Irritability
* Cardiac Complications in 5-20%
* Occasional Intermittent Colicky ABD Pain Associated with MI
* Rash Over Trunk & Perineal Area

Acute stage: Fever; red throat; swollen hands, feet; enlarged cervical lymph nodes

Subacute stage: Cracking lips and fissures; desquamation of skin on tips of fingers and toes; joint pain; cardiac manifestations; thrombocytosis

- Assess vital signs, heart sounds and rhythm
- Assess extremities for edema, redness, desquamation
- Assess mucous membranes for inflammation
- Daily weights
- Administer soft foods
- Provide passive range of motion
- Coronary artery aneurysms are the most serious potential sequelae in untreated clients, leading to complications such as myocardial infarction and death.
- Echocardiography is used to monitor these cardiovascular complications.
- Intravenous immunoglobulin (IVIG) along with aspirin is used to prevent coronary aneurysms and subsequent occlusion.

Cardiovascular Medications

Anticoagulants

- Prevent extension and formation of clots by inhibiting factors in clotting cascade and decreasing blood coagulability
- Side effects: Bleeding: Implement bleeding precautions

Heparin sodium

- Normal activated partial thromboplastin time (aPTT) 20 to 30 seconds – Therapeutic: 1.5 to 2.5 times the control value
- Antidote is protamine sulfate

Warfarin sodium (Coumadin)

- Normal PT is 11 to 12.5 seconds
- Therapeutic level of INR with warfarin = 2-3
- Avoid green leafy vegetables??? – don't change routines
- Antidote is vitamin K (phytonadione [AquaMEPHYTON])

Thrombolytic, Antiplatelet

- Thrombolytic: Dissolve clots
- Antidote: Aminocaproic acid (Amicar) is antidote for streptokinase
- Antiplatelet - Inhibit aggregation of platelets and prolong bleeding time – Aspirin
- Side effects: Bleeding
- Interventions: Monitor for bleeding, Implement bleeding precautions.
- Contraindications to thrombolytics: Prior intracranial bleed, Arteriovenous malformations, Ischemic stroke, or head trauma in last 3 months, aortic dissection, active bleeding.

Antihypertensive Medications

Diuretics

- Blocks the reabsorption of sodium, chloride, and water
- Loop: furosemide (Lasix), Bumetanide (Bumex), Torsemide (Demadex)

- Thiazide Diuretic: work in the early distal convoluted tubule
- Hydrochlorothiazide (Hydrodiuril), Indapamide (Lozide, Lozol) Chlorthalidone (Hygroton), Metolazone (Zaroxolyn)
- Lasix – Ototoxicity, Dig toxicity with Hypokalemia
- Electrolyte imbalance: hypokalemia, hyponatremia, hypocalcemia, hyperglycemia, hypomagnesemia
- Monitor vital signs (orthostatic hypotension), appropriate laboratory values, I&O, Daily Weight
- High-potassium foods (BP DC NS) bananas, potatoes, dried fruits, citrus fruit, nuts, and spinach).
- Avoid nighttime administrations- nocturia
- Diabetic clients- monitor glucose

Potassium-Sparing Diuretics

- spironolactone (Aldactone), triamterene (Dyrenium), amiloride (Midamor)
- Block the action of aldosterone (sodium and water retention), which results in potassium retention and the secretion of sodium and water.
- S/E; Hyperkalemia, Endocrine effects (impotence in male clients; irregularities of menstrual cycle in female clients)
- Low K foods: carrot, broccoli, beans, peas, cabbage, corn, wheat, popcorn, marshmallow, mints, grape, apple, pear, herbal tea, rice, oat milk, spices like chili, garlic.
- Teach clients to avoid salt substitutes that contain potassium.
- Triamterene (Dyrenium): Blue urine

Osmotic diuretics – Manitol

- Reduce ICP - drawing off fluid from the brain into the bloodstream.
- Use a filter needle when drawing from the vial and a filter in the IV tubing (To prevent administering microscopic crystals)
- Monitor daily weight, I&O, and serum electrolytes.

Alpha -Adrenergic Blockers

- Causes vasodilation and decrease the blood pressure. Ends with "zosin"

- Example: prazosin, doxazosin mesylate (Cardura), terazosin
- Side effects: Hypotension, Tachycardia, Sodium, and water retention
- GI disturbances: Take the initial dose at bedtime to decrease "first-dose" hypotensive effect
- Interventions: Monitor blood pressure and apical heart rate
- Monitor for fluid retention and edema

Alpha2 Agonists

- Clonidine, Methyldopa: Act on CNS and decrease the cardiac output
- S/E: Drowsiness and sedation – Safety precautions
- Dry mouth: Encourage clients to chew gum or suck on hard candy, and to take small amounts of water or ice chips
- Rebound hypertension: if abruptly discontinued
- Transdermal patches are applied every seven days.
- Advise clients to apply patch on hairless, intact skin on torso or upper arm

Angiotensin-Converting Enzyme (ACE) Inhibitors and Angiotension II Receptor Blockers (ARB)

- Prevent peripheral vasoconstriction
- ACE - Ends in "prill": captopril, Enalapril Fosinopril, Lisinopril, Ramipril, Moexipril
- ARB – Ends in "sartan": losartan, Valsartan, Irbesartan, Candesartan, Olmesartan
- Hyperkalemia and hypotension are contraindications for giving ACE inhibitors

Side effects

- ACE: Persistent dry cough, Angioedema (swelling -tongue and oral pharynx- airway obstruction)
- First-dose orthostatic hypotension (start low dose, monitor other meds? diuretics? BP?)
- Hypotension, Tachycardia, Hyperkalemia, Hypoglycemia in diabetic client
- Captorpil – neutropenia, Rash and dysgeusia (altered taste)

Interventions:

- Avoid use with potassium supplements and potassium-sparing diuretics
- NSAIDs may decrease the antihypertensive effect of ACE inhibitors. Avoid concurrent use.
- Captopril and moexipril should be taken at least 1 hr before meals. Other ACE inhibitors can be taken with or without food.
- Monitor vital signs and for signs of hyperkalemia, Instruct diabetic client about the risk for hypoglycemia
- Instruct client to report persistent dry cough, ACE inhibitors can increase levels of lithium

Renin Inhibitors -Aliskiren

- S/E – Diarrhea, Angioedema, Hyperkalemia
- High-fat meals interfere with absorption

Nitroprusside - a centrally acting vasodilator

- Avoid prolonged use, use separate IV line. Light brown color is normal.
- Plasma level at less than 10 mg/dL.
- Monitor for Cyanide poisoning (headache and drowsiness, and may lead to cardiac arrest – D/C med.

Calcium Channel Blockers

- Many ends with "dipine." E.g.- Nifedipine, Amlodipine
- Other meds: Verapamil & Diltiazem
- Consuming grapefruit juice can lead to toxicity
- Nifedipine: Reflex tachycardia, Peripheral edema
- Verapamil: constipation, dig toxicity
- Verapamil and Diltiazem: Orthostatic hypotension, peripheral edema, bradycardia, heart failure, heart block

Beta Adrenergic Blockers

- Ends with "lol"

- Propranolol and nadolol affects both heart and lungs. Bronchoconstriction can occur. Avoid in asthma pts.
- S/E – Bradycardia, AV block, orthostatic hypotension (avoid sudden changes in position), sexual dysfunction
- Client needs to monitor blood glucose levels carefully; medication may mask symptoms of hypoglycemia or prolong the effect of insulin.

Nesiritide

- Dilates arteries and veins and is used to treat decompensated heart failure
- Side effects: Hypotension, Dysrhythmias
- Interventions: Monitor apical heart rate and blood pressure, urine output, and body weight. Monitor for signs of resolving heart failure

Digoxin

- Increased force of myocardial contraction, and decreased Heart Rate
- Avoid hypokalemia (nausea/vomiting, general weakness) - Risk for Dig Toxicity
- Therapeutic serum levels: 0.5 to 2.0 ng/mL. Toxic – HAD DNV (Halo, Anorexia, Diarrhea, Dizziness, N/V)
- Don't miss dose –don't take double if missed.
- Check apical pulse, hold if < 60

Nitroglycerin

- Nitroglycerin (NTG) dilates veins and decreases venous return (preload), which decreases cardiac oxygen demand.
- Headache – give acetaminophen (Tylenol)/ may reduce dose of NTG.
- Orthostatic hypotension – safety. Reflex tachycardia – may need beta blocker
- Nitro Ointment: Avoid touching ointment with the hands.
- Do not crush or chew oral nitroglycerin or isosorbide tablets.
- Nitro S/L: Prophylactic.
    - Place under the tongue and allow it to dissolve. A tingling sensation under tongue is OK

- o Use Light resistant container. Store in original bottles, and in a cool, dark place.
- One tab * three times, 5 mts apart. If pain not relieved by first tablet, call 911, then take a second tablet.
- Nitro patch:
  - o To ensure an appropriate dose, patches should not be cut.
  - o Place the patch on a hairless area of skin (chest, back, or abdomen) and rotate sites to prevent skin irritation.
  - o Remove old patch, wash skin with soap and water, and dry thoroughly before applying new patch.
  - o Remove the patch at night to reduce the risk of developing tolerance to nitroglycerin. Be medication-free between 10 and 12 hr/day.

Ranolazine (Ranexa)

- Anti anginal (reduces cardiac oxygen demand)
- S/E: QT prolongation: Get ECG baseline. Contraindicated in clients -liver dysfunction. Monitor the client's vital signs and ECG frequently.

Sodium channel blockers

- Stabilize cardiac membranes, Procainamide, Quinidine
- S/E Systemic lupus syndrome (fever, painful and swollen joints, butterfly-shaped rash on face).

Potassium channel blockers

- Prolong cardiac cycle: Amiodarone, sotalol Amiodarone - Pulmonary toxicity. Obtain baseline chest x-ray and pulmonary function tests.
- Visual issues, photophobia. Avoid grapefruit juice (toxicity)
- Adverse effects may continue for an extended period of time after the medication is discontinued.

Statins

- Antilipemic agents (lower cholesterol), Hepatotoxic, Renal toxic
- Baseline liver and kidney function tests should be obtained and monitored periodically throughout the course of therapy.

- Myopathy can occur – Monitor CK levels
- Rhabdomyolysis.: Advise clients to report muscle aches, pain, and tenderness
- Evening dosing is best as most cholesterol is synthesized during the night.

Adenosine

- Drug of choice for the treatment of SVT
- The half-life is <5 seconds, so adenosine should be administered rapidly as a 6-mg bolus IV over 1-2 seconds followed by a 20-mL saline flush.
- The injection site should be as close to the heart as possible (ex: antecubital area). Central line is not required.
- The client's ECG should be monitored continuously. A brief period of asystole may happen due to adenosine slowing impulse conduction through the atrioventricular node.
- The client should be monitored for flushing, dizziness, chest pain, or palpitations during and after administration (vasodilation)

Neurology

Central Nervous System

Brain and Spinal cord

- Brain - Normal contents are 80% brain tissue, 10% blood, 10% CSF
- Meninges: Dura mater, Arachnoid mater, and Pia mater.
- Dura: strong, thick membrane that closely lines the inside of the skull
- Arachnoid: thin, web-like membrane that covers the entire brain.
- The space between Dura and Arachnoid = Subdural space.
- Pia: Hugs the surface of the brain and has many blood vessels that reach deep into the brain.
- The space between arachnoid and pia = Subarachnoid space -CSF
- BROCA – (Frontal) - production of speech.
- WERNICKE's - (Temporal)- comprehension of speech.

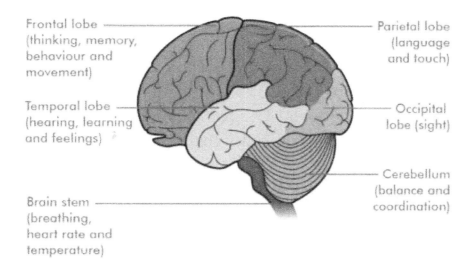

Frontal lobe
(thinking, memory,
behaviour and
movement)

Temporal lobe
(hearing, learning
and feelings)

Brain stem
(breathing,
heart rate and
temperature)

Parietal lobe
(language
and touch)

Occipital
lobe (sight)

Cerebellum
(balance and
coordination)

Source: Sulaiman et al, 2020. Doi: 10.1007/978-981-15-3270-2_29

Cerebral circulation

- Receives 15% to 20% of cardiac output (750 ml per min)
- Carotid arteries (anterior circulation)
- Vertebral arteries (posterior circulation)
- Cerebral veins empty into venous sinuses- jugular veins
- The sole source of cellular energy for the brain is glucose. As the brain is unable to store glucose, it requires a constant supply.
- Brain metabolism
    - Cerebral glucose < 70 mg/dL = confusion
    - Cerebral glucose < 20 mg/dL = damage

Blood Brain Barrier

- Helps to maintain a stable environment at brain
- OK to pass water, oxygen, CO_2, glucose, Vitamins, minerals
- Not OK: Waste: urea, creatinine, toxins, most drugs
- Antidepressants, anti-anxiety medications, alcohol and cocaine might pass.
- Infection, radiation, hypertension, trauma can alter BBB

Neurological Assessment

- Risk factors, Cranial nerves, Level of alertness, Level of consciousness, Glasgow Coma Scale
- Vital signs
- Pupils - Normal pupils are 3-5 mm in diameter - PERRLA
- Motor function, Posturing
    - Decorticate position – Flexion
    - Decerebrate position – Extension
- Reflexes, Sensory function
- DTR – Deep Tendon Reflexes
- A) Biceps, B) Brachioradial, C) Triceps, D) Patellar, E) Achilles, F) Evaluation of ankle clonus

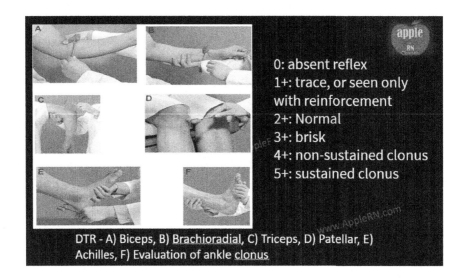

DTR - A) Biceps, B) Brachioradial, C) Triceps, D) Patellar, E) Achilles, F) Evaluation of ankle clonus

Glasgow Coma Scale: Best response=15, No response =3

Feature	Response	Score
Best eye response	Open spontaneously	4
	Open to verbal command	3
	Open to pain	2
	No eye opening	1
Best verbal response	Orientated	5
	Confused	4
	Inappropriate words	3
	Incomprehensible sounds	2
	No verbal response	1
Best motor response	Obeys commands	6
	Localising pain	5
	Withdrawal from pain	4
	Flexion to pain	3
	Extension to pain	2
	No motor response	1

Source: Nursing Standard. 19, 33, 56-67.

Cranial Nerves

Number	Name	Function
I	Olfactory	Sense of smell
II	Optic	Vision
III	Oculomotor	Motor control of some eye muscles and eyelid
IV	Trochlear	Motor control of some eye muscles
V	Trigeminal	Chewing muscles and some facial sensation
VI	Abducent	Motor control of some eye muscles
VII	Facial	Motor control of facial muscles, salivation. Taste and cutaneous sensations.
VIII	Acoustic	Equilibration, static sense and hearing
IX	Glossopharyngeal	Salivation, sensations of skin, taste and viscera
X	Vagus	Motor control of the heart and viscera, sensation from the thorax, pharynx and abdominal viscera
XI	Accessory	Motor impulses to the pharynx and shoulder
XII	Hypoglossal	Motor control of the tongue, some skeletal muscles, some viscera, sensation from skin and viscera

Source: ATI nursing

1. Olfactory
2. Optic
3. Oculomotor
4. Trochlear
5. Trigeminal
6. Abducens
7. Facial
8. Acoustic
9. Glossopharyngeal
10. Vagus
11. Spinal Accessory
12. Hypoglossal

Sarah Martin, 2011

10
The Cranial Nerves

Meningitis

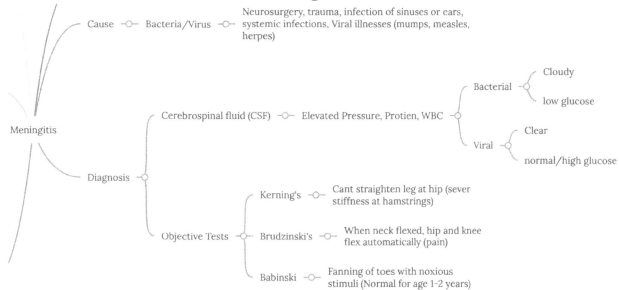

Cause — Bacteria/Virus — Neurosurgery, trauma, infection of sinuses or ears, systemic infections, Viral illnesses (mumps, measles, herpes)

Meningitis

Diagnosis

Cerebrospinal fluid (CSF) — Elevated Pressure, Protien, WBC

Bacterial — Cloudy / low glucose

Viral — Clear / normal/high glucose

Objective Tests

Kerning's — Cant straighten leg at hip (sever stiffness at hamstrings)

Brudzinski's — When neck flexed, hip and knee flex automatically (pain)

Babinski — Fanning of toes with noxious stimuli (Normal for age 1-2 years)

Meningitis Signs and Symptoms

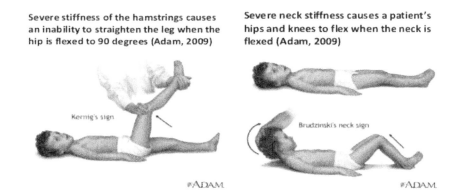

Severe stiffness of the hamstrings causes an inability to straighten the leg when the hip is flexed to 90 degrees (Adam, 2009)

Severe neck stiffness causes a patient's hips and knees to flex when the neck is flexed (Adam, 2009)

Kernig's sign

Brudzinski's neck sign

#ADAM

#ADAM

- Babinski reflex can be present up to age 1-2 years and is a normal, expected finding

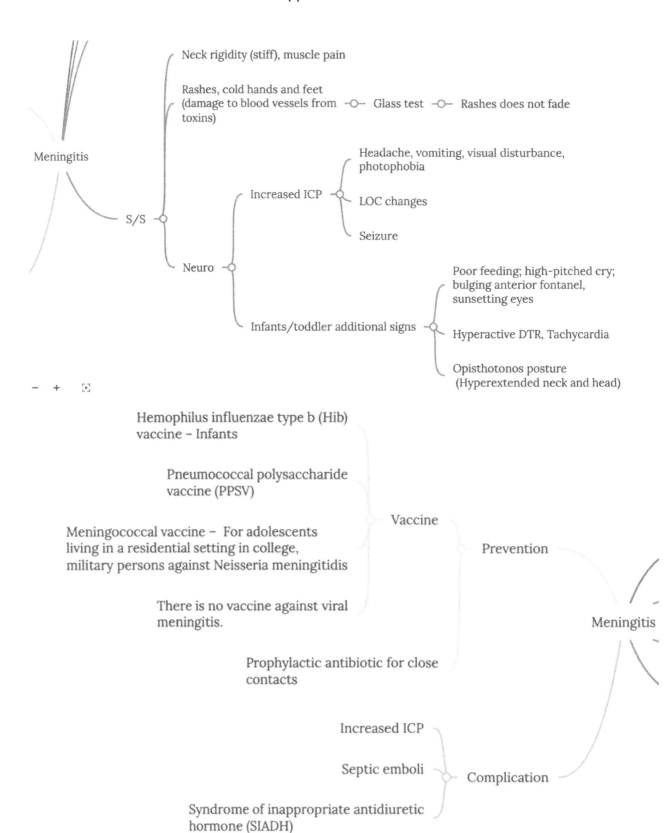

Meningitis

S/S
- Neck rigidity (stiff), muscle pain
- Rashes, cold hands and feet (damage to blood vessels from toxins) —O— Glass test —O— Rashes does not fade
- Neuro
  - Increased ICP
    - Headache, vomiting, visual disturbance, photophobia
    - LOC changes
    - Seizure
  - Infants/toddler additional signs
    - Poor feeding; high-pitched cry; bulging anterior fontanel, sunsetting eyes
    - Hyperactive DTR, Tachycardia
    - Opisthotonos posture (Hyperextended neck and head)

Meningitis

Prevention
- Vaccine
  - Hemophilus influenzae type b (Hib) vaccine – Infants
  - Pneumococcal polysaccharide vaccine (PPSV)
  - Meningococcal vaccine – For adolescents living in a residential setting in college, military persons against Neisseria meningitidis
  - There is no vaccine against viral meningitis.
- Prophylactic antibiotic for close contacts

Complication
- Increased ICP
- Septic emboli
- Syndrome of inappropriate antidiuretic hormone (SIADH)

Complications

- Increased ICP (possibly to the point of brain herniation)
  - Meningitis can cause ICP to increase.
  - Nursing Actions : Monitor for signs of increasing ICP (LOC changes, pupillary changes, impaired extraocular movements). Provide interventions to reduce ICP (positioning and avoidance of coughing and straining). Mannitol can be administered via IV.
- Septic emboli (leading to disseminated intravascular coagulation or cardiovascular accident)
  - Septic emboli can form during meningitis and travel to other parts of the body, particularly the hands and feet.
- Syndrome of inappropriate antidiuretic hormone (SIADH)
  - SIADH can be a complication of meningitis by abnormal stimulation to the hypothalamic area of the brain, causing excess secretion of antidiuretic hormone (vasopressin).

Meningitis Nursing Actions :

- Monitor for signs and symptoms (dilute blood, concentrated urine). Provide interventions, such as the administration of demeclocycline (diuretic type property)and restriction of fluid.
- Isolate the client as soon as meningitis is suspected
- Droplet isolation for bacterial meningitis
- for first 24 hrs of antibiotics and when oral and nasal secretions are no longer infectious.
- Standard – all clients who have meningitis
- Tubercular meningitis with lung involvement?? - Airborne
- Report meningococcal infections to the public health department.
- Decrease environmental stimuli.
- Implement fever-reduction measures, such as a cooling blanket, if necessary
- Minimize exposure to bright light (natural and electric).
- Maintain bed rest with the HOB elevated to 30°.
- Monitor the client for increased intracranial pressure (ICP).

- Tell the client to avoid coughing and sneezing, which increase ICP.
- Maintain client safety, such as seizure precautions.
- Replace fluid and electrolytes
- Older adult clients are at an increased risk for secondary complications, such as pneumonia.
- Prophylactic antibiotics given to individuals in close contact with the client.

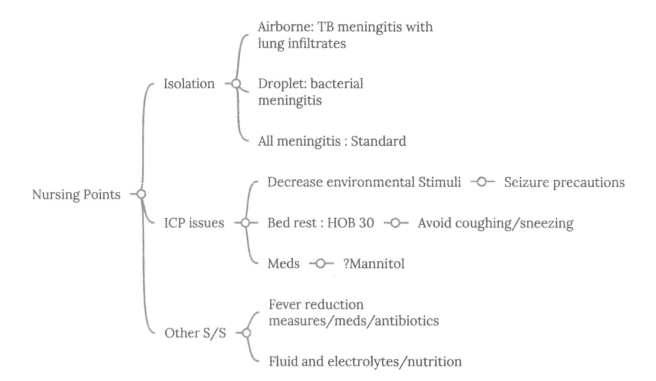

Intracranial Pressure

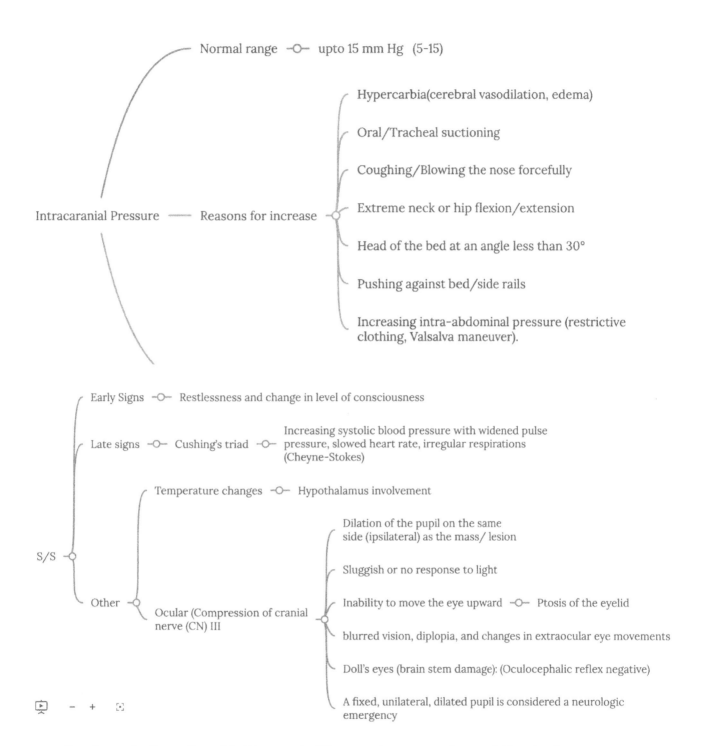

- Oculocephalic reflex (doll's eyes): The test is not performed if spinal trauma is suspected. Negative response, i.e., absence of eye movement and remain fixed at midline, shows damage to the brainstem.

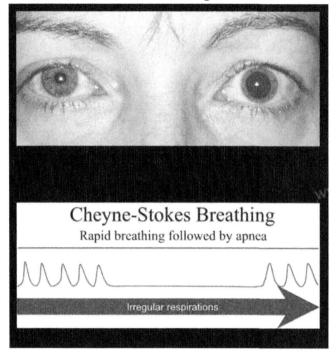

Cheyne-Stokes Breathing
Rapid breathing followed by apnea

Irregular respirations

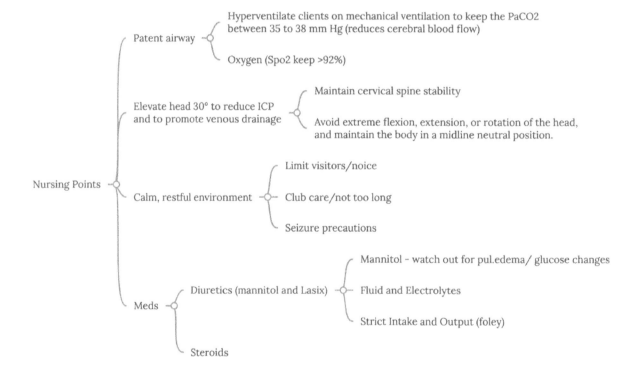

Nursing Points

- Patent airway
  - Hyperventilate clients on mechanical ventilation to keep the PaCO2 between 35 to 38 mm Hg (reduces cerebral blood flow)
  - Oxygen (Spo2 keep >92%)
- Elevate head 30° to reduce ICP and to promote venous drainage
  - Maintain cervical spine stability
  - Avoid extreme flexion, extension, or rotation of the head, and maintain the body in a midline neutral position.
- Calm, restful environment
  - Limit visitors/noice
  - Club care/not too long
  - Seizure precautions
- Meds
  - Diuretics (mannitol and Lasix)
    - Mannitol - watch out for pul.edema/ glucose changes
    - Fluid and Electrolytes
    - Strict Intake and Output (foley)
  - Steroids

Head Injury

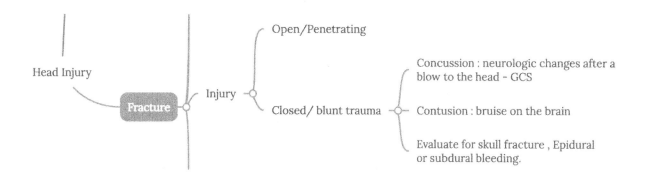

Head Injury — Fracture — Injury
- Open/Penetrating
- Closed/ blunt trauma
  - Concussion : neurologic changes after a blow to the head - GCS
  - Contusion : bruise on the brain
  - Evaluate for skull fracture , Epidural or subdural bleeding.

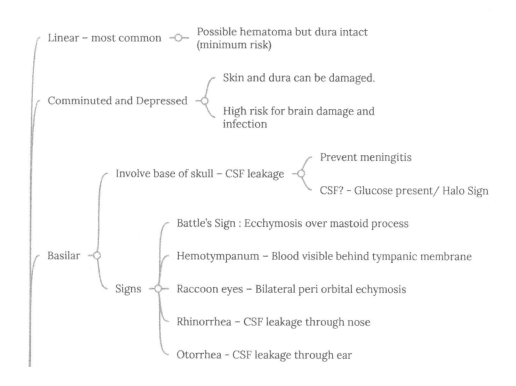

- Linear – most common — Possible hematoma but dura intact (minimum risk)
- Comminuted and Depressed
  - Skin and dura can be damaged.
  - High risk for brain damage and infection
- Basilar
  - Involve base of skull – CSF leakage
    - Prevent meningitis
    - CSF? - Glucose present/ Halo Sign
  - Signs
    - Battle's Sign : Ecchymosis over mastoid process
    - Hemotympanum – Blood visible behind tympanic membrane
    - Raccoon eyes – Bilateral peri orbital echymosis
    - Rhinorrhea – CSF leakage through nose
    - Otorrhea - CSF leakage through ear

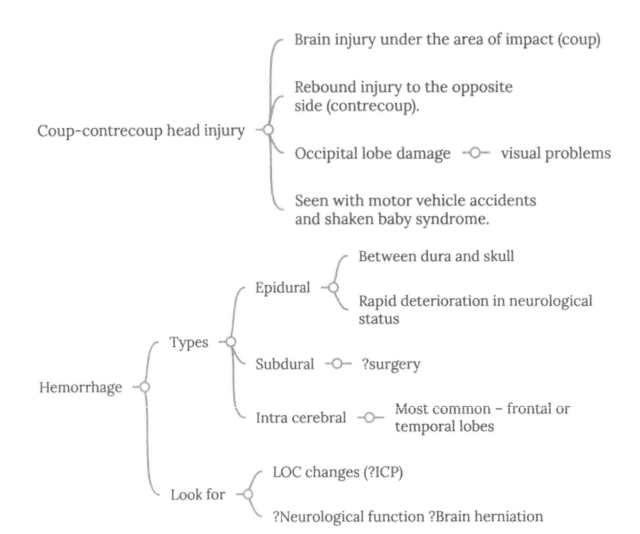

Coup-contrecoup head injury
- Brain injury under the area of impact (coup)
- Rebound injury to the opposite side (contrecoup).
- Occipital lobe damage — visual problems
- Seen with motor vehicle accidents and shaken baby syndrome.

Hemorrhage
- Types
  - Epidural
    - Between dura and skull
    - Rapid deterioration in neurological status
  - Subdural — ?surgery
  - Intra cerebral — Most common – frontal or temporal lobes
- Look for
  - LOC changes (?ICP)
  - ?Neurological function ?Brain herniation

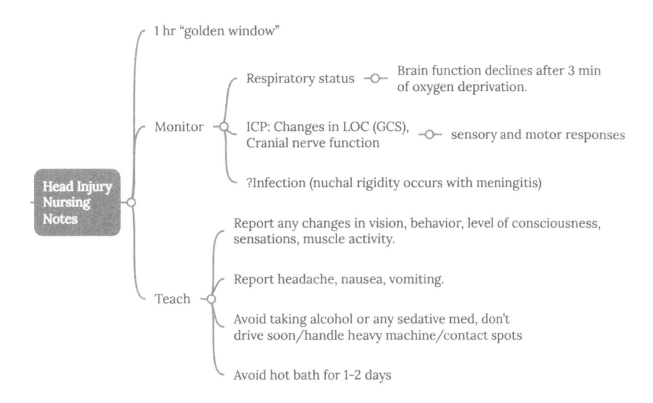

Head Injury Nursing Notes

- 1 hr "golden window"
- Monitor
  - Respiratory status — Brain function declines after 3 min of oxygen deprivation.
  - ICP: Changes in LOC (GCS), Cranial nerve function — sensory and motor responses
  - ?Infection (nuchal rigidity occurs with meningitis)
- Teach
  - Report any changes in vision, behavior, level of consciousness, sensations, muscle activity.
  - Report headache, nausea, vomiting.
  - Avoid taking alcohol or any sedative med, don't drive soon/handle heavy machine/contact spots
  - Avoid hot bath for 1-2 days

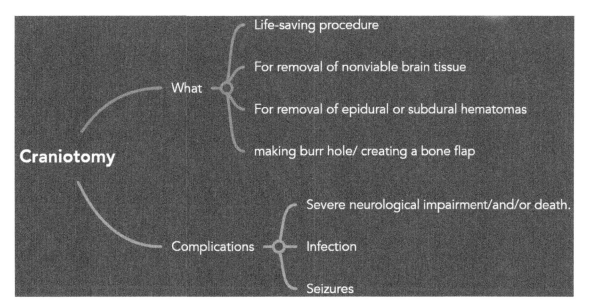

Craniotomy

- What
  - Life-saving procedure
  - For removal of nonviable brain tissue
  - For removal of epidural or subdural hematomas
  - making burr hole/ creating a bone flap
- Complications
  - Severe neurological impairment/and/or death.
  - Infection
  - Seizures

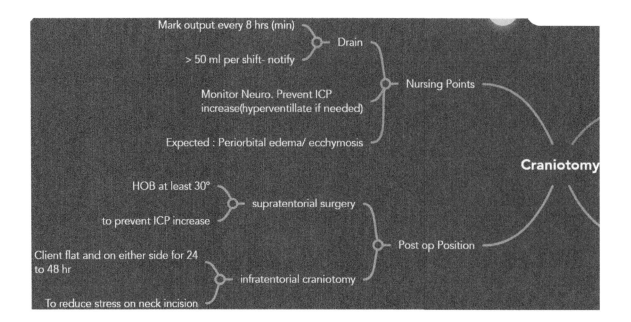

Arteriovenous malformation (AVM)

- Weak and dilated connections in Artery and Vein in Brain
- AVM can cause neurologic deficits. Treatment - blood pressure control
- AVMs - high risk for intracranial bleed - report any neurologic changes immediately: Sudden severe headache, nausea, and vomiting

Seizure

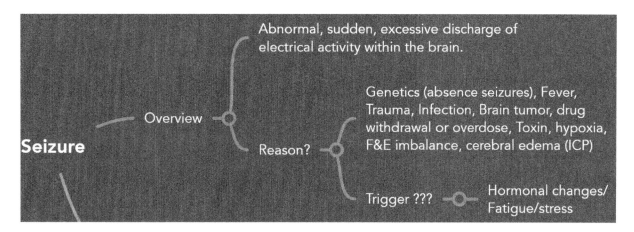

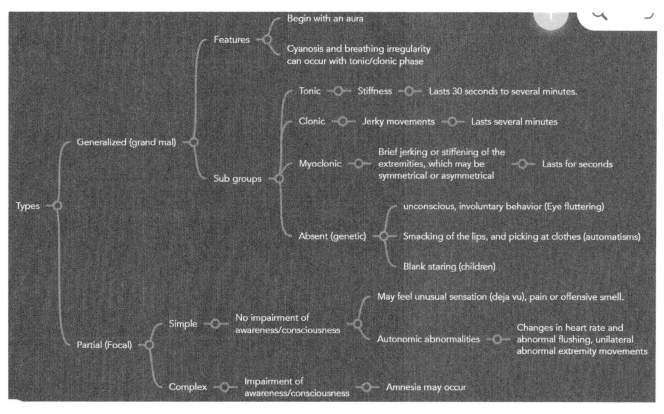

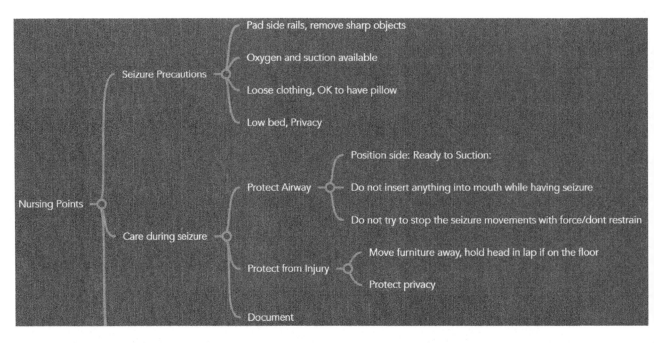

Nursing Points
- Seizure Precautions
  - Pad side rails, remove sharp objects
  - Oxygen and suction available
  - Loose clothing, OK to have pillow
  - Low bed, Privacy
- Care during seizure
  - Protect Airway
    - Position side: Ready to Suction:
    - Do not insert anything into mouth while having seizure
    - Do not try to stop the seizure movements with force/dont restrain
  - Protect from Injury
    - Move furniture away, hold head in lap if on the floor
    - Protect privacy
  - Document

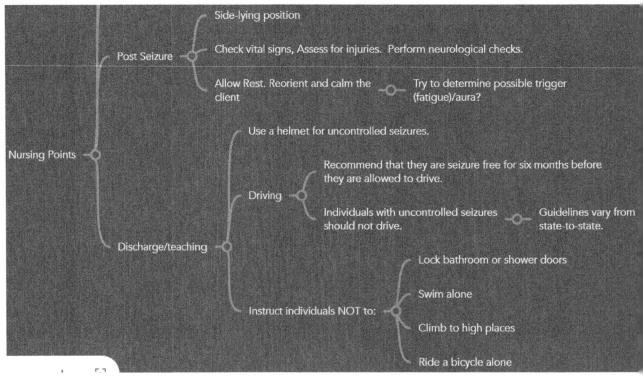

Nursing Points
- Post Seizure
  - Side-lying position
  - Check vital signs, Assess for injuries. Perform neurological checks.
  - Allow Rest. Reorient and calm the client
    - Try to determine possible trigger (fatigue)/aura?
- Discharge/teaching
  - Use a helmet for uncontrolled seizures.
  - Driving
    - Recommend that they are seizure free for six months before they are allowed to drive.
    - Individuals with uncontrolled seizures should not drive.
      - Guidelines vary from state-to-state.
  - Instruct individuals NOT to:
    - Lock bathroom or shower doors
    - Swim alone
    - Climb to high places
    - Ride a bicycle alone

Status Epilepticus

- Prolonged seizure activity occurring over a 30-min time frame.
- Complications: Hypoxia
- The usual causes: withdrawal from drugs or alcohol, sudden withdrawal from antiepileptic medication, head injury, cerebral edema, infection, and fever.
- Nursing Actions: Maintain an airway, provide oxygen, establish IV access, perform ECG monitoring, and monitor pulse oximetry and ABG results. Give medications.

Phenytoin

- S/E: gingival hyperplasia: need good oral hygiene
- Folic acid deficiency- need supplementation
- Therapeutic range 10-20 mcg/mL.
- Need regular blood test
- Early signs of toxicity: nystagmus and unsteady gait
- Late signs: lethargy, confusion, coma.
- Others: Increase in body hair, rash, and osteoporosis

Stroke

- Sudden, focal neurological deficit
- Risk factors: Cerebral aneurysm, AVM, DM, HTN, Obesity, Atherosclerosis, Hyperlipidemia, Hypercoagulability, Atrial fibrillation, Use of oral contraceptives, Smoking, Cocaine use
- Assessment: Depends on area of brain affected
- Airway patency is priority

Thrombotic -Ischemic	Embolic - Ischemic	Hemorrhagic
Blood clot	Emboli	bleeding
Most common, atherotic plaque	Thrombolytic enzyme (rtpa) is helpful	Poor prognosis
HTN, DM	Rheumatic heart disease (younger), Atherosclerosis (older)	Occur secondary to a ruptured artery or aneurysm, HTN
TIA common	Warning signs are less common	Sudden onset of symptoms
Symptoms over several hours to days	Sudden, rapid occurrence of severe clinical manifestations. (neurologic deficits or a loss of consciousness instantly occur)	Fifty percent of the deaths occur within the first 48 hours.

Left Sided Stroke

- The left cerebral hemisphere is responsible for language, mathematics skills, and analytic thinking.
- Symptoms consistent with a left-hemispheric stroke include the following:
- Expressive and receptive aphasia (inability to speak and understand language respectively)
- Agnosia (unable to recognize familiar objects)
- Alexia (reading difficulty)
- Agraphia (writing difficulty)
- Right extremity hemiplegia (paralysis) or hemiparesis (weakness)
- Slow, cautious behavior
- Depression, anger, and quick to become frustrated
- Visual changes, such as hemianopsia (loss of visual field in one or both eyes)

Normal   Hemianopsia

- Dysphasia - impaired ability to communicate – speech problem
- Apraxia - loss of the ability to perform a learned movement (e.g., whistling, clapping, dressing) due to neurological impairment.

Right Sided Stroke

- The right cerebral hemisphere is responsible for visual and spatial awareness and proprioception.
- Altered perception of deficits (overestimation of abilities)
- One-sided neglect syndrome (ignore left side of the body – cannot see, feel, or move affected side, so client unaware of its existence). Can occur with left-hemispheric strokes but is more common with right-hemispheric strokes.
- Loss of depth perception, Poor impulse control and judgment
- Left hemiplegia or hemiparesis
- Visual changes, such as hemianopsia

Nursing Care

- Monitor the client's vital signs every 1 to 2 hr.
- HTN - Notify the provider immediately (crisis 180/110)
- Monitor temperature. Fever – ICP increase
- Provide oxygen (Spo2 >92%)
- cardiac assessment, Tele monitor (arrhythmias)

- ICP? – LOC changed, position HOB 30, seizure precaution.
- Communication
- Assist with safe feeding.
    - Assess swallowing and gag reflexes before feeding.
    - Consult Speech therapy
    - Use thickener to avoid aspiration.
    - Position upright: swallow with the head and neck flexed slightly forward.
    - Place food in the back of the mouth on the unaffected side.
    - Have suction on standby.
    - Maintain a distraction-free environment during meals.
- Prevent complications of immobility.
    - Passive ROM every 2 hr to the affected extremities and active ROM every 2 hr to the unaffected extremities
    - Elevate, SCD, TED hose, PT
- Maintain skin integrity.
    - Reposition the client frequently and use padding.
    - Monitor bony prominences, paying particular attention to the affected extremities.
- Care of unilateral neglect.
    - Unilateral neglect is the loss of awareness of the side affected by the stroke. (Forgets that it exists)
    - Observe for injury. Apply an arm sling
    - Ensure the footrest is on the wheelchair and an ankle brace is on the affected foot.
    - Instruct the client to dress the affected side first.
    - Teach the client how to care for the affected side: pull the affected extremity to midline to avoid injury
    - Teach the client to look over the affected side periodically.
- Maintain a safe environment to reduce the risk of falls.
- Use assistive devices: transfer belts and sliding boards.
- Impaired balance: Leaning towards affected side while sitting – provide support.

- Shoulder subluxation - painful dislocation of the shoulder from its socket due to weight of unused arm. Use arm sling or pillows.
- Client with homonymous hemianopsia (loss of the same visual field in both eyes)
  - instruct to use a scanning technique (turning head from the direction of the unaffected side to the affected side) when eating and ambulating.
- Provide assistance with ADLs as needed.

Prism Adaptation Treatment (PAT)

- For Brain Injury clients (stroke/occipital damage): Spatial Neglect/ Unilateral neglect
- PAT: patients wear goggles with prism lenses that shift the visual field.
- With goggles, patient repeatedly perform arm-reaching tasks for about 20 minutes. (Need multiple sessions/weeks)
- After removing goggles, there is an adaptation process– and certain part of brain function restores with neural connections. This help brain to readjust to "look" at the neglected side.

Medications

- Anticoagulants (heparin sodium, enoxaparin [Lovenox], warfarin
  - Use of anticoagulants is controversial and not recommended due to the high risk of intracerebral bleeding.
- Antiplatelets (aspirin)
  - Low-dose aspirin is given within 24 to 48 hr following a stroke to prevent further clot formation.
- Thrombolytic medications reteplase recombinant (rtPA [Retavase])
  - Give within 4.5 hours of the initial symptoms.
- Antiepileptic medications (phenytoin [Dilantin], gabapentin [Neurontin])
  - These medications are given if client develops seizures.
- Gabapentin can be given for paresthetic pain in an affected extremity.

Multiple Sclerosis

- Neurological disease resulting in impaired and worsening function of voluntary muscles.
- Autoimmune disorder characterized by development of plaque in CNS, it damages the myelin sheath.
- Relapses and remission occur many times. Finally leading to quadriplegia.
- Triggers: Viruses, infectious, cold climate, injury, stress, Pregnancy, Fatigue, Hot shower/bath

Signs and Symptoms

- Fatigue – especially of the lower extremities
- Pain or paresthesia, Spasticity (rigid muscle)
- Visual changes, diplopia, nystagmus
- Uhthoff's sign (temporary worsening of vision & neurological functions)
- Dysphagia, Dysarthria (slurred and nasal speech)
- Bowel, bladder, and sexual dysfunction
- Cognitive changes (memory loss, impaired judgment)
- Meds: Azathioprine and cyclosporine: Immunosuppressive agents are used to reduce the frequency of relapses. Monitor for long-term effects. Assess for manifestations of infection, hypertension, kidney dysfunction.

Teaching Points

- Avoid triggers
- Apply alternating eye patches to treat diplopia (double vision).
- Teach scanning techniques.
- Fluids-to prevent urinary tract infection.
- Bladder and Bowel training (might need catheterization)
- Promote energy conservation by grouping cares and planning rest periods.
- Safety precautions

Myasthenia gravis (MG)

- Progressive autoimmune disease - severe muscular weakness.
- It is characterized by periods of exacerbation and remission.
- Muscles are stronger in the morning and become weaker with the day's activity as the supply of available acetylcholine is depleted. Muscle weakness improves with rest and worsens with increased activity.
- It is caused by antibodies that interfere with the transmission of acetylcholine at the neuromuscular junction.
- Therapeutic procedure: Plasmapheresis (removing antibodies from blood)

Factors that trigger exacerbations

- Infection, Stress, emotional upset, fatigue, Pregnancy
- Increases in temperature (fever, sunbathing, hot tubs).

Diagnostic Procedures: Tensilon testing

- Do baseline assessment of cranial muscle strength
- Give Edrophonium (Tensilon): inhibits the breakdown of acetylcholine, making it available for use at the neuromuscular junction.
- A positive test results in marked improvement in muscle strength that lasts approximately 5 min.
- Have atropine available, which is the antidote for edrophonium (bradycardia, sweating, and abdominal cramps, V fib)

Subjective Data

- Progressive muscle weakness, Diplopia
- Difficulty chewing and swallowing (bulbar sign)
- Respiratory dysfunction, Bowel, and bladder dysfunction
- Poor posture, Fatigue after exertion

Assessment

- Impaired respiratory status (difficulty managing secretions, decreased respiratory effort. Decreased swallowing ability.
- Decreased muscle strength, especially of the face, eyes, and proximal portion of major muscle groups.
- Incontinence
- Drooping eyelids – unilateral or bilateral

Nursing Care

- Patent airway (muscle weakness of diaphragm, respiratory, and intercostal)
- Conserve energy /Allow for periods of rest.
- Assess swallowing to prevent aspiration.
- oxygen, endotracheal intubation, suctioning equipment, and a bag valve mask available at the client's bedside.
- Provide small, frequent, high-calorie meals and schedule at times when medication is peaking.
- Sit upright when eating, use thickener in liquids. Soft food is better.
- Lubricating eye drop during the day and ointment at night if the client is unable to completely close his eyes. Patch or tape his eyes shut at night to prevent damage to the cornea.
- Patient to wear a medical id band
- Medications: Anticholinesterase agents are the first line in therapy.
- Ensure that the medication is given at the specified time, usually four times a day.
- If periods of weakness are observed, discuss change in administration times with the provider.
- Use cautiously in clients who have a history of asthma or cardiac dysrhythmias.
- Client Education
    - Take with food to address gastrointestinal side effects.
    - Eat within 45 min of taking the medication to strengthen chewing and reduce the risk for aspiration.

- Stress the importance of maintaining therapeutic levels and taking the medication at the same time each day.
- Pyridostigmine and neostigmine: Anticholenesterase
  - Used to increase muscle strength in the symptomatic treatment of MG. It inhibits the breakdown of acetylcholine and prolongs its effects.
- Nursing Considerations
  - Assess the client for a history of seizures.
  - Use cautiously in clients who have a history of asthma and cardiovascular disease.

Complications

- Myasthenic crisis occurs when the client is experiencing a stressor that causes an exacerbation of MG (infection, under medication)
- Cholinergic crisis occurs when the client has taken too much cholinesterase inhibitor (over medication)
- The manifestations of both can be very similar (Muscle weakness - bowel and bladder incontinence, absent cough and swallow reflex, respiratory distress/hypoxia/cyanosis).
- An edrophonium test may be performed to determine the crisis
- Worsening of the symptoms after the test dose of medication is administered indicates a cholinergic crisis.

Trigeminal Neuralgia:(tic douloureux)

- Sensory disorder of trigeminal cranial nerve
- Severe pain on lips, gums, nose, or across cheeks.
- Pain is severe, intense, burning, or electric shock-like
- Interventions: Avoiding hot or cold fluids or foods, Chew food on unaffected side
- Administer medications- The drug of choice is carbamazepine (risk of infection)

- Triggers can include washing the face, chewing food, brushing teeth, yawning, or talking.

Bell's Palsy (Facial Paralysis)

- Lower motor lesion of facial nerve that results in paralysis on one side of face - Inflammation of the facial nerve (cranial nerve VII)
- Assessment
    - Unilateral facial paralysis
    - Inability to raise eyebrows, frown, smile, close eyelids, or puff out cheeks on the affected side
- Interventions
    - Protect eye from dryness –patch eye
    - Prevent client injury, Supportive care
- Vision, balance, consciousness, and extremity motor function are not impaired with Bell's palsy.

Guillain-Barré Syndrome (GBS)

- Acute, infectious neuronitis of cranial and peripheral nerves
- Assessment: Motor weakness and flaccid paralysis, which starts from lower extremities- "Ground to brain"
- Gradual progressive weakness of upper extremities, facial muscles, and possible progression to respiratory failure- Report Shallow respirations, Dyspnea, hypoxia, Inability to cough/lift the head/eyebrows.
- Interventions
    - Prepare to initiate respiratory support
    - Provide supportive care

Amyotrophic Lateral Sclerosis (Lou Gehrig's disease)

- ALS is a disease of the upper and lower motor neurons that results in deterioration and death of the motor neurons.
- This results in progressive paralysis and muscle wasting that eventually causes respiratory paralysis and death

- ALS does not involve sensory alterations or cognitive changes.

Assessment

- Fatigue, Twitching and cramping of muscles
- Muscle weakness – usually begins in one part of the body
- Muscle atrophy, Dysphagia, Dysarthria
- Hyperreflexia of deep tendon reflexes

Interventions ALS

- Care is directed toward treatment of symptoms.
- Maintain a patent airway, and suction and/or intubate as needed.
- Monitor ABGs, and administer oxygen
- Keep the head of the bed at 45°; turn, cough, and deep breathe every 2 hr; and conduct incentive spirometry/chest physiotherapy.
- Assess swallow reflex and ensure safety with oral intake. Thicken fluids as needed. Meet nutritional needs for calories, fiber, and fluids.
- When no longer able to swallow, provide enteral nutrition as prescribed.
- Facilitate effective communication. Use energy conservation measures.

Huntington Disease

Overview	Symptoms	Treatment/care points
Rare, genetic Affects Brain (Neuro)	Personality/mood changes	No cure
	Forgetfulness & impaired judgment	Safety issues (chorea)
	Unsteady gait & involuntary movements (chorea)	Multidisciplinary collaboration (dietitian, PT/OT, Speech)
	Slurred speech, difficulty in swallowing, weight loss	Case management/full time caregiver

Spinal cord injuries

- Spinal cord injuries (SCIs) involve the loss of motor function, sensory function, reflexes, and control of elimination.
- Cervical region injury - quadriplegia (tetraplegia)/ paralysis/ paresis of all four extremities and trunk.
- T1 below- result in paraplegia – paralysis/paresis of the lower extremities.
- The level of cord involved determines the consequences of spinal cord injury

Nursing Care

- Respiratory status: First priority.
- oxygen and suction: intubation / mechanical ventilation
- Assist the client to cough - apply abdominal pressure
- incentive spirometer, coughing and deep breathing
- Intake and output
- Fluids and nutritional support -? NPO
- Neurological status, Muscle strength and tone
- Treatment: Patient may be placed in traction (Halo)

Bladder Issues

- Clients with upper motor neuron injury (above L1 & L2)
    - Spastic muscle tone after neurogenic shock - spastic bladder – fills with urine- reflex trigger automatic emptying- always leak.
- With lower motor neuron injuries (below L1 and L2)
    - A flaccid type of paralysis- a flaccid bladder – slow/absent reflex – patient won't feel fullness – urine back up (reflux)- damage kidney
- Bladder management
    - Intermittent catheterization
    - Crede's method (downward pressure placed on the bladder to manually express the urine).

Neurogenic shock/spinal shock

- Check Reflex - Areflexia characterizes spinal shock.
- Other Symptoms: bradycardia, hypotension, paralysis and paralytic ileus, dependent edema, and loss of temperature regulation.

Nursing Actions

- Monitor vital signs for hypotension and bradycardia (IVF, meds: vasopressors/atropine).
- Monitor the client for signs of thrombophlebitis (anticoagulants)
- Gastrointestinal function –Ileus- Monitor for bowel sounds.
- Skin Integrity – Changing the client's position every 2 hr is critical (every 1 hr when in a wheelchair).
- Encourage active range-of-motion (ROM) exercises. Pressure-relief devices in both the bed and the wheelchair must be consistently used.
- Orthostatic hypotension
    - Change the client's positioning slowly and place the client in a wheelchair that reclines.
    - Use thigh-high elastic hose or elastic wraps to increase venous return.
    - Elastic wraps may need to extend all the way up the client's legs and include the client's abdomen.

Autonomic dysreflexia

- Imbalanced reflex discharge, leading to potentially life-threatening hypertension.
- Symptoms: Sudden severe headache, pallor below the level of the spinal cord's lesion, blurred vision, diaphoresis, restlessness, nausea, and piloerection (goose bumps)
- It is considered a medical emergency and must be recognized immediately. Can cause seizures, retinal hemorrhage, pulmonary edema, renal insufficiency, myocardial infarction, cerebral hemorrhage, and death.

- Triggers: bladder distention, bowel distention, visceral distention, or stimulation of pain on skin.
- Position – High fowlers- sit up (decreases BP)
- Clients who have lesions below T6 do not experience dysreflexia: because the parasympathetic nervous system is able to neutralize the sympathetic response.

Steps: Autonomic dysreflexia – neurological emergency – hypertensive crisis

1. Elevate head of bed
2. Loosen tight clothing on client
3. Check for kinks in foley catheter
4. Contact the health care provider
5. Administer antihypertensive medication
6. Document client's response

Parkinson's disease (PD)

- Progressively debilitating disease that grossly affects motor function.
- It is characterized by four primary symptoms: tremor, muscle rigidity, bradykinesia (slow movement), and postural instability.
- These symptoms occur due to overstimulation of the basal ganglia by acetylcholine (and depletion of dopamine)
- Clients with PD have an imbalance between dopamine and acetylcholine in which dopamine is not produced in high enough quantities to inhibit acetylcholine.

Medication

- May take several weeks of use before improvement of symptoms is seen.
- Levodopa: converted to dopamine in the brain.
  - Give with food to minimize GI side effects
  - May be combined with carbidopa (Sinemet) to decrease peripheral metabolism of levodopa
- Anticholinergics: help control tremors and rigidity
  - Monitor for anticholinergic effects (dry mouth, constipation, urinary retention, acute confusion, acute glucoma).

Nursing Care

- Monitor swallowing and maintain adequate nutrition.
  - Maintain client mobility for as long as possible.
- Monitor client's mental and cognitive status
  - Observe for signs of depression and dementia.

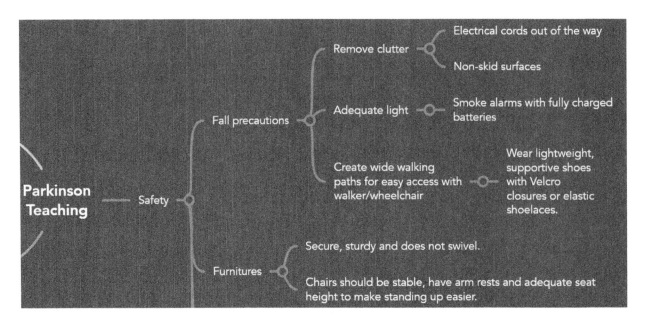

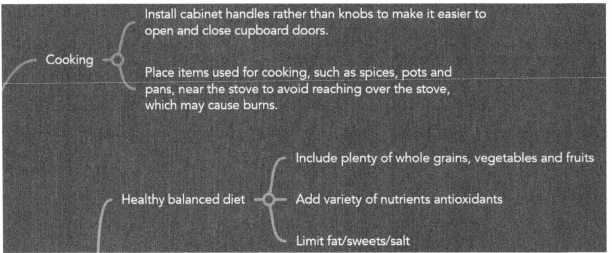

- Provide a safe environment (no throw rugs, encourage the use of an electric razor).
- Promote client communication
  - Teach the client facial muscle strengthening exercises.
  - Encourage the client to speak slowly and to pause frequently.
  - Use alternate forms of communication as appropriate.
  - Refer client to a speech-language pathologist

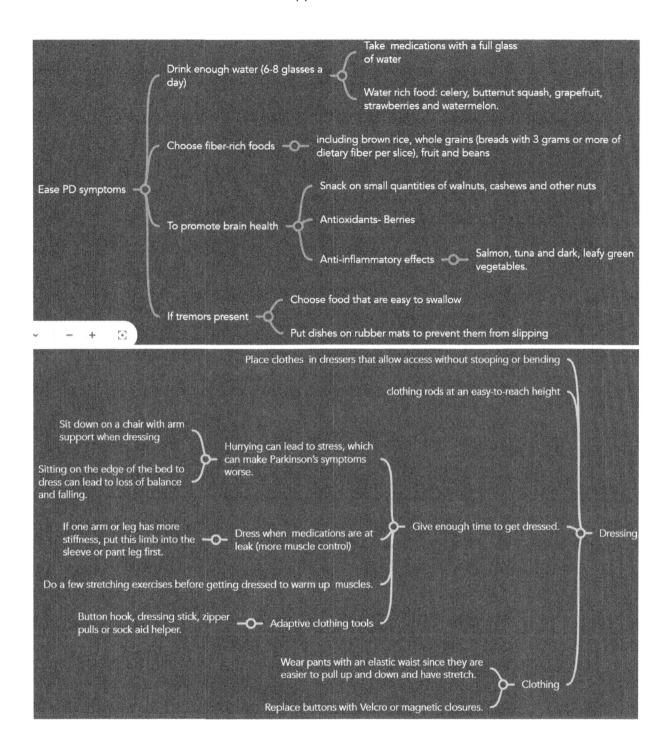

Ease PD symptoms

- Drink enough water (6-8 glasses a day)
  - Take medications with a full glass of water
  - Water rich food: celery, butternut squash, grapefruit, strawberries and watermelon.
- Choose fiber-rich foods
  - including brown rice, whole grains (breads with 3 grams or more of dietary fiber per slice), fruit and beans
- To promote brain health
  - Snack on small quantities of walnuts, cashews and other nuts
  - Antioxidants- Berries
  - Anti-inflammatory effects
    - Salmon, tuna and dark, leafy green vegetables.
- If tremors present
  - Choose food that are easy to swallow
  - Put dishes on rubber mats to prevent them from slipping

Dressing

- Place clothes in dressers that allow access without stooping or bending
- clothing rods at an easy-to-reach height
- Give enough time to get dressed.
  - Sit down on a chair with arm support when dressing
  - Sitting on the edge of the bed to dress can lead to loss of balance and falling.
  - Hurrying can lead to stress, which can make Parkinson's symptoms worse.
  - If one arm or leg has more stiffness, put this limb into the sleeve or pant leg first.
    - Dress when medications are at leak (more muscle control)
  - Do a few stretching exercises before getting dressed to warm up muscles.
  - Button hook, dressing stick, zipper pulls or sock aid helper.
    - Adaptive clothing tools
- Clothing
  - Wear pants with an elastic waist since they are easier to pull up and down and have stretch.
  - Replace buttons with Velcro or magnetic closures.

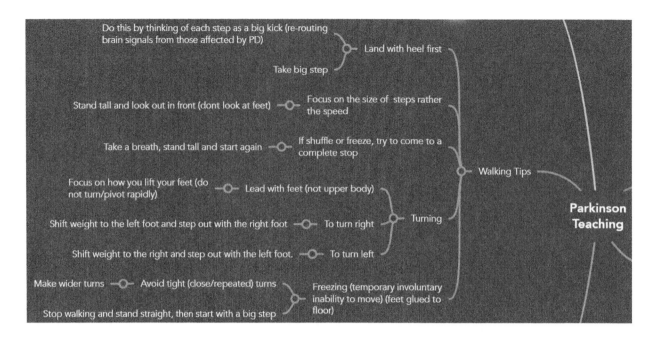

Alzheimer's disease

- Nonreversible type of dementia
- Characterized by memory loss, problems with judgment, and changes in personality leading to severe physical decline
- Sundowning: increased confusion experienced by an individual with dementia at night, when lighting is inadequate, or when the client is excessively fatigued – use simple commands
- Meds- Aricept – Prevent breakdown of Ach result in increased nerve impulses at the nerve sites.
    - Antipsychotics, anxiolytics, antidepressants
    - Ginkgo biloba – herbal- memory improvement
- Alzheimer disease and eating
    - Clients may forget that they have eaten recently.
    - Do not argue/ make them feel guilty
    - Give clients something to eat when they say they are hungry.
    - Smaller meals throughout the day, Provide low-calorie snacks
- Home Safety
    - Remove scatter rugs, lock cleaning supplies
    - Install door locks and place alarms on doors.

- Keeping a lock on the water heater and thermostat
- Provide good lighting, especially on stairs.
- Place mattress on the floor.
- Install handrails on stairs, mark step edges with colored tape.
- Remove clutter and clearing hallways for walking.
- Secure electrical cords to baseboards.
- Install handrails in the bathroom, at bedside, and in the tub, placing a shower chair in the tub.
  - Having the client wear a medical identification bracelet
- Monitoring for improvement in memory and the client's quality of life.

Pediatric considerations: Neurology

Hydrocephalus

- Results in head enlargement (prior to fontanels closing), increased ICP

Types

- Communicating: Result of impaired absorption within subarachnoid space
- Noncommunicating: Obstruction of cerebrospinal fluid (CSF) flow within brain

Assessment

- Infant: Increased head circumference; widening sutures; bulging fontanel; dilated scalp veins; frontal bossing; sunsetting eyes
- If the head circumference is greater than or equal to 4 cm larger than the chest circumference, this can be an indication of hydrocephalus
- Child: Irritability; lethargy; headache on awakening; nausea and vomiting; ataxia; nystagmus

Ventriculoperitoneal (VP) shunt

- Cerebral shunt that drains excess cerebrospinal fluid (CSF) when there is an obstruction in the normal outflow or there is a decreased absorption of the fluid. Has a one-way valve
- Hydrocephalus – usually placed at 3-4 months of age
- Shunts drain the CSF into the peritoneal cavity- VP shunt.
- A VP shunt is placed in the operating room under general anesthesia by a neurosurgeon.
- Contraindication - Infection over the entry site, Infection of the CSF, Allergy to any of the catheter components (silicone)

Hydrocephalus

Surgical interventions

- Goal - to prevent further CSF accumulation by bypassing blockage, draining fluid from ventricles to location where it may be reabsorbed – Ventriculoperitoneal shunt/ventriculostomy

Preoperative interventions

- NPO status,
- Reposition head frequently to prevent pressure sores
- Prepare the child and family for surgery

Postoperative interventions

- Position on nonoperative side to prevent pressure on shunt valve
- Keep flat as prescribed
- Observe for increased ICP; if present, elevate head of bed 15 to 30 degrees

Cerebral Palsy

- Disorder characterized by impaired movement and posture, results from abnormality in extrapyramidal or pyramidal motor system

Assessment

- Abnormal posturing, such as opisthotonos (exaggerated arching of back)
- Stiff and rigid arms and legs, Feeding difficulties
- Delayed gross motor activity, Alterations of muscle tone
- Persistence of primitive infantile reflexes

Interventions

- Assess developmental level, Encourage early intervention programs
- Prepare for use of mobilizing devices
- Provide safe environment, Provide safe, developmentally appropriate toys
- Position upright after meals, Administer muscle relaxants as prescribed

Spina Bifida

- Central nervous system (CNS) defect occurs as result of neural tube failure to close during embryonic development
- Types: Spina Bifida Occulta, Spina Bifida Cystica - Meningocele, Myelomeningocele
- Assessment: Depends on spinal cord involvement; visible spinal defect; flaccid paralysis of legs; altered bladder, bowel function; hip, joint deformities

Spina bifida occulta

- Mildest form
- Incomplete formation of posterior arch of the spinal column
- Usually incidental finding
- Seen in LS spine, commonest S1
- Occasionally patient may have fatty deposit, hemangioma or tuft of hair

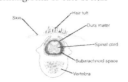

Image credit: Health and medicine

Spina bifida cystica

↗Two types:
- **Meningocele**- protrusion of only the dura and arachnoid through the defect in the vertebral lamina forming a cystic swelling usually in lumbosacral area
- Spinal cord remains in the vertebral canal

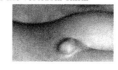

Spina bifida cystica

Myelomeningocele-
- 10 times more frequent
- portion of the spinal cord or the nerve roots are displaced through the spina bifida defect into the sac

- Interventions: Protect sac by covering with sterile, moist, nonadherent dressing as prescribed; change every 2 to 4 hours as prescribed
- Prone position, Aseptic technique

Attention-Deficit/Hyperactivity Disorder

- Developmental disorder with following types of symptoms
- Inattention—having difficulty paying attention
- Hyperactivity—having too much energy or moving and talking too much
- Impulsivity—acting without thinking or having difficulty with self-control
- Treatment: Meds/Cognitive Behavioral Therapy

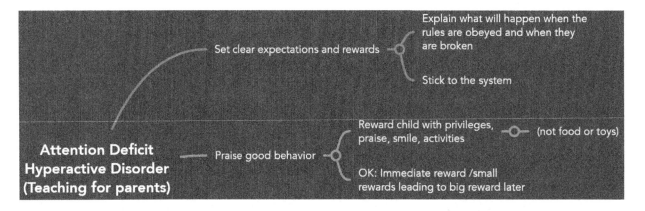

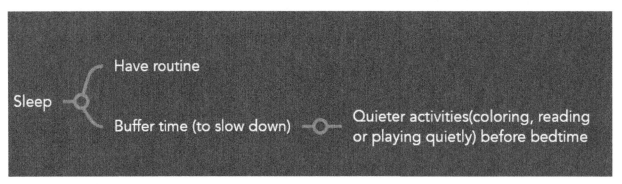

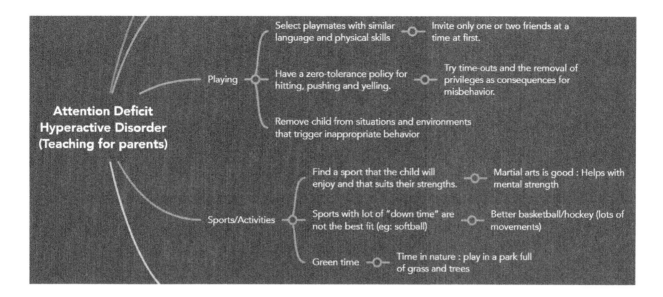

Reyes Syndrome

- Acute encephalopathy that follows viral illness: cerebral edema, fatty changes in liver
- Administration of aspirin not recommended for children with varicella or influenza. Use Acetaminophen.
- Goal of treatment: Maintenance of effective cerebral perfusion, control of increasing ICP
- Assessment: History of systemic viral illness 4 to 7 days preceding onset of symptoms; malaise; nausea and vomiting; progressive neurological deterioration

Interventions

- Frequent monitoring of neurological status, Monitor intake and output,
- Provide rest, Decrease environmental stimuli
- Monitor for signs of bleeding, impaired coagulation
- Monitor liver function studies

Renal System

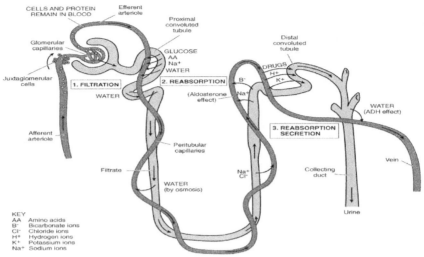

Fig. 18-4 Schematic illustration of formation of urine.
Copyright © 2014, 2011, 2006, 2002, 1997 by Saunders, an imprint of Elsevier Inc.

Hemodialysis

- Hemodialysis shunts the client's blood from the body through a dialyzer and back into circulation.
- Vascular access is needed for hemodialysis
- Central line
- AV fistula (requires several weeks to months to mature before it can be used)
- AV Graft (can be used 2-4 weeks after placement)
- Maturing of the fistula is aided by having the client perform hand exercises, such as squeezing a rubber ball, which increase blood flow through the vein

Nursing Considerations – Dialysis

- Obtain Consent, Medications- might be on hold
- Assess Vitals and Lab works, Obtain daily weight
- Assess patency of AV fistula/ graft
    - Presence of bruit, palpable thrill, distal pulses
- Restrictions on the extremity with AVF/G
    - Avoid taking blood pressure, do not administer injections through AVF/G. Do not perform vein punctures or insert IV lines

- Assess for the following:
  - Complications (hypotension, clotting of vascular access, headache, muscle cramps, bleeding)
  - Indications of bleeding, and/or infection at the access site
  - Signs of disequilibrium syndrome (due to too rapid decrease in BUN and fluids – can result in cerebral edema and ICP- Signs include N/V, headache, fatigue, confusion, convulsion, coma)
  - Signs of Hypovolemia (hypotension, dizziness, tachycardia)

Peritoneal Dialysis

- Instill dialysate solution into peritoneal cavity and drain.
- The peritoneum serves as the filtration membrane.
- The client may feel fullness when the dialysate is dwelling.
- Continuous ambulatory peritoneal dialysis (CAPD) is usually done 7 days a week for 4 to 8 hr.
- Clients may continue normal activities during CAPD.
- Continuous-cycle peritoneal dialysis (CCPD)- The exchange occurs at night while the client is sleeping.
- Nursing Considerations
  - Access site care: strict sterile technique
  - Monitor weight, serum electrolytes, creatinine, BUN, and blood glucose (might need insulin).
  - Warm the dialysate prior to instilling.
  - Avoid the use of microwaves, which cause uneven heating.
  - Monitor the color (clear, light yellow is expected) and amount (expected to equal or exceed amount of dialysate inflow) of outflow: Cloudy - infection
  - Reposition the client if inflow or outflow is inadequate: Movement of the client will help disseminate the fluid throughout the abdomen
  - Monitor for signs of infection (fever; bloody, cloudy, or frothy dialysate return; drainage at access site) and for complications (peritonitis, respiratory distress, abdominal pain, insufficient outflow, discolored outflow).

Renal Disorders

Acute Kidney Injury (Renal Failure)

- Sudden cessation of renal function - when blood flow to the kidneys is significantly compromised.
- AKI is comprised of four phases:
  - Onset – Begins with the onset of the event, ends when oliguria develops, and lasts for hours to days.
  - Oliguria – Begins with the kidney insult, urine output is 100 to 400 mL/24 hr with or without diuretics and lasts for 1 to 3 weeks.
  - Diuresis – Begins when the kidneys start to recover, diuresis of a large amount of fluid occurs, and can last for 2 to 6 weeks.
  - Recovery – Continues until kidney function is fully restored and can take up to 12 months.

Acute Renal Injury Causes

Pre-Renal	Intra-Renal	Post-Renal
Hypo perfusion, Obstructed renal artery blood flow	Prolonged renal ischemia	Ureteral obstruction
Hypovolemia, Water and electrolyte loss	Nephrotoxins	Edema, tumor, stones, clots
Hemorrhage, loss of plasma volume	Intra tubular obstruction/Necrosis	Bladder outlet obstruction
Cardiac failure, PE	Immunological damage	BPH, ureteral stricture
Hypotension , sepsis, shock	pyelonephritis	Neurogenic bladder

Nursing Considerations

- Monitor urine, input and output, urine color, characteristics
- Monitor daily weight, signs of infection
- Monitor lungs for wheezes, rhonchi, edema
- Administer prescribed diet
    - Restrict dietary intake of potassium, phosphate, and magnesium during oliguric phase.
    - Potassium and sodium are regulated according to the stage of kidney injury.
    - High-protein diet to replace the high rate of protein breakdown due to stress from the illness. Possible total parenteral nutrition (TPN).

Chronic Renal Failure

- A slow, progressive, irreversible loss in kidney function
- Primary causes
    - May follow acute renal failure
    - Diabetes mellites and other metabolic disorders
    - Hypertension
    - Chronic urinary obstruction

Assessment – entire body functions

- Decreased sodium (dilutional hyponatremia) and calcium (vit D receptors), increased potassium, phosphorus, and magnesium.
- Decreased hemoglobin and hematocrit from anemia secondary to the loss of erythropoietin
- Neurologic – lethargy, decreased attention span, slurred speech, tremors, seizures, coma
- Cardiovascular – fluid overload, hypertension, dysrhythmias, heart failure, orthostatic hypotension

- Respiratory – uremic halitosis (NHC03- by product in saliva –urea) with deep sighing, yawning, shortness of breath, tachypnea, hyperpnea, Kussmaul respirations, crackles, pleural friction rub, frothy pink sputum
- Hematologic – anemia (pallor, weakness, dizziness), ecchymoses, petechiae, melena
- Gastrointestinal – ulcers in mouth and throat, foul breath, blood in stools, nausea, vomiting
- Musculoskeletal – thin fragile bones
- Renal – urine contains protein, blood, particles; change in the amount, color, concentration
- Skin – decreased skin turgor, yellow cast to skin, dry, pruritus, urea crystal on skin (uremic frost)

Special considerations

- For anemia, administer epoetin alfa (Epogen, Procrit), darbepoetin alfa (Aranesp)
- Give if Hb is less than 10g/dl
- S/E: Hypertension, blood clots
- Contains albumin – check for hypersensitivity
- Blood transfusions - for anemia.
- Instruct the client to avoid antacids containing magnesium.
- Avoid acetylsalicylic acid (aspirin) or NSAIDS – GI bleed
- Avoid nephrotoxic (antimicrobial medications (e.g., aminoglycosides, amphotericin B), ACE inhibitors and angiotensin-receptor blockers, IV contrast dye)

Nursing Considerations

- Monitor for hypervolemia, hypovolemia, dehydration, congestive heart failure, pulmonary edema.
- Monitor for signs of infection
- Monitor for signs of peripheral neuropathy
- Monitor for hyperkalemia - cardiac monitoring (dysrhythmias)

- Provide low-potassium diet if prescribed for hyperkalemia
- Avoid potassium-sparing diuretics
- Sodium polystyrene (Kayexalate) to eliminate serum potassium
- Diet: Restrict the client's dietary sodium, potassium, phosphorous, and magnesium.
- Provide the client a diet that is high in carbohydrates and moderate in fat.
- Low-protein diet helps prevent kidney disease progression. But if the client is already on dialysis, liberal protein intake is recommended to prevent malnutrition.
- Protect client's eyes from ocular irritation
- Provide end-of-life care for client with end-stage renal disease
  - Avoid diuretics for end stage if possible. It increases destruction of the remaining nephrons in the kidney.

Glomerulonephritis

- Inflammation of the glomerular capillaries.
- Risk Factors
  - Group A beta-hemolytic streptococcal infection of pharynx or skin
  - History of pharyngitis or tonsillitis 2 to 3 weeks before symptoms
  - HTN, DM, Excessively High protein, and high sodium diet
- Types
  - Acute - usually has fever
  - Chronic (cause not known) – Usually has pruritis
- Labs:
  - Antistreptolysin-O (ASO) titer (positive indicating the presence of strep antibodies), Elevated RFT
  - Urinalysis (proteinuria, hematuria, casts, specific gravity increases)

Symptoms and care

- Renal symptoms
  - Decreased urine output, Smoky or coffee-colored urine (hematuria)
  - Proteinuria

- Fluid volume excess symptoms (edema, shortness of breath, weight, crackles, Hypertension) - severe hypertension must be identified early.
- LOC (Level of consciousness) changes
- Older adult clients may report vague symptoms (nausea, fatigue, joint aches) which may mask glomerular disease.

Nursing care

- Daily weight, Intake, and output, Assess for urinary pattern change
- Labs - serum electrolytes, BUN, and creatinine. Creatinine clearance: Male: 97 to 137 ml/min. Female: 88 to 128 ml/min.
- Skin – manage pruritus.
- Bed rest to decrease metabolic demands.
- Maintain prescribed dietary restrictions.
    - Fluid restriction (24 hr output + 500 to 600 mL)
    - Sodium restriction (1 to 3 g/day) begins when fluid retention occurs
    - Protein restriction (if azotemia is present = increased BUN)

Other Complications

- Uremia
    - Monitor the client for muscle cramps, fatigue, pruritus, anorexia, and a metallic taste in mouth.
    - Maintain skin integrity.
    - Encourage mouth rinses, chewing gum, or hard candy.
- Pulmonary edema, congestive heart failure, pericarditis
- Anemia
    - Therapeutic Procedures - Plasmapheresis (filters antibodies out of circulating blood volume by removing the plasma)
    - Weigh the client before and after the procedure
    - Monitor for hypovolemia
    - Administer replacement fluids - albumin
    - Monitor for signs of tetany if too much calcium is removed.

Ileal conduit

- Surgery – Use a piece of the client's ileum to create an outlet (No bladder)
- The client's ureters are connected to the ileal conduit, then to abdominal stoma, then to the bag to pass urine.
- A healthy stoma should be pink to brick-red and moist.
  - Dusky or any shade of blue: Impaired perfusion: Contact the HCP immediately. - medical emergency

Renal Calculi

- Urolithiasis -calculi (stones) in the urinary tract.
  - Most common (75%) calcium phosphate / calcium oxalate.
  - Others - (uric acid, struvite, cystine).
- Most – no need for invasive procedures.
- Severe pain (renal colic) - priority
  - Pain intensifies as the stone moves
  - Murphy's punch sign -Tenderness at the costovertebral angle due to percussion. Flank pain – stone in kidney/ ureter.
  - Flank pain radiates to abdomen, scrotum, testes, vulva - stones in ureter or bladder.
- Urinary frequency or dysuria (stones in the bladder)
- Nausea, vomiting, Diaphoresis, Pallor, Fever
- Oliguria/anuria - urinary tract obstruction - medical emergency

Nursing Considerations

- Strain all urine - laboratory analysis.
- Increased oral intake to 3 L/day unless contraindicated. IV fluids.
- Encourage ambulation - passage of the stone.
- Surgical Interventions
  - Ureteroscopy (dilate ureter using scope)
  - Ureterolithotomy – with lithotripter - grasp and extract the stone.
  - Open Surgery (large stone)

Therapeutic Procedures

- Extracorporeal shock wave lithotripsy (ESWL)
    - Sound, laser, or shock-wave energies to break stones into fragments.
    - Moderate (conscious) sedation and ECG monitoring during the procedure.
- Nursing Actions
    - Client Education: Bruising is normal at the site.
    - Mild hematuria post-procedure is expected.
    - Assess for GROSS hematuria and strain urine following the procedure. Analgesics as needed
- Uric acid stone
    - Decrease intake of purine sources (organ meats, poultry, fish, gravies, red wine, sardines).
- Calcium Stone
    - Limit intake of food high in animal protein (reduction of protein intake decreases calcium precipitation).
    - Avoid oxalate sources: Spinach, black tea, rhubarb, cocoa, beets, pecans, peanuts, okra, chocolate, wheat germ, lime peel, and Swiss chard.

Urinary Tract Infections

Upper UTI: pyelonephritis.

- Infection and inflammation of the kidney pelvis, calyces, and medulla.
- Fever, flank pain, nausea, vomiting, Costovertebral tenderness
- May start as lower UTI – Cystitis (bladder) – dysuria, frequency, urgency, suprapubic discomfort
- Meds- antipyretic and opioid analgesics
- UA: Bacteria, sediment, white blood cells (WBC), and red blood cells (RBC). (Cloudy urine)
- Positive leukocyte esterase and nitrates (68% to 88% positive results indicates UTI)

Nursing Considerations

- Fluid intake: up to 3 L daily
- Antibiotics
- Frequent voiding: urinate every 3 to 4 hrs.
- Warm sitz bath: comfort.
- Body hygiene: Wipe from front to back after urination.
- Avoid urinary catheters if possible.
- Hand washing

Kidney Transplant

- Risk: immunosuppression, organ rejection
  - Immunosuppressants (steroids, Cyclosporine)
  - Early signs of organ rejection: fever, hypertension, pain
- Post procedure
  - Signs of infection???
  - Measure abdominal girth
  - Other complications: cardiovascular disease; recurrence; Steroid side effects, malignancies.
- Diet recommendations:
  - Low fat, high fiber, increased protein
  - Steroid diet – Low CHO, Low Na
  - Magnesium supplements (cyclosporine can reduce magnesium levels)
  - Avoid grapefruit (interfere absorption).
- Activity - Avoid contact sports

Nephrotic Syndrome

- Kidney disorder - massive proteinuria, hypoalbuminemia, edema
- No specific treatment- supportive - steroids
- Might develop into end stage renal disease (ESRD).
- Can be genetic (child lives < 2 yrs.)
- Assessment

- Weight gain, edema (Periorbital, facial, dependent)
- Oliguria, Dark and frothy urine
- Abdominal swelling
- Blood pressure normal or slightly decreased, or hypertensive later

Nursing Care

- Monitor vital signs, intake and output, edema, daily weight
- Watch for ICP increase
- Monitor urine for protein, specific gravity
- High protein, high calorie, and restricted sodium diet
- corticosteroids / immunosuppressants and/or diuretics
- Monitor - infection, avoid contact with others who may be infectious

Wilms tumor (Nephroblastoma)

- Kidney tumor - children age <5.
- Usual sign: unusual contour/bulging/swelling in one side of abdomen.
- Post the sign "Do not palpate abdomen" at the bedside
- Handle the child carefully.
- Need nephrectomy in 1-2 days

Benign Prostatic Hyperplasia (BPH)

- BPH - impair the outflow of urine from the bladder
- Urinary infection (from reflux) and urinary retention.

Symptoms:

- Urinary frequency, urgency, incomplete emptying of the bladder, urinary hesitancy, urinary incontinence, dribbling post-voiding,
- Nocturia, diminished force of urinary stream (miss the toilet bowl)
- Straining with urination, painless hematuria

Teaching

- Avoid drinking large amounts of fluids at one time
- Urinate when the urge is initially felt.
- Avoid bladder stimulants (alcohol/caffeine) and medications that cause decreased bladder tone (anticholinergics, decongestants, and antihistamines)

Transurethral resection of the prostate (TURP)

- CBI: continuous bladder irrigation: indwelling three-way catheter.
- The rate - keep the irrigation return pink or lighter.
- If the catheter becomes obstructed (bladder spasms, reduced irrigation outflow), turn off the CBI and irrigate with 50 mL of irrigation solution using a large piston syringe.
- Contact the surgeon if unable to dislodge the clot.
- Record the amount of irrigating solution instilled (generally very large volumes) and the amount of return. The difference =urine output.
- Avoid kinks in the tubing.

Hysterectomy

- Removal of the uterus.
- salpingo oophrectomy -removal of the ovaries and fallopian tubes.
- Three methods for hysterectomy
    - Abdominal approach, also known as a total abdominal hysterectomy
    - Vaginal approach (TVA)
    - Laparoscopy-assisted vaginal hysterectomy (LAVH)

Pre-Procedure

- Meds- Discontinue anticoagulants /aspirin/nonsteroidal anti-inflammatory drugs (NSAIDs), or vitamin E
- Rule out pregnancy.
- Preoperative antibiotics, antiembolism stockings.
- Complete psychological assessment.

- NPO status. Informed consent
- Client Education
    - turn, cough, and deep breathe, importance of early ambulation.
    - use of incentive spirometer.
    - preoperative and postoperative medications.

Postoperative Care

- Monitor bleeding, vital signs, breath sounds, bowel sounds, urine output
- Provide IV fluid and electrolyte replacement
- Incision: infection, integrity, risk of dehiscence.
- Complication: DVT?
- Monitor the client's blood loss (Hgb and Hct).
- Discharge Education
    - Well-balanced diet: high in protein, iron, vitamin C
    - Oophorectomy - Hormone Replacement Therapy
    - Activity restriction for 6 weeks: (heavy lifting, strenuous activity, driving, stairs, sexual activity)
    - Notify s/s infection: fever, drainage, UTI

Menstrual Disorders

- Dysfunctional uterine bleeding (DUB): due to a hormonal imbalance and may include menorrhagia and metrorrhagia.
- Menorrhagia is excessive bleeding (in amount and duration), possibly with clots and for longer than 7 days.
- Metrorrhagia is bleeding between menstrual periods more frequently than every 21 days.
- Treatment: Dilatation and curettage
- Endometrial ablation
    - Used to remove endometrial tissue in the uterus.
    - The tissue may be removed by laser, heat, electricity, or cryotherapy.
    - Hysterectomy if other treatments are unsuccessful

Premenstrual syndrome (PMS)

- Caused by an imbalance between estrogen and progesterone.
- Symptoms can vary: Common symptoms:
    - irritability, impaired memory, depression, poor concentration, mood swings, binge eating, breast tenderness, bloating, weight gain, headache, and back pain.
- Continue daily activities and maintain the normal schedules as much as possible

Endometriosis

- Overgrowth of endometrial tissue: into the fallopian tubes, onto the ovaries, and into the pelvis.
- Common cause of infertility - Blockage of the fallopian tubes by endometrial tissue
- CA-125: may be elevated – also high in ovarian cancer.
- NSAIDs – ibuprofen - to inhibit production of prostaglandins
- Laparoscopic removal of ectopic tissue and adhesions

Renal/GU Medications

Finasteride (Proscar)

- For BPH: It decrease the production of testosterone in the prostate gland, reduce the size.
- Reinforce that it may take 6 months to 1 year before effects of the medication are evident.
- Inform the client that impotence and a decrease in libido are possible side effects.
- Report breast enlargement to the provider.
- Finasteride is teratogenic to a male fetus.
    - The medication can be absorbed through the skin. Pregnant women should not be in contact with tablets that are crushed or broken.

Tamsulosin (Flomax)

- Relaxation of the bladder outlet and prostate gland.
- Postural hypotension may occur, and that changes in position must be made slowly.
- Warn the client that concurrent use with cimetidine (Tagamet) can potentiate the hypotensive effect.

Hormone Therapy

- To suppress hot flashes associated with menopause, to prevent atrophy of vaginal tissue, and to reduce the risk of fractures due to osteoporosis.
- Short term treatment – less than 5 yrs.
- At risk for a number of adverse conditions, including coronary heart disease, myocardial infarction, deep-vein thrombosis, stroke, and breast cancer.
- Teach the client how to prevent and assess the development of venous thrombosis.
    - Avoid wearing knee-high stockings and clothing or socks that are restrictive.

- Note and report symptoms of unilateral leg pain, edema, warmth, and redness.
- Avoid sitting for long periods of time.
- Take short walks throughout the day to promote circulation

Oral contraceptive

- Usually taken for twenty-one consecutive days, stopped for 7 days; cycle then repeated.
- One pill daily at the same time every day.
- The client must be instructed to use a second birth control method during the first pill cycle of contraceptives.
- If miss one pill, take as soon as the client remembers and continue the daily dose.
- If miss two pills, take them both, as soon as possible, and take two pills the next day also.
- If she misses three pills, she will need to discontinue pill use for that cycle and use another birth control method.
- Instruct client to report signs of thromboembolic complications
- Advise client to use alternative form of birth control when taking antibiotics
- Instruct client to perform breast self-examination (BSE) monthly.
- Oral contraceptives may increase growth of a pre-existing breast cancer. Do not give to women who have breast cancer.
- If client decides to discontinue contraceptive to become pregnant, recommend alternative form of birth control for 2-month period
- If using patch and it remains off for less than 24 hours, reapply
- If using patch and it is off longer than 24 hours, new 4-week cycle must be started immediately

Eyes

Assessment of Vision

- Acuity – eye chart - The American Academy of Ophthalmology recommends getting a baseline eye examination at age 40
- Extraocular muscle function
- Color vision
- Pupils: PERRLA
- Ophthalmoscopy: An ophthalmoscope is used to examine the back part of the eyeball (fundus), including the retina, optic disc, macula, and blood vessels.
- Tonometry: Tonometry is used to measure IOP. IOP (expected reference range is 10 to 21 mm Hg)

Snellen chart

- To measure visual acuity
- Children –10 ft, Adults – 20 ft
- If child has glasses, keep it. Both eyes open – cover one eye at a time
- Test each eye separately – the 'bad' eye first
- Correctly say 4 of 6 letters in each line before moving to the next.
- Higher referral: cannot identify 4 correct letters on 20/30 vision with either eye.

Disorders of the Eye

- Risk factors related to eye disorders
  - Aging process, Congenital, Hereditary
  - Medications – dry eyes: Diuretics, Antihistamines, Antidepressants, Cholesterol-lowering drugs, Beta-blockers.
  - Trauma, Diabetes mellitus, HTN
  - Diet – Vit A deficiency, low carotene

- Legally blind: In United States, this refers to a medically diagnosed central visual acuity of 20/200 or less in the better eye with the best possible correction
- Provide safe environment, Orient client to environment
- Promote independence as much as possible
- Vitamin A Foods: Eye Must Feel Very Lively
- Eggs; Milk (cheese, butter); Fruits /Fish: sweet potato &tropical fruits; Vegetable (Carrots, Kale, Spinach, Broccoli), Liver (beef).
- Vitamin A - fat soluble vitamin, Better when taken with fat

Macular degeneration

- Central loss of vision that affects the macula of the eye.
- The macula is a small area in the retina that is responsible for central vision, allowing to see fine details clearly.
- Gradual blockage in retinal capillary arteries, which results in the macula becoming ischemic and necrotic due to the lack of retinal cells.
- There is no cure for macular degeneration.
- No. 1 cause of vision loss in people over the age of sixty.
  - Risk Factors: Smokers, Hypertension, Female, Family history, Diet lacking carotene and vitamin A

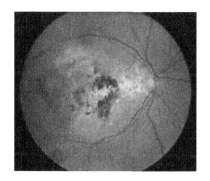 

Macular degeneration

- Client Education

- Encourage clients to consume foods high in antioxidants: Vit A, vitamin E, and B12.
  - Retinol- Vitamin A from animal sources
  - Beta carotene – Vitamin A from plant sources
- Monthly eye exams are essential in managing this disease.
- As loss of vision progresses, clients will be challenged with the ability to eat, drive, write, and read, as well as other activities of daily living.
- Refer clients to community organizations that can assist with transportation, reading devices, and large-print books.
- High Antioxidant Foods: Berries, Dark chocolate, Pecans, Artichoke, Elderberries, Kidney beans, Cranberries

Cataracts

- Opacity in the lens of an eye impairs vision.
- Encourage annual eye examinations and good eye health, especially in adults over the age of forty.
- S/S: Decreased visual acuity (prescription changes, reduced night vision), Blurred vision, Diplopia – double vision
- Glare and light sensitivity – photo sensitivity, Halo around lights, Progressive and painless loss of vision
- Absent red reflex: A red reflex test can detect cataract, retinal and other ocular problems

Glaucoma

- Normal IOP = 10-21 mm Hg: changes throughout day- high in morning
- Glaucoma is a disturbance of optic nerve, mostly due to Increased intraocular pressure (IOP)
- Increased IOP Causes atrophic changes of the optic nerve and visual defects.
- IOP increase due to Decreased fluid drainage / increased fluid secretion
- Two kinds: Open angle and Closed angle
- Loss of peripheral vision = tunnel vision

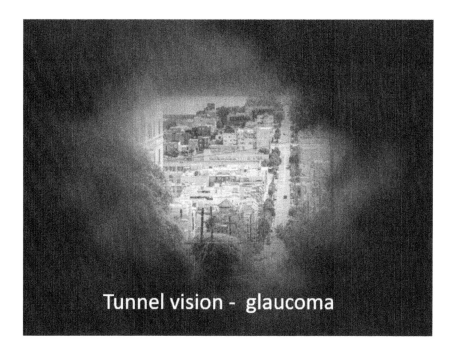

Tunnel vision - glaucoma

- Diabetes is a risk factor for the development of glaucoma.
- Familial tendency – African American ethnicity

Open-angle glaucoma: Most common

- The aqueous humor outflow is decreased due to blockages in the eye's drainage system causing a rise in IOP.
- S/S: Headache, Mild eye pain, Loss of peripheral vision, decreased accommodation, Elevated IOP (greater than 21 mm Hg)

Angle-closure glaucoma

- less common form of glaucoma. IOP rises suddenly.
- Decreased or blurred vision, halos, Pupils are nonreactive to light
- Severe pain and nausea, Photophobia

Treatment

- Surgery
- Medication: Client teaching should include the following:
- Prescribed eye medication is beneficial if used every 12 hr.

- Instill one drop in each eye twice daily. Wait 10 to 15 min in between eye drops if more than one is prescribed by the provider. Avoid touching the tip of the application bottle to the eye. Always wash hands before and after use.
- Once eye drop is instilled, apply pressure (placing pressure on the inner corner of the eye).
- The older client is instructed to lie down on a bed or sofa to instill the eye drops (balance issues, tremors)

Cataract and Glaucoma

- Teach clients to wear sunglasses while outside and wear protective eyewear
- Magnifying lens and large print books/newspapers

Postoperative interventions

- Elevate head of bed 30 to 45 degrees, turn client to back or non-operative side, Report severe pain or nausea (increased IOP - hemorrhage).
- Avoid activities that increase IOP
- Bending over at the waist, Sneezing and Coughing, Straining, Head hyperflexion, Restrictive clothing, avoid tilting the head back to wash hair.
- Limit cooking and housekeeping. Avoid rapid, jerky movements (vacuuming /sports)
- Best vision is not expected until 4 to 6 weeks following the surgery.
- Glaucoma - Instruct client on need for lifelong medication use

Conjunctivitis

- "Pinkeye," indicating inflammation of conjunctiva
- Usually caused by allergy, infection, trauma
- Bacterial or viral—extremely contagious
- Assessment: Itching, burning, scratchy eyelids; redness; edema; discharge

Interventions

- Instruct parents regarding infection control measures, such as good hand washing, no sharing of towels, washcloths
- Administer antibiotic or antiviral eye drops, ointment as prescribed
- Instruct parents, child in proper administration of eye medication
- Cool compresses to eye(s) as prescribed
- Instruct child to avoid rubbing eyes, wear contact lenses, wear dark glasses if in sun

Retinal detachment (Medical emergency)

- Sensations of flashes of light, floaters or curtain being drawn over eye
- Immediate interventions: Provide bed rest, Cover both eyes with patches.
- Postoperative interventions
  - Maintain eye patches
  - Position – area of detachment should be down (inferior/dependent) to maintain pressure of the repaired retinal area and improve contact with choroid
  - Avoid activities which increase IOP, notify physician if sudden, sharp eye pain occurs

Other Disorders of the Eye

- Hyphema (Bleeding into eye): Encourage rest in semi-Fowlers' position, bedrest, eye patches
- Contusions: Place ice on eye immediately
- Foreign bodies: If dust or dirt, remove carefully with a cotton applicator
- Penetrating objects: Do not remove, Client should be seen by physician immediately
- Chemical burns: Flush eyes at site of injury with water for at least 15 to 20 minutes

Refractive errors

- Myopia: nearsightedness- OK to see near
- Hyperopia: farsightedness- OK to see far
- Presbyopia: loss of near vision with age due to decreased elasticity of lens
- Astigmatism: an imperfection (irregular) in the curvature of cornea

Strabismus

- Misalignment of eyes - lack of eye muscle coordination
- Normal in young infant, but not after 4 months of age
- Assessment: Loss of binocular vision; impairment of depth perception; frequent headaches; squinting or tilting of head to see

Interventions

- Corrective lenses may be indicated
- Patching "good" eye to strengthen weak eye. (Good eye patched 1-2 hrs. daily)
- Eye drops to good eye to induce blurred vision

Retinoblastoma

- Retinal tumor
- Common in children under age 2 and is usually first recognized when parents report a white "glow" of the pupil
- Light reflecting off the tumor will cause the pupil to appear white instead of displaying the usual red reflex
- Can be hereditary

Eye Irrigation

- For accidental eye exposure to body fluids (e.g., blood, urine) or chemicals

- Immediately flush the affected eye with water or saline for at least 10 minutes to reduce exposure to potentially infected material and prevent/reduce injury (e.g., burn).

Ear

- Functions
    - Hearing and maintenance of balance (vestibular)
- Parts: External ear (pinna), Middle ear, Inner ear

Auditory Screening tests

TEST	TECHNIQUE	EXPECTED FINDING
Whisper test 8th Cranial Nerve	› Occlude one ear and test the other to see if the client can hear whispered sounds without seeing your mouth move. › Repeat with the other ear.	› The client can hear you whisper softly from 30 to 60 cm (1 to 2 ft) away.
Rinne test	› Place a vibrating tuning fork firmly against the mastoid bone and note the time. › Have the client state when he can no longer hear the sound, note the time, and then move the tuning fork in front of the ear canal. When the client can no longer hear the tuning fork, note the time.	› Air conduction (AC) greater than bone conduction (BC); 2-to-1 ratio.
Weber test	› Place a vibrating tuning fork on top of the client's head. Ask whether the client can hear the sound best in the right ear, the left ear, or both ears equally.	› The client hears sound equally in both ears (negative Weber test).

Source: ATI nursing education

Assessment of the Ear

- Otoscope
    - Properly sized speculum
    - Ear pinna - pull up and back for adults, and down and back for children

- Tympanic Membrane (ear drum) should be a pearly gray color and intact.
  - Inner ear problems are characterized by tinnitus (continuous ringing in ear), vertigo (whirling sensation), and dizziness
- Black cerumen - presence of blood - unexpected finding
- May irrigate with warm sterile solution
- Auditory assessment – Whisper test
- Tuning fork tests – Rinne Test, weber test
- Romberg test for equilibrium
- Presbycusis - part of the aging process - progressive sensorineural hearing loss - hearing aid
- Swimmer's ear – otitis externa

Otitis Media

- Infection of the middle ear secondary to blocked eustachian tube
- Common in children (Infants eustachian tubes -ineffective drainage and protection from respiratory secretions)

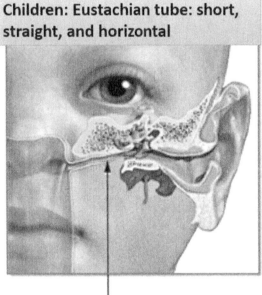
Children: Eustachian tube: short, straight, and horizontal

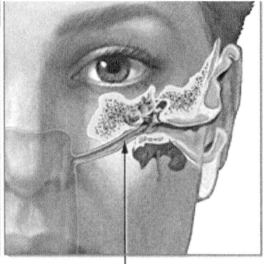
Image credit: National Library of Medicine

- Child at Risk – secondary smoking (respiratory inflammation)

Assessment

- Fever, Irritability, Anorexia, rolling of head from side to side, Pulling or rubbing on ear
- Earache or pain, Signs of hearing loss
- Purulent ear drainage
- Red, opaque, bulging, or retracting tympanic membrane

Interventions

- Feed infants in upright position; prevents reflux, avoid excessive pacifier use.
- Immunization should be current
- Instruct parents about procedure for administering ear medications
- Untreated OM – Mastoiditis
- Adults OM- Apply local heat three times per day for 20 mts. Antibiotics - Amoxicillin
- Myringotomy
    - Surgery of tympanic membrane to allow drainage
    - Insertion of tympanostomy tubes into middle ear to equalize pressure and keep ear aerated
    - After the insertion - avoid getting water in the ears.
    - Use shower cap or earplug if needed
    - Avoid swimming, showering without a shower cap or ear plugs, and washing the hair – until OK by surgeon
    - After ear surgery - for 3 weeks: - Avoid bending over, rapid movements of the head or bouncing, straining when having a bowel movement; drinking through a straw, air travel, excessive coughing.
    - Stay away from individuals with colds
    - Blow the nose gently, one side at a time, with the mouth open
    - Avoid wetting the head and showering for 1 week
    - Keep the ear dry for 6 weeks by placing a ball of cotton coated with petroleum jelly in the ear (this should be changed daily).
    - Report excessive drainage to the health care provider immediately.

Meniere's Disease (Idiopathic Endolymphatic hydrops)

- Inner ear – fluid accumulation - Endolymph
- Severe vertigo, tinnitus, nausea, headache
- Drop attack - Tumarkin's otolithic crisis- sudden fall that may occur without warning and without any loss of consciousness.
- Unilateral hearing impairment might be present
- Trigger – salt intake, allergy, stress
- Meds- diuretics, Meclizine (Antivert)
- Patient education
  - Low salt diet, avoid sugar and stimulants (alcohol, coffee, nicotine)
  - Avoid sudden movements, position changes
  - Safety

Management of Vertigo

- Clutter-free home
- Remove throw rugs - because the effort of trying to regain balance after slipping could trigger the onset of vertigo.
- Change position slowly
- Turn the entire body, not just the head, when spoken to.
- Avoid driving and using public transportation. The sudden movements could precipitate an attack.
- If vertigo does occur, the client should immediately sit down or lie down (rather than walking to the bedroom) or grasp the nearest piece of furniture.

Ear Drops (Adults)

- Client is placed on the side with the affected ear upward.
- The solution is warmed to room temp before use.
- The nurse pulls the pinna backward and upward and instills the medication by holding the dropper about 1 cm above the ear canal.
- The dropper is not allowed to touch any object or any part of the client's skin.

Epistaxis (Nosebleeds)

- Nose bleeding secondary to direct trauma, presence of foreign body, nose picking, underlying disease

Interventions

- Have client sit up, lean forward, apply continuous pressure to nose with thumb and forefinger for at least 10 minutes.
- Insert cotton into each nostril; if still bleeding, apply cold compress to bridge of nose
- Packing or cauterization may be prescribed for uncontrollable bleeding
- Use humidified air, After nosebleed- (for 3-4 days)
    - Client should not bend forward, Avoid hot liquids, hot shower
    - Avoid excessive exercise

Special Pediatric considerations

Routine hearing test

- Toddlers with hearing deficits may appear shy, timid, or withdrawn, often avoiding social interaction.
- They may seem extremely inattentive when given directions and appear "dreamy."
- Speech is usually monotone, difficult to understand, and loud.
- Increased use of gestures and facial expressions is also common.

Hearing aid facts

- Hearing aid - If the earmold is too small, sounds from the hearing aid may leak out, making a whistling sound.
- Sometimes adjusting the earmold in child's ear will be enough to stop whistling.
- But if the whistling doesn't stop after adjusting the earmold, it might be too small- child need to see audiologist.

- To avoid falling out - a cord can be attached to the hearing aid and then clipped to child's clothing. An ear hook can also be used.
- Battery lock – child lock on hearing aid batteries- for safety

Tips – communicating with babies (with hearing difficulty)

- Don't shout. Hold the baby close so that he or she can focus on your face. Make eye contact often.
- Try to minimize background noises (TV, music)
- Use good lighting (Dim light may be too low)
- Imitate the movements and sounds the baby makes, then wait for him or her to repeat them.
- Give you and your child some quiet time. If your child becomes fussy, he or she may be overwhelmed by all of the communication!

Acoustic Neuroma (vestibular schwannoma)

- A rare noncancerous tumor – affect ear
- Tumor presses on the hearing and balance nerves in the inner ear – acoustic nerve – cranial nerve eight
- A large tumor can press on the facial nerve or brain structures.
- Treatment can include observation (watching and waiting), surgery or radiation.
- caused by: Genetic - People with neurofibromatosis (tumor of nerves)
- Constant or continuous exposure to loud noise (such as music or work-related noise)
- Neck or face radiation can lead to acoustic neuroma many years later.

Ototoxic Medications

- Multiple antibiotics – gentamicin, amikacin, or metronidazole (Flagyl)
- Diuretics – furosemide (Lasix). NSAIDs – ibuprofen (Advil)
- Aspirin – Antiplatelet. Chemotherapeutic agents – cisplatin

Rhytidectomy is "Face- lift" surgery

- Mild to moderate bruising and swelling is expected up to 1-2 weeks
- Some numbness around ear lobes, face and neck for several weeks is expected
- Mild pain – expected – take pain med. A significant pain is a warning sign – notify doctor (don't wait for pain med to work)
- Do not take any aspirin or any anti-inflammatory compounds for 2 weeks
- Sleep with the head elevated for 3 weeks after surgery.
- Do not rub, wash, or massage face until cleared by doctor
- No vigorous exercise and should avoid any significant physical exertion, lifting or straining for a minimum of 3 weeks

Gastrointestinal System

Blood supply

- Celiac artery - Stomach and duodenum
- Superior mesenteric artery (SMA) - Distal small intestine to mid-large intestine
- Inferior mesenteric artery (IMA)- Distal large intestine through anus
- Venous blood empties into the portal vein and then perfuses the liver

Assessment

- Abdominal assessment
- Inspect - color, abnormalities, contour, tautness, abdominal distention
- Auscultate - bowel sounds
- Percuss for air (tympany) or solids (Dull)
- Palpate for tenderness or masses – Referred pain
- Bowel sounds
  - Auscultate prior to percussion and palpation
  - Normal bowel sounds occur 5 to 30 times/min

- Auscultate in all four quadrants
- Listen at least 5 minutes in each quadrant before assuming sounds are absent
- Bowel sounds are normally intermittent (every 5-15 seconds)

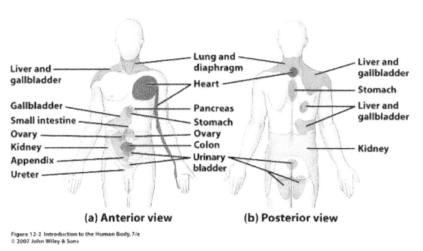

Borborygmi sounds

- Borborygmi sounds are loud, gurgling sounds
- Usually normal - suggesting increased peristalsis.
- Abnormal – Gastroenteritis and the early phases of mechanical obstruction.
- Vomiting: NCLEX Tips: Look for Metabolic alkalosis and hypokalemia

Gastro Esophageal Reflux Disease (GERD)

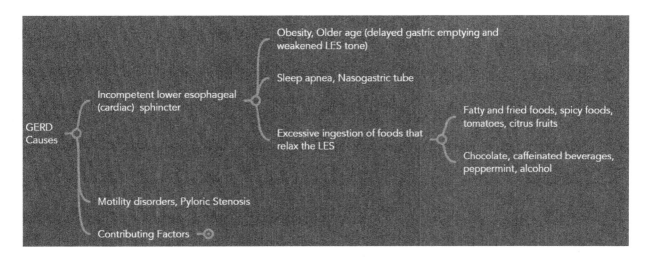

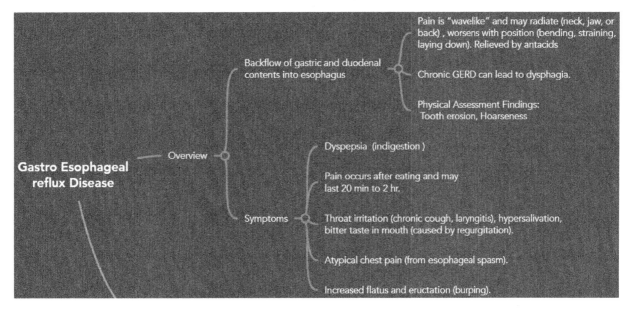

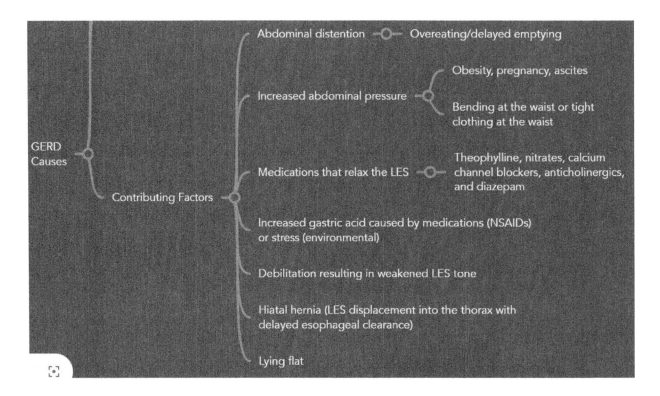

- Fundoplication: The fundus of the stomach is wrapped around and behind the esophagus through a laparoscope to create a physical barrier.

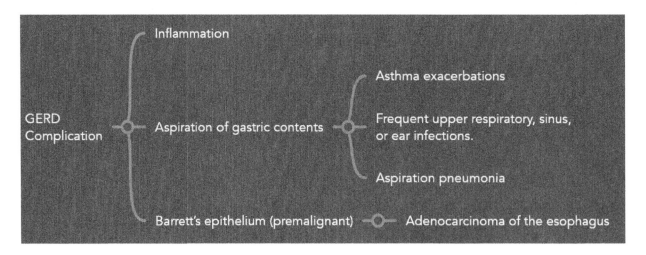

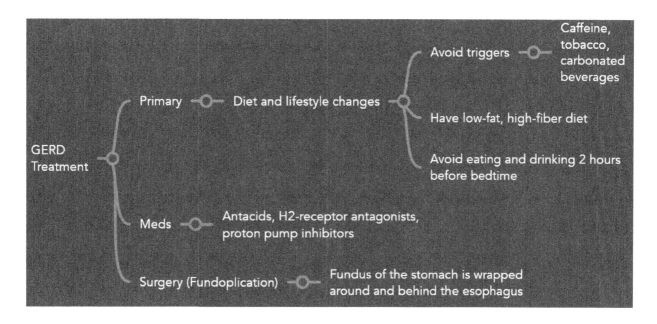

Esophageal Varices

- Dilated, tortuous veins in submucosa of esophagus caused by portal hypertension

Assessment

- Hematemesis; melena; tarry stools; ascites; jaundice; hepatosplenomegaly; dilated abdominal veins

Physical Assessment Findings (Bleeding Esophageal Varices)

- Hypotension and Tachycardia
- The client may experience no manifestations until the varices begin to bleed.
- Activities that precipitate bleeding are the Valsalva maneuver, lifting heavy objects, coughing, sneezing, and alcohol consumption.

Risk Factors

- Portal hypertension
- Collateral circulation - creating varices in the upper stomach and esophagus. Varices are fragile and can bleed easily.

- Portal hypertension is the primary risk factor for the development of esophageal varices
- Alcoholic cirrhosis, Viral hepatitis.
- Older adult clients frequently have depressed immune function, decreased liver function, and cardiac disorders that make them especially vulnerable to bleeding

If bleeding is suspected

- Establish IV access with a large bore needle
- Monitor vital signs and hematocrit
- Type and crossmatch for possible blood transfusions
- Monitor for overt and occult bleeding.

Medications

- Nonselective Beta-Blockers
    - Propranolol - to decrease heart rate and hepatic venous pressure.
    - Used prophylactically (not for emergency hemorrhage).
- Vasoconstrictors
    - IV synthetic vasopressin and natural somatostatin to increase portal inflow.
- Nursing Considerations – Vasopressin cannot be given to clients who have coronary artery disease due to resultant coronary constriction.
- Potent vasoconstriction may also cause problems with peripheral and cerebral circulation.

Procedures

- Endoscopic injection sclerotherapy or variceal band ligation
- Ligating bands / injection sclerotherapy
- Used only for active bleeding and not prophylactically.
- Nursing Actions:
    - Administer preprocedural sedation.
    - After care - vital signs and take measures to prevent aspiration.

- Sclerotherapy - greater risk of postoperative hemorrhage.
- Antacids and/or H2 receptor blockers are administered postoperatively.
- Esophagogastric balloon tamponade
    - An esophagogastric tube with esophageal and gastric balloons - to compress blood vessels in the esophagus and stomach.
    - Check balloons before inserting
    - Semi fowlers or high fowlers position is best for insertion.
    - Prevent airway obstruction/aspiration
    - Oral Suction as needed
    - Balloon pressure – avoid necrosis
    - Irrigate tube – document output /color
    - Confused patients- careful not to pull on tube

Complications

- Hypovolemic Shock – due to hemorrhage from varices
- Nursing Actions
    - Observe for manifestations of hemorrhage and shock (tachycardia, hypotension).
    - Monitor vital signs, Hgb, Hct, and coagulation studies.
    - Replace losses and support therapeutic procedures to stop and control bleeding.

Cirrhosis

- Cirrhosis is extensive scarring of the liver
- Normal liver tissue is replaced with fibrotic tissue that lacks function.
- Affect the liver's ability to handle the flow of bile -Jaundice
- The three types of cirrhosis
    - Post necrotic: caused by viral hepatitis or certain medications or toxins.
    - Laennec's: caused by chronic alcoholism.
    - Biliary: caused by chronic biliary obstruction or autoimmune disease.
- Stay current on immunizations.
- Encourage the client to avoid drinking alcohol

- Alcohol recovery program.

Risk Factors

- Alcohol abuse, Hepatitis – Autoimmune/ Hep B, C, D/Biliary
- Steatohepatitis (fatty liver disease causing chronic inflammation)
- Damage - by drugs, toxins, and other infections
- Cardiac cirrhosis: severe right heart failure inducing necrosis and fibrosis due to lack of blood flow

Subjective Data and assessment findings

- Fatigue, Weight loss, abdominal pain, distention, Pruritus
- Confusion or difficulty thinking – hepatic encephalopathy
- Personality and mentation changes: emotional lability/ euphoria/depression
- Altered sleep/wake pattern
- Gastrointestinal bleeding– Varices
- Other bleeding signs: Petechiae, ecchymoses, nosebleed
- Palmar erythema, Spider angiomas (telangiectasia)

Physical Assessment Findings

- Dependent peripheral edema of extremities and sacrum
- Asterixis (liver flapping tremor) – coarse tremor characterized by rapid, nonrhythmic extension and flexion of the wrists and fingers
- It is assessed by having the client extend the arms and dorsiflex the wrists
- Correlates with progression into hepatic encephalopathy
- Fetor hepaticus (liver breath) – fruity or musty odor

Nursing Care

- Respiratory status – Monitor oxygen saturation levels and distress.
    - Position: sit in a chair or elevate the head of the bed to 30° with feet elevated.
- Skin integrity – Monitor for skin breakdown.

- Prevent pressure ulcers.
  - Pruritus: Wash with cold water, apply lotion
- Fluid balance – Monitor for signs of fluid volume excess.
  - Keep strict intake and output, obtain daily weights, and assess ascites and peripheral edema.
  - Restrict fluids and sodium if prescribed.
- Vital signs – Monitor vital signs and pain level
- Neurological status
  - Hepatic encephalopathy: Lactulose
- Nutritional status – give diet education
  - High-carbohydrate, low-protein, moderate-fat, and low-sodium diet with vitamin supplements such as thiamine, folate, and multivitamins.
- Gastrointestinal status
  - Ascites: measure abdominal girth daily over the largest part of the abdomen.
  - Mark the location of tape for consistency. Observe the client for potential bleeding complications.
- Medications
  - Avoid opioids, sedatives, and barbiturates.
  - Give Diuretics: Decrease excessive fluid in the body.
  - Give Beta-blocking agent: to prevent bleeding varices
  - Lactulose: Used to promote excretion of ammonia from the body through the stool.
  - Nonabsorbable antibiotic: Rifaximin: Can be used in place of lactulose.
- Surgery – Liver transplant
- Procedure – Paracentesis
- Complication – Encephalopathy, Varices

Client Education: Diet

- Encourage the client to abstain from alcohol and engage in alcohol recovery program. Helps prevent further scarring and fibrosis of the liver.
- Allows healing and regeneration of liver tissue.
- Prevents irritation of the stomach and esophagus lining.

- Helps decrease the risk of bleeding.
- Helps to prevent other life-threatening complications.
- Consult with provider prior to taking any over-the-counter medications or herbal supplements.

Vitamin B12 Deficiency

- Pernicious Anemia
- Inadequate intake of vitamin B12 /lack of absorption from intestinal tract
- Vegan Diet -Vegetarians who avoid all animal and animal-derived products, Gastric surgery
- Assessment: Smooth, beefy red tongue, Paresthesia of hands and feet, Disturbance in gait and balance

- Interventions: Administer vitamin B12 (Cyanocobalamin) injections for life

Hiatal Hernia

- Portion of stomach herniates through diaphragm and into thorax
- Assessment
  - Heartburn; regurgitation or vomiting; dysphagia; feeling of fullness
- Interventions
  - small frequent meals, Limit liquid with meals
  - Do not to recline for 1 hour after feeding

Appendicitis

- Assessment
  - Abdominal pain most intense at McBurney's point
  - Client in side-lying position, with abdominal guarding
  - Constipation or diarrhea
- Peritonitis
  - Increased fever; chills; pallor; progressive abdominal distention; abdominal pain; restlessness; right guarding of abdomen; tachycardia; tachypnea

- Surgery – Appendectomy
- Signs in Appendicitis
  - Rovsing sign (RLQ pain with palpation of the LLQ): Suggests peritoneal irritation
  - Obturator sign (RLQ pain with internal and external rotation of the flexed right hip): Suggests the inflamed appendix is located deep in the right hemipelvis
  - Psoas sign (RLQ pain with extension of the right hip or with flexion of the right hip against resistance): Suggests that an inflamed appendix is located along the course of the right psoas muscle
  - Dunphy sign (sharp pain in the RLQ elicited by a voluntary cough): Suggests localized peritonitis
- Preoperative interventions
  - Monitor --? ruptured appendix, peritonitis
  - Position - right side-lying / low to semi-Fowler's position
  - No heat to abdomen / laxatives/ enemas
- Postoperative interventions
  - NPO - until bowel function returns
  - ? Penrose drain - care
  - Position - right side-lying or low to semi-Fowler's position, legs flexed - to facilitate drainage

Ruptured Appendix – Peritonitis

Clinical manifestations

- Distended abdomen; a rigid, board like abdomen.
- Diminished bowel sounds: inability to pass flatus
- Abdominal pain (localized, poorly localized, or referred to the shoulder or thorax), anorexia, nausea, and vomiting
- Rebound tenderness in the abdomen
- High fever; tachycardia; dehydration from the high fever
- Decreased urinary output
- Hiccups, possible compromise in respiratory status.

Lactose intolerance

- Due to not enough lactase from small intestine
- Lactase: the enzyme that digests the milk sugar lactose.
- S/S: Pain, abdominal cramps, bloating, and diarrhea.
- Test to diagnose: Hydrogen breath test
- More hydrogen is produced due to fermentation of lactose in colon (which is not absorbed in small intestine)
- Treatment – lactose-free dairy products, supplements

Peptic Ulcer Disease

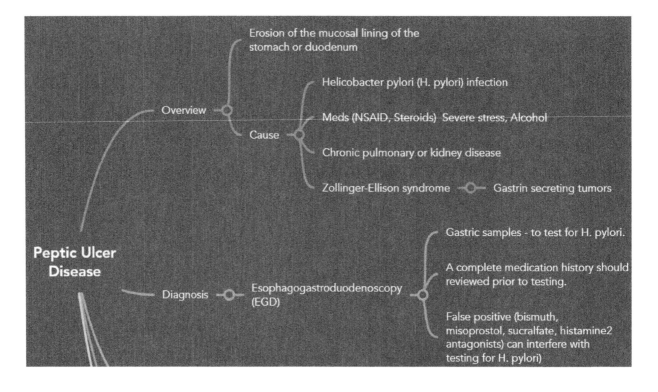

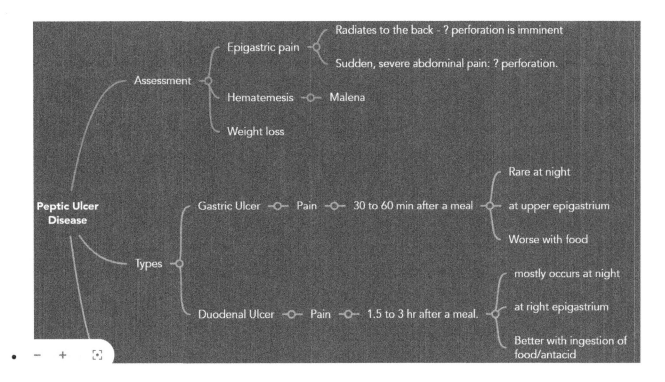

Gastritis

- Gastritis is an inflammation in the lining of the stomach.
- Acute gastritis - sudden onset - GI bleeding if severe.
- Chronic gastritis - slow onset -pernicious anemia.
- Erosive gastritis: Black, tarry stools; coffee-ground emesis, Acute abdominal pain
- Medications and surgery – same as PUD
- NPO (ice chips OK) until symptoms of acute gastritis subside, then advance diet as prescribed
- Monitor for signs of hemorrhage (hematemesis, tachycardia, hypotension).
- Avoid irritating foods (spicy foods, caffeine, alcohol, nicotine)

Gastric surgeries

- Gastrectomy – All or part of the stomach is removed with laparoscopic or open approach.
- Antrectomy – The antrum portion of the stomach is removed.

- Gastroduodenal reconstruction
- Gastrojejunostomy (Billroth II procedure) – The lower portion of the stomach is excised, the remaining stomach is anastomosed to the jejunum, and the remaining duodenum is surgically closed.
- Vagotomy –severs only the nerve fibers that disrupt acid production.
- Pyloroplasty – The opening between the stomach and small intestine is enlarged to increase the rate of gastric emptying.

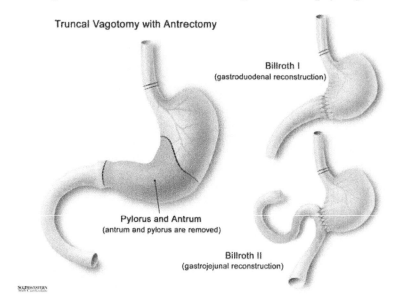

-

Bariatric Surgery

- Size of stomach reduced using various procedures
- Obese clients - increased postoperative risk for pulmonary, thromboembolic complications, death

Nursing Actions

- Monitor incision for evidence of infection.
- Position: semi-Fowler's position to facilitate lung expansion.
- NG tube: Scant blood may be seen in first 12 to 24 hr.
- Notify the provider before repositioning or irrigating the nasogastric tube (disruption of sutures).
- Monitor bowel sounds. Advance diet as tolerated.

- Administer medication (analgesics, stool softeners), vitamin and mineral supplements: vitamin B12, vitamin D, calcium, iron, and folate.
- Consume small, frequent meals while avoiding large quantities of carbohydrates as directed – No concentrated sweets

Complications

- Perforation/Hemorrhage: it is an emergency situation.
  - Severe epigastric pain spreading across the abdomen.
  - The abdomen is rigid, board-like, hyperactive to diminished bowel sounds, and there is rebound tenderness.
- Shock (hypotension, tachycardia, dizziness, confusion), and decreased hemoglobin.
  - Perform frequent assessments. Report findings
  - Prepare the client for endoscopic or surgical intervention
  - Replace fluid and blood losses to maintain blood pressure
  - Insert nasogastric tube and provide saline lavages.
- Pernicious anemia

Dumping syndrome

- After gastric surgery- occur following eating, Rapid gastric emptying
- Assist/instruct the client to lie down when vasomotor manifestations occur

	EARLY MANIFESTATIONS	LATE MANIFESTATIONS
Onset	Within 30 min after eating	1.5 to 3 hr after eating
Cause	› Rapid emptying	› Excessive insulin release
Symptoms	› Nausea, vomiting, and dizziness › Tachycardia › Palpitations	› Hunger, dizziness, and sweating › Tachycardia and palpitations › Shakiness and feelings of anxiety › Confusion

Source: ATI nursing education

Prevention and management of dumping syndrome

- Lying down after a meal slows the movement of food within the intestines.
- Limit the amount of fluid ingested at one time.
- Eliminate liquids with meals, for 1 hr prior to, and following a meal.
- Consume a high-protein, high-fat, low insoluble fiber, and low- to moderate-carbohydrate diet.
- Avoid milk, sweets, or sugars (fruit juice, sweetened fruit, milk shakes, honey, syrup, jelly).
- Consume small, frequent meals rather than large meals.

Client teaching points about diet after bariatric surgery (general points)

- small frequent meals, low in calories
- Eat/ drink fluids at separate times during meal
- Take chewable or liquid multivitamin daily as prescribed

Hemorrhoids

- Distended or edematous intestinal veins - from increased intra-abdominal pressure (straining, obesity).
- Pregnancy increases the risk of hemorrhoids.
- Assessment: Bright red bleeding with defecation
- Surgery – hemorrhoidectomy
- Pain is a priority as patient will dread having BM: Manage Pain
- Prone / side-lying position
- Maintain ice packs over dressing as prescribed
- Monitor for urinary retention
- limit sitting to short periods, Ok to use sitz baths 3 to 4 times a day

Irritable Bowel Syndrome

- IBS causes changes in bowel function (chronic diarrhea, constipation, or abdominal pain). IBS is difficult to diagnose with specific tests
- Client education:
  - Avoid foods that contain dairy, eggs, and wheat products.

- Avoid alcoholic and caffeinated beverages and other fluids containing fructose and sorbitol.
- Drink 2 to 3 L of fluid per day from food and fluid sources.
- Increase daily fiber intake (approximately 30 to 40 g/day).

Cholecystitis

- Inflammation of the gallbladder that may occur as an acute or chronic process
- Assessment
    - Epigastric pain radiating to scapula 2 to 4 hours after eating fatty foods
    - Feeling of abdominal fullness, dyspepsia
    - Pain localized in right upper quadrant
    - Guarding, rigidity, rebound tenderness
- Mass palpated in right upper quadrant
- Murphy's sign
- Biliary obstruction:
    - Jaundice; dark orange and foamy urine
    - Steatorrhea; clay-colored stools; pruritus
- Pruritis Management: Apply cool wet cloths to skin, apply lotion – calamine, lanolin, use gloves (cotton), Long sleeved shirt, no hot shower, cut nails short, Use mild soap

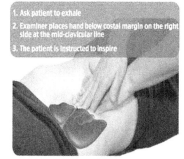

Positive Murphy's Sign [Acute cholecystitis]
The patient **stops breathing in** and **winces** with a 'catch' in breath
(Due to the inflamed gallbladder being palpated as it descends on inspiration)

Interventions

- NPO during nausea or vomiting episodes
- Administer analgesics as prescribed (morphine sulfate or codeine sulfate generally avoided because they cause spasm of sphincter of Oddi, increase pain
- Instruct client to eat small, low-fat meals, avoiding gas-forming foods
- Pruritis management
- Surgical interventions: Cholecystectomy, Choledochotomy

Postoperative interventions

- Monitor for respiratory complications – sims position to expel co2 gas used in lap surgery
- Encourage coughing, deep breathing
- Maintain NPO status, NG tube suction as prescribed
- Advance diet from clear liquids to solids as prescribed
- Instruct client about splinting abdomen to prevent discomfort during coughing

Intestinal Obstruction

- Bowel sounds are hyperactive above the obstruction and hypoactive below.
- Mechanical (90%) or nonmechanical (10%) causes.
- Mechanical obstruction
    - Adhesions, tumors, fibrosis, Hernia, Fecal impactions

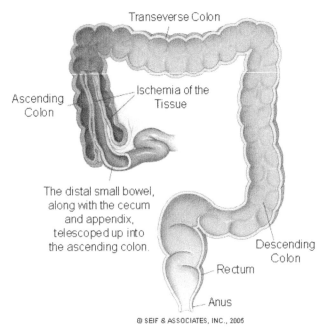

Transeverse Colon

Ascending Colon

Ischemia of the Tissue

The distal small bowel, along with the cecum and appendix, telescoped up into the ascending colon.

Descending Colon

Rectum

Anus

@ SEIF & ASSOCIATES, INC., 2005

- Volvulus (twisting) or intussusception (telescoping) of bowel segments
- Nonmechanical obstructions (paralytic ileus) result from decreased peristalsis secondary to:
- Neurogenic disorders (manipulation of the bowel during major surgery and spinal fracture)
- Vascular disorders (vascular insufficiency and mesenteric emboli)
- Electrolyte imbalances (hypokalemia)
- Inflammatory responses (peritonitis or sepsis)

Intussusceptions in Children

- The classic clinical triad is

- 1. intermittent, severe, crampy abdominal pain.
- 2. A palpable "sausage-shaped" mass on the right side of the abdomen.
- 3. "currant jelly" stools: mixture of blood and mucus
- Other manifestations include inconsolable crying, drawing the knees up to the chest during episodes of pain, and vomiting.
- The child may appear normal and comfortable between episodes.
- A contrast enema is used for diagnostic purposes and often reduces the intussusceptions. An air enema is considered safer than a barium enema.
- Small bowel obstruction: Rapid onset of Nausea, vomiting, intermittent abdominal pain, abdominal distention.
    - Delay in treatment can lead to vascular compromise, bowel ischemia, perforation
- Large bowel obstruction: Gradual onset of symptoms, cramping pain, abdominal distention, absolute constipation, lack of flatus

Nursing Care: Nonmechanical cause of obstruction

- Nothing by mouth with bowel rest.
- Assess bowel sounds.
- Provide oral hygiene.
- Administer IV fluid and electrolyte replacement (particularly potassium).
- Pain management, as prescribed (once diagnosis identified).
- Encourage ambulation

Mechanical obstruction

- Usually requires surgery – Exploratory laparotomy
- Monitor for hemodynamic instability.
- Administer IV fluid replacement and maintenance as prescribed.
- Monitor bowel sounds.
- Maintain NG tube patency and measure output.
- Clamp NG tube as prescribed to assess the client's tolerance prior to removal.

- Advance diet as tolerated when prescribed, beginning with clear liquids – clamp tube after eating for 1 to 2 hr.
- Instruct client to report intolerance of intake following NG tube removal (nausea, vomiting, increasing distention).

Complications

- Dehydration (potential hypotension); Electrolyte Imbalance
- Metabolic Alkalosis (vomiting)
- Perforation - Peritonitis. This condition can be fatal if it is not treated quickly.

Ulcerative Colitis

- Ulcerative and inflammatory disease of bowel (large intestine)- Results in poor absorption of nutrients

Assessment

- Severe diarrhea; may contain blood, mucus
- Dehydration, electrolyte imbalances, anemia from blood loss.
- Nonsurgical interventions
- Administer intravenous (IV) fluids, TPN
- Restrict activity level as prescribed
- Monitor bowel function, abdominal distention
- Low-residue diet as prescribed, bulk-forming agents as prescribed

Postoperative colostomy

- Monitor for color changes in stoma (pink to bright red, shiny is normal)
- Expect liquid stool in immediate postoperative period, depending on area of colostomy
- Instruct client to avoid foods that cause excess gas formation, odor (broccoli, Brussels sprouts, cabbage, cauliflower, cucumbers, mushrooms, and peas, should be avoided)

- Foods that help eliminate odor with a colostomy include yogurt, buttermilk, cranberry juice, and parsley.

Postoperative ileostomy - Normal stool is liquid

- Monitor for dehydration, electrolyte imbalances
- No suppositories administered through ileostomy

Peristomal skin care

- Clean skin with mild soap and water
- Ostomy appliance - fits well
- Trimming the appliance opening to one-eighth inch (0.32 cm) larger than the stoma so that it "hugs" the stoma without touching stoma tissue
- OK to wear the pouch 4 to 7 days.

Ileostomy Diet

- Diet- immediate post op period – low fiber – to prevent obstruction of the narrow lumen of small intestine and stoma.
- OK: white rice, refined grains, pasta, Most canned or well-cooked vegetables and fruits without skins or seeds
- After the ileostomy heals, add fibrous foods one at a time.
- Patient should chew thoroughly. Use cooked vegetables
- Avoid – high fiber (popcorn, coconut, brown rice, multigrain bread, Dried fruits, prune juice, Raw fruit, Raw or undercooked vegetables, including corn, Dried beans, peas, and lentils)
- Avoid stringy vegetables (celery, broccoli, asparagus)
- Avoid Seeds/pits (strawberry, raspberry, olives)

Crohn's Disease

- Inflammatory disease: can occur anywhere in GI tract, but most often affects terminal ileum

Assessment

- Cramp-like, colicky pain after meals
- Diarrhea (semisolid); may contain mucus, pus
- Dehydration, electrolyte imbalances
- Interventions: Similar to ulcerative colitis

Colostomy irrigation

- Daily irrigation: more control over passage of stool.
- Do not use an enema set. Use cone tipped applicator
- Fill chamber with 500-1000 ml lukewarm water, flush tubing, reclamp, hang the container in IV pole
- Client sits on toilet, place irrigation sleeve over stoma. Place irrigation container 18-24 inch above stoma
- Lubricate cone tipped irrigator and insert gently into stoma, hold in place
- Slowly open clamp, clamp if cramping occurs

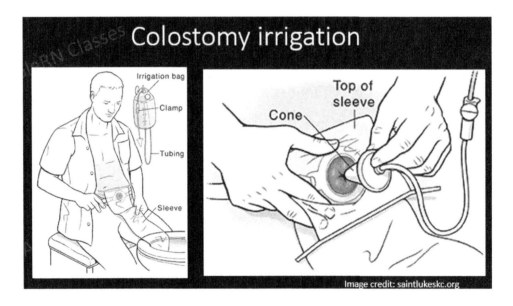

Diverticulosis and Diverticulitis

- Outpouching or herniation of intestinal mucosa
- Diverticulosis becomes diverticulitis with inflammation of one or more diverticula; results when diverticulum perforates

Assessment

- Left lower quadrant abdominal pain, increasing with coughing, straining, lifting
- Palpable, tender rectal mass, Melena

Interventions

- Provide bed rest during acute phase
- Maintain NPO status, clear fluids during acute phase
- Monitor for perforation, hemorrhage, fistulas, abscess formation
- Instruct client to avoid gas-forming foods, foods containing indigestible roughage, seeds, nuts, high-fiber foods (when inflammation occurs)
- A low-residue diet, which avoids all high-fiber foods, may be used in treating acute diverticulitis. However, after symptoms have resolved, a high-fiber diet is resumed to prevent future episodes.

Surgical interventions

- Colon resection with primary anastomosis
- Temporary or permanent colostomy may be required

Pancreatitis

- Autodigestion of the pancreas by pancreatic digestive enzymes
- The islets of Langerhans - insulin and glucagon.
- Digestive enzymes break down carbohydrates, proteins, and fats.
- Risk – Gallbladder stones, alcohol, smoking, high triglycerides

Acute pancreatitis

- Pain – sudden, severe, constant, knifelike pain abdominal / mid epigastric radiating to back / pain aggravated by fatty meal or alcohol
- Inflammation can vary from mild edema to severe necrosis

- Pancreatic abscess: Report immediately any signs of sudden fever. (Leads to peritonitis)
- The abscess must be treated promptly to prevent sepsis.

Acute pancreatitis Nursing Care

- Assess and manage pain (meperidine hydrochloride)
- Assess for Cullen's sign, Turner's sign (Seepage of blood-stained exudates into tissue as a result of pancreatic enzyme actions)
- Assess for absent or decreased bowel sounds, respiratory

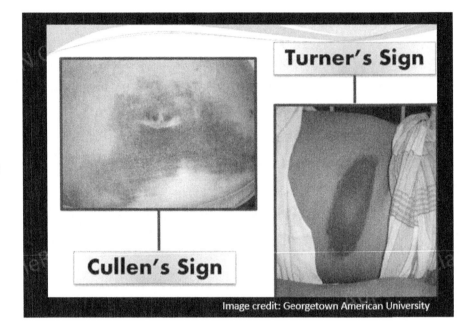

complications (ARDS, pleural effusion atelectasis- activated pancreatic enzymes and cytokines released into circulation causing systemic inflammation)
- Assess for lab tests, Tetany (low calcium)
- Trousseau's sign (hand spasm when blood pressure cuff is inflated)
- Chvostek's sign (facial twitching when facial nerve is tapped)
- Maintain NPO status; hydrate with IV fluids
- Instruct client to comply with follow-up visits
- Notify physician if client develop
    - Acute abdominal pain and fever (pancreatic abscess)
    - Dark-colored stools, or urine – biliary obstruction

Chronic pancreatitis

- Assess for abdominal pain, tenderness, left upper quadrant mass
- Assess for steatorrhea, signs, and symptoms of diabetes mellitus
- Instruct client in prescribed dietary measures
- Administer pancreatic enzymes as prescribed; fat, protein intake may be limited. Have bland diet
- Administer insulin or oral hypoglycemics as prescribed
- Instruct client to notify physician if increased steatorrhea, abdominal distention, cramping, or fever occur
- Monitor for respiratory infections

Hepatitis

- Inflammation of liver caused by virus, bacteria, exposure to medications or hepatotoxins
- Types of viral hepatitis: Hepatitis A, B, C, D, E
- Stages of viral hepatitis
  - Preicteric stage: Flu-like symptoms; precedes jaundice
  - Icteric stage: Appearance of jaundice; elevated bilirubin levels; dark or tea-colored urine; clay-colored stools
  - Posticteric stage: Jaundice decreases; color of stool, urine returns to normal
- Laboratory assessment
  - Elevated levels of alanine aminotransferase, aspartate aminotransferase, alkaline phosphatase, bilirubin
- Encourage hepatitis prevention activities:
  - Aseptic technique for the preparation and administration of parenteral medications.
  - Sterile, single-use, disposable needle, and syringe for each injection.
  - Use single-dose vials as often as possible.
  - Use needleless systems or safety caps.
  - Use personal protective equipment, such as gown, gloves, and goggles, appropriate to the type of exposure.

- Proper hand hygiene (before preparing and eating food, after using the toilet or changing a diaper).
- When traveling to underdeveloped countries, drink purified water, and avoid sharing eating utensils and bed linens.
- It is important to explain to the client with hepatitis that the majority of calories should be eaten in the morning hours because nausea most often occurs in the afternoon and evening.
- Clients should select a diet high in calories because energy is required for healing.
- Changes in bilirubin interfere with fat absorption so low-fat diets are better tolerated.

TYPE	ROUTE OF TRANSMISSION	RISK FACTORS
Hepatitis A (HAV)	› Fecal-oral route	› Ingestion of contaminated food or water › Close personal contact with an infected individual
Hepatitis B (HBV)	› Blood	› Unprotected sex with infected individual › Infants born to infected mothers › Contact with infected blood › Injection drug users
Hepatitis C (HCV)	› Blood	› Drug abuse › Sexual contact
Hepatitis D (HDV)	› Coinfection with HBV	› Injection drug users › Unprotected sex with infected individual
Hepatitis E (HEV)	› Fecal-oral route	› Ingestion of contaminated food or water

Source: ATI nursing education

Client and Family Home Care

- Strict and frequent hand washing
- Do not share bathrooms unless the client strictly adheres to personal hygiene measures. Use of individual towels, eating utensils, toothbrushes, razors
- Client should not be food preparer for family. Avoid over-the-counter medications, alcohol
- Client should increase activity gradually
- Client should consume small, frequent high-carbohydrate, low-fat foods

- Client should not donate blood
- Discourage close personal contact, such as kissing
- Client should keep follow-up appointments

Probiotics: Health purpose

- Prevention of antibiotic-associated diarrhea (including diarrhea caused by Clostridium difficile)
- Prevention of necrotizing enterocolitis and sepsis in premature infants
- Treatment of infant colic, Treatment of periodontal disease
- Maintenance of remission in ulcerative colitis, IBS
- Take the probiotic supplement at least 2 hr after taking an antibiotic or antifungal medication. Antibiotics and antifungal medications destroy bacteria and yeast found in probiotic supplements.

GI Pediatric Considerations

- Esophageal Atresia and Tracheoesophageal Fistula
- Esophagus terminates before it reaches the stomach and/or fistula present those forms unnatural connection with trachea
- Assessment: Three Cs: Coughing, choking, cyanosis

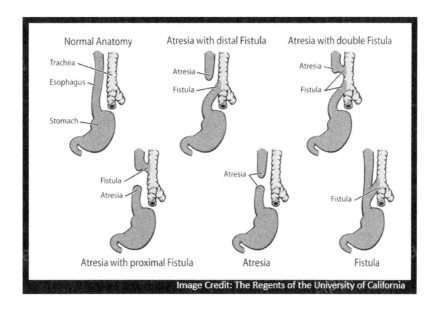

Preoperative interventions

- NPO, IV fluids, Suction mouth, pharynx PRN, antibiotics as prescribed
- Maintain upright position, Maintain esophageal catheter to low suction/ gastrostomy tube

Postoperative interventions

- Monitor respiratory status, I&O, daily weights, surgical site, pain, signs of dehydration
- Maintain IV fluids, total parenteral nutrition, antibiotics as prescribed
- Maintain gastrostomy tube, Suction PRN,
- Begin oral feedings with sterile water as prescribed

Hypertrophic Pyloric Stenosis

- Narrowing of pyloric canal between stomach and duodenum

Assessment

- Visible peristaltic waves from left to right across epigastrium during and immediately following feeding
- Olive-shaped mass in epigastrium, just right of umbilicus
- Projectile Vomiting (Hungry baby – Poor weight gain)

Interventions

- Monitor vital signs, I&O
- Signs of dehydration, Signs of electrolyte imbalances (skin that is dry and/or pale, cool lips, dry mucous membranes, decreased skin turgor, diminished urinary output, concentrated urine, thirst, rapid pulse, sunken eyes)
- Pyloromyotomy: Incision through muscle fibers of pylorus
- Postoperatively, feed infant slowly, burp frequently, handle minimally following feeding

Celiac Disease

- Intolerance to gluten, protein component of, barley, rye, oats, wheat. BROW
- Assessment: acute diarrhea; anorexia; abdominal pain, distention; muscle wasting (buttocks and extremities) vomiting; anemia

Celiac crisis

- Precipitated by fever, infection, gluten ingestion
- Electrolyte imbalances; rapid dehydration; severe acidosis; profuse watery diarrhea; vomiting

Interventions

- Maintain gluten-free diet, substituting corn, rice, millet as grain sources. Potato is OK
- Instruct in lifelong elimination of gluten sources: Beer, pasta, crackers, cereals, and many more substances contain gluten.

Abdominal Wall Defects

Omphalocele

- Herniation of abdominal contents through umbilical ring
- Immediately after birth, sac covered with sterile gauze soaked in normal saline. Handle infant carefully
- Preop- NPO, IV fluids, monitor for signs of infection

Gastroschisis

- Herniation of intestine, lateral to umbilical ring
- Exposed bowel covered loosely in saline-soaked pads, with abdomen wrapped in plastic drape
- Surgery performed within several hours after birth.
- Postoperatively: Perform measures to control pain, infection, fluid, and electrolyte imbalances; provide nutrition as prescribed

Hirschsprung's Disease

- Congenital anomaly; aganglionic megacolon
- Complication - Enterocolitis - presents with fever, gastrointestinal bleeding, explosive, watery diarrhea
- Assessment
  - Newborn: Delayed passage or absence of meconium stool
  - Abdominal distention, Bilious vomiting, tight anal sphincter.
  - Children: Ribbon-like, foul-smelling stools
- Interventions
  - Medical management
  - Dietary management; administer stool softeners as prescribed; perform daily rectal irrigations with normal saline as prescribed

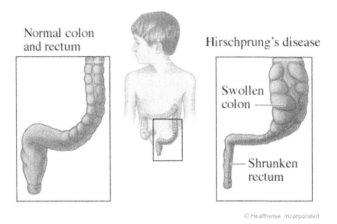

- Preoperative interventions
  - Assess bowel function, I&O, abdominal girth, weight; administer antibiotics as prescribed; no rectal temperatures
- Postoperative interventions
  - Monitor vital signs, with no rectal temperatures
  - Measure abdominal girth
  - Assess surgical site and stoma
  - Maintain NPO until bowel sounds return, NG tube suction as prescribed
  - Monitor for fluid, electrolyte imbalances

Necrotizing Enterocolitis

- In preterm babies (immature GI and immunity)
- Enteral feeding activates bacterial proliferation, leading to inflammation and ischemia of bowel
- Important Nursing Actions:
  - Measure abdominal girth, NPO, NG tube to suction

Nutrition and Therapeutic Diets

- Healthy diet – variety of nutrients
- Minimize salt, sugar, and saturated fat • BMI and weight management
- Overall indicator of nutritional level – Albumin
- Special concern – pregnancy, adolescent, elderly

Therapeutic Diets

Clear-liquid diet

- Intended for short-term use or as transition diet • Liquids that leave little residue (clear fruit juices, gelatin, broth) • Consists of clear fluids or foods that are relatively transparent to light, liquid at body temperature
- Foods include water, fat-free broth, bouillon, clear carbonated beverages, gelatin, hard candy, lemonade, frozen fruit bars, diluted juices, regular or decaffeinated coffee or tea
- Do not give "red" color liquids to post surgery patient (if vomits, unable to determine blood)

Full liquid diet

- Clear liquids plus liquid dairy products, all juice, pureed vegetables
- The full liquid diet is often used as a step between a clear liquid diet and a regular diet, for example, after surgery or fasting.
- It may also be used after certain procedures.

- This diet may also be appropriate for patients who have swallowing and chewing problems.

Mechanically altered diet

- Foods to be avoided include nuts, dried fruits, raw fruits and vegetables, fried foods, chocolate products, smoked or salted meats, foods with coarse textures
- Soft diet: Avoid foods that contain seeds or nuts

High protein and/ calorie

- Whole milk and dairy products (e.g., milkshakes), fruit smoothies
- Granola, muffins, biscuits
- Potatoes with sour cream and butter
- Meat, fish, eggs, dried beans, almond butter
- Pasta/rice dishes with cream sauce

Low-residue, low-fiber diet

- Foods include white bread, refined cooked cereals, cooked potatoes without skins, white rice, refined pasta
- Avoid raw fruits, vegetables, nuts, seeds, plant fiber, whole grains –

High-fiber diet

- Consists of fruits and vegetables and whole-grain products
- Increase fiber gradually, provide adequate fluids

Cardiac diet: Restrict saturated fat, trans-fat, cholesterol, sodium

Fat-restricted diet: Restrict amount of total fat, including saturated, trans-, polyunsaturated, monounsaturated fats

High-calorie, high-protein diet

- Foods include whole milk and milk products, peanut butter, nuts, seeds, beef, chicken, fish, pork, eggs, sugar, cream, mayonnaise, milkshakes, nutritional supplements

Carbohydrate-consistent diet

- Used in management of diabetes mellitus, hypoglycemia, lactose intolerance, dumping syndrome, obesity and galactosemia (a rare genetic metabolic disorder that affects an individual's ability to metabolize the sugar galactose properly)

Protein-restricted diet: Used to treat renal and liver disease

Renal diet: Used to treat acute renal failure, chronic renal failure

Sodium-restricted diet

- Used to treat hypertension, congestive heart failure, cardiac and liver disease
- Encourage intake of fresh rather than processed foods
- Avoid canned, boxed, microwaved foods

Potassium-modified diet

- Foods low in potassium include applesauce, green beans, cabbage, lettuce, grapes, blueberries, summer squash
- Foods high in potassium include - BP DC NS avocado, carrots, fish, raisins, tomatoes

High-calcium diet: Lactose-intolerant clients should incorporate nondairy sources of calcium in their diet regularly

Low-purine diet: Restrict such foods as anchovies, herring, mackerel, sardines, glandular meats, gravies, meat extracts, goose

High-iron diet

- Foods include organ meats, egg yolks, whole-wheat products, green leafy vegetables, dried fruits
- Eating foods rich in vitamin C (e.g., citrus fruits, potatoes, tomatoes) with iron-rich foods will enhance iron absorption

Magnesium

- Help with: Bone nourishment, nerve/muscle function, CV support.
- Source: Green leafy vegetables, nuts, grains, meat, milk
- Incompatible with some antibiotics. Give PO, 2 hr apart.

Enteral Nutrition

- Provides liquefied foods into gastrointestinal tract via tube• Continuous or bolus
- Indications
    - Clients who have functional gastrointestinal system, but oral intake not possible
    - For clients with swallowing problems, burns, major trauma, liver failure, severe malnutrition – Nursing considerations
- Monitor weight, labs (metabolic issues)
- Check tube placement, check residual
- Intake and output, Flush tube with water before and after (prevent dehydration)
- Head of the bed at 30 degrees

Nursing Interventions

- Assist in advancing the diet as appropriate.
- Instruct clients about the appropriate diet regimen.
- Provide interventions to promote appetite (good oral hygiene, favorite foods, minimal environmental odors).
- Educate clients about medications that may affect nutritional intake.
- Assist clients with feeding to promote optimal independence.
- Assist with preventing aspiration.

- Position in Fowler's position or in a chair.
- Support the upper back, neck, and head.
- Have clients tuck their chin when swallowing to help propel food down the esophagus.
- Observe for aspiration and pocketing of food in the cheeks or other areas of the mouth.
- Observe for signs of dysphagia, such as coughing, choking, gagging, and drooling of food.
- Keep clients in semi-Fowler's position for at least 1 hr after meals.
- Provide oral hygiene after meals and snacks

Parenteral Nutrition Overview

- Supplies all necessary nutrients via veins
- Indications
  - Severe dysfunctional or nonfunctional gastrointestinal (GI tract, or unable to process nutrients
  - Limited oral intake
  - AIDS, cancer, burn injuries, malnutrition, or receiving chemotherapy

Components

- Carbohydrates: Mainly in the form of glucose; ranges from 5% glucose solution for peripheral parenteral nutrition to 50% to 70% glucose solution for TPN
- Amino acids, Vitamins, Minerals and trace elements, Water
- Electrolytes: sodium, potassium, magnesium, calcium
- Insulin
- Heparin: May be added to reduce buildup of fibrinous clot at catheter tip
- Fat emulsion (lipids): Most fat emulsions prepared from soybean or safflower oil, with egg yolk for emulsification

Pre TPN-Consideration

- Review the client's medical record. TPN also includes administration of lipids (egg allergy)
- Document patient's weight (daily), BMI, nutritional status, diagnosis, and current laboratory data.
- Blood test: - serum chemistry profile, PT/aPTT, iron, total iron-binding capacity, lipid profile, liver function tests, electrolyte panel, BUN, prealbumin and albumin level, creatinine, blood glucose, and platelet count.
- Use IV pump and special filter for administering TPN solution.
- No additives to solution

Ongoing Care

- I&O, daily weights, vital signs
- Lab values (e.g., serum electrolytes, blood glucose)
- Ongoing evaluation of the client's underlying condition. This data is used to determine the client's response to therapy.
- Monitor serum and urine glucose – insulin sliding scale
- Presence of oily appearance or a layer of fat on top of the solution –DONOT USE
- The bag and tubing should be changed every 24-hr. new tubing is used with every bag.
- Discontinuation should be done gradually. Use D10W if there is discontinuation.

Complications

- Air embolism, Hypervolemia
- Hyperglycemia
  - Monitor blood glucose levels every 4 to 6 hours
  - Administer regular insulin as prescribed
- Infection
- Pneumothorax – catheter correct place

Gastrointestinal medications

Antiemetics

Prochlorperazine, Metoclopramide (Reglan)

- Extrapyramidal symptoms (Restlessness, anxiety, spasms of face and neck)
  - Protruding and twisting of the tongue, Lip smacking
  - Puffing of cheeks, chewing movements
  - Frowning or blinking of eyes, Twisting fingers
  - Twisted or rotated neck (torticollis)
- Stop medication
- Administer an anticholinergic medication, such as diphenhydramine (Benanadryl) or benztropine (Cogentin), to treat symptoms.
- Anticholinergic effects (dry mouth, urinary retention, constipation)
- Instruct clients to increase fluid intake.
- Instruct clients to increase physical activity by engaging in regular exercise.
- Tell clients to suck on hard candy or chew gum to help relieve dry mouth.
- Advise clients to void every 4 hr. Monitor I&O and palpate the lower abdomen area every 4 to 6 hr to assess the bladder.

Ondansetron (Zofran)

- Side Effect: Headache, diarrhea, dizziness

Scopolamine

- Side Effects: sedation, anticholinergic effect

Laxatives

- Psyllium (Metamucil): Bulk-forming, act like dietary fiber, Take with full glass of water. Full effect may take up to 2-3 days
- Docusate sodium (Colace): Stool softener (allow more water in stool)
- Bisacodyl (Dulcolax): Stimulate intestinal peristalsis

- Milk and antacids can destroy the enteric coating of bisacodyl. (Take 1 hr apart)
  - Take on empty stomach for maximum effectiveness.
  - Administer at bedtime for morning effect. (PO will take 6-12 hrs.)
- Magnesium hydroxide (Milk of Magnesia): Increase mass of stool and increase peristalsis, can lead to accumulation of toxic levels of magnesium, may cause dehydration
- Other Medications: senna (Senokot), lactulose
- Lactulose aids in the clearance of ammonia via the gastrointestinal tract.
  - Reduces ammonia levels: Hepatic encephalopathy
  - Administered orally or rectally, Cause Diarrhea
- Laxatives are contraindicated in clients who have fecal impaction, bowel obstruction, and acute surgical abdomen to prevent perforation.

Antidiarrheals

- Diphenoxylate plus atropine (Lomotil)
  - Administer initial dose of diphenoxylate, 4 mg. Follow each loose stool with additional dose of 2 mg, but do not exceed 16 mg/day.
- loperamide (Imodium)
  - Patient to drink small amounts of clear liquids or a commercial oral electrolyte solution to maintain electrolyte balance for the first 24 hr
  - Advise clients to avoid caffeine.
  - Caffeine exacerbates diarrhea by increasing GI motility.
  - Follow BRAT diet: Banana, Rice, Applesauce, Tea/Toast – to reduce diarrhea

Antacids

- Should be taken on regular schedule; some as prescribed
- To be taken 1 and 3 hours after each meal or at bedtime
- Tablets should be chewed thoroughly, followed with glass of water or milk
- Allow 1 hour between antacid administration, administration of other medications

Aluminum hydroxide preparations

- Contain significant amounts of sodium; use with caution in clients with hypertension, heart failure
- Constipation most common side effect
- Can reduce effects of tetracyclines, warfarin sodium (Coumadin), digoxin (Lanoxin); reduce phosphate absorption; can cause hypophosphatemia
- Calcium carbonate preparations: rapid acting, can cause constipation

Magnesium hydroxide preparations

- Also, saline laxative; most common side effect diarrhea
- Contraindicated in clients with intestinal obstruction, appendicitis, undiagnosed abdominal pain
- In clients with renal impairment, magnesium can accumulate, leading to toxicity

Sodium bicarbonate

- Can cause systemic alkalosis in clients with renal impairment.
- Use with caution in clients with hypertension, heart failure

Gastric Protectants

- Misoprostol (Cytotec):
  - Administer with meals.
  - Causes diarrhea, abdominal pain
- Sucralfate (Carafate):
  - Administered orally on empty stomach, May cause constipation
  - May impede absorption of warfarin sodium, phenytoin (Dilantin), theophylline, digoxin, some antibiotics
  - Administer 2 hours apart from these medications

Histamine 2 Receptor Antagonists

- Suppress secretion of gastric acid
- Should be used with caution in clients with impaired renal or hepatic failure

Cimetidine (Tagamet)

- Food reduces rate of absorption
- Administer 1 hour apart from antacids
- Passes blood-brain barrier; central nervous system side effects may occur
- Reduced dosage in clients with renal impairment necessary
- IV administration can lead to hypotension and dysrhythmias.
- If administered IV, need to be diluted and infused over 15 to 20 minutes

Ranitidine

- Side effects uncommon
- Does not penetrate blood-brain barrier
- For IV administration, dilute and administer slowly
- Famotidine (Pepcid), nizatidine (Axid)
- Do not need to be administered with food

Proton Pump Inhibitors

- Example: Omeprazole, Pantoprazole, Lansoprazole (Prevacid)
- Suppress gastric acid secretion
- Used to treat active ulcer disease, erosive esophagitis, pathological hypersecretory conditions
- Contraindicated in hypersensitivity
- Common side effects include headache, diarrhea, abdominal pain, nausea
- PPIs impair intestinal calcium absorption and therefore are associated with decreased bone density, which increases the possibility of fractures of the spine, hip, and wrist.

- PPIs cause acid suppression that otherwise would have prevented pathogens from more easily colonizing the upper gastrointestinal tract. This leads to increased risk of pneumonias.
- PPI use may also increase the risk for clostridium difficile-associated diarrhea (CDAD); currently the cause is unclear

Helicobacter pylori Infections

- Antibacterial agent alone not effective in eradicating bacterium
- Dual, triple, quadruple therapy with variety of combinations used
- Combinations include antibacterial agents, proton pump inhibitors, histamine two receptor antagonists, antacids
- Common treatment protocol is triple therapy with two antibacterial agents, one proton pump inhibitor
- If triple therapy fails, quadruple therapy recommended, with two antibiotics, one proton pump inhibitor, one bismuth or histamine two receptor antagonist

Gastrointestinal (GI) Stimulants

- Stimulate motility of upper GI tract, increase rate of gastric emptying
- Used to treat gastroesophageal reflux, paralytic ileus.
- May cause restlessness, drowsiness, extrapyramidal reactions, insomnia, headache.
- Usually administered 30 minutes before meals or at bedtime
- Contraindicated in clients with sensitivity, mechanical obstruction, perforation, GI hemorrhage.
- Can precipitate hypertensive crisis in clients with pheochromocytoma
- Metoclopramide (Reglan) can cause parkinsonian symptoms
- Anticholinergics, opioid analgesics antagonize effects of metoclopramide
- Alcohol, sedatives, cyclosporine (Sandimmune), tranquilizers produce additive effect

Bile Acid Sequestrants

- Act by absorbing, combining with intestinal bile salts, which are then secreted in feces, preventing intestinal reabsorption
- Used to treat hypercholesterolemia, biliary obstruction, pruritus associated with biliary disease
- Taste, palatability causes for noncompliance
- Should be used cautiously in clients with bowel obstruction, severe constipation
- Side effects include nausea, bloating, constipation
- Stool softeners, other sources of fiber can be used to relieve side effects

Pancreatic Enzyme Replacements

- Used to supplement, replace pancreatic enzymes
- Should be taken with meals or snack.
- High-fiber diet may increase efficacy of medication.
- Side effects include abdominal cramps, pain, nausea, diarrhea
- Products that contain calcium carbonate or magnesium hydroxide interfere with action of enzyme replacement

Endocrine System

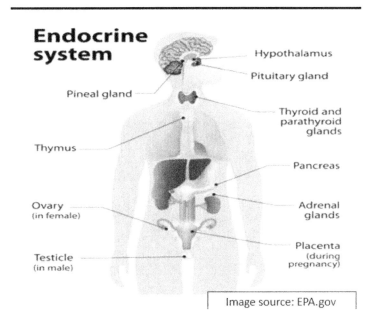

Image source: EPA.gov

- Hormone transport: Two kinds of Travel
- 1. Lipid soluble: Made from cholesterol: Ex: corticosteroids, sex hormones, thyroid hormones, need plasma proteins to travel
- 2. Water Soluble - circulate freely in the blood, Ex: insulin, growth hormone, and prolactin

Hypothalamus

- Control center – Release hormones to stimulate/inhibit pituitary
- Makes releasing hormones (thyrotropin-releasing hormone, gonadotropin releasing hormone, corticotropin-releasing hormone) and inhibiting hormones (Melanocyte inhibiting hormones, growth hormone inhibiting hormones, Prolactin inhibiting hormones)
- SAT: Sleep, Appetite Temperature

Posterior Pituitary (Neurohypophysis)

ADH (Antidiuretic hormone/Vasopressin)	Conserve water	Promote reabsorption of water at renal tubules
Oxytocin	Stimulate Uterine contraction	Stimulate lactation

Anterior Pituitary (Adenohypophysis)

Hormone Acronym	Hormone	Stimulating Effect
ACTH	Adrenocorticotropic hormone	Glucocorticoids production –adrenal cortex
MSH	Melanocyte-stimulating hormone	Skin Pigment production -Melanine
GH	Growth hormone	Promote growth of body tissues (muscle, bone, liver)
TSH	Thyroid-stimulating hormone	Production and release of T3, T4 from thyroid
FSH	Follicle-stimulating hormone	Maturation of ovarian follicles (female) spermatogenesis (male)
LH	Luteinizing hormone	Ovary- estrogen, progesterone Testes- Androgen
	Prolactin	Breast milk secretion (breast)

Pituitary Disorders

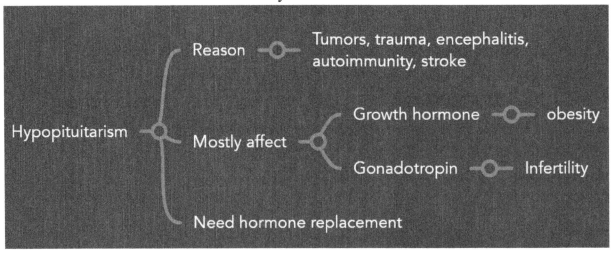

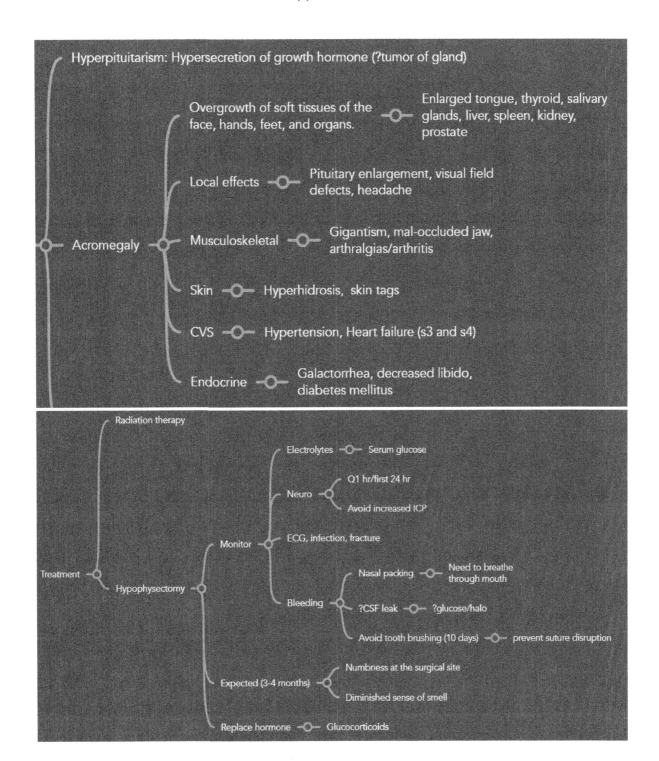

Hyperpituitarism: Hypersecretion of growth hormone (?tumor of gland)

Acromegaly
- Overgrowth of soft tissues of the face, hands, feet, and organs. — Enlarged tongue, thyroid, salivary glands, liver, spleen, kidney, prostate
- Local effects — Pituitary enlargement, visual field defects, headache
- Musculoskeletal — Gigantism, mal-occluded jaw, arthralgias/arthritis
- Skin — Hyperhidrosis, skin tags
- CVS — Hypertension, Heart failure (s3 and s4)
- Endocrine — Galactorrhea, decreased libido, diabetes mellitus

Treatment
- Radiation therapy
- Hypophysectomy
  - Monitor
    - Electrolytes — Serum glucose
    - Neuro
      - Q1 hr/first 24 hr
      - Avoid increased ICP
    - ECG, infection, fracture
    - Bleeding
      - Nasal packing — Need to breathe through mouth
      - ?CSF leak — ?glucose/halo
      - Avoid tooth brushing (10 days) — prevent suture disruption
  - Expected (3-4 months)
    - Numbness at the surgical site
    - Diminished sense of smell
  - Replace hormone — Glucocorticoids

Page 362

Posterior Pituitary Disorders

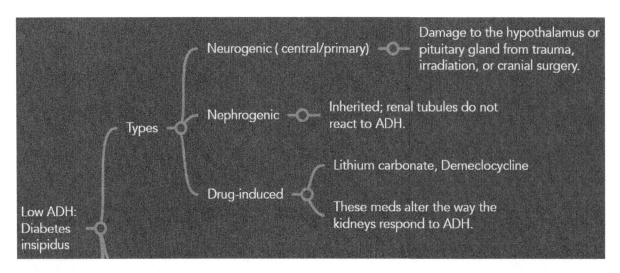

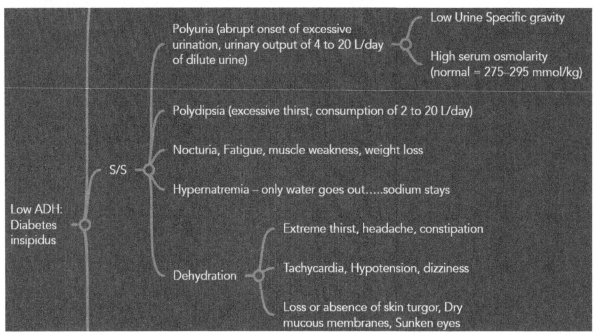

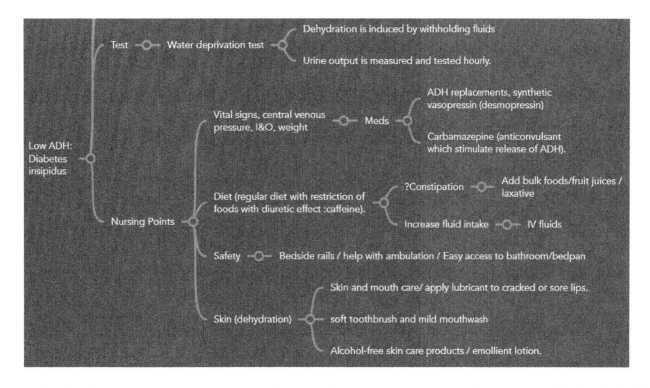

Low ADH: Diabetes insipidus

- **Test** — Water deprivation test
  - Dehydration is induced by withholding fluids
  - Urine output is measured and tested hourly.
- **Nursing Points**
  - Vital signs, central venous pressure, I&O, weight — **Meds**
    - ADH replacements, synthetic vasopressin (desmopressin)
    - Carbamazepine (anticonvulsant which stimulate release of ADH).
  - Diet (regular diet with restriction of foods with diuretic effect :caffeine).
    - ?Constipation — Add bulk foods/fruit juices / laxative
    - Increase fluid intake — IV fluids
  - Safety — Bedside rails / help with ambulation / Easy access to bathroom/bedpan
  - Skin (dehydration)
    - Skin and mouth care/ apply lubricant to cracked or sore lips.
    - soft toothbrush and mild mouthwash
    - Alcohol-free skin care products / emollient lotion.

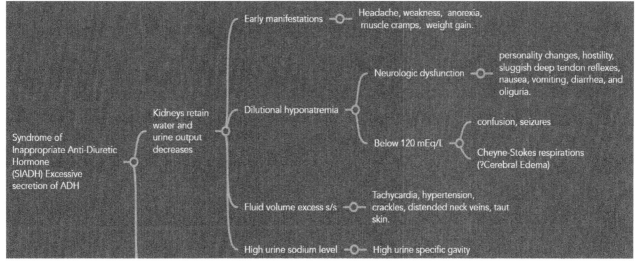

Syndrome of Inappropriate Anti-Diuretic Hormone (SIADH) Excessive secretion of ADH

- Kidneys retain water and urine output decreases
  - Early manifestations — Headache, weakness, anorexia, muscle cramps, weight gain.
  - Dilutional hyponatremia
    - Neurologic dysfunction — personality changes, hostility, sluggish deep tendon reflexes, nausea, vomiting, diarrhea, and oliguria.
    - Below 120 mEq/L
      - confusion, seizures
      - Cheyne-Stokes respirations (?Cerebral Edema)
  - Fluid volume excess s/s — Tachycardia, hypertension, crackles, distended neck veins, taut skin.
  - High urine sodium level — High urine specific gavity

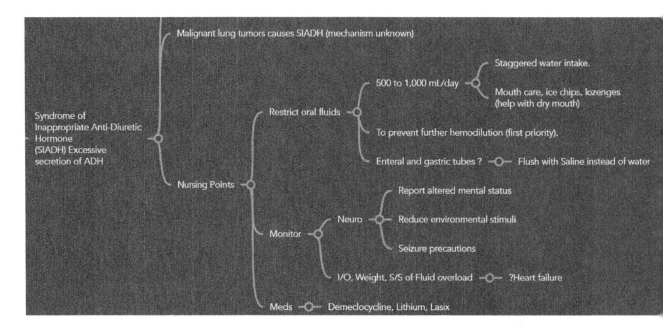

Thyroid and parathyroid

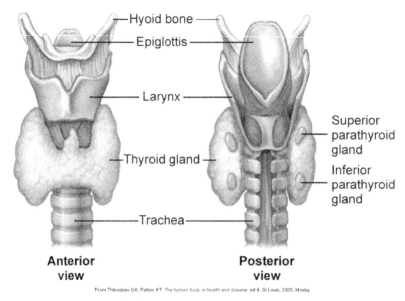

Hyoid bone

Epiglottis

Larynx

Thyroid gland

Superior parathyroid gland

Inferior parathyroid gland

Trachea

Anterior view

Posterior view

From Thibodeau GA, Patton KT: *The human body in health and disease*, ed 4, St Louis, 2005, Mosby.

Fig. 48-8. Thyroid and parathyroid glands. Note the surrounding structures.

- Thyroid Hormones: T3, T4 and Calcitonin

Thyroxin (T3, T4)	Increase metabolism
Calcitonin	Lower serum calcium

- Parathyroid hormone: Increase serum calcium

- The thyroid gland is difficult to palpate: Anterior or posterior palpation techniques can be used.
- In many normal people, the thyroid is not palpable. If it is palpable, it usually feels smooth with a firm consistency, but it is not tender with gentle pressure. If nodules, enlargement, asymmetry, or hardness (abnormal findings) are present, refer the patient for further evaluation.

Diagnostic Studies of Thyroid

- 1. Ultrasonography? fluid filled nodule or solid tumor?
- 2. Thyroid scan: For nodules. Radioactive isotopes PO/ IV.
    - Benign nodules - warm spots (take up radionuclide)
    - Malignant tumors - cold spots (do not to take up radionuclide)
- 3. Radioactive iodine uptake (RAIU)
    - Direct measure of thyroid activity.
    - Radioactive iodine- PO or IV. The uptake by the thyroid gland is measured in intervals such as 2 to 4 hours and at 24 hours.
- Client Teaching
    - Drink more fluids for 24 to 48 hours unless this is contraindicated.
    - Radionuclide will be eliminated in 6 to 24 hours.

Levothyroxine

- Levothyroxine: Adjust dose – blood test
- High levels of TSH – start/increase Levothyroxine
- Dose - Once daily – an empty stomach
- Usually - lifelong therapy.
- Can take up to 8 weeks to see the full effect

Characteristics	Hypothyroidism	Hyperthyroidism
Metabolism	Decreased	Increased
Weight	Gain	Loss
Intolerance	Cold (decreased sweating)	Heat (Increased sweating)
GI	Constipation/ not hungry	Diarrhea /increased appetite
CVS	Low cardiac output/low HR	Increased CO/HR, palpitations
Respiration	Hypoventilation	Tachypnea, Dyspnea
Muscle tone/reflex	Decreased	Increased
Complication	Myxedema	Exophthalmos/Graves Disease/Thyroid Storm/Thyroid Crisis
Skin	Dry	Increased perspiration

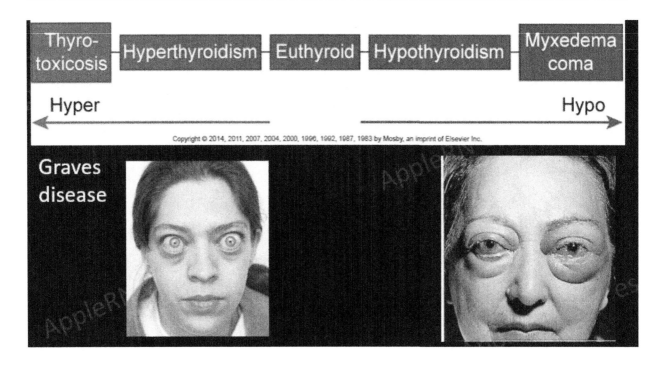

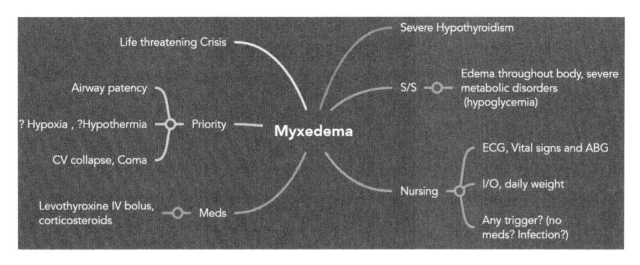

Myxedema

- Life threatening Crisis
- Severe Hypothyroidism
- S/S — Edema throughout body, severe metabolic disorders (hypoglycemia)
- Priority
  - Airway patency
  - ? Hypoxia , ?Hypothermia
  - CV collapse, Coma
- Meds — Levothyroxine IV bolus, corticosteroids
- Nursing
  - ECG, Vital signs and ABG
  - I/O, daily weight
  - Any trigger? (no meds? Infection?)

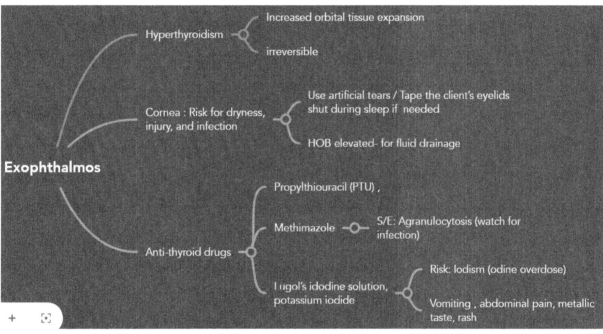

Exophthalmos

- Hyperthyroidism
  - Increased orbital tissue expansion
  - irreversible
- Cornea : Risk for dryness, injury, and infection
  - Use artificial tears / Tape the client's eyelids shut during sleep if needed
  - HOB elevated- for fluid drainage
- Anti-thyroid drugs
  - Propylthiouracil (PTU) ,
  - Methimazole — S/E: Agranulocytosis (watch for infection)
  - Lugol's iodine solution, potassium iodide
    - Risk: Iodism (iodine overdose)
    - Vomiting , abdominal pain, metallic taste, rash

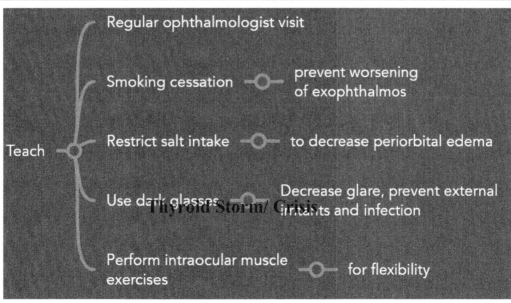

Teach
- Regular ophthalmologist visit
- Smoking cessation — prevent worsening of exophthalmos
- Restrict salt intake — to decrease periorbital edema
- Use dark glasses — Decrease glare, prevent external irritants and infection
- Perform intraocular muscle exercises — for flexibility

Thyroid Storm/ Crisis

- From a sudden surge of large amounts of thyroid hormones into the blood
- Greater increase in body metabolism - medical emergency
- Precipitating factors - infection, trauma, emotional stress, diabetic ketoacidosis, and digitalis toxicity.
- It also can occur following a surgical procedure or a thyroidectomy as a result of manipulation of the gland during surgery.
- Findings - hyperthermia, hypertension, hyperglycemia, dysrhythmias, chest pain, palpitations, delirium, vomiting, abdominal pain, and dyspnea

Nursing Care

- Maintain a patent airway. Start oxygen
- Continuous cardiac monitoring
- Hyperthermia management- Medicine, cool sponge, cooling blanket
- Avoid Aspirin (salicylates increases thyroid hormone availability)
- Administer Meds: Anti-thyroid drugs- thionamides (Propylthiouracil (PTU) methimazole)
  - Propranolol to block sympathetic nervous system effects (tachycardia, palpitations). Glucocorticoids to treat shock. IV fluids to provide hydration
  - Insulin.

Thyroidectomy

- Airway swelling is a life-threatening complication of thyroid surgery.
- Signs of respiratory distress such as stridor and dyspnea require rapid intervention.
- Have tracheostomy set, oxygen, suctioning at bedside at all times
- Position client in semi-Fowler's position
- Assess neck dressing for bleeding, Monitor for hypocalcemic crisis
- Assess for signs of potential tetany, Monitor for laryngeal nerve damage

Diet with Hyperthyroidism

- Hyperthyroidism leads to a high metabolic rate:

- Diet high in calories (high in protein, carbohydrates, vitamins, and minerals) to satisfy hunger and prevent weight loss and tissue wasting.
- Avoidance of high-fiber foods due to the constant hyperstimulation of the gastrointestinal (GI) tract. However, high-fiber diets are recommended if the client with hyperthyroidism has constipation.
- Avoidance of stimulating substances: caffeinated: coffee, tea, soft drinks).
- Avoidance of spicy foods as these can also increase GI stimulation.

Parathyroid Disorders

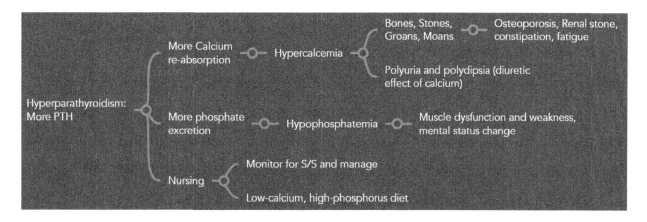

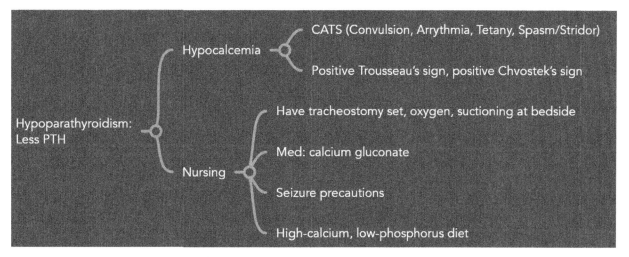

Adrenal Disorders

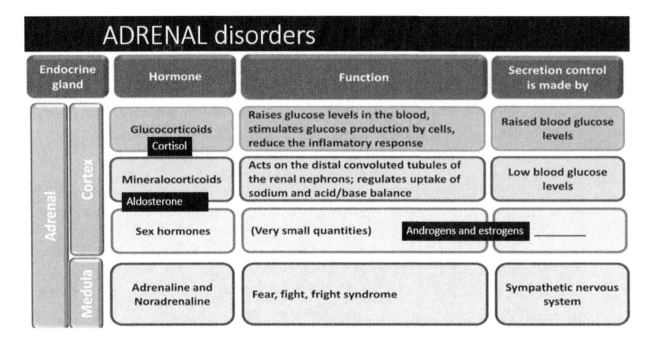

Cushing's disease / Cushing's syndrome

- Over secretion of ACTH by pituitary /or hormones by adrenal cortex /or by long-term use of glucocorticoids
- Clinical Manifestations
  - Moon Face, Buffalo hump, Weakness, fatigue, sleep issues, weight gain, Back and joint pain, thin fragile bone
  - Frequent infections, poor wound healing
  - Altered emotional state (may include irritability or depression)
- Lab test – Cortisol (salivary cortisol also elevated)
  - K and Calcium – low
  - Na and Glucose – High
- Diet: Decreased sodium intake and increased intake of potassium, protein, and calcium.

Nursing Care

- Monitor I/O, and daily weight.

- Assess hypervolemia (edema, distended neck veins, shortness of breath, presence of adventitious breath sounds, hypertension, tachycardia).
- Low calcium: Fractures
- Prevent Infection and skin trauma.
- Medications – suppress /inhibit adrenal cortex (Mitotane, Ketoconazole, aldectone)
- Surgery - Surgical removal of the pituitary gland (Hypophysectomy) or Adrenalectomy

Adrenalectomy

- Steroid and Hormonal replacement
- Monitor for adrenal crisis due to an abrupt drop in cortisol level (hypotension, tachycardia, tachypnea, nausea, and headache)
- Vital signs and hemodynamic levels (every 15 min initially).
- Fluids and electrolytes/ bleeding at incision site
- Bowel sounds. Slowly introduce foods/ pain meds/ stool softeners Assess the abdomen for distention and tenderness.
- Monitor the incision site for redness, discharge, and swelling.

Adrenal Crisis

- Sudden drop in corticosteroids due to sudden withdrawal of medication or tumor removal. Medical Emergency – Life threatening.
- Precipitating Factors: Sepsis, Trauma, Stress (myocardial infarction, surgery, anesthesia, hypothermia, volume loss, hypoglycemia), Adrenal hemorrhage and Steroid withdrawal.
- Indications include hypotension, tachycardia, hypoglycemia, hyperkalemia, hyponatremia, confusion, abdominal pain, weakness, and weight loss.
- Administration of glucocorticoids treats acute adrenal insufficiency.
- Instruct the client to gradually taper steroid medications.
- Additional glucocorticoids may be needed to prevent adrenal crisis.

Addison's disease

- Adrenocortical insufficiency
- Decreased production of mineralocorticoids and glucocorticoids: resulting in decreased aldosterone and cortisol.
- Lab tests - K+, calcium, BUN, and creatinine – increased
- Na, Glucose, and cortisol decreased.
- Bronze color skin – Likely due to ACTH interference with MSH

Nursing Care

- Monitor F&E, Give IV fluids. Observe for dehydration, orthostatic vitals
- Administer hydrocortisone (IV bolus /continuous /intermittent IV bolus)
- Hyperkalemia: Obtain a serum potassium/ ECG / Kayexalate
- Monitor for and treat hypoglycemia.
- Safe environment: assistance ambulating, Raise side rails/fall precaution
- Meds- Steroids: Report signs and symptoms of infection, even a low-grade fever
- Situations -corticosteroid adjustment- fever, influenza, extraction of teeth, rigorous physical activity (playing tennis on a hot day or running a marathon)
- Tachycardia, moon face, and weight gain - side effects of long-term corticosteroid therapy.

Pheochromocytoma (Adrenal medulla tumor)

- Catecholamines increase (adrenalin, noradrenaline) resulting in paroxysmal hypertensive crisis.
- 6 P: Pounding Pain (Headache), Perspiration, Pallor, Panic, Palpitation, Pressure
- Meds: nitroprusside or another vasodilator: Hypertension is difficult to treat and is often resistant to multiple drugs.
- Avoid activities that can precipitate a hypertensive crisis (bending, lifting, Valsalva maneuver).

- Abdominal palpation should be avoided as manipulation of the adrenal gland and release of catecholamines can precipitate a hypertensive crisis.

Pancreatic Disorders

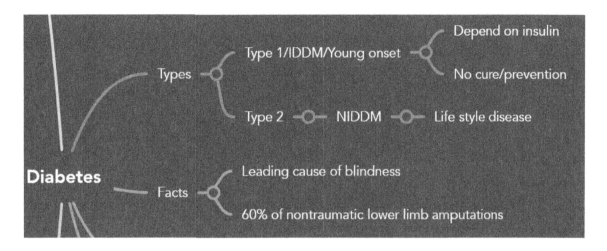

Criteria	Diabetes Type 1	Diabetes Type 2
Onset	Young	Adult
Etiology	Genetic/Autoimmune	Risk factor combination
Use of insulin	Required	Oral drugs, insulin combo
Control by lifestyle changes	No	Yes
DKA	More likely	Not usually
Weight	Normal/underweight	Usually, overweight

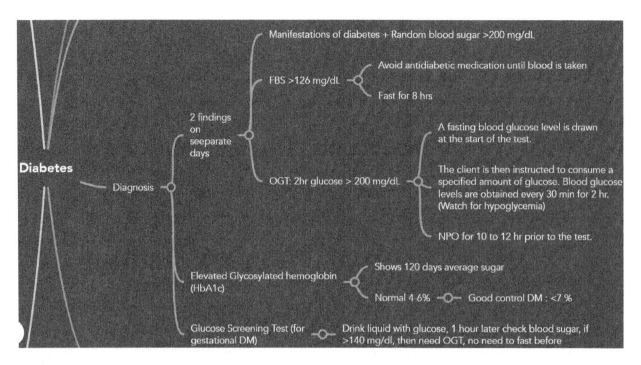

Diabetes

Diagnosis

2 findings on seeparate days

Manifestations of diabetes + Random blood sugar >200 mg/dL

FBS >126 mg/dL
- Avoid antidiabetic medication until blood is taken
- Fast for 8 hrs

OGT: 2hr glucose > 200 mg/dL
- A fasting blood glucose level is drawn at the start of the test.
- The client is then instructed to consume a specified amount of glucose. Blood glucose levels are obtained every 30 min for 2 hr. (Watch for hypoglycemia)
- NPO for 10 to 12 hr prior to the test.

Elevated Glycosylated hemoglobin (HbA1c)
- Shows 120 days average sugar
- Normal 4-6% — Good control DM : <7 %

Glucose Screening Test (for gestational DM) — Drink liquid with glucose, 1 hour later check blood sugar, if >140 mg/dl, then need OGT, no need to fast before

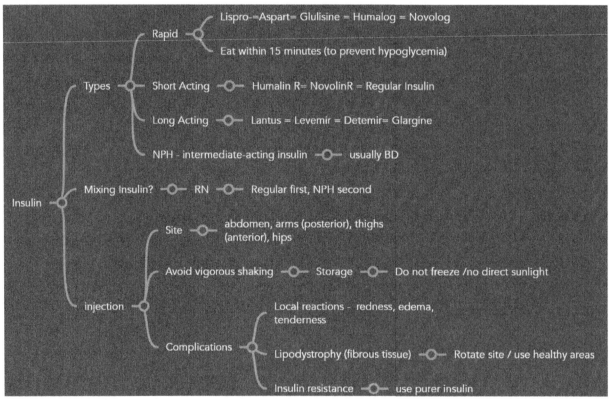

Insulin

Types

Rapid
- Lispro-=Aspart= Glulisine = Humalog = Novolog
- Eat within 15 minutes (to prevent hypoglycemia)

Short Acting — Humalin R= NovolinR = Regular Insulin

Long Acting — Lantus = Levemir = Detemir= Glargine

NPH - intermediate-acting insulin — usually BD

Mixing Insulin? — RN — Regular first, NPH second

injection

Site — abdomen, arms (posterior), thighs (anterior), hips

Avoid vigorous shaking — Storage — Do not freeze /no direct sunlight

Complications
- Local reactions - redness, edema, tenderness
- Lipodystrophy (fibrous tissue) — Rotate site / use healthy areas
- Insulin resistance — use purer insulin

Insulin

Source: ATI nursing education

CLASSIFICATION	GENERIC (TRADE NAME)	ONSET	PEAK	DURATION
Rapid-acting	› Lispro insulin (Humalog)	15 to 30 min	0.5 to 2.5 hr	3 to 6 hr
Short-acting	› Regular insulin (Humulin R)	0.5 to 1 hr	1 to 5 hr	6 to 10 hr
Intermediate-acting	› NPH insulin (Humulin N)	1 to 2 hr	6 to 14 hr	16 to 24 hr
Long-acting	› Insulin glargine (Lantus)	70 min	None	24 hr

Premixed insulins
• 70% NPH and 30% regular (Humulin 70/30) – mixture of intermediate-acting and short-acting insulin
•When mixing short-acting insulin with longer-acting insulin, draw the short-acting insulin up into the syringe first, then the longer-acting insulin.

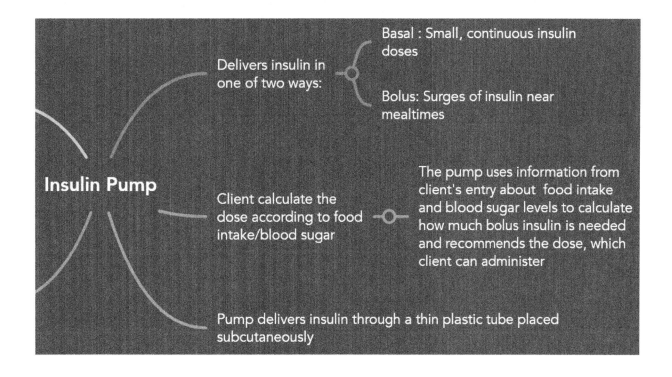

Insulin Pump

Delivers insulin in one of two ways:
- Basal : Small, continuous insulin doses
- Bolus: Surges of insulin near mealtimes

Client calculate the dose according to food intake/blood sugar — The pump uses information from client's entry about food intake and blood sugar levels to calculate how much bolus insulin is needed and recommends the dose, which client can administer

Pump delivers insulin through a thin plastic tube placed subcutaneously

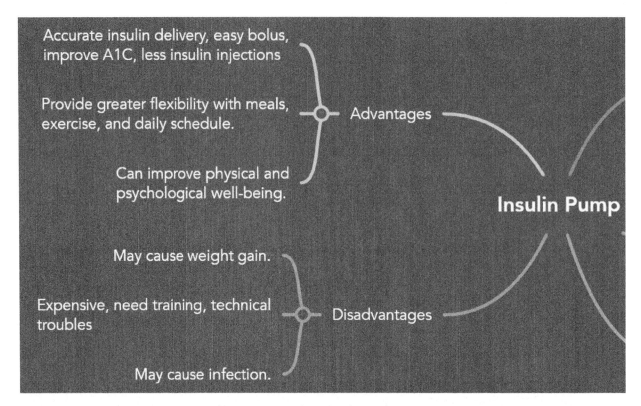

Accurate insulin delivery, easy bolus, improve A1C, less insulin injections

Provide greater flexibility with meals, exercise, and daily schedule.

Can improve physical and psychological well-being.

Advantages

Insulin Pump

May cause weight gain.

Expensive, need training, technical troubles

Disadvantages

May cause infection.

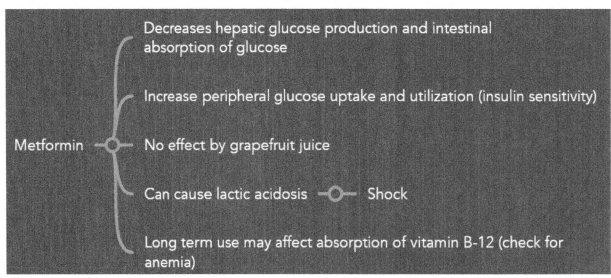

Metformin

Decreases hepatic glucose production and intestinal absorption of glucose

Increase peripheral glucose uptake and utilization (insulin sensitivity)

No effect by grapefruit juice

Can cause lactic acidosis — Shock

Long term use may affect absorption of vitamin B-12 (check for anemia)

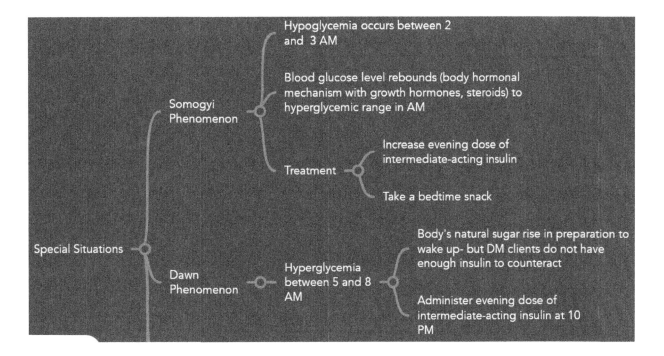

Signs and Symptoms of Diabetes

- Polyuria: Urinate (pee) a lot, often at night
- Polydipsia: Intense thirst despite drinking plenty of fluids.
- Polyphagia: Excessive eating from excess hunger or increased appetite.
- Lose weight without trying
- Blurry vision
- Have numb or tingling hands or feet
- Feel very tired
- Have very dry skin
- Have sores that heal slowly
- Have more infections than usual

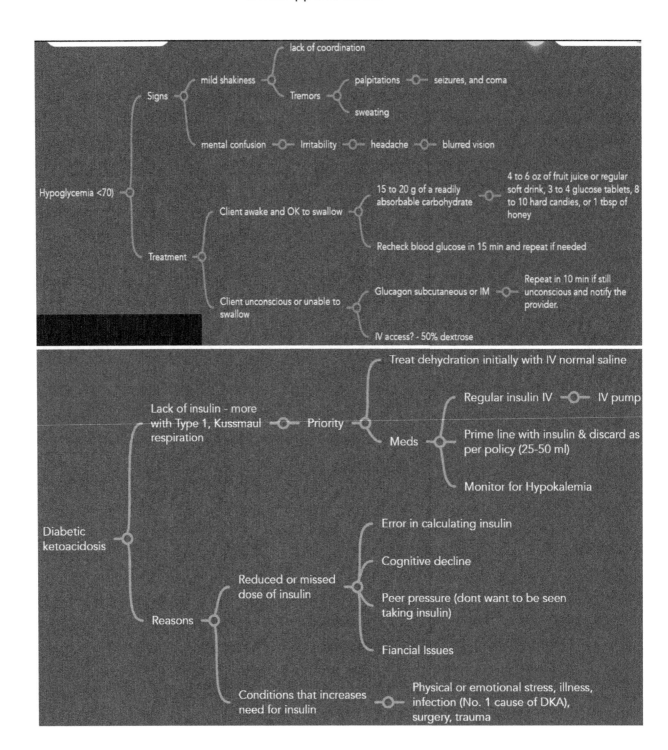

Hypoglycemia <70)

Signs
- mild shakiness — lack of coordination
  - Tremors — palpitations — seizures, and coma
  - sweating
- mental confusion — Irritability — headache — blurred vision

Treatment
- Client awake and OK to swallow
  - 15 to 20 g of a readily absorbable carbohydrate — 4 to 6 oz of fruit juice or regular soft drink, 3 to 4 glucose tablets, 8 to 10 hard candies, or 1 tbsp of honey
  - Recheck blood glucose in 15 min and repeat if needed
- Client unconscious or unable to swallow
  - Glucagon subcutaneous or IM — Repeat in 10 min if still unconscious and notify the provider.
  - IV access? - 50% dextrose

Diabetic ketoacidosis

- Lack of insulin - more with Type 1, Kussmaul respiration — Priority
  - Treat dehydration initially with IV normal saline
  - Meds
    - Regular insulin IV — IV pump
    - Prime line with insulin & discard as per policy (25-50 ml)
    - Monitor for Hypokalemia

- Reasons
  - Reduced or missed dose of insulin
    - Error in calculating insulin
    - Cognitive decline
    - Peer pressure (dont want to be seen taking insulin)
    - Fiancial Issues
  - Conditions that increases need for insulin — Physical or emotional stress, illness, infection (No. 1 cause of DKA), surgery, trauma

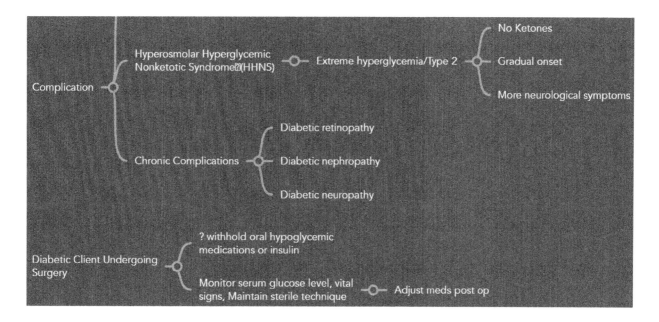

- Diabetic neuropathy = Nerve damage
- Sensory neuropathy – most common
- Autonomic neuropathy – affecting autonomic nervous system – controls all involuntary body functions (Heart rate, Blood pressure, Sexual function, Digestion, Perspiration)
- Signs: Postural hypotension, tachycardia, impotence, bowel and bladder dysfunction, sexual dysfunction, diarrhea

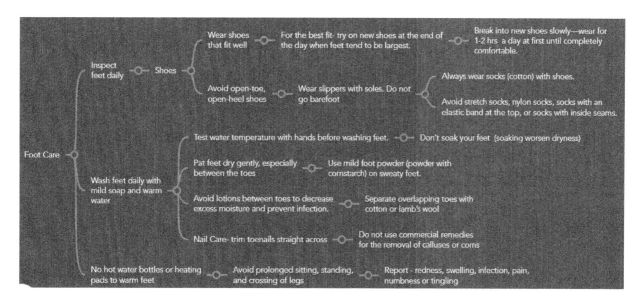

A note on Carbohydrates in diet

- Three kinds of carbohydrates

  1. Sugars: such as the natural sugar in fruit and milk or the added sugar in soda and many other packaged foods. Raises blood sugar.
  2. Starches: including wheat, oats, and other grains; starchy vegetables such as corn and potatoes; and dried beans, lentils, and peas. Raises blood sugar.
  3. Fiber: the part of plant foods that isn't digested but helps to stay healthy. It will not raise blood sugar.

- 1 carb serving is about fifteen grams of carbs (4 calories per gram)

- American Diabetic Association recommend: 1800 Cal/day (general) People with diabetes should aim to get about only half of their calories from carbs (about 800 to 900 calories can come from carbs)

- Plate method: Portion Size - A portion is the amount of food a person chooses to eat at one time

1. Check the **Serving size** first. All the numbers on this label are for a 2/3-cup serving.

2. **This package has 8 servings.** If you eat the whole thing, you are eating 8 times the amount of calories, carbs, fat, etc., shown on the label.

3. **Total Carbohydrate** shows you types of carbs in the food, including sugar and fiber.

4. Choose foods with **more fiber, vitamins, and minerals.**

5. Choose foods with **lower calories, saturated fat, sodium, and added sugars.** Avoid *trans* fat.

Source: CDC

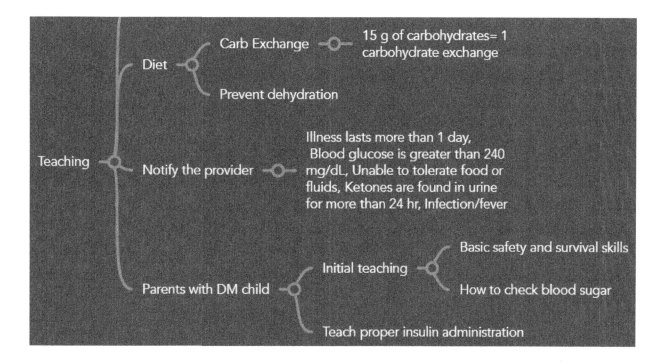

Endocrine Medications

Pituitary Medications

- Administered to replace deficient amounts of hormones secreted by the anterior and posterior pituitary gland
- Growth hormones and related medications
    - Assess child's physical growth; compare with standards
    - Monitor blood glucose levels, thyroid function tests
    - Teach client, family signs of hyperglycemia, importance of follow-up blood tests

Antidiuretic Hormones

Desmopressin

- Enhance reabsorption of water in kidneys, promoting antidiuretic effect, regulating fluid balance
- Side effects • Include flushing, headache, water intoxication, hypertension

Interventions

- Monitor strict intake and output, urine osmolality
- Monitor daily weights, vital signs, Monitor electrolyte serum levels
- Restrict fluid intake as prescribed
- Monitor for signs of water intoxication (hyponatremia), including drowsiness, listlessness, headache
- Instruct client how to use intranasal spray medication
- Instruct client to report any signs of water intoxication, dyspnea, shortness of breath, headache to primary health care provider

Thyroid Hormones

- Control metabolic rate of tissues; accelerate heat production, oxygen consumption
- Should be given at least 4 hours apart from multivitamins, aluminum hydroxide, magnesium hydroxide, simethicone, calcium carbonate, bile acid sequestrants, iron, sucralfate (Carafate)
- Side effects: weight loss, nervousness, insomnia, diaphoresis, tachycardia, hypertension, chest palpitations, chest pain
- Interventions
    - Instruct client to take medication at same time each day, preferably in morning, without food
    - Advise client to report symptoms of hyperthyroidism (tachycardia, chest pain, palpitations, diaphoresis)

Antithyroid Medications

- Inhibit synthesis of thyroid hormone
- Ex: Lugol's iodine solution, potassium iodide (risk-iodine overdose)
- Other meds: Methimazole and propylthiouracil
- Methimazole is associated with an increased risk of congenital defects, and thus propylthiouracil (PTU) is preferred in managing hyperthyroidism during pregnancy.

- PTU: Advise clients that therapeutic effects may take 1 to 2 weeks to be evident. PTU does not destroy the thyroid hormone that is present, but rather prevents continued synthesis of TH.
- Side effects: Agranulocytosis with leukopenia, thrombocytopenia, hypothyroidism (toxic response), iodism

Interventions

- Instruct client how to take pulse
- Advise client to contact physician if fever, sore throat develops
- Instruct client regarding importance of medication compliance
- Advise client to consult physician before eating iodized salt, foods containing iodine
- Instruct client to avoid acetylsalicylic acid (aspirin), medications containing iodine
- Monitor for signs of thyroid storm (fever, flushed skin, confusion, behavioral changes, tachycardia, dysrhythmias, signs of heart failure)

Parathyroid Medications

- Regulate serum calcium levels
- Hyperparathyroidism results in high serum calcium levels, bone demineralization
- Hypoparathyroidism results in low serum calcium levels, neuromuscular excitability

Interventions

- Assess for symptoms of tetany in client with hypocalcemia
- Instruct client to maintain intake of vitamin D if receiving oral calcium supplements
- Instruct client receiving calcium regulators to
  - Swallow tablet whole with water at least 30 minutes before breakfast

- Not to lie down for at least 30 minutes
- Instruct client using antihypercalcemic agents to avoid foods rich in calcium, including green leafy vegetables
- Instruct client not to take other medications within 1 hour of taking calcium salts

Corticosteroids

Mineralocorticoids

- Used for replacement therapy in primary or secondary adrenal insufficiency in Addison's disease
- Side effects: sodium and water retention, hypokalemia, hypertension, weight gain
- Interventions • Instruct client not to stop medication abruptly • Instruct client to take medication with food or milk • Instruct client to consume diet high in potassium as prescribed • Instruct client to notify physician if signs of infection, muscle aches, sudden weight gain, headache occur • Instruct client not to take aspirin products without consulting physician

Glucocorticoids

- Alter the normal immune response, suppress inflammation
- Promote sodium and water retention, potassium excretion
- Produce anti-inflammatory, antiallergic, antistress effects
- May be used as replacement for adrenocortical insufficiency
- Side effects: hyperglycemia, sodium and fluid retention, weight gain, mood swings, moon face and buffalo hump, increased susceptibility to infection, hirsutism.
- Contraindications and cautions
  - Should be used with caution in clients with DM
  - Use with extreme caution in clients with infections
- Interventions

- Instruct client to take medication with food
- Instruct client to avoid individuals with infections
- Instruct client to eat diet high in potassium as prescribed
- Instruct client to report signs of Cushing's syndrome

Important notes – steroids

- Corticosteroids are catabolic to bone (osteoporosis) and muscle (muscle weakness).
- Do not discontinue abruptly
- Report any signs and symptoms of infection to the HCP immediately (sore throat, fever, redness and swelling, discharge, pain)
- No live vaccines (varicella-zoster, MMR, rotavirus, yellow fever, nasal flu vaccine)

Estrogens and Progestins

- Preparations may be used to stimulate endogenous hormones to restore hormonal balance; treat hormone-sensitive tumors; for contraception

Contraindications and cautions

- Estrogens – Contraindicated in clients with breast cancer, endometrial hyperplasia, endometrial cancer, history of thromboembolism, known or suspected pregnancy or lactation
- Barbiturates, phenytoin (Dilantin), rifampin decrease effectiveness
- Progestins: Contraindicated in clients with thromboembolic disorders; should be avoided in clients with breast tumors, hepatic disease
- Side effects: Hypertension, stroke, myocardial infarction, thromboembolism

Interventions

- Instruct client not to smoke
- Instruct client to undergo routine breast and pelvic examinations

Oral Antidiabetics

Sulfonylureas:

- Help with Insulin release from the pancreas
- Chlorpropamide, glipizide, tolzamide, glyburide, glimepiride
- Side Effects: Gastrointestinal symptoms, hypoglycemia
- Chlorpropamide can cause disulfiram type reaction when alcohol ingested

Sitagliptin

- Help hormones to promote release of insulin and decrease secretion of glucagon.
- Lowers fasting and postprandial blood glucose levels

Biguanides: Metformin

- Reduces the production of glucose within the liver, increases use of glucose by muscle
- Side Effects: GI distress, Lactic acidosis (hyperventilation, myalgia, sluggishness)

Nursing Care: Diabetic Medications

- Obtain medication history
- Instruct client not to ingest alcohol with sulfonylureas
- Inform client that insulin may be needed during stress, surgery, infection
- Teach client about signs and symptoms of hypoglycemia and hyperglycemia

Musculoskeletal System

Lab studies related to MS

- ANA – Anti nuclear antibodies- to detect autoimmune disorders (RA, Scleroderma, SLE)
- Ca++ and Ph
    - Calcium High: cancer, fracture, immobilization
    - Calcium Low: osteomalacia / Rickets
- ESR: normal <20 mm/hr – High: RA (Rheumatoid Arthritis), osteomyelitis
- RF: Rheumatoid factor: antibodies
- Uric Acid – High: Gout

Fracture

- Types
    - Open (compound) vs Closed (simple)
    - Complete (break completely through bone) Vs Incomplete (bone still in one piece)
- Initial care of extremity fracture
    - Immobilize (injury to blood vessels, nerves/PE/Fat embolism)
    - Cover an open wound
    - Assess neurovascular status
    - Cast/Traction/Surgery

Proper fit of the sling

- Elbow is flexed at 90 degrees: shoulder support, prevent swelling
- Hand slightly above the level of the elbow: prevent venous pooling
- Bottom of the sling ends in the middle of the palm with the fingers visible: for assessment
- Sling supports the wrist joint with the thumb facing upward or inward toward the body: to maintain proper alignment

Cast and Care

- Clean and dry area first
- Tubular Cotton Web roll underneath casting material
- Monitor neurovascular status and assess pain.
- Apply ice for 24 to 48 hr.
- Handle a plaster cast with the palms, not fingertips, until the cast is dry to prevent denting the cast. Avoid setting the cast on hard surfaces or sharp edges.
- Fiberglass cast is available
    - Synthetic cast – water resistant- dry in 20 mts
    - Plaster cast - not water resistant– dry in 24-72 hrs.
- Use gloves to touch the cast until it is completely dry.
- Elevate the cast above the level of the heart during the first 24 to 48 hr to prevent edema of the affected extremity. Monitor for drainage
- Special consideration - Older adult clients (fragile skin)
- Do not place any foreign objects under the cast.
- Itching? - blow cool air from a hair dryer under the cast. (Not Hot air – skin burn). Plastic coverings to avoid soiling from urine or feces. Report "hot spot": painful/ drainage/warm/ foul odor areas under the cast - infection.
- Instruct the client to report immobility / complications - shortness of breath, skin breakdown, and constipation.

Traction (Skin/Skeletal)

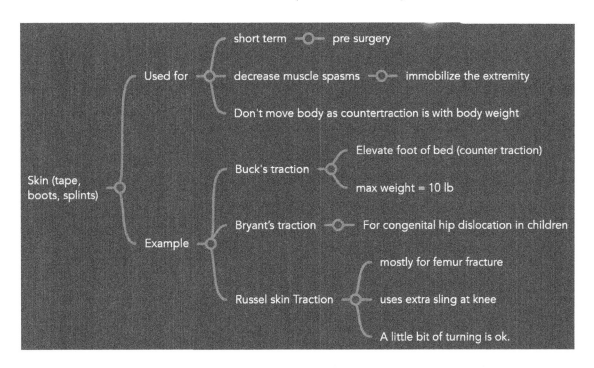

Skin (tape, boots, splints)

Used for
- short term ─○─ pre surgery
- decrease muscle spasms ─○─ immobilize the extremity
- Don't move body as countertraction is with body weight

Example
- Buck's traction ─○─ Elevate foot of bed (counter traction) / max weight = 10 lb
- Bryant's traction ─○─ For congenital hip dislocation in children
- Russel skin Traction ─○─ mostly for femur fracture / uses extra sling at knee / A little bit of turning is ok.

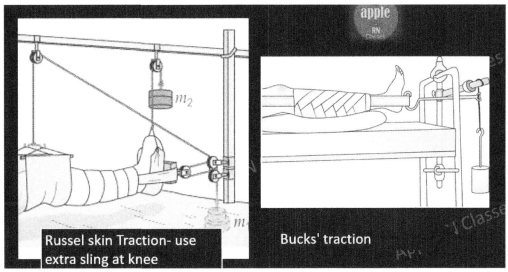

Russel skin Traction- use extra sling at knee

Bucks' traction

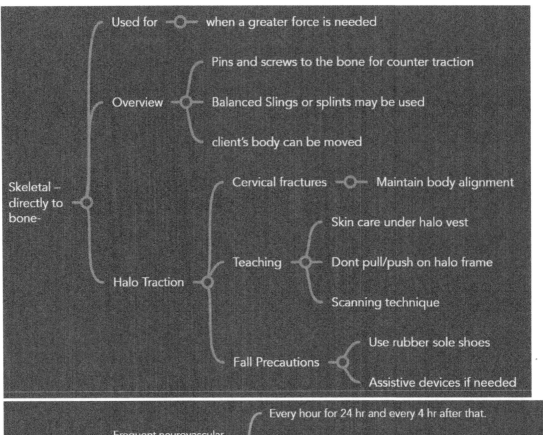

Skeletal – directly to bone-

- Used for — when a greater force is needed
- Overview
  - Pins and screws to the bone for counter traction
  - Balanced Slings or splints may be used
  - client's body can be moved
- Halo Traction
  - Cervical fractures — Maintain body alignment
  - Teaching
    - Skin care under halo vest
    - Dont pull/push on halo frame
    - Scanning technique
  - Fall Precautions
    - Use rubber sole shoes
    - Assistive devices if needed

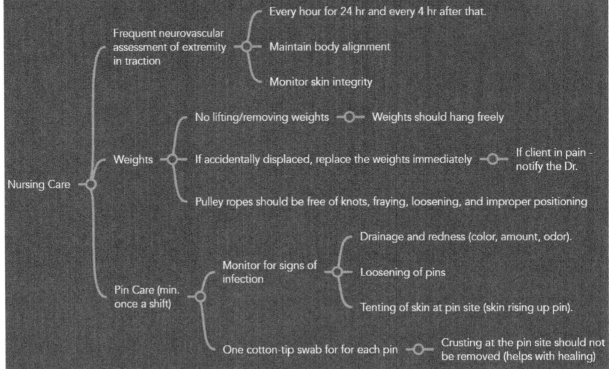

Nursing Care

- Frequent neurovascular assessment of extremity in traction
  - Every hour for 24 hr and every 4 hr after that.
  - Maintain body alignment
  - Monitor skin integrity
- Weights
  - No lifting/removing weights — Weights should hang freely
  - If accidentally displaced, replace the weights immediately — If client in pain - notify the Dr.
  - Pulley ropes should be free of knots, fraying, loosening, and improper positioning
- Pin Care (min. once a shift)
  - Monitor for signs of infection
    - Drainage and redness (color, amount, odor).
    - Loosening of pins
    - Tenting of skin at pin site (skin rising up pin).
  - One cotton-tip swab for for each pin — Crusting at the pin site should not be removed (helps with healing)

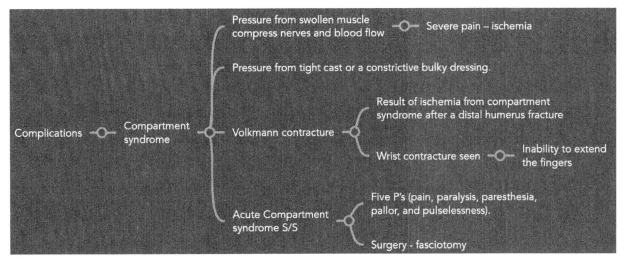

Open Reduction and Internal Fixation (ORIF)

- Visualization of a fracture through an incision in the skin, and internal fixation with plates, screws, pins, rods, and prosthetics as needed.
- After the bone heals, the hardware may be removed, depending on the location and type of hardware.
- Care: Skin integrity, prevent complications
- Skin breakdown – position, mobility, skin care, nutrition

Complications

- DVT and PE - Prevention
  - Anticoagulants
  - Early Ambulation
- Fat embolism – minimize movement
  - When a long bone is fractured, pressure within the bone marrow leads to release of fat globules into the bloodstream.
  - Cutaneous petechiae –on the neck, chest, upper arms, and abdomen (from the blockage of the capillaries by the fat globules).
  - Only in fat embolism. This is a discriminating finding from pulmonary embolism and is a late sign.
- Osteomyelitis

Spinal Abnormalities

- Terms for abnormal spinal curvatures
  - Scoliosis – Exaggerated **lateral** (side)curvature
  - Kyphosis – Exaggerated curvature of the **thoracic spine** (common among older adults)
  - Lordosis – Exaggerated curvature of the **lumbar spine** (common during the toddler years and pregnancy)

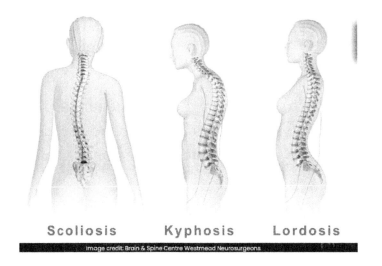

Scoliosis   Kyphosis   Lordosis

Image credit: Brain & Spine Centre Westmead Neurosurgeons

Braces and Care

- Braces **do not cure -** but prevent further worsening
- Worn around the trunk of the body under the client's outer clothing.
- Wear cotton t-shirt under the brace to decrease skin irritation and absorb sweat.
- Compliance/psychological support for children (Conformity issues)
- Types
  - The Boston brace
  - Wilmington brace
  - Thoracolumbosacral orthosis (TLSO) brace
  - Milwaukee brace: should be worn about 23 hours a day. Ok to be out for 1 hour –showering/ exercising

Spinal immobilization

- Indications
    - Abnormal neurological findings (Paresthesia)
    - Mechanism of injury (fall/accident)
    - Tenderness/ Painful over the spine.
    - Pain: patient may not report pain if: -
    - Change in LOC (Level of consciousness)
    - Intoxication (impaired decision making/lack of awareness)
    - Distracting injury (another big injury somewhere- lose focus)

Peroneal Nerve Injury

- Can happen with knee/leg fracture, dislocation, degenerative neurological issues (ALS, MS, Parkinson's)
- Peroneal nerve branches from the sciatic nerve and provides sensation to the front and sides of the legs and to the top of the feet.
- S/S: Tingling, Numbness (leg, thigh, toes),
    - Tripping or being clumsy (Difficulty moving foot in different directions)
    - Foot drop: the affected foot drags on the floor.
    - Weakness in pointing foot/toes up toward ceiling. Difficulty walking.
    - Muscle loss (atrophy) in the outer edge of the leg.

Crutches and Care

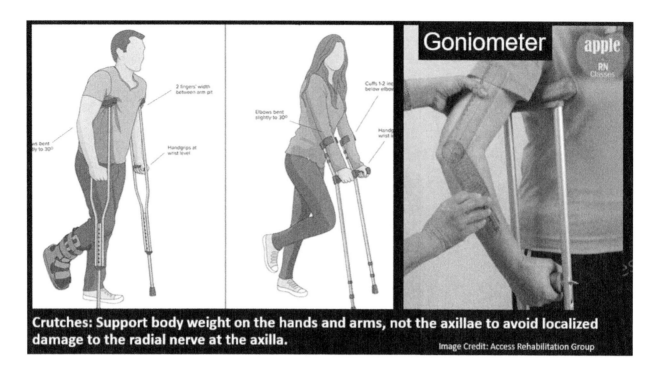

Crutches: Support body weight on the hands and arms, not the axillae to avoid localized damage to the radial nerve at the axilla.

Image Credit: Access Rehabilitation Group

Crutch walking

- Four-point gait (Reciprocal walking – each leg moved separately)
    - WB on both legs, Slow gait, maximal support
    - Move each foot and crutch forward separately
    - Right crutch-left foot- left crutch-right foot
- Two-point gait (reciprocal)
    - Partial WB on each foot – opposite leg and opposite crutch moved together
    - Move Lt crutch and Rt foot forward together; move Rt crutch and Lt foot forward together
- Three-point gait (Swing –to-gait / Swing – through- gait: moving both legs together)
    - Two crutches and unaffected leg bear weight alternatively
    - Weaker leg and both crutches move together, followed by stronger leg

Crutch Walking Stairs

- Sitting or standing from chair – hold crutches on affected side- hand.
- Need to use unaffected hand for holding chair
- Going Up Stairs - UP WITH GOOD FIRST
  - Weight on crutches and move good leg into step
  - Transfer weight to good (unaffected) leg and move crutches and bad (affected) leg together
- Going Downstairs - DOWN WITH BAD FIRST
  - Transfer weight to good (unaffected) leg
  - Move crutches and bad (affected) leg together to first downward step
  - Transfer weight on crutches and move good leg into step

Cane

- Cane length should equal the distance from the greater trochanter to the floor. Elbow bent slightly (15 degree)
- Maintain two points of support on the ground at all times.
- Keep the cane on the stronger side (unaffected) of the body.
- Support body weight on both legs, move the cane forward six inches (lateral to fifth toe) while advancing the weaker leg.
- Move the stronger leg after.

Some Terms

- Ankylosis – Stiffness and fixation of a joint
- Ankylosing spondylitis: Inflammatory rheumatic disorder of spine – stiff/fused spinal joints– bamboo spine- do stretching and breathing exercise daily
- Ataxia – Staggering, uncoordinated gait
- Tennis elbow – Lateral epicondylitis: Dull ache along outer aspect of elbow, worsens with twisting and grasping movements.
- Subluxation- partial dislocation of joint

Total Knee Replacement

- Implantation of a device to substitute for the knee joint
- Postoperative interventions: Monitor for infection
- Continuous passive motion (CPM) as prescribed: CPM provides passive range of motion from full extension to the prescribed amount of flexion
- Avoid weight-bearing as prescribed and instruct in crutch-walking

Amputation of a Lower Extremity

- Below-knee amputation (BKA) /above-knee amputation (AKA)
- Postoperative interventions
    - Keep tourniquet at bedside
    - Elevate foot of bed to control edema (first 24 hrs.).
    - Evaluate phantom limb sensation, pain
- Rehabilitation
    - Instruct in crutch-walking, range of motion and upper body strengthening
    - Prepare residual limb for prosthesis
    - The patient lies in the prone position several times daily to prevent flexion contractures of the hip (after first 24-48 hrs.)
    - Do not use lotion on the stump.
    - The residual limb should not be elevated – to prevent flexion contracture

Osteoporosis

- Demineralization of bone, Fragile bone, and fractures

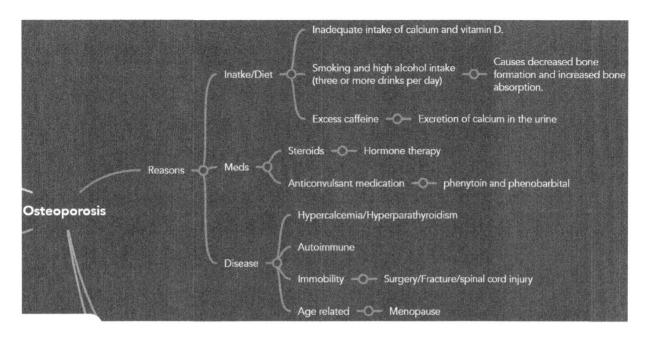

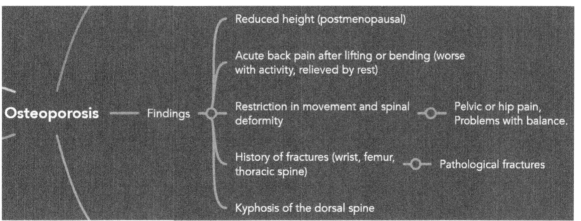

- Colles' fracture and Smith Fracture: Common with osteoporosis (when falling)

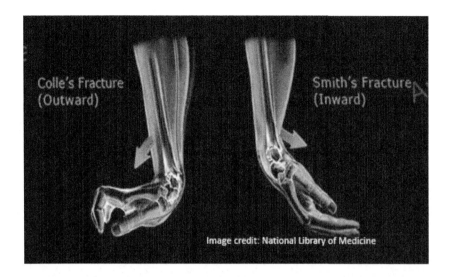

Image credit: National Library of Medicine

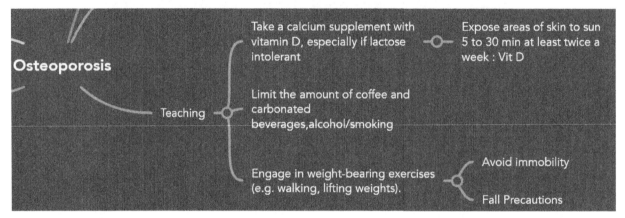

Osteomyelitis

- Osteomyelitis: Infection of the bone, bone marrow and surrounding soft tissue. Most common: Staphylococcus aureus.
- Bone pain that is constant, pulsating, localized, and worse with movement.
- Erythema and edema at the site of the infection
- Osteomyelitis is caused by bacteria and frequently is found after an internal infection, such as an ear infection.
- Bone scan/radioisotope /gallium scan. Laxative may be given.
  - Flush toilet three times after use
- Treatment: Chronic: Long course (3 months) of IV and oral antibiotic therapy, Hyperbaric oxygen treatments, if fails, amputation

Hip Fracture

- S/S: external rotation, shortened extremity, pain, muscle spasm
- Maintain alignment - prevent internal or external rotation
- Turn client to unaffected side (affected side if prescribed only)
- Avoid weight bearing on affected leg. Use walker to avoid WB
- Avoid hip flexion greater than 90 degrees, avoid low chairs when out of bed.
- Neurovascular assessment of affected extremity: check color, pulses, capillary refill, movement, and sensation
- Instruct client to avoid crossing legs and activities that require bending over

Hip Fracture Client Teaching

- Do not bend the hip more than 90 degrees
- Do not cross legs or feet
- Do not roll or lie on your unoperated side for the first 6 weeks
- Do not twist the upper body when standing
- Sleep on the back for the first 6 weeks
- The patient may benefit from a shower chair or elevated seat for home use
- Avoid bathing for 8 to 12 weeks (flexed and bent down in the tub)
- Use aids to put on underwear/socks/shoes for 6 weeks to avoid deep hip flexion angles - never bend at the waist more than 90 degree

Rheumatoid Arthritis (RA)

- Chronic systemic inflammatory disease that leads to destruction of connective tissue and synovial membrane within joints
- Assessment
    - Inflammation, tenderness, and stiffness of joints
    - Moderate to severe pain with morning stiffness lasting longer than 30 minutes
- Rheumatoid factor: A blood test used to diagnose rheumatoid arthritis
- Pain – more with morning stiffness
- Physical mobility: Finger/hand deformity: (Swan neck and boutonnière)

- A balanced diet and weight control are important
- Range of motion exercises -more effective after warm bath/shower- decrease stiffness - flexibility.
- NSAID- take with food
-

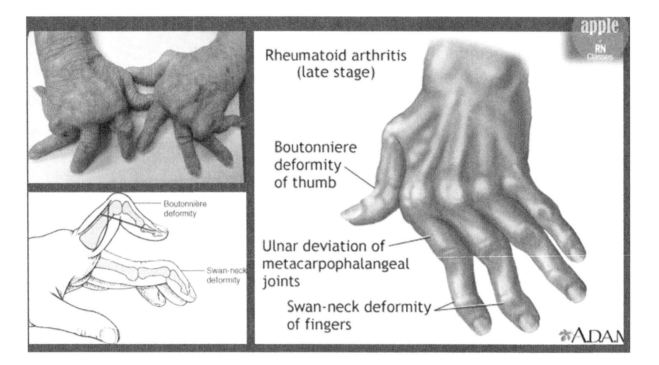

Client Teaching Points for RA

- Maintain joint in neutral position to minimize deformity.
- Use strongest joint available for any task
- Distribute weight over many joints rather than few – don't lift, slide
- Change positions frequently, Avoid repetitious movements
- Modify chores to avoid stress on joints – sit instead of standing when cooking/ talking
- Nursing Points: OK to use Inspection, Palpation, and strength testing. No ROM- on swollen stiff joints – this will increase pain

Juvenile Idiopathic Arthritis (JIA)

- A chronic autoimmune inflammatory disease affecting joints and other tissues.
- Physical Assessment Findings
    - Joint swelling, stiffness: worse in the morning or after naps
    - Fever, Rash, enlarged lymph nodes, Delayed growth
    - Uveitis: eye inflammation and swelling that can destroy eye tissues: Need regular eye exams

Interventions

- Pain management – relaxation techniques, nonpharmacological therapy, analgesics
- Exercise: PT, encourage activity as tolerated.
    - Apply heat or warm moist packs to the child's affected joints prior to exercise.
- Teach parents to apply splints for nighttime sleep. Splints should be applied to knees, wrists, and hands to decrease pain and prevent flexion deformities.
    - Encourage proper positioning with sleep, provide firm mattress and discourage use of pillows under knees.
    - Use no pillow or/ flat pillow for head
- Encourage the use of electric blankets or sleeping bags for extra warmth.

Osteoarthritis (Degenerative Joint Disease)

- A progressive degeneration of joints as a result of wear and tear that causes formation of bony buildup and loss of articular cartilage in joints
- Assessment
    - Joint pain that diminishes after rest, intensifies after activity.
    - Crepitus, Physical mobility issues: Heberden's and Bouchard's nodes
    - Not much systemic involvement like RA.

Septic arthritis (infectious arthritis)

- Acute joint inflammation due to an infection.
- Severe, pulsating pain, usually with sudden onset and exacerbated by movement
- Pathogens may enter the joint from the bloodstream, direct penetration (e.g., intraarticular injection), or infected adjacent tissue (e.g., osteomyelitis).
- Septic arthritis can lead to irreversible joint damage

Gout

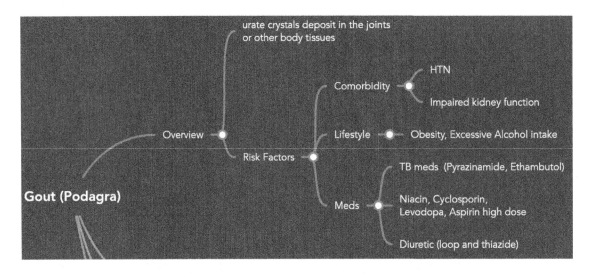

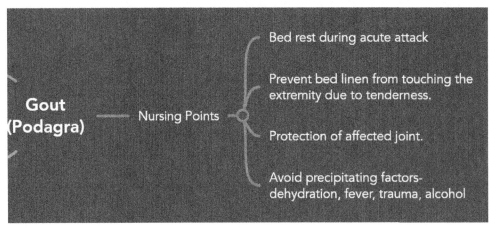

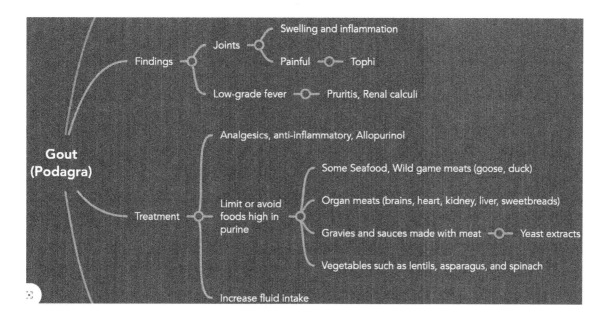

Carpel Tunnel Syndrome

- Pain, numbness, and tingling in the hand and arm due to median nerve compression
- Tinel's sign
- Phalen's sign

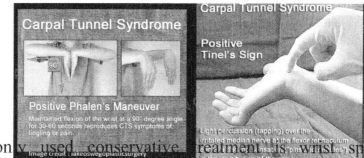

- The most commonly used conservative treatment is wrist splinting, particularly at nighttime. Splinting of the wrist prevents excessive flexion or extension, which could narrow the carpal tunnel.

Sprains and Strains

- Sprain – A stretch and/or tear of a ligament
- Ligaments – connects bone to bone
- Tendons- attach muscle to bone
- Strain – A twist, pull and/or tear that may involve both muscles and tendons
- Nursing care: Assess – neurovascular
    - RICE approach to recovery
    - Rest, Ice, Compression elastic bandage, Elevate

- Ligaments and tendon have relatively poor blood supply – take more time to heal.

Paget's disease of bone

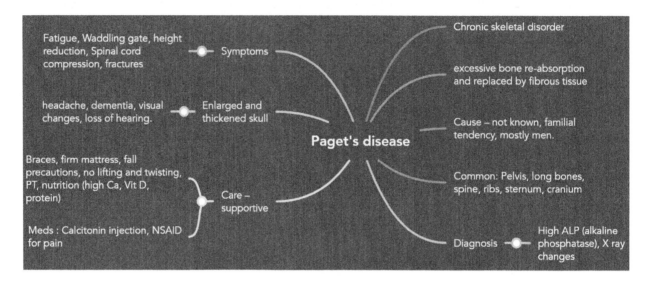

Clubfoot

- A complex deformity of the ankle and foot. Series of castings starting shortly after birth
- ROM exercise, Assess neurovascular status. Perform cast care- keep dry, assess, elevate foot. Monitor growth and development

Legg-Calve-Perthes Disease

- Aseptic necrosis of the femoral head (lack of blood supply)
- Can be unilateral or bilateral.
- Subjective and Objective Data
  - Intermittent painless limp, Hip stiffness, Limited ROM,
  - Thigh pain, Shortening of the affected leg, Muscle wasting,
- Maintain rest and non-weightbearing (crutches)
- Need crutches/braces/cast/traction/surgery as needed

Duchenne muscular dystrophy

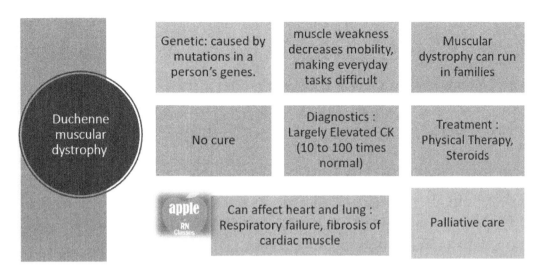

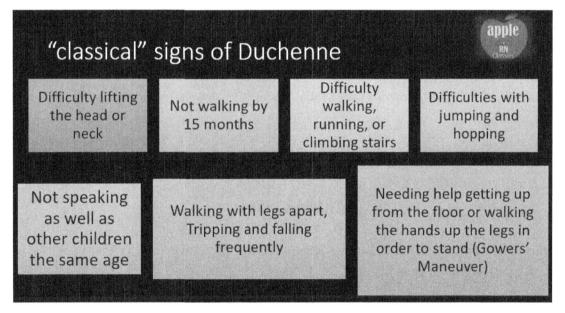

Developmental dysplasia of the hip

- A variety of disorders resulting in abnormal development of the hip structures that can affect infants or children.
- Infant
    - Asymmetry of gluteal and thigh folds
    - Limited hip abduction
    - Shortening of the femur (knows as Galeazzi sign/Allis sign)

- Positive Ortolani test (hip is reduced by abduction)
- Positive Barlow test (hip is dislocated by adduction)
- Child
  - One leg shorter than the other
  - Walking on toes on one foot, Walk with a limp

Pavlic Harness- points

- It keeps infant's hips slightly flexed and abducted.
- Skin Assessment: 2-3 times daily
- Lightly massage skin under the straps daily to promote circulation
- Dress: Shirt and knee socks under the harness to protect the skin
- Apply diapers underneath the straps - keep the harness clean and dry. No lotions.
- Always leave the harness on, unless said by the HCP
- Pavlik harnesses are typically worn for 3-5 months or until the hip joint is stable. (Afterwards spica cast/ surgery)
- Straps assessed and adjusted only by health care provider every 1-2 weeks

Musculoskeletal Medications

Muscle Relaxants

- Act directly on neuromuscular junction or indirectly on CNS
- Centrally acting muscle relaxants: diazepam, Baclofen, Cyclobenzaprine, Tizanidine
- Peripherally acting muscle relaxants: dantrolene
- Contraindicated in clients with severe liver, renal, heart disease
- Side effects: Drowsiness, Dizziness, Muscle weakness, Hypotension
- Interventions: Assess involved joints, muscles for pain, mobility. Monitor liver and renal function test results, instruct client to take with food
- Nursing considerations
  - Dantrolene: Liver damage most serious adverse effect. Instruct client to notify physician if rash, bloody, tarry stool, jaundice develops

- Cyclobenzaprine (Flexeril): Contraindicated in clients receiving MAO inhibitors within 14 days of initiation of cyclobenzaprine therapy
- Methocarbamol (Robaxin): Parenteral form can cause hypotension, bradycardia, anaphylaxis, seizures
  - May turn urine brown, black, or green. Inform client to notify physician if blurred vision, nasal congestion, urticaria, rash develops

Nursing consideration:

- Tizanidine (Zanaflex) – Hepatotoxic – Obtain LFT
- Baclofen (Lioresal): S/E – constipation, N/V, Urinary retention
  - Can be administered by physician via intrathecal infusion
  - increase intake of high-fiber foods. Monitor I/O
- All muscle relaxants and antispasmodics: CNS depression (sleepiness, lightheadedness, fatigue)
- Advise clients to avoid hazardous activities, such as driving and concurrent use of other CNS depressants, including alcohol.

Antigout Medications

- Allopurinol (Zyloprim): can increase effects of warfarin &oral hypoglycemic agents
- Side effects: Blood dyscrasias, Uric acid kidney stones, Hypersensitivity reaction, fever, and rash, eye pain

Nursing Consideration:

- Maintain fluid intake of at least 2000 to 3000 mL/day
- Do not take large doses of vitamin C concurrently- interaction
- Avoid foods high in purine (red meat, scallops, cream sauces). Instruct client to take with food – GI distress
- Have yearly eye exam. Minimize exposure to sunlight.
- Do not take aspirin concurrently- interaction. Use acetaminophen (Tylenol) instead of aspirin

Antiarthritic Medications

- Inflammation control is key to preserving joint function
- Nonsteroidal anti-inflammatory medications (NSAIDs).
  - Ibuprofen (Motrin, Advil), Diclofenac, Indomethacin, Meloxicam, Naproxen, Celecoxib (Celebrex)

Disease-modifying antirheumatic drugs (DMARDs)

- They slow joint degeneration and progression of rheumatoid arthritis.
- Full therapeutic effect will take several months.
- Etanercept, Infliximab, Adalimumab, Rituximab
- Hydroxychloroquine sulfate (Plaquenil) (antimalarial drug)
  - S/E – Retinal damage – Eye exam. Report blurred vision
- Methotrexate
  - S/E: Hepatotoxic, Bone marrow suppression, GI issues
  - Prevent infection, Baseline CBC, LFT
  - Inspect mouth, gums, and throat daily for ulcerations, bleeding, or color changes. Report Anorexia, abdominal fullness
  - Take the medication with food or a full glass of water
- Gold salts
  - Monitor client for 30 minutes after injection for anaphylaxis, allergic reaction
  - Teach client about signs and symptoms of gold toxicity. If toxicity develops, dimercaprol (BAL in Oil) may be prescribed

Calcium

- Calcium citrate, Calcium carbonate (Tums, Rolaids), Calcium acetate
- For IV: Calcium chloride, Calcium gluconate
- Monitor serum calcium levels to maintain between 9.0 to 10.5 mg/dL.
- Spinach, rhubarb, bran, and whole grains may decrease calcium absorption.

Raloxifene

- Work like estrogen. Decreases bone reabsorption
- Prevent and treat postmenopausal osteoporosis and prevent spinal fractures in female clients
- S/E: Hot flashes, Increases risk for PE and DVT
- Clients should undergo a bone density scan every 12 to 18 months
- Monitor liver function tests. Raloxifene levels may be increased in clients with hepatic impairment.
- Encourage clients to perform weight-bearing exercises daily, such as walking 30 to 40 min each day.

Alendronate (Fosamax):

- Decrease the number and action of osteoclasts and inhibits bone resorption.
- Other Medications: Ibandronate (Boniva), Risedronate (Actonel), zoledronic
- S/E: Esophagitis, GI disturbances, Visual disturbances,
- Instruct client to sit upright or ambulate for 30 min after taking this medication orally.
- Take the medication first thing in the morning after getting out of bed.
- Take with lots of water, but no food or calcium tablets together

Integumentary System

- Largest sensory organ of body
  - Function: First line of defense against infections, protection, receives stimuli, regulate temperature, fluid, and electrolyte balance (excrete water, salt, waste), synthesize vit D, store nutrients
- 3 Layers:
  - Epidermis- Outer -waterproof barrier
  - Dermis –Hair follicles and sweat glands.
  - Hypodermis -fat and connective tissue (subcutaneous)
- Epidermal appendages: Nails, hair, glands
- Normal bacterial flora is helpful

Skin Diagnostic Studies

- Wood's light examination
  - Ultraviolet light – produce specific colors -? skin infection.
  - Dark room

Skin culture and sensitivity

- Culture refers to isolation of the pathogen on culture media. Sensitivity refers to the effect that antimicrobial agents have on the micro-organism.
- A culture and sensitivity can be done on a sample of purulent drainage from a skin lesion. Viral culture? place sample on ice.
- Cultures should be done prior to initiating antimicrobial therapy. Results of a culture and sensitivity test usually are available preliminarily within 24 to 48 hr, and final results in 72 hr.
- Indications
  - Skin lesions, which may be infectious, may appear raised, reddened, edematous, and/or warm. There may be purulent drainage and/or fever.
  - Infected wound with pus? – first irrigate it with saline- to get from wound bed

Contact dermatitis

- Elevate extremity to reduce edema
- Apply cool, wet dressings as prescribed
- Poison ivy & poison
- Cleanse skin of plant oils immediately (urushiol)

Psoriasis

- Scaly, dermal patches (silvery) - by an overproduction of keratin.
- Autoimmune disorder - periods of exacerbations and remissions.
- Can also affect the joints, causing arthritis-type changes and pain.
- Treatments: - Meds- antihistamines, antibiotic, steroids, chemo meds, phototherapy (UVL)
- Skin Care:
    - Not to scratch affected areas, lubricate skin to minimize itching.
    - Pat dry (no rubbing), Apply emollient lotions immediately after bath
    - Use antibacterial soaps for handwashing
    - Avoid wool or constrictive clothing (itching, trap sweats)

Eczema (Atopic dermatitis)

- Inflammatory skin disorder, unknown cause
- Main s/s: pruritus, erythema, and dry skin.
- Triggers – stress, humidity, allergens, irritants (soap, detergent, wool)
- Red raised lesions start from cheek, spread to forehead, arm and legs.
- Identify and control triggers, keep skin dry and lubricated. – Tepid bath, Pat dry, apply emollient
- Skin care as psoriasis
- Infants- keep fingernails clean and short, place cotton gloves or socks to prevent scratching.

Impetigo

- Highly contagious bacterial infection of skin
- Caused by beta-hemolytic streptococci, staphylococci, or both
- Assessment: Lesions: Honey color crust; pruritus; burning; secondary lymph node involvement
- Interventions
    - Contact isolation, teach to prevent spread of infection
    - Inform of need to use separate towels, linens, dishes
    - All linens, clothes of infected client need to be washed with detergent and hot water, separately from others in family
    - Administer topical and oral antibiotics as prescribed-Scabs or crusts must be carefully removed for the antibiotic ointment to be effective.
    - Apply warm compresses to lesions 2 or 3 times/day as prescribed

Pediculosis Capitis (Lice):

- Infestation of hair and scalp with lice
- Assessment intense pruritus; small gray specks in hair; visible nits, firmly attached to hair shaft near scalp
- Interventions
    - Pediculicide- Do not use a combination shampoo/conditioner, or conditioner before using lice medicine. Do not re–wash the hair for 1–2 days after the lice medicine is removed.
    - Permethrin (Nix)
        - Bedding, clothing used by child should be changed daily, laundered in hot water with detergent, dried in hot dryer for 20mts
        - Seal toys that cannot be washed or dried in plastic bag for 2 weeks
        - Teach child not to share clothing, headwear, brushes, combs

Scabies

- Parasitic skin disorder caused by infestation of Sarcoptes scabiei (itch mite)
- Assessment: Intense pruritus, especially at night; burrows (straight or wavy lines) beneath skin

Interventions

- Scabicide- Lindane should not be used in children younger than 2 years (neurotoxic/seizures)
- Household members, contacts of infected child need to be treated at same time.
- Instruct parents that all clothing, bedding used by child need to be changed daily, washed in hot water and detergent, dried in hot dryer, ironed before reuse for 1 week
- Instruct parents that non-washable toys, other items should be sealed in plastic bags for 4 days

Toxic Epidermal Necrolysis

- Cause: medication reaction
- S/S: erythema, blistering, skin erosion and shedding, eye inflammation, sepsis
- Management:
  - Wound care: Sterile, moist dressings
  - Eye care: Sterile, cool compresses, Lubricants
  - Reverse isolation
  - Fluids, nutrition, Prevent hypothermia (warm room)

Skin Disorders

- Paronychia: Infection of tissue around nail plate,
- Assist client with warm soaks as prescribed
- Folliculitis: Deep bacterial inflammation of hair follicles caused by Staphylococcus, Give Antibiotics

- Boils- Folliculitis with pus:
- Apply warm compresses as prescribed until drainage occurs

Acne vulgaris

- Administer topical or oral antibiotics as prescribed
- Administer Isotretinoin (Accutane) or other medications as prescribed
  - Made with Vit A. (do not take extra vitamin A)
  - Vitamin A toxicity (increased ICP, GI upset, liver damage, and changes in skin and nails)
  - Monitor triglyceride levels (med elevate trig level)
  - No Blood donation up to a month after treatment ends.
  - Teratogenic – birth defects – No pregnancy: Encourage client to take 2 forms of contraception to prevent pregnancy.

Frostbite

- Numbness and paresthesia; may progress to necrosis, gangrene
- Re-warm affected tissue rapidly, continuously with warm water (immerse for about thirty mts) or use warm washcloths
- Avoid debriding blisters

Pressure ulcer

- Prevention of skin breakdown major role of nurse
- Risk factors: malnutrition, incontinence, immobility, decreased sensory perception
- Institute measures to prevent pressure ulcers
- Stage 1: Ulcer is reddened area; returns to normal color after 15 to 20 minutes of pressure relief
- Stage 2: Ulcer is area with top layer of skin missing; shallow with pink-red base; white-yellow eschar may be present
- Stage 3: Deep ulcer; extends into dermis, subcutaneous tissue; white-gray-yellow eschar usually present at bottom of ulcer; purulent drainage common

- Stage 4: Deep ulcer; extends into muscle, bone; foul-smelling; brown or black eschar present; purulent drainage common
- Risk Score for pressure ulcer- Braden Scale
- Very High Risk: Total Score 9 or less
- High Risk: Total Score 10-12
- Moderate Risk: Total Score 13-14
- Mild Risk: Total Score 15-18
- No Risk: Total Score 19-23

Braden Risk Assessment Scale
(abridged version)

Sensory Perception	1 Completely limited	2 Very limited	3 Slightly limited	4 No impairment
Moisture	1 Constantly moist	2 Very moist	3 Occasionally moist	4 No impairment
Activity	1 Bedfast	2 Chairfast	3 Walks Occasionally	4 Walks frequently
Mobility	1 Completely immobile	2 Very limited	3 Slightly limited	4 No limitation
Nutrition	1 Very poor	2 Probably inadequate	3 Adequate	4 Excellent
Friction & Shear	1 Problem	2 Potential problem	3 No apparent problem	

Image credit: Ecri.org

Skin integrity and wound care

- Isotonic saline or wound cleansers to clean
- Warm or body temperature solutions
- Clean wound at every dressing change if contaminated
- Avoid cotton balls – shed fibers. Use gauze
- Daily assessment
- Nutrition and mobility
- High-protein nutritional supplements (1.25-1.5 g/kg/day)

Preventive methods

- The primary focus: optimal nutrition and hydration.
- Assess all clients regularly: Braden scale.
- Keep skin clean, dry, and intact.
- Bathe with tepid water (not hot) and minimal scrubbing.
- Reposition, Ambulate, raise heels off the bed, Avoid donut pillows
- Lift patient don't pull or push (reduce friction). Use Hoyer lift
- Use pressure-reducing surfaces and devices.
- Provide a firm, wrinkle-free foundation with wrinkle-free linens.
- Lab test – albumin, vitamins, nutrients

Scleroderma

- Overproduction of collagen: tight and hard skin and connective tissue.
- No cure.
- Heartburn and dysphagia are common
- Complications
    - Raynaud phenomenon (vasospasm)
    - Pulmonary fibrosis
    - Renal crisis (life-threatening): Malignant hypertension

Burns

- Thermal burns: exposure to flames, steam, or hot liquids.
    - (CDC: Hot water heaters should be set at 120° F (to minimize the growth of Legionella. A hotter water temperature of 130–140°F can kill many harmful germs, but also increases the risk of scalding.)
- Chemical burns: occur when there is exposure to a caustic agent. (Drain cleaner, bleach) and agents used in the industrial setting (caustic soda, sulfuric acid)
- Electrical burns: loss of organ function, tissue destruction with subsequent need for amputation of a limb, and cardiac and/or respiratory arrest.

- Radiation burns: most frequently occur as a result of therapeutic treatment for cancer or from sunburn.

Burn Process

- Injured tissue releases vasoactive substances – they let plasma to come out of capillaries into surrounding tissues – causing edema (but reduced circulatory volume – reduced organ perfusion- decreased cardiac output)
- Metabolism increases to maintain body heat- more need for O2
- The severity of the burn is based on:
    - Percentage of total body surface area (TBSA)
    - Depth of the burn – Burns are classified according to the layers of skin and tissue involved.
    - Body location of the burn – In areas where the skin is thinner, there is more damage to underlying tissue (any part of the face, hand, perineum, feet).

Burn Assessments

- Rule of Nines – Quick method to approximate the extent of burn by dividing the body into multiples of nine. The total of the sum is equal to the total body surface area (TBSA). This determines the measurement and the extent of the burn.
- Lund and Browder Method – A more exact method estimating the extent of burn by the percentage of surface area of anatomic parts. Dividing body into smaller parts and providing a TBSA for each body part, an estimate of TBSA can be determined.
- Palmer Method – Quick method to approximate scattered burns using the palm of the client's hand. The palm of the client's hand (excluding the fingers) is equal to 0.5% TBSA. This method can be used for all age groups.

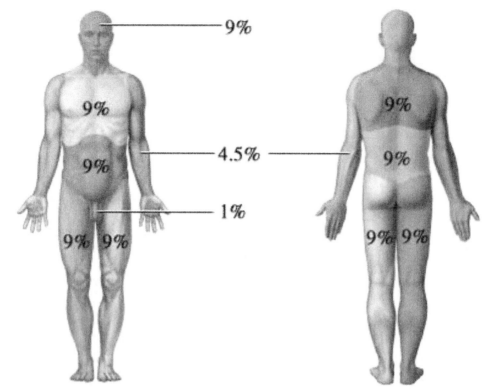

Image Credit: health.state.mn.us

Fluid Formula

- Parkland Formula using Lactated Ringers fluid
- Volume of LR = 4ml * % burned body surface area * Weight of client in Kg
- Give half of the volume in the first 8 hours. The rest through next 16 hours

Depth of Burn:

- Epidermis – superficial (1st degree)
- Dermis – partial thickness (superficial/deep) (2-degree) with blisters
- Hypodermis- Full thickness- (nerve endings may get affected – may not be painful) (3rd degree)

- Goes beyond skin- to muscles, tissues -Deep full thickness (4th degree)

ASSESS DEPTH OF INJURY		
AREA INVOLVED/APPEARANCE	SENSATION/HEALING	EXAMPLE
Superficial – damage to epidermis		
› Pink to red, tender, no blisters, mild edema, and no eschar	› Painful › Heals within 3 to 6 days › No scarring	› Sunburn
Superficial partial thickness – damage to the entire epidermis and some parts of the dermis		
› Pink to red, blisters, mild to moderate edema, and no eschar	› Painful › Heals within 10 to 21 days › No scarring	› Flame or burn scalds
Deep partial thickness – damage to entire epidermis and deep into the dermis		
› Red to white, with moderate edema, free of blisters, and soft and dry eschar	› Painful and sensitive to touch › Heals within 3 to 6 weeks › Scarring likely › Possible grafting involved	› Flame and burn scalds › Grease, tar, or chemical burns › Exposure to hot objects for prolonged time

ASSESS DEPTH OF INJURY		
AREA INVOLVED/APPEARANCE	SENSATION/HEALING	EXAMPLE
Full thickness – damage to the entire epidermis and dermis, and may extend into the subcutaneous tissue. Nerve damage also occurs.		
› Red to tan, black, brown, or white › Free from blisters, severe edema, and hard and inelastic eschar	› Pain may or may not be present › As burn heals, painful sensations return and severity of pain increases › Heals within weeks to months › Scarring › Grafting required	› Burn scalds › Grease, tar, chemical, or electrical burns › Exposure to hot objects for prolonged time
Deep full thickness – damage to all layers of skin and extends to muscle, tendons and bones		
› Black, no edema	› Heals within weeks to months › Scarring › Grafting required	› Chemical burns

Source: ATI nursing education

Management of Burn

- Extensive burns result in generalized edema, decreased circulating intravascular blood volume, leading to hypotension.
- Fluid replacement is important during the first 24 hr. (LR)
- Hypovolemia and shock may result when injury to at least 20% to 30% TBSA occurs.
- Decrease in organ perfusion secondary to fluid losses – oliguria
- urine output is the greatest indicator of adequate fluid resuscitation.
- Laboratory Tests – Due to fluid shift,
- First 24 hrs.: - H&H and K High, Na-Low
- 48 to 72 hr after injury- H&H, K and Na-Low; Glucose-high

Minor Burns

- Stop the burning process.
- Remove clothing or jewelry that might conduct heat (If not stuck to skin)
- In a chemical burn injury, the burning process continues as long as the chemical is in contact with the skin.
- All clothing, including gloves and shoes, is immediately removed and water lavage is instituted before and during the transport to the emergency department.
- Apply cool water soaks or run cool water over injury; do not use ice.
- Flush chemical burns with large volume of water.
- Cover the burn with clean cloth to prevent contamination and hypothermia.
- Provide warmth. No butter, ointment, lotion etc.
- Provide analgesics. Cleanse with mild soap and tepid water (avoid excess friction).
- Use antimicrobial ointment - if prescribed by a health care provider.
- Apply dressing (nonadherent, hydrocolloid) if the burn area is irritated by clothing.
- Educate the family to avoid using greasy lotions or butter on burn.
- Educate family to monitor for evidence of infection.
- Check immunization status for tetanus and determine need for immunization

Moderate and Major Burns

- Maintain airway and ventilation.
- A nasogastric tube may be indicated for clients at risk for aspiration.
- Assist client to cough and deep breathe every hour.
- Suction every hour or as needed. Keep the head of bed elevated at all times.
- Provide humidified supplemental oxygen as prescribed.
- Monitor vital signs. Pain management. Avoid IM or subcutaneous injections
- Maintain cardiac output – IV fluids, Blood products, Albumin.
- Monitor for manifestations of shock.
  - Alterations in sensorium (confusion), Increased capillary refill time
  - Urine output less than 30 mL/hr, Rapid elevations of temperature
  - Decreased bowel sounds
- Psychological Support of Client and Family
- Prevent Infection
- Nutrition – High Calorie, High Protein, TPN
- NPO till bowel sound returns- then start with clear liquids.

Restoration of Mobility

- Maintain correct body alignment, splint extremities, and facilitate position changes to prevent contractures.
- Maintain active and passive range of motion.
- Assist with ambulation as soon as the client is stable.
- Apply pressure dressings to prevent contractures and scarring.
- Monitor areas at high risk for pressure sores (heels, sacrum, back of head).

Wound Care

- Hyperbaric Oxygen - By helping the body fight infection, hyperbaric oxygen can improve healing, lessen damage from infection, and thereby decrease the chance of death associated with severe burns
- Biologic skin coverings: promote healing of large burns, reduce pain by covering nerve endings, help in retaining water and proteins.

- Hydrotherapy – Place the client in a warm tub of water or use warm running water, as if to shower, to cleanse the wound.
  - 30 mts max (to prevent heat loss/sodium loss/pain). Use mild soap or detergent to gently wash burns and then rinse with room-temperature water. Whirlpool: for the removal of necrotic cellular debris

Wound Graft

- Autografting: Permanent coverage created from client's own unburned skin
- Allograft -homograft – human tissue (cadaver/postmortem)
- Xenograft – heterograft – animal tissue (pig)
- Care of graft site: Elevate, immobilize site; keep free from pressure; monitor for signs of infection; protect site from direct sunlight
- Care of donor site: Moist gauze dressing as prescribed; keep site clean, dry; keep free from pressure; educate client not to scratch site; apply lubricating lotions to healed site as prescribed

Rehabilitation phase

- Begins after the client's wounds have fully healed and lasts about 12 months
- Counseling or other psychosocial support
- Gentle massage with water-based lotion to alleviate itching and minimize scarring. Planning for reconstructive surgery
- Pressure garments to prevent hypertrophic scars and promote circulation
- Range-of-motion exercises to prevent contractures
- Sunscreen and protective clothing to prevent sunburns and hyper pigmentation

Dressing materials for general wound care

Dressing Type	Feature	Best for
Transparent (see through)	Porous/allows passage of oxygen and moisture but does not let fluid and bacteria enter into wound.	Small, superficial wounds, peripheral and central IV insertion sites, stage I or II pressure ulcers or partial-thickness wounds such as skin tears
Hydrocolloid	Has gel forming agent, absorbs exudates from wound, waterproof, doesnot stick to wound, can be used on difficult to dress area like elbow (duoderm)	Deep dermal wounds, venous or arterial ulcers and pressure ulcers stage 3/4. No need to change everyday (3-4 days)
Hydrogel	Saturated with high water content gel, rehydrate the wound and maintain wound humidity, ok to use on infected wound, will need another dressing over it to cover	Partial- or full-thickness wounds, burns, deep or necrotic wounds or radiation-damaged skin, donor sites.
Alginate	forms a soft gel when mixed with wound fluid	Moderate to heavily draining wounds, partial- and full-thickness wounds, pressure ulcers, dermal wounds, surgical incisions or dehisced wounds, sinus tracts, tunnels, cavity wounds, and infected wounds.

Pediatric considerations

- Very young child with severe burn- higher mortality. Increased risk for fluid and heat loss, dehydration, metabolic acidosis versus adult. Scarring more severe in children. Burns involving more than 10% of total body surface area require some form of fluid resuscitation
- Parameters such as vital signs, urine output, adequacy of capillary filling, sensorium status determine adequacy of fluid resuscitation
- Extent of burn injury: Modified rule of nines may be used for pediatric population
- Pain management: Administer pain medications, including opioid analgesics prior to any procedure or activity involving high risk for pain

Hematological Concepts

Blood Cells Formation

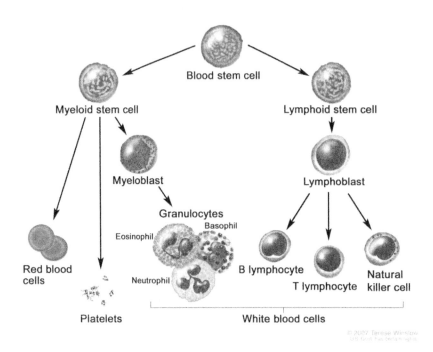

Bone Marrow Aspiration/Biopsy

- To diagnose causes of blood disorders, such as anemia or thrombocytopenia, or to rule-out diseases, such as leukemia and other cancers, and infection.
- Usual sites – Post. Sup. Iliac spine, Iliac Crust
- Nursing: Ensure consent, Hold anticoagulants

Blood Transfusion

Transfusion Types

- Homologous transfusions – Blood from donors is used.
- Autologous transfusions – The client's blood is collected in anticipation of future transfusions (elective surgery); this blood is designated for and can be used only by the client.
- Clients may donate blood 5 weeks in advance up to 72 hr prior to surgery.

- Intraoperative blood salvage – blood loss during certain surgeries can be recycled through a cell saver machine and transfused intraoperatively or postoperatively (orthopedic surgeries, Coronary Artery Bypass Graft).

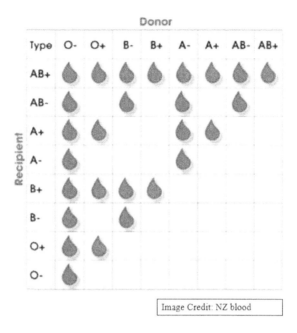

Image Credit: NZ blood

- The Rh system is based on a third antigen, D, which is also on the RBC membrane.
    - Rh-positive people have the D antigen, Rh-negative people do not.
    - A Coombs test is used to evaluate the person's Rh status.
- Rh and Pregnancy: RH Negative mothers are given Rho(D) immune globulin (RhoGAM) within 72 hours of birth of Rh-positive baby

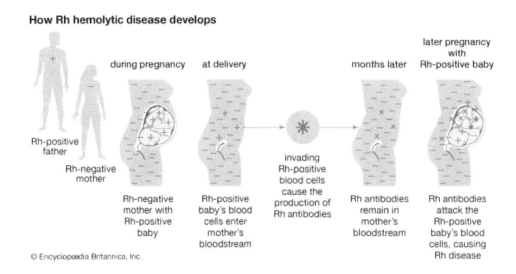

How Rh hemolytic disease develops

© Encyclopædia Britannica, Inc.

Blood Transfusion: Precautions and Nursing Responsibilities

- Need doctor's order
- Need Consent – Telephone consent (2 nurses)
- Type and Cross match, Initiate large-bore IV access
- Obtain blood products from the blood bank. Inspect the blood for discoloration, excessive bubbles, or cloudiness.
- Two RNs may check blood bag against client's blood identification band.
- Measure vital signs, lung sounds before and after 15 minutes of transfusion, then every hour until completed.
- Remain with the client for the first 15 to 30 min of the infusion
- Blood must be administered as soon as possible after being received from blood bank, within 20 to 30 minutes. Check blood bag for date of expiration; inspect bag for leaks, abnormal color, clots, bubbles
- Blood administration sets should be changed every 4 to 6 hours or according to agency policy
- Blood should not be infused rapidly unless platelets, which may be infused rapidly, with caution. No medications should be added to blood bag or piggybacked into blood transfusion
- Only normal saline should be infused or added to blood components

TRANSFUSION REACTIONS	
ONSET	SIGNS AND SYMPTOMS
Acute hemolytic	
› Immediate	› This reaction may be mild or life-threatening. Clinical findings include chills, fever, low back pain, tachycardia, flushing, hypotension, chest tightening or pain, tachypnea, nausea, anxiety, and hemoglobinuria. › This reaction may cause cardiovascular collapse, kidney failure, disseminated intravascular coagulation, shock, and death.
Febrile	
› 30 min to 6 hr after transfusion	› Clinical findings include chills, fever, flushing, headache, and anxiety. › Use WBC filter. Administer antipyretics.
Mild allergic	
› During or up to 24 hr after transfusion	› Clinical findings include itching, urticaria, and flushing. › Administer antihistamines, such as diphenhydramine (Benadryl).
Anaphylactic	
› Immediate	› Clinical findings include wheezing, dyspnea, chest tightness, cyanosis, and hypotension. › Maintain airway; administer oxygen, IV fluids, antihistamines, corticosteroids, and vasopressors.

Source: ATI nursing education

Transfusion Reaction Interventions

- Stop the transfusion.
- Keeping vein open with 0.9% normal saline. Notify physician and blood bank
- Monitor client closely, prepare to administer emergency medications (e.g., antihistamines, vasopressors, corticosteroids)
- Send urine specimen to laboratory
- Return all blood tubing and bags to blood bank,
- Document

Complications

- Disease Transmission – HIV, Hep C, Hep B, malaria
- Hyperkalemia
  - The older the blood, the greater the risk for hyperkalemia, because hemolysis causes potassium release
  - Monitor for muscle weakness, paresthesia, abdominal cramps, diarrhea, dysrhythmias

- Septicemia: Rapid onset of chills and high fever, vomiting, diarrhea, hypotension, shock
  - Obtain blood cultures and cultures from blood bag
  - Administer oxygen, IV fluids, antibiotics, vasopressors, and corticosteroids as prescribed
- Circulatory overload: Monitor for: cough, dyspnea, chest pain, wheezing, hypertension, tachycardia (fluid volume excess signs)
- Interventions
  - Slow rate of infusion, Place client upright with feet in dependent position, Notify physician
  - Administer oxygen, diuretics, and morphine sulfate as prescribed
  - Monitor for dysrhythmias

Anemia

- Anemias are due to:
  - Blood loss
  - Inadequate RBC production (renal failure, bone marrow depression, malignancy, radiation)
  - Increased RBC destruction (hemolytic, sickle cell, autoimmune disorder)
  - Deficiency of necessary components such as folic acid, iron, erythropoietin, and/or vitamin B12 (pernicious anemia after gastric surgery)
- Iron-deficiency anemia: Due to inadequate intake, Due to blood loss (such as from a gastrointestinal ulcer)
- Bone-marrow aspiration/biopsy is used to diagnose aplastic anemia (failure of bone marrow to produce RBCs as well as platelets and WBCs).
- S/S: Fatigue, weakness, dizziness, shortness of breath, hypotension, tachycardia, palpitation, chest pain, splenomegaly, pale/cold/yellow skin, jaundice (eyes)

Iron Deficiency Anemia

- Normally Iron formed in intestine – converted to ferritin and stored in liver, spleen, bone marrow.
- Duodenum – most iron absorption happens here
- In this anemia, Iron stores are depleted
- Assessment
    - Pallor; weakness; fatigue; Irritability, SOB, dizziness
    - Brittle spoon like nails, Cheilosis (cracks in corner of mouth)
- Interventions
    - Oral iron supplements- Give with orange juice/vit c
    - Antacids interfere with absorption.
    - Liquid iron preparations stain teeth; should be given through a straw. Rinse mouth thoroughly
    - Instruct the client to take iron supplements empty stomach (or between meals). Food delays absorption
    - Stool – greenish tarry color. Constipation common (fluids and fiber)
    - Parenteral iron supplements (iron dextran) are only given for severe anemia (Z track method)

Sickle Cell Anemia

- Autosomal recessive blood disorder -abnormal sickled hemoglobin present- sRBC- 20 days life span
- Precipitating sickling conditions
    - Fever, emotional and physical stress, conditions that increase the need for oxygen, weather
- Assessment of crisis
    - Pain in abdomen, long bones; painful and swollen joints; possibly dyspnea, chest pain
- Splenomegaly – priority- shock.
- Interventions
    - Hydration, oxygen, analgesics as prescribed

- Prevent sickling - no dehydration, high altitude, infection (get flu and pneumonia vaccine), stress, extreme weather
- Avoid meperidine (Demerol); may cause seizures

Aplastic Anemia

- Deficiency of circulating erythrocytes due to suppression of bone marrow cells (congenital/radiation/toxins/viral and bacterial infection)
- Assessment
  - Pancytopenia; petechiae; purpura; pallor, weakness, fatigue, tachycardia, bleeding from gums, nose
- Interventions
  - Prepare for bone marrow transplantation, if planned
  - Reverse isolation, limit visitors, bleeding precautions
  - Frequent rest periods, hand washing
  - Administer immunosuppressive medications, Blood
  - Educate about wearing Medic-Alert bracelet

Polycythemia vera

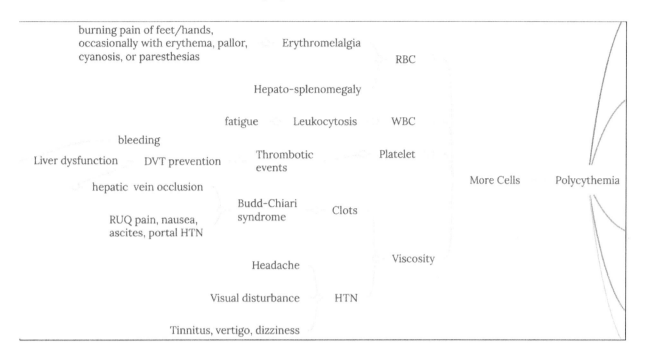

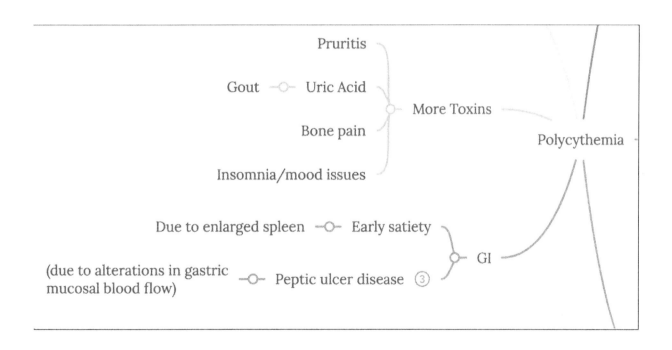

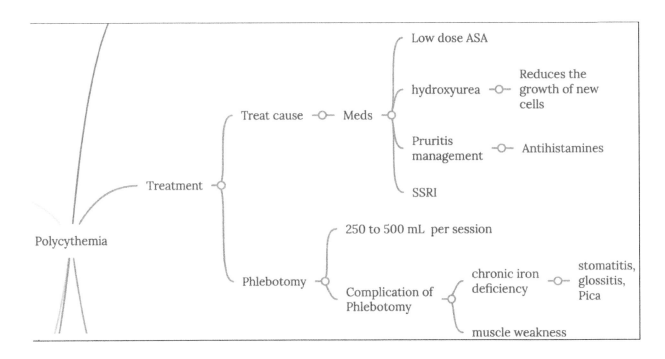

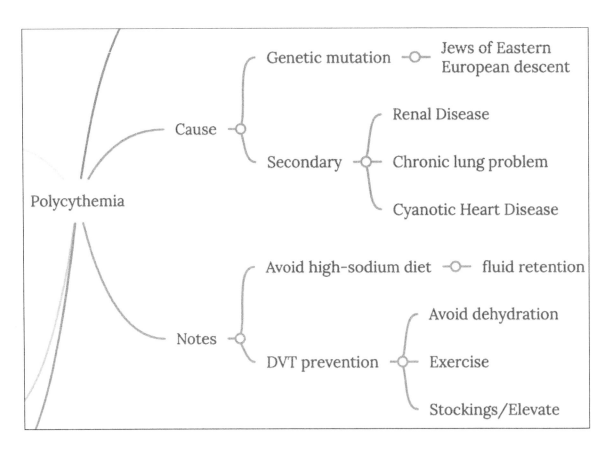

Coagulation Disorders

Idiopathic thrombocytopenic purpura (ITP)

- An autoimmune disorder
- The life span of platelets is decreased by anti-platelet antibodies although platelet production is normal
- In ITP, platelets are coated with antibodies- when they reach the spleen, the antibody-coated platelets are recognized as foreign and are destroyed by macrophages.
- This can result in severe hemorrhage following a cesarean birth or lacerations.

Disseminated intravascular coagulation (DIC)

- A life-threatening coagulopathy in which clotting and anti-clotting mechanisms occur at the same time.
- The client who has DIC is at risk for both internal and external bleeding, as well as damage to organs resulting from ischemia caused by micro clots – need anticoagulants
- Signs and Symptoms
    - Unusual spontaneous bleeding from the client's gums and nose (epistaxis)
    - Oozing, trickling, or flow of blood from incisions or lacerations, Petechiae and ecchymoses
    - Excessive bleeding from venipuncture, injection sites, or slight traumas
    - Tachycardia, hypotension, and diaphoresis
    - Organ failure secondary to micro emboli - DIC
- Medications
    - ITP – Corticosteroids and immunosuppressants
    - DIC – Anticoagulants (heparin)

- Nursing Considerations
  - Vital signs, hemodynamic status.
  - Monitor for signs of organ failure or intracranial bleed (oliguria, decreased level of consciousness).
  - Lab values: Give blood, platelets, and other clotting products.
  - Oxygen, fluids
  - Avoid use of NSAIDs. Provide protection from injury.
  - Instruct client to avoid Valsalva maneuver (could cause cerebral hemorrhage).
  - Implement bleeding precautions (avoid use of needles).
- Bleeding Precautions
  - Monitor: signs of bleeding
  - Gentle Handling, no heat
  - Avoiding injections and IV. Use smallest gauge needle
  - 5 to 10 mts pressure to needle stick site
  - No rectal temperatures, enemas, and suppositories
  - Use electric razor (not straight)
  - Use soft-bristled toothbrush, avoid flossing or chewing on hard food
  - Avoid nose blowing; hard sneezing, contact sports.

Hemophilia

- Bleeding disorder; results from deficiency of specific coagulation proteins
- Transmitted as X-linked recessive genetic disorder
- Assessment
  - Abnormal bleeding in response to trauma, surgery; epistaxis
  - Ecchymoses, Purpura, Pain, swelling, tenderness in joints
  - Normal platelet count, but abnormal coagulation factor results
- Interventions
  - Bleeding precautions, Protect from trauma
  - Administer replacement factors as prescribed
  - Immobilize affected joints, if applicable
  - Assess neurological status for changes secondary to bleeding
  - Monitor for hematuria

- Educate child, parents in signs of internal bleeding and how to control bleeding, if occurs
- Dental hygiene is necessary to prevent gum bleeding, and soft toothbrushes should be used.

Other Hematological Disorders

- Von Willebrand disease (VWD): A genetic disorder caused by missing or defective von Willebrand factor (VWF), a clotting protein.
- Beta thalassemia: A blood disorder that reduces the production of hemoglobin.
- B thalassemia major- is also known as Cooley's anemia – need blood transfusion to sustain life
  - Bone marrow transplant/splenectomy may be needed

Oncology

- Cancer: Neoplastic disorder that can involve all body organs
- Metastasis: Cancer cells that move from original location to other sites

Cancer classification

- Solid tumors: Originate from organs, such as breast
- Hematological cancers: Originate from blood tissues
- Grading and staging: TNM
- Methods used to describe tumor, including extent of tumor, node involvement, metastasis

Stage	Level of involvement
Tumor	
T1	Limited to mucosa and submucosa
T2	Extension into but not through muscularis propria
T3	Invasion of perirectal fat
T4	Invasion of adjacent structures
Nodes	
N0	No involved lymph nodes
N1	Fewer than four regional nodes involved
N2	More than four regional nodes involved
N3	Distant nodes involved
Metastasis	
M0	No metastasis
M1	Distant metastasis

- TX: Main tumor cannot be measured.
- T0: Main tumor cannot be found.

- NX: Cancer in nearby lymph nodes cannot be measured.

- MX: Metastasis cannot be measured.

AppleRN Classes

- Carcinoma In Situ (CIS)
    - A condition in which abnormal cells that *look like cancer cells under a microscope* are found *only in the place where they first formed.*
    - Also called stage 0 disease.
    - CIS is not cancer, but it may become cancer.
    - At some point, these cells may become cancerous and spread

Factors that influence cancer development

- Environmental, dietary, genetic predisposition, age, immune function, substance abuse
- Exposure to certain viruses and bacteria
- Human papillomavirus (HPV) increases the risk for cancers of the cervix, penis, vagina, anus, and oropharynx.
- Hepatitis B and hepatitis C viruses increase the risk for liver cancer.
- Epstein-Barr virus - increased risk of lymphoma
- HIV increases the risk of lymphoma and Kaposi's sarcoma.
- Helicobacter pylori may increase the risk of gastric cancer
- A diet high in fat and red meat, and low in fiber – colorectal cancer
- Sun, ultraviolet light, or radiation exposure
- Presence of autosomal dominant gene- Lynch syndrome – causes various cancers.

Cancer Screening

- C – Change in bowel or bladder
- A – A sore that does not heal
- U – Unusual bleeding or discharge
- T – Thickening or lump
- I – Indigestion or difficulty swallowing
- O – obvious change in a wart or mole
- N – nagging cough or hoarseness

Surgery

- Prophylactic surgery: Performed in clients with existing premalignant condition or known family history that strongly predisposes person to cancer development
- Curative surgery: All gross and microscopic tumor removed, destroyed
- Control surgery: Removal of part of tumor; decreases number of cancers cells, increases chances of success of other therapies

- Palliative surgery: Performed to improve quality of life during survival time
- Reconstructive or rehabilitative surgery: Performed to improve quality of life by restoring maximal function and appearance, such as breast reconstruction
- Side effects of surgery
    - Loss or loss of function of specific body part
    - Reduced function as result of organ loss
    - Scarring or disfigurement
    - Grieving about altered body image, change in lifestyle

Chemotherapy

- Kills or inhibits reproduction of neoplastic cells, but also attacks and kills normal cells. Effects are systemic
- Normal cells profoundly affected include those of skin, hair, lining of gastrointestinal (GI) tract, spermatocytes, hematopoietic cells
- Usually, several medications used in combination to increase therapeutic response
- May be combined with other therapies, such as radiation or surgery
- Side effects include alopecia, nausea and vomiting, mucositis, immuno-suppression, anemia, thrombocytopenia

Neutropenic precautions

- Have the client remain in his room unless he needs to leave for a diagnostic procedure or therapy. In this case, place a mask on him during transport.
- Protect the client from possible sources of infection (live plants, water in equipment, uncooked food).
- Have client, staff, and visitors perform frequent hand hygiene. Restrict visitors who are ill.
- Avoid invasive procedures that could cause a break in tissue unless necessary (rectal temperatures, injections).
- Keep dedicated equipment in the client's room (blood pressure machine, thermometer, stethoscope).

- Administer medicine Filgrastim (Neupogen, Neulasta) as prescribed to stimulate WBC production

Complication

Immuno-suppression:

- due to bone marrow suppression by chemo medications is the most significant adverse effect of chemotherapy.
- Nursing Actions
  - Monitor temperature and white blood cell (WBC) count.
  - A fever greater than 37.8° C (100° F) should be reported to the provider immediately.
  - Monitor skin and mucous membranes for infection (breakdown, fissures, abscess).
  - Cultures should be obtained prior to initiating antimicrobial therapy.
  - Neutropenic precautions (WBC drops below 1,000/uL)

Mucositis (stomatitis)

- Inflammation of tissues in the mouth, such as the gums, tongue, roof, and floor of the mouth, and inside the lips and cheeks.
- Very common with radiation therapy to the head and neck.

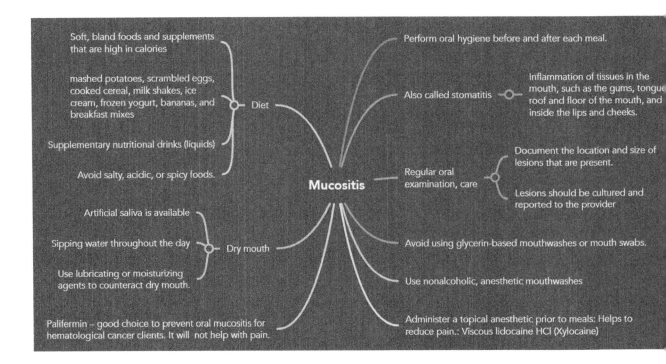

Health Education (on chemo)

- Avoid crowds. Take temperature daily and report elevation
- Avoid food sources that could contain bacteria (fresh fruits and vegetables; undercooked meat, fish, and eggs; pepper and paprika).
- Avoid yard work, gardening, or changing a pet's litter box.
- Avoid fluids that have been sitting at room temperature for longer than 1 hr.
- Wash all dishes in hot, soapy water or dishwasher.
- Always wash glasses and cups after one use.
- Wash toothbrush daily in dishwasher or rinse in bleach solution.
- Do not share toiletry or personal hygiene items with others.
- Report fever greater than 37.8° C (100° F) or other manifestations of bacterial or viral infections immediately to the provider.

Oncology Clients: Taste alterations and thick saliva

- Try adding foods that are tart (citrus juices).
- Include cold or room temperature foods in the diet.
- Try using sauces for added flavor. Use plastic utensils for eating.
- Suck on mints, candy, or chew gum to remove bad taste in mouth.

Radiation Therapy

Radiation Therapy

RT: External beam radiation

Client does not emit radiation — Given over several weeks — Bone marrow depression

Care

Skin

Gentle wash with mild soap and water. Pat dry — Do not remove or wash off radiation "tattoos"

No powders, ointments, lotions, deodorants, or perfumes to the irradiated skin. — Wear soft clothing; avoid tight clothes.

Use soft cotton bed sheets and towels — Do not expose the irradiated skin to sun or a heat source

Diet — Provide a well-balanced diet — Limit red meat (difficult to eat/digest)

Activity — Manage fatigue
- Schedule activities with rest periods in between
- Use energy-saving measures (sitting during showers and ADLs).

Radiation Injury
- Skin – blanching, erythema, desquamation, sloughing, hemorrhage
- Mouth/neck - mucositis, xerostomia (dry mouth), dysphagia
- Abdomen – gastroenteritis

Radiation Therapy

Brachytherapy

Internally with an implants — Client's body fluids are contaminated with radiation

Activity — Bedrest
- Prevent dislodgment (cervical/ endometrial)
- Keep a lead container and tongs in client's room

care
- Place the client in a private room away from other clients
- Place appropriate sign on the door warning of the radiation source.
- Limit visitors to 30-min visits
  - visitors maintain a distance of 6 ft from the source.
  - people <16yrs age : better not visit/contact with client

Staff
- Dosimeter film badge and lead apron for staff.
- No pregnant caretakers

Cancer disorders

Skin Cancer

- Sunlight exposure - leading cause of skin cancer (Avoid ultraviolet rays, Tanning beds)
- At risk: Light skin/red or blond hair/blue or green eyes/family history/ personal history of skin cancer, age above 60

SKIN CANCER TYPE	ASSESSMENT	CHARACTERISTICS
Squamous cell (epidermis)	› Rough, scaly lesion with central ulceration and crusting › Bleeding (possible)	› Localized; may metastasize.
Basal cell (basal epidermis or nearby dermal cells)	› Small, waxy nodule with superficial blood vessels, well-defined borders › Erythema and ulcerations	› Invades local structures (nerves, bone, cartilage, lymphatic and vascular tissue); rarely metastatic but high rate of recurrence.
Malignant melanoma (cancer of melanocytes)	› New moles or change in an existing mole (can occur in intestines or any other body structure that contains pigment cells) › Cracks, ulcerations, or bleeding (possible)	› Teach clients the "ABCDE" system to evaluate moles. Source: ATI nursing education

Melanoma

ABCDEs of suspicious lesions

- A – Asymmetry: One side does not match the other
- B – Borders: Ragged, notched, irregular, or blurred edges
- C – Color: Lack of uniformity in pigmentation (shades of tan, brown, or black)
- D – Diameter: Width greater than 6 mm, or about the size of a pencil eraser or a pea
- E – Evolving: Or change in appearance (shape, size, color, height, texture) or condition (bleeding, itching)

Treatment

- Excision, immunotherapy, chemotherapy, radiation therapy

- Cryotherapy/surgery: For small, clinically well-defined primary tumors (Nonmelanoma)- tissue freezing-cause cell death
  - Permanent pigment loss at the treatment site.
  - Edema is common after treatment.
  - Treated tumors usually exude necrotic material, after which an eschar forms and persists for about 4 weeks.
  - Topical antibiotic may be given
  - Avoid placing ice on site post procedure.
  - Warm, damp washcloth to the site can be applied for comfort

Leukemia

- Leukemias -cancers of white blood cells or of cells that develop into white blood cells.
- These white blood cells are not functional and destroy bone marrow (blast cells)
- Overgrowth of leukemic cells prevents growth of other blood components (platelets, erythrocytes, mature leukocytes).
- Leukemias
  - Acute lymphocytic leukemia (ALL)
  - Acute myelogenous leukemia (AML)
  - Chronic lymphocytic leukemia (CLL)
  - Chronic myelogenous leukemia (CML)

Symptoms of Leukemia (general)

- Symptoms arise from sequelae of bone marrow suppression and/or from leukemic cell organ infiltration.
- B symptoms: fever, weight loss, night sweats
- Anemia: fatigue, shortness of breath, light-headedness, angina, headache, pallor
- Thrombocytopenia: easy bruising or bleeding, petechiae, ecchymoses, epistaxis, retinal hemorrhages
- Neutropenia: fever, infection

- Lymphocytosis: bone pain, lymphadenopathy; splenomegaly
- CNS: confusion, cranial nerve palsies, meningeal signs
- Nadir – Period of greatest bone marrow depression during leukemia. (Lowest WBC count, platelet count). If platelet goes below 20,000, they need platelet transfusion.

Infection

- Major cause of death in immunosuppressed client
- Monitor for evidence of infection.
- Assess for other physiological indicators of infection (lung crackles, cough, urinary frequency or urgency, oliguria, lesions of skin or mucous membrane).
- Prevent infection. (Implement neutropenic precautions.)
    - Frequent, thorough hand hygiene, Private room. Screen visitors carefully.
    - Allow only well visitors; when unavoidable, visitors - wear a mask.
    - Restrict foods with possible bacteria (no fresh or raw fruits, vegetables).
    - Monitor WBC. Avoid bacteria and viruses (no live plants, fresh flowers)
    - Eliminate standing water (humidifiers, denture cups, vases) to prevent bacteria breeding.
    - Encourage good personal hygiene (oral care). Avoid crowds.
- Complication: Splenic rupture!!!

Prevent injury.

- Monitor platelets.
- Assess frequently for obvious and occult bleeding.
- Protect the client from trauma (avoid injections and venipunctures, apply firm pressure, increase vitamin K intake).
- Teach the client how to avoid trauma (use electric shaver, soft bristled toothbrush, avoid contact sports).

Lymphomas

- Malignancy of lymph nodes; originates in single lymph node or single chain of nodes.
- S/S: Painless enlarged lymph node, Unexplained fever, weight loss, night sweats, itching, fatigue
- Hodgkin's lymphoma (HL) Reed Sternberg cells present.
  - Most cases involve young adults.
  - Possible causes include viral infections (Epstein Barr) and exposure to chemical agents.
- Non-Hodgkin's lymphoma (NHL)
  - More common in clients older than 50.
  - Possible causes include gene damage, viral infections, autoimmune disease, and exposure to radiation or toxic chemicals.
- Lymphomas can metastasize to almost any organ.
- Radiation and chemotherapy are the treatment of choice

Multiple Myeloma

- Malignant tumors within bone
- Assessment
  - Bone, skeletal pain, especially in ribs, spine, pelvis
  - Osteoporosis
  - Recurrent infections; fatigue; anemia; thrombocytopenia; granulocytopenia; elevated uric acid and calcium serum levels
- Interventions
  - Monitor for signs of bleeding, infection, skeletal fractures, renal failure (Bence Jones proteins in urine)
  - Encourage fluids, at least 2 L/day
  - Encourage ambulation, Provide skeletal support during movement

Gastric Cancer

- Malignant growth in stomach
- Assessment
  - Fatigue; anorexia; indigestion; epigastric discomfort; sensation of pressure in stomach; dysphagia; ascites; anemia; palpable mass
- Cause- no single cause.
- Risk: H pylori, gastric ulcer, diet (smoked/highly salted/processed/spicy), smoking and alcohol
- Interventions
  - Monitor vital signs, Monitor weight (malnourishment)
  - Monitor hemoglobin, hematocrit levels (anemia)
  - Administer analgesics as prescribed
  - Administer pre-, post chemotherapy, and/or radiation care as prescribed, Prepare client for surgery as prescribed
- Postoperative interventions
  - Place in Fowler's position (comfort)
  - Do not irrigate or remove nasogastric tube
  - Monitor fluid, electrolyte balance. Administer IV fluids and electrolytes
  - Monitor for signs of dumping syndrome, diarrhea, hypoglycemia, vitamin B_{12} deficiency

Pancreatic Cancer

- Most common neoplasm of pancreas; more common in Black people than whites, in smokers, in men
- Assessment
  - Nausea, vomiting; unexplained weight loss; clay-colored stools; dark urine, glucose intolerance.
  - Pain - abdominal pain, Pain that radiates to the back and is unrelieved by change in position and is more severe at night.
  - Jaundice (late finding)
  - Ascites, Pruritus (buildup of bile salt)

- Early satiety or anorexia

Nursing Care

- Administer pre-, post chemotherapy as prescribed.
- Palliative care – nutrition –Jejunostomy/TPN (Total parenteral nutrition)
- Monitor blood glucose and give insulin.
- Partial pancreatectomy – small tumors
- Prepare client for Whipple's procedure (pancreaticoduodenectomy)
- Removal of the "head" (wide part) of the pancrea along with duodenum, a portion of the common bile duct, gallbladder, and sometimes part of the stomach

Thyroid Cancer

- Monitor airway patency: tumor affecting or compressing the trachea.
- Assess swallowing: tumor affecting or compressing the esophagus.
- Clients who are treated for thyroid cancer are hypothyroid.
- Monitor vital signs for impaired oxygenation, hypotension, or bradycardia.
- Use ECG monitoring to detect dysrhythmias.
- Assess mental status and provide a safe environment.

Thyroidectomy care

- Support neck with pillows or sandbags.
- Maintain a humidifier to promote airway clearance.
- Assess damage- to parathyroid glands or laryngeal nerve
- Monitor for hemorrhage (incision site, hypotension, tachycardia, increased swallowing, or throat "tickling").
- Monitor for respiratory distress (caused by tetany, swelling, or laryngeal nerve damage).
- Monitor for parathyroid injury (decreased PTH, hypocalcemia, tetany).

Radioactive iodine (RAI) therapy

- The client ingests RAI (liquid/ tablet) – absorbed by thyroid cells which are then destroyed.
- Radioactive precautions to reduce risk of radiation exposure.
- Chew gum or hard candy to relieve dry mouth or reduced salivation.
- Alteration in taste is expected.

RAI Precautions

- Avoid close proximity to pregnant women or children
- Do not breastfeed (RAI may be excreted through breast milk)
- Do not share utensils with others or use bare hands to handle food that is to be served to others
- Isolate personal laundry (e.g., bed linens, towels, daily clothes) and wash it separately
- Use a separate toilet from the rest of the family and flush 2-3 times after each use
- Wash hands frequently and thoroughly, especially after restroom use
- Drink plenty of fluids
- Sleep in a separate bed from others and do not sit near others in an enclosed area for a prolonged period of time (e.g., train or flight travel)

Lung Cancer

- One of the leading causes of cancer-related deaths.

Risk Factors

- Cigarette smoking (80% to 90%): both firsthand and secondhand smoke
- Low dose CT scan recommended yearly for (a) Have a history of heavy smoking, and (b) Smoke now or have quit within the past 15 years, and (c) are between 55 and 80 years old.
- Radiation exposure

- Chronic exposure to inhaled environmental irritants (air pollution, asbestos, other talc dusts)
- Older adult clients, clients with structural abnormality
- Determine the pack-year history (number of packs of cigarettes smoked per day times the number of years smoked).
- Monitor for a cough that changes in pattern, hoarseness

Criteria	Non–Small-Cell Lung Cancer	Small-Cell Lung Cancer (SCLC)
Prevalence	80%	20%
Sub types	Squamous Ca, Adeno Ca, large cell carcinoma	SCLC
Growth rate	Depends (Sq-slow, Ad-Moderate, Large cell- rapid)	Very rapid
Complication	Large cell- more mets	Associated SIADH, mets to brain, Poor prognosis
Treatment	Surgery, Chemo, Radiation	Chemotherapy and radiation, prophylactic RT to brain

Types of Lung cancer

Ca Lung Management

- Chemotherapy - primary choice - might combine with radiation and/or surgery.
- Removal of a lung (pneumonectomy), lobe (lobectomy) or segment (segmentectomy)
- Monitor vital signs, oxygenation (SaO2, ABG values), and for evidence of hemorrhage.
- Manage chest tube /oxygen / ventilator if appropriate.
- Educate – avoid crowds, report to doc any complications and increase in pain
- Use upright position, Teach pursed lip breathing
- Bronchodilators and corticosteroids - to help decrease inflammation /dry secretions.

Head and Neck Cancers

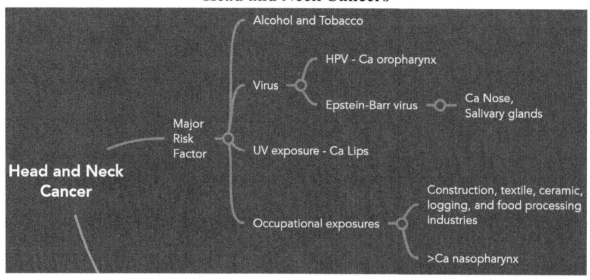

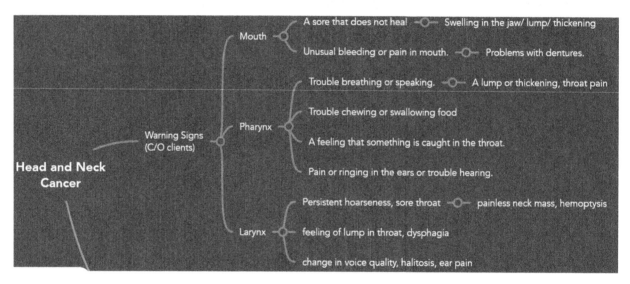

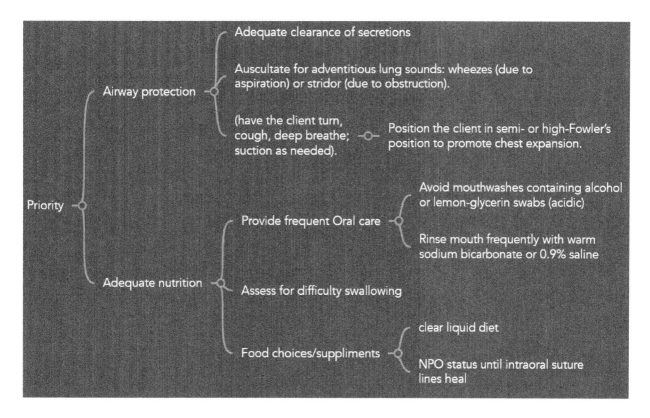

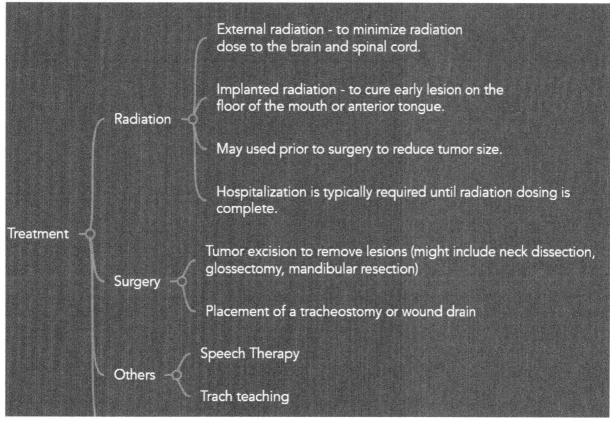

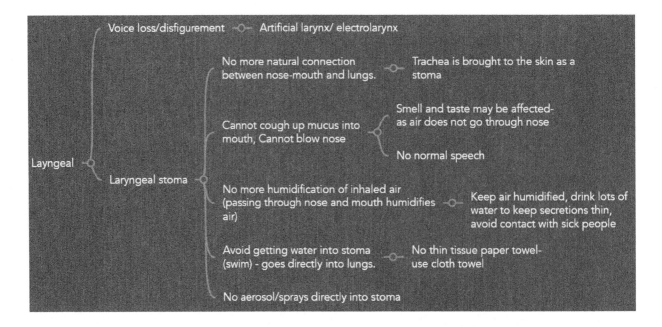

Special Situation: Varicocele (not cancer)

- A varicocele is abnormal dilation and enlargement of the scrotal Veins which drains blood from each testicle.
- Usually, painless, and asymptomatic ("bag of worms" appearance)
- Diagnostics: Physical examination, Ultrasound
- Can be associated with male infertility issues – can impair the production, structure, and function of sperm.
- No effective medical treatments – analgesics, scrotal support
- Surgery - Varicocelectomy

Testicular Cancer

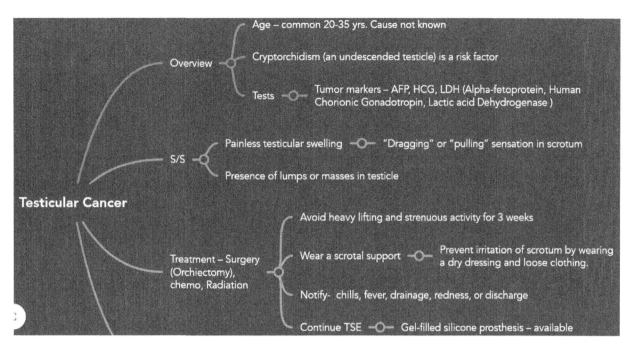

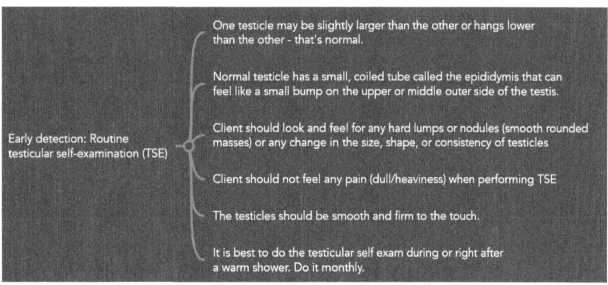

Prostate Cancer

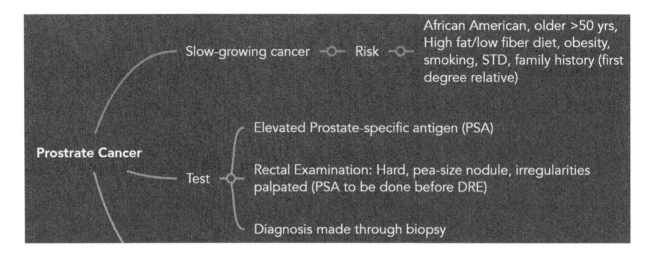

PSA is not recommended as a routine test. Done on a case-to-case basis

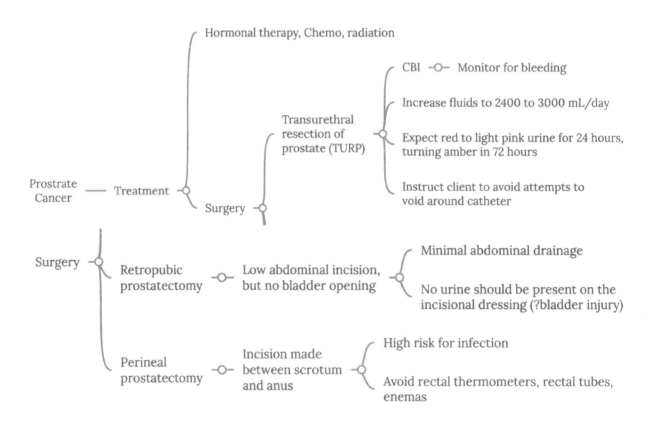

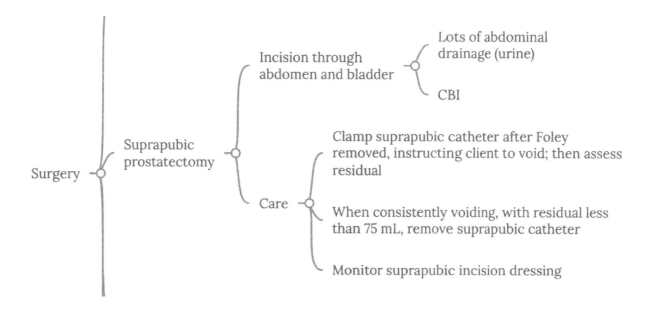

Surgery — Suprapubic prostatectomy

- Incision through abdomen and bladder
  - Lots of abdominal drainage (urine)
  - CBI
- Care
  - Clamp suprapubic catheter after Foley removed, instructing client to void; then assess residual
  - When consistently voiding, with residual less than 75 mL, remove suprapubic catheter
  - Monitor suprapubic incision dressing

Ovarian Cancer

- Cancer of ovaries; grows rapidly, spreads quickly CA-125
- Often bilateral: Metastasis occurs by direct spread to organs in pelvis or through lymphatic drainage (distal spread)
- Assessment
  - Abdominal discomfort; abdominal swelling; early satiety, gastrointestinal disturbances; dysfunctional vaginal bleeding; abdominal mass
- Interventions
  - Administer pre-, post radiation and/or chemotherapy care as prescribed, prepare client for total hysterectomy if prescribed

Cervical cancer

- Risk: Multiple sex partners, Smoking, Oral contraceptive use, STD infections, Human papilloma virus, early age sexual activity (<18)
- Two tests are used for cervical cancer screening, the Pap test, and the test for HPV.
- Assessment: Painless vaginal bleeding, foul-smelling vaginal discharge; pelvic, lower back, leg, or groin pain; anorexia; dysuria; hematuria
  - Treatment options: Chemotherapy, RT, Surgery
- Post op precautions
  - Assist with coughing, deep-breathing exercises
  - Apply antiembolism stockings, Monitor bowel sounds
  - Avoid stair climbing for 1 month, avoid sitting for long
  - Avoid strenuous activity or lifting more than 20 lb

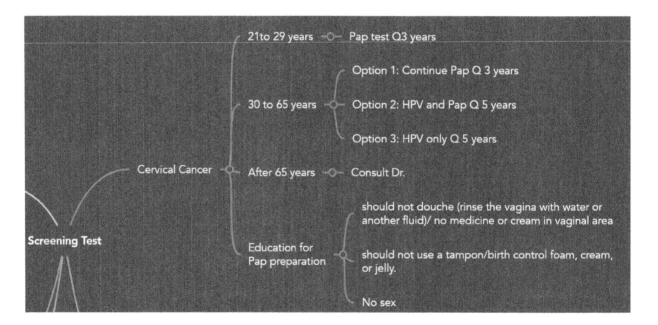

Endometrial Cancer

- Slow-growing tumor; associated with menopausal years
- Risk factors
  - History of uterine polyps; nulliparity; polycystic ovary disease; family history

- Prolonged estrogen stimulation (infertility treatments/ Tamoxifen/ early menarche/late menopause)
- Assessment: Postmenopausal bleeding; water, sero-sanguineous discharge; low back, pelvic, abdominal pain; enlarged uterus in advanced stages
- Nonsurgical interventions
  - Administer pre-, post chemotherapy, and/or radiation therapy
  - Medroxyprogesterone - for estrogen-dependent tumors

Breast Cancer

- Invasive when it penetrates tissue surrounding mammary duct, grows in irregular pattern.
- Second most common malignancy and death in women

Risk Factors

- Family history; BRCA gene mutations, early menarche, and late menopause; previous cancer of breast, uterus, or ovaries; nulliparity; obesity; high doses of radiation exposure to chest

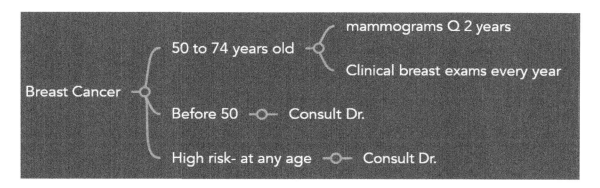

- Types: Lobular (milk glands) or ductal (milk passages), pagets, inflammatory (peau d'organge)
- Peau d'orange: pink, reddish purple, or bruised - caused by cancer cells blocking lymph vessels in the skin causing buildup of fluid (lymph) in the skin of the breast
- Mass felt usually in upper outer quadrant, beneath nipple or axilla.

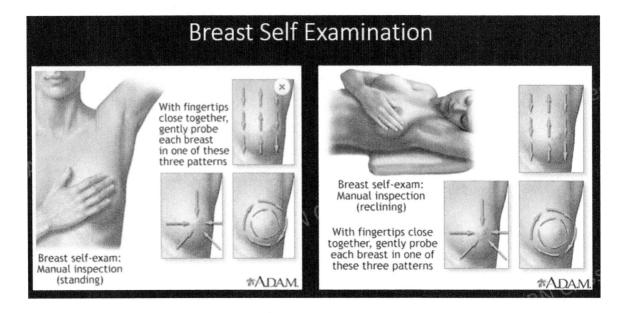

- Histology: 3 receptors: estrogen, progesterone, HER2 (human epidermal growth factor receptor)

- Surgery
    - Lobectomy
    - Simple mastectomy – breast and few lymph nodes
    - Modified radical mastectomy – Breast and axillary lymph nodes
    - Radical mastectomy – Breast, axillary nodes, pectoral muscle
- Nonsurgical interventions: Hormonal manipulation: Tamoxifen for estrogen-dependent tumors
- Postoperative interventions
    - Place client in semi-Fowler's position, turning from back to nonoperative side, with affected arm elevated above level of heart.
    - Assess axillary region along with surgical wound.
    - If drain, maintain suction; note drainage characteristics
    - Sign above bed, "No IVs, No Injections, No BP in Affected Arm"
    - Prophylactic oophorectomy and mastectomy in women with BRCA1 or BRCA2 mutations

Paget's Disease

- Rare malignancy of breast (areola and nipple)
- Persistent lesion of the nipple and areola with or without palpable mass
- Different from Paget's disease of the bone (abnormal bone growth and deformity)
- Itching, burning, bloody nipple discharge
- Superficial skin erosion and ulceration may also be present.
- Treatment - mastectomy

Lymphedema management

- Massage to mobilize fluid
- Compression sleeves or intermittent pneumatic compression sleeves
- Clothing should be less constrictive at the proximal arm and over the chest.
- Elevation of arm above the heart
- Arm exercises

Injury prevention to affected arm

- The client is at risk for edema and infection as a result of lymph node dissection. Use gloves when working in the garden
- Use an electric razor to shave under the arm
- Use potholders when cooking to prevent burns
- Avoid activities that increase edema – heavy load/BP/Injections on the arm

Breast Cancer Home Care

- Avoid overuse of affected arm for first few months
- Keep affected arm elevated
- Provide incision care with lanolin as prescribed
- Instruct client about BSE: monthly regular

- Always protect affected arm and hand from trauma, cuts, bruises – use gloves, use lanolin cream for skin
- Avoid wearing constrictive clothing on affected side
- Call physician if signs of inflammation occur
- Prevent infection – use mosquito repellant
- Wear Medic-Alert bracelet stating lymphedema arm
- Do not cut the cuticles on the nails

Tamoxifen

- It has different action on different tissues (mixed agonist/antagonist).
- In the breast, they block estrogen (antagonist) and are therefore helpful in inhibiting the growth of estrogen-receptive breast cancer cells.
- In uterus – it is estrogen-stimulating (agonist)- resulting in excessive endometrial proliferation (endometrial hyperplasia) – can lead to endometrial cancer.
- Risk for thromboembolic events (e.g., stroke, pulmonary embolism, deep vein thrombosis).

Intestinal Tumors

- Malignant lesions; develop in cells lining bowel wall or as polyps in colon or rectum
- Risk factors for colorectal cancer
    - Age older than 50 years; history of ulcerative colitis or Crohn's disease; family history of intestinal cancer, genetic (lynch syndrome), lifestyle (obesity, a diet high in red meat, cigarette smoking, and alcohol)
- Assessment
    - Blood in stools; anorexia; weight loss; vomiting; malaise; anemia; diarrhea or constipation; abdominal distention; abdominal mass (late sign)

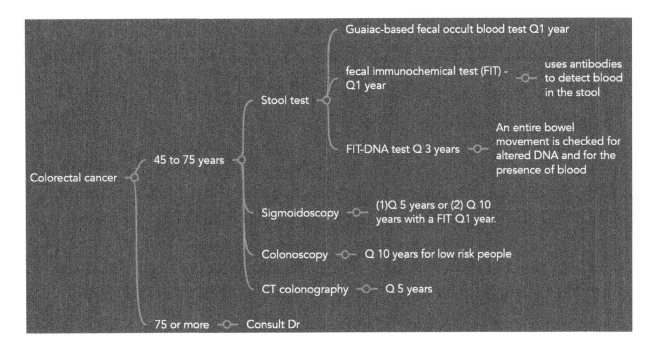

- Non-surgical interventions
  - Monitor for complications: bowel perforation, abscess or fistula formation, hemorrhage, complete intestinal obstruction
  - Administer pre-, post radiation, chemotherapy care as prescribed
- Surgical interventions: Colostomy, ileostomy, administer intestinal antiseptics, antibiotics as prescribed preoperatively

Bladder Cancer

- Papillomatous growth in bladder urothelium; undergoes malignant changes, may infiltrate bladder wall
- Assessment: Gross, painless hematuria; frequency; urgency; dysuria; bladder biopsy confirms diagnosis
- Radiation: Usually need high doses.
- Surgery
- Chemotherapy: Treat urine as biohazard
  - For 6 hours following intravesical chemotherapy, disinfect toilet with bleach after each voiding

General Cancer Complications

- Malnutrition: Increased risk for weight loss and anorexia.
- Increased metabolic function, Impaired digestion
- Management
    - Anti emetics, antacids
    - Megestrol to increase the appetite
    - Labs (albumin, ferritin, transferrin).
    - Encourage frequent oral hygiene.
    - Incorporate client preferences into meal planning
    - Perform calorie counts to determine intake. Provide liquid nutritional supplements as needed. Add protein powders to food or tube feedings

Health Education (nutrition)

- Administer antiemetics and schedule them prior to meals.
- Encourage the client to eat several small meals a day if better tolerated.
- Nausea? - Have Low-fat and dry foods (crackers, toast). Avoid drinking liquids during meals. Select foods that are served cold and do not require cooking, which can emit odors that stimulate nausea.
- Have high-protein, high-calorie, nutrient-dense foods, meal supplements
- Metallic Taste? - use plastic eating utensils, suck on hard candy, and avoiding red meats to prevent or reduce the sensation of metallic taste.
- Create a food diary to identify items that can trigger nausea.

General Cancer Complications and Nursing care

- Paraneoplastic syndromes
    - T cells in the body attack normal cells rather than cancerous ones, resulting in changes in neurological function (movement, sensation, mental function).
- Management
    - Recognize manifestations of paraneoplastic syndrome.
    - Administer medications (steroids, immune suppressants)

- Provide a safe environment until client returns to baseline mental status.
- Use aids for vision or hearing deficits, as indicated.

Oncological Emergencies

- Sepsis, disseminated intravascular coagulation (DIC)
  - Maintain strict aseptic technique; administer antibiotics, anticoagulants, clotting factors as prescribed
- Syndrome of inappropriate antidiuretic hormone (SIADH)
- Spinal cord compression
  - Occurs when tumor directly enters spinal cord
  - Assess for back pain, neurological deficits; prepare client for radiation, chemotherapy as prescribed
- Hypercalcemia
  - Late manifestation of extensive malignancy, often in clients with bone cancer
  - Monitor serum calcium level: give fluids, administer medications to lower calcium levels as prescribed
- Superior vena cava syndrome
  - Occurs when vein compressed, obstructed by tumor growth
  - Neurological symptoms
  - Prepare client for radiation therapy as prescribed
- Tumor lysis syndrome
  - Occurs when large numbers of tumor cells destroyed rapidly, indicating cancer treatment is effective
  - hyperuricemia, hyperkalemia, hyperphosphatemia, hypocalcemia, and acute renal failure.
- Encourage oral hydration; administer diuretics as prescribed

Chemo precautions

- Extravasations: the leakage of medication into surrounding skin and subcutaneous tissue.
  - Stop the infusion, Leave the needle in place
  - Attempt to aspirate any residual medication from the site (the needle would be removed after treatment of the event)
  - Administer an antidote if available
  - Direct pressure is not applied to the site because it could further injure tissues exposed to the chemotherapeutic agent.
  - Assess the site for complications.

Chemo Home Care

- The client may excrete the chemotherapeutic agent for 48 hours or more after administration.
- Blood, emesis, and excreta may be considered contaminated during this time.
- Client should not share a bathroom with children or pregnant women during this time.
- Any contaminated linens or clothing should be washed separately and then washed a second time, if necessary.
- All contaminated disposable items should be sealed in plastic bags and disposed of as hazardous waste.

Bone marrow suppression

- One of the common side effects
- low WBC count or neutropenia,
- bleeding caused by thrombocytopenia or low platelet count,
- Anemia or low RBCs
- Hormonal agents are effective against tumors that are supported or suppressed by hormones.

Immunology

Sjögren's syndrome

- Chronic autoimmune disorder
- Moisture-producing exocrine glands of the body are attacked by white blood cells
- The most commonly affected glands are the salivary and lacrimal glands, leading to dry eyes (xerophthalmia) and dry mouth (xerostomia).
- Dryness in these areas can lead to corneal ulcerations, dental caries, and oral thrush.
- Skin - dry skin and rashes
- Throat and bronchi - chronic dry cough
- Management
    - Supportive care: Alleviate symptoms
    - Over the counter or prescribed drops are used to relieve itching, burning, dryness, and gritty sensation in the eyes.
    - Wear goggles
    - Dry mouth: sugarless gum and candy or artificial saliva.
    - Lukewarm water and mild soap when showering can prevent dry skin.
    - Use humidifier, avoid decongestants

Systemic lupus erythematosus

- Chronic multisystem inflammatory autoimmune disease
- No cure – treatment is supportive. More common in women
- Remissions and relapses (Flares).
- Anti-Nuclear Antibody and ESR will be elevated
- Most commonly affects skin, muscles, lining of lungs, heart, nervous tissue, and kidneys
- Arthritis occurs in more than 90% of patients with SLE: Painful/swollen joints, morning stiffness
- Lupus nephritis: serious complication of SLE: Look for abnormal KFT

Multisystem Involvement of SLE

- Health Promotion and SLE. Infection is a major cause of death for patients with SLE, Pneumonia being the most common infection.
- Vaccination is essential, avoid contact with sick people.
- Follow a healthy lifestyle (e.g., 7-8 hours of sleep, no smoking).
- Balanced exercise with alternating periods of rest (no extreme fatigue)
- Rash: Sunlight – Avoid exposure between 10 AM-4 PM, Apply sunscreen. Wash with mild soap and water (no harsh soap)
- Treatment: Corticosteroids – immunosuppression
- Antimalarial drugs (hydroxychloroquine and chloroquine) and antileprosy drugs (dapsone) might also be used to treat fatigue and moderate skin and joint problems.
- Antimalarial drug will take long time to be effective (issue of noncompliance)
- Retinal toxicity and visual disturbances can occur with hydroxychloroquine – need regular ophthalmic check ups
- Supportive treatment

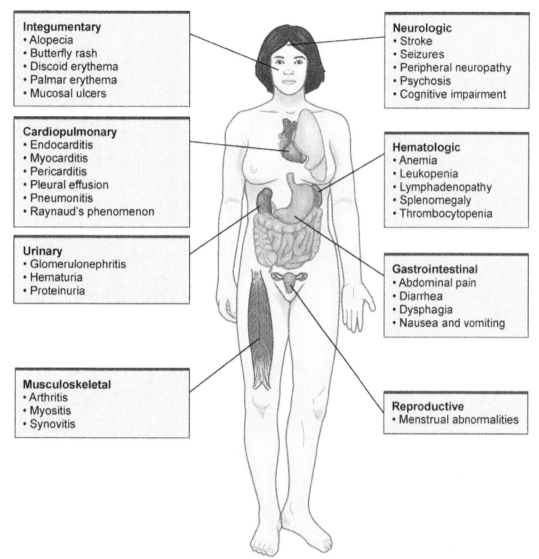

Integumentary
• Alopecia
• Butterfly rash
• Discoid erythema
• Palmar erythema
• Mucosal ulcers

Cardiopulmonary
• Endocarditis
• Myocarditis
• Pericarditis
• Pleural effusion
• Pneumonitis
• Raynaud's phenomenon

Urinary
• Glomerulonephritis
• Hematuria
• Proteinuria

Musculoskeletal
• Arthritis
• Myositis
• Synovitis

Neurologic
• Stroke
• Seizures
• Peripheral neuropathy
• Psychosis
• Cognitive impairment

Hematologic
• Anemia
• Leukopenia
• Lymphadenopathy
• Splenomegaly
• Thrombocytopenia

Gastrointestinal
• Abdominal pain
• Diarrhea
• Dysphagia
• Nausea and vomiting

Reproductive
• Menstrual abnormalities

Copyright © 2014, 2011, 2007, 2004, 2000, 1996, 1992, 1987, 1983 by Mosby, an imprint of Elsevier Inc.

• The SLE increased risk for: spontaneous abortion, stillbirth, and intrauterine growth retardation.
  • Infertility can be present
  • Renal involvement. Women with serious SLE should be counseled against pregnancy.
  • Exacerbation is common during the postpartum period

Fibromyalgia

- Fibromyalgia (FM) results from abnormal central nervous system pain transmission and processing.
- Signs: Chronic musculoskeletal pain, Multiple tender points, Fatigue, Sleep/cognitive disturbances.
- Treatment: Duloxetine (Cymbalta) and amitriptyline (Antidepressant): Help with neuropathic pain-relief, sleep issues and fatigue
- Tender Points in Fibromyalgia

Anaphylactic shock

- Acute onset, and manifestations usually develop quickly (20-30 minutes).
- Common Causes
    - Drugs (e.g., antibiotics), Foods (e.g., shellfish, peanuts)
    - Diagnostic agents (e.g., contrast), Biologic agents (e.g., blood, vaccines)
    - Poison - venom (e.g., bees, snakes)
- Manifestations
    - Cardiovascular: Vasodilation → hypotension and tissue edema, Tachycardia
    - Respiratory: Upper airway edema → stridor & hoarseness, Bronchospasm → wheezing
    - Cutaneous: Urticarial rash, pruritus, flushing
    - Gastrointestinal: Nausea, vomiting, abdominal pain
- Management
    - Airway and Oxygen. Remove insect stinger if present
    - IM epinephrine: Repeat every 5 to 15mts if needed
    - Place in recumbent position and elevate legs, maintain BP with IV fluids and meds
    - Bronchodilator (albuterol), Antihistamine (diphenhydramine)
    - Corticosteroids (methylprednisolone)
    - Anticipate tracheostomy with severe laryngeal edema

EpiPen

- The EpiPen is designed to be administered through clothing. Do not waste the precious time to save the client.
- Use a swing and firm push against the mid-outer thigh until the injector clicks.
- Hold the position for 10 seconds to allow the entire contents to be injected
- The site should be massaged for an additional 10 seconds.

Important Notes on Vaccination

- Assess for allergies to vaccine components (e.g., neomycin, gelatin, yeast, eggs)
- Screen for an allergy to latex (e.g., lips swelling from contact with bananas, kiwis, or latex balloons).
- Severely immunocompromised children (e.g., corticosteroid therapy, chemotherapy, AIDS) generally should not receive live vaccines
- Common Live vaccines are varicella-zoster vaccine, measles-mumps-rubella, rotavirus, flu vaccine (nasal) and yellow fever
    - OK to give even if allergic to Penicillin
- Mild illness (with or without an elevated temperature) is not a contraindication
- Mild site reactions (e.g., swelling, erythema, soreness) are expected

Childhood Vaccination Guidelines

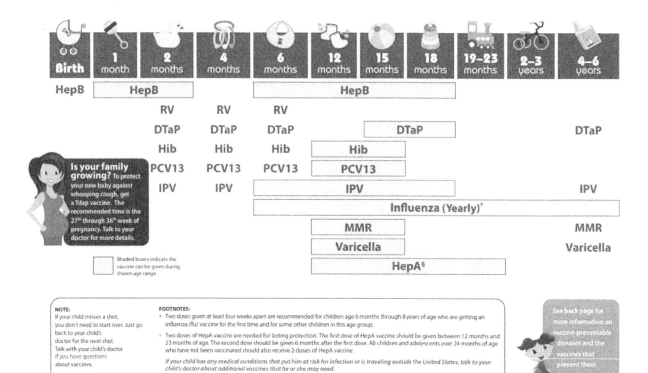

Birth	1 month	2 months	4 months	6 months	12 months	15 months	18 months	19–23 months	2–3 years	4–6 years
HepB	HepB				HepB					
		RV	RV	RV						
		DTaP	DTaP	DTaP	DTaP					DTaP
		Hib	Hib	Hib	Hib					
		PCV13	PCV13	PCV13	PCV13					
		IPV	IPV	IPV						IPV
				Influenza (Yearly)*						
					MMR					MMR
					Varicella					Varicella
					HepA§					

Is your family growing? To protect your new baby against whooping cough, get a Tdap vaccine. The recommended time is the 27th through 36th week of pregnancy. Talk to your doctor for more details.

Shaded boxes indicate the vaccine can be given during shown age range.

NOTE:
If your child misses a shot, you don't need to start over. Just go back to your child's doctor for the next shot. Talk with your child's doctor if you have questions about vaccines.

FOOTNOTES:
- Two doses given at least four weeks apart are recommended for children age 6 months through 8 years of age who are getting an influenza (flu) vaccine for the first time and for some other children in this age group.
- Two doses of HepA vaccine are needed for lasting protection. The first dose of HepA vaccine should be given between 12 months and 23 months of age. The second dose should be given 6 months after the first dose. All children and adolescents over 24 months of age who have not been vaccinated should also receive 2 doses of HepA vaccine.

If your child has any medical conditions that put him at risk for infection or is traveling outside the United States, talk to your child's doctor about additional vaccines that he or she may need.

See back page for more information on vaccine-preventable diseases and the vaccines that prevent them.

For more information, call toll-free
1-800-CDC-INFO (1-800-232-4636)
or visit
www.cdc.gov/vaccines/parents

**U.S. Department of
Health and Human Services**
Centers for Disease
Control and Prevention

Hematology/Oncology Medications

Anticoagulants

- Prevent clotting
- Ex: Heparin, Enoxaparin (Lovenox)
- Nursing Interventions: Monitor vital signs.
- Advise clients to observe for bleeding (Hypotension, tachycardia, bruising, petechiae, hematomas, black tarry stools). Use an electric razor for shaving and brush with a soft toothbrush. Use gloves when working in garden

Heparin

- Use an infusion pump for continuous IV administration.
- Monitor rate of infusion every 30 to 60 min.
- Monitor activated partial thromboplastin time (aPTT).
- Keep value at 1.5 to 2 times the baseline. Therapeutic level is 60 to 80 seconds. Apply gentle pressure for 1 to 2 min after the injection.
- Rotate and record injection sites.
- In the case of overdose, stop heparin, administer protamine, and avoid aspirin.
- Do not rub the site for 1 to 2 min after the injection

Enoxaparin (Lovenox)

- Mild pain, bruising, irritation, or redness of the skin at the injection site is common. Do NOT rub the site with the hand.
- Using an ice cube on the injection site can provide relief
- Avoid taking aspirin, nonsteroidal anti-inflammatory drugs (NSAIDs), and herbal supplements (Ginkgo biloba, vitamin E) - increase the risk of bleeding. Monitor CBC for thrombocytopenia

warfarin (Coumadin)

- Monitor levels of PT and international normalized ratio (INR) periodically.

- Therapeutic range of INR = 2-3
- INR of 3 to 3.5 (?4) for mechanical heart valve or recurrent systemic embolism.
- Overdose? – Give Vit. K
- Hepatotoxic - Monitor liver enzymes. Assess for jaundice
- Minimize changes with Vit K food: dark green leafy vegetables (lettuce, cooked spinach), cabbage, broccoli, Brussels sprouts, mayonnaise, canola, and soybean oil
- Full therapeutic effect is not achieved for 3 to 5 days.

Antiplatelets

- Inhibit platelet aggregation   Ex: Aspirin, clopidogrel
- Meds may be discontinued a week before surgery.
- Aspirin: GI effects (nausea, vomiting, dyspepsia), Tinnitus, hearing loss.
- Use cautiously - peptic ulcer disease and severe renal and/or hepatic disorders.
- Do not give to children or adolescents with fever or recent chickenpox (Reye's syndrome – swelling of liver and brain)

Reye's syndrome (Aspirin)

- Reye's syndrome most often affects children and teenagers recovering from a viral infection, most commonly the flu or chickenpox.
- Signs and symptoms such as confusion, seizures and loss of consciousness require emergency treatment. Early diagnosis and treatment of Reye's syndrome can save a child's life.
- Aspirin has been linked with Reye's syndrome, so use caution when giving aspirin to children or teenagers

Thrombolytic Medications

- Alteplase (tPA) – Give within 3 hrs. (stroke pts)

- Serious risk of bleeding from different sites – internal bleeding (GI or GU tracts and cerebral bleeding), as well as superficial bleeding (wounds, IV catheter sites).
- Obtain baseline platelet counts, hemoglobin (Hgb), hematocrit (Hct), aPTT, PT, INR, and fibrinogen levels, and monitor periodically.
- Limit venipunctures and injections. Apply pressure dressings to recent wounds.
- Monitor for changes in vital signs, alterations in level of consciousness, weakness, and indications of intracranial bleeding.
- Notify the provider if symptoms occur. Monitor aPTT and PT, Hgb, Hct.

Rivaroxaban (Xarelto)

- Provides anticoagulation selectively and directly by inhibiting factor Xa.
- Prevents DVT and pulmonary embolism in clients who are undergoing total hip or knee arthroplasty surgery.
- S/E: Hepatotoxic, bleeding (GI/GU/Retinal/Cranial)
- Teach client to report bleeding, bruising, headache, eye pain.
- Monitor hemoglobin and hematocrit.
- Wait at least 18 hr following last dose to remove an epidural catheter and wait 6 hr after removal before starting rivaroxaban again.
- No antidote is available for severe bleeding; not removed by dialysis.

Dabigatran (Pradaxa)

- Works by directly inhibiting thrombin
- S/E; Bleeding, GI discomfort, Hypotension, and headache
- Take dabigatran with food.
- Client may need a proton pump inhibitor, such as omeprazole (Prilosec) or an H2 receptor antagonist, such as ranitidine (Zantac) for GI manifestations.

Erythropoietic Growth Factors

- Act on the bone marrow to increase production of red blood cells. Used for Renal failure, chemo, HIV patients

- EX: Epoetin alfa (Epogen, Procrit), Aranesp
- S/E: Hypertension, Headache. Not to be used if Hb> 11 (risk for thrombus)

Neupogen

- Stimulate the bone marrow to increase production of neutrophils.
- S/E: Bone pain, Splenomegaly, risk of splenic rupture with long-term use
- Monitor CBC two times per week.

Name	Action	Side effect	Nursing Tips
	Antimetabolites		
methotrexate	Stops cell reproduction by inhibiting folic acid conversion	Bone marrow suppression,	Monitor WBC, absolute neutrophil count, platelet count, Hgb, and Hct.
	Contraindicated in renal or hepatic failure, blood dyscrasias, pregnancy, lactation		›› Assess clients for bruising and bleeding gums.
	Administer with leucovorin rescue to reduce toxicity to healthy cells.		›› Instruct clients to avoid crowds and contact with infectious individuals.
	gastric ulcers, perforation	GI discomfort	Monitor for GI bleed (coffee-ground emesis or tarry black stools).
	Advise female clients to use birth control during and for 6 months after completing	Mucositis (GI tract),	Assess the client's mouth for sores.
			›› Provide frequent oral hygiene using soft toothbrushes and avoid
			alcohol mouthwashes.
		Reproductive toxicity	Advise female clients against becoming pregnant while taking these
			medications and 6 months after
		Renal damage	Monitor kidney function, BUN, creatinine, and I&O.
			›› Encourage adequate fluid intake of 2 to 3 L/day.
			›› Administer allopurinol if uric acid level is elevated.

Name	Action	Side effect	Nursing Tips
cytarabine	Inhibits RNA and DNA synthesis of cancer cells	neurotoxicity, such as nystagmus	
	Cytarabine may reduce digoxin (Lanoxin) level.		Monitor digoxin level and ECG.
Fluorouracil	Inhibits RNA and DNA synthesis of cancer cells	Pulmonary edema	Monitor breath sounds. Advise clients to notify the provider of shortness of breath.
Capecitabine	Inhibits RNA and DNA synthesis of cancer cells	Arachnoiditis (include nausea, headache,and fever)	Advise clients to notify the provider of nausea, vomiting, headache, or fever. Manifestations may be treated with dexamethasone
Floxuridine	Inhibits RNA and DNA synthesis of cancer cells	Liver disease	Monitor liver enzymes. Monitor for indications of jaundice.
mercaptopurine	Interrupts RNA and DNA synthesis of cancer cells	Liver toxicity, GI, Reproductive	
	Mercaptopurine may either increase or decrease anticoagulant effect of warfarin.		Monitor PT and INR.
	Antitumor Antibiotics	Bone marrow suppression	
		Severe tissue damage due to extravasations of vesicants	
		Alopecia	
doxorubicin	Binds to DNA, altering its structure	Acute cardiac toxicity, dysrhythmias	Monitor ECG and echocardiogram.
		Cardiomyopathy, heart failure	The client may be treated with ACE inhibitors
		Red coloration to urine and sweat	Advise clients that this effect is not harmful

Name	Action	Side effect	Nursing Tips
		Doxorubicin may reduce phenytoin (Dilantin) levels.	Monitor phenytoin level
Daunorubicin			
dactinomycin			
Bleomycin			
Mitomycin		Mitomycin may increase risk for bronchospasm	Monitor breath sounds
	Antimitotics		
vincristine	Stops cell division	Peripheral neuropathy effects (weakness, paresthesia)	Advise clients to report manifestations. Use caution to prevent injury.
	Vincristine may reduce effects of digoxin. Moniter dig level	Severe tissue damage due to extravasations of vesicants	Stop chemotherapeutic medications if extravasation occurs.Only clinically trained personnel should give these medications, ›› Use
		Alopecia	
paclitaxel		Bone marrow suppression	
docetaxel		Bradycardia, heart block, MI	Monitor for cardiac effects.
		Alopecia	
	Alkylating Agents	Bone marrow suppression, GI discomfort, Alopecia	

Name	Action	Side effect	Nursing Tips
cyclophosphamide	Kills rapid growing cells		
Carmustine		Crosses the blood-brain barrier	
		Pulmonary fibrosis	Monitor lung function. The client may be treated with corticosteroids
		Liver and kidney toxicity	Monitor liver and kidney function
cisplatin		Acute hemorrhagic cystitis	Increase fluids (3 L daily).
		Renal toxicity	››Monitor for blood in urine.
			››Mesna (Mesnex) may be given if needed. Mesna is a uroprotectant agent
			that detoxifies metabolites to reduce hematuria
		Hearing loss	Monitor for tinnitus and hearing loss.

Other Antineoplastic Agents

Name	Action	Side effect	Nursing Tips
Asparaginase	May decrease effect of antidiabetic medication	Hypersensitivity reaction	Premedicate if needed. Monitor for wheezing and/or rash. Give test dose. Monitor closely.
		CNS effects ranging from confusion to coma; temporary tremor may	Monitor for CNS effects and evaluate frequently for changes
		Liver and pancreas toxicity	Monitor liver enzymes. Monitor for indications of jaundice, Monitor pancreatic enzymes

Name	Action	Side effect	Nursing Tips
		Renal toxicity	Monitor kidney function. Increase fluids and administer a diuretic if indicated
Hydroxyurea		Bone marrow suppression	
Procarbazine		Bone marrow suppression, Peripheral neuropathy symptoms	

Hormonal agents

	Prostate Cancer Medications	Hot flushes, decreased libido,and gynecomastia,	
leuprolide, triptore	Testes stop producing testosterone	Decreased bone density,Arrhythmias, pulmonary edema	Palliative treatment for advanced prostate cancer. Advise clients to increase calcium and vitamin D intake. Advise clients to increase bone mass with weight-bearing exercises. Monitor for arrhythmias and assess breath sounds.
flutamide	Blocks testosterone at receptor site	GI disturbances, Hepatitis	Contraindicated in clients who have severe liver disease.

	Breast Cancer		
tamoxifen	Stops growth of breast cancer cells	Endometrial cancer	Monitor for abnormal bleeding. Advise clients to have a yearly gynecological exam and PAP smear
	Contraindicated in clients taking warfarin and in clients who have a history of blood clots or	Hypercalcemia	Monitor calcium level.
	Tamoxifen may increase the anticoagulation action of warfarin.	Nausea and vomiting	Monitor fluid status. Administer fluids and antiemetics as prescribed

Name	Action	Side effect	Nursing Tips
		Pulmonary embolus	Assess breath sounds. Advise clients to report chest pain or shortness of breath.
		Hot flushes	Warn clients about adverse effects
		Vaginal discharge or bleeding	Monitor bleeding and discharge
anastrozole	Contraindicated in women before menopause and in severe liver disease	Muscle and joint pain, headache	Treat pain with a mild analgesic as prescribed.
		Nausea, Hot flushes	
		Vaginal bleeding	Monitor bleeding and CBC
		Increased risk for osteoporosis	Advise clients to take calcium and vitamin D supplements and perform weight-bearing exercises.
trastuzumab		Cardiac toxicity, tachycardia,heart failure	
		Hypersensitivity reaction	Monitor closely during infusion. Have resuscitation equipment nearby.
	Targeted Antineoplastic		
cetuximab	colorectal and solid tumors of the head and neck	Infusion reaction, rash,hypotension, wheezing	Monitor carefully for indications of a reaction, Premedicate if needed with diphenhydramine or corticosteroids, Stop treatment and administer antihistamines as prescribed.
		Pulmonary emboli	Monitor breath sounds. Monitor SaO2.
	Sun exposure may increase skin toxicity.	Skin toxicity, rash	Monitor for rash over 2 weeks of treatment. Treat with topical antibiotics if needed.

Name	Action	Side effect	Nursing Tips
imatinib	Treat chronic myeloid leukemia	›› GI discomfort	Administer antiemetic before chemo, Take med with food
	Acetaminophen may increase chance of liver failure.	Flulike symptoms (fever, fatigue, headache, chills, myalgia)	Supportive treatment (tylenol)
		Edema, Hypokalemia	Closlely monitor
		Neutropenia, anemia	Monitor CBC. Assess for bruising and bleeding gums, Instruct clients to avoid crowds and contact with infectious individuals.
rituximab	non-Hodgkin's lymphoma	Infusion reaction, rash, hypotension, wheezing, flu like	Monitor carefully for indications of a reaction. Premedicate if needed with diphenhydramine or corticosteroids. Stop treatment and administer
	antihypertensive medications increase chance of hypotension	Tumor lysis syndrome due to rapid cell death may lead to kidney	Monitor kidney function, dialyze if needed. Monitor fluids and electrolytes. Teach the client to report manifestations, which begin 12 to 24
bevacizumab		Thromboembolism, cerebrovascular accident, myocardial	Monitor for thromboembolic disorders.
	Contraindicated in clients who have a low WBC, nephrotic syndrome, recent surgery or	Hemorrhage – GI, vaginal, nasal, intracranial, or	
		Hypertension, Gastric perforation	

Psychosocial Concepts

Overview

- Each encounter with a client involves an ongoing assessment.
- Psychosocial History: Includes
  - Perception of own health, beliefs about illness and wellness
  - Activity/leisure activities/Use of substances/support system/Stress level and coping abilities /Cultural beliefs and practices/ Spiritual beliefs
- Admission:
  - Voluntary commitment – The client or client's guardian chooses commitment to a mental health facility in order to obtain treatment. (competent)
  - Involuntary (civil) commitment – The client enters the mental health facility against her will, based on the client's need for psychiatric treatment, the risk of harm to self or others, or the inability to provide self-care (food/shelter/clothing/medical care/personal safety)
  - Determined by Court/Judge/2 doctors/state policies
  - The client is still considered competent unless declared as incompetent by authority. If incompetent, the client will have a guardian (family member/person appointed by court)

Mental Status Examination and Assessment

- Physical appearance: personal hygiene, grooming, and clothing choice
- Behavior: voluntary and involuntary body movements, and eye contact.
- Assess the client's orientation to time, person, and place.
- Abstract thinking (higher thought process) and Judgment
- Assess the client's memory, both recent and remote.
  - Immediate – Ask the client to repeat a series of numbers or a list of objects.

- Recent – Ask the client to recall recent events, such as visitors from the current day, or the purpose of the current mental health appointment or admission.
- Remote – Ask the client to state a fact from his past that is verifiable, such as his birth date or his mother's maiden name

Level of consciousness

- Alert – The client is responsive and able to fully respond by opening her eyes and attending to a normal tone of voice and speech. She answers questions spontaneously and appropriately.
- Lethargy – The client is able to open her eyes and respond but is drowsy and falls asleep readily.
- Stupor – The client requires vigorous or painful stimuli (pinching a tendon or rubbing the sternum) to elicit a brief response. She may not be able to respond verbally.
- Coma - NO response can be achieved from repeated painful stimuli.
- Glasgow Coma Scale

Safety

- No access to sharp or otherwise harmful objects
- Restriction of client access to restricted or locked areas
- Monitoring of visitors
- Restriction of alcohol and illegal substance access or use
- Rapid de-escalation of disruptive and potentially violent behaviors through planned interventions by trained staff
  - Seclusion rooms and restraints should be set up for safety and used only after all less restrictive measures have been exhausted. When used, facility policies and procedures must be followed.
- Plan for safe access to recreational areas, occupational therapy, and meeting rooms.

Therapeutic Nurse-Client Relationship

- Phases of therapeutic relation: Pre-interaction (getting ready), Orientation (introductory), Working phase (interventions), Termination (separation)
- Consistently focus on the client's ideas, experiences, and feelings.
- Identify and explore the client's needs and problems.
- Discuss problem-solving alternatives with the client.
- Help to develop the client's strengths and new coping skills.
- Encourage positive behavior change in the client.
- Assist the client to develop a sense of autonomy and self-reliance.
- Portray genuineness, empathy, and a positive regard toward the client.
- The nurse practices empathy by remaining nonjudgmental and attempting to understand the client's actions and feelings.
- This differs from sympathy, in which the nurse allows herself to feel the way the client does and is non-therapeutic.

Therapeutic Communication

- Client centered – not social or reciprocal (taking advantage)
- Purposeful, planned, and goal-directed
- Attending behaviors, caring, active listening
- Nonjudgmental attitude, trust, honesty, empathy
- Children
    - Use simple, straightforward language. Be aware of own nonverbal messages, as children are sensitive to nonverbal communication.
    - Enhance communication by being at the child's eye level.
    - Incorporate play in interactions
- Older Adult Clients
    - Recognize that the client may require amplification.
    - Minimize distractions and face the client when speaking.
    - Allow plenty of time for the client to respond.
    - When impaired communication is assessed, ask for input from caregivers or family to determine the extent of the deficits and how best to communicate.

Effective Skills and Techniques for therapeutic communication

- Silence: Allows time for meaningful reflection.
- Active listening: The nurse is able to hear, observe, and understand what the client communicates and to provide feedback.
- Open-ended questions: This technique facilitates spontaneous responses and interactive discussion
- Showing acceptance and recognition
- Focusing: helps client to concentrate on what is important
- Asking questions
- Summarizing: emphasizes important points and reviews what has been discussed.

Clarifying techniques

- To determine if the message received was accurate:
- Restating – uses the client's exact words.
- Reflecting – directs the focus back to the client in order for the client to examine his feelings.
- Paraphrasing – restates the client's feelings and thoughts for the client to confirm what has been communicated.
- Exploring – allows the nurse to gather more information regarding important topics mentioned by the client.

Barriers to Effective Communication

- Asking irrelevant personal questions -Why didn't you marry yet?
- Offering personal opinions -If it was me, I would have opted for DNR
- Giving advice, giving false reassurance: "No reason to worry"
- Minimizing feelings – "You should not be this depressed over it"
- Changing the topic. Asking "why" questions
- Offering value judgments: You form an opinion about it based on your principles and beliefs and not on facts which can be checked or proved.
- "You should not accept blood transfusion. It's not right"

- Excessive questioning
- Responding approvingly or disapprovingly – "Abortion is women's right"

Terms to know

- Transference: Transference occurs when the client views a member of the health care team as having characteristics of another person who has been significant to the client's personal life.
- Counter transference: Counter transference occurs when a health care team member displaces characteristics of people in her past onto a client.

Mental Health Nursing Interventions

Counseling	›› Using therapeutic communication skills ›› Assisting with problem solving, Crisis intervention ›› Stress management
Milieu therapy	›› Management of total environment of the mental health unit to provide the least amount of stress: **Patient could cope adaptively, interact more effectively and appropriately, and strengthen relationship skills** ➤Orienting the client to the physical setting ›› **Identifying rules and boundaries of the setting** ›› Ensuring **a safe environment** for the client ›› Assisting the client to participate in appropriate **activities**
Promotion of self-care activities	››Offering assistance with self-care tasks ›› Allowing time for the client to complete self-care tasks ›› Setting incentives to promote client self-care

Health promotion & health maintenance	››Assisting the client with cessation of smoking ››Monitoring other health conditions
Psychobiological interventions	›› Administering prescribed medications ›› Providing teaching to the client/family about medications ››Monitoring for adverse effects and effectiveness of pharmacological therapy
Cognitive and behavioral therapies (CBT)	5 components

CBT :5 components:

- Education about the client's specific disorder
- Self-observation and Monitoring - the client learns how to monitor anxiety, identify triggers, and assess the severity.
- Physical control strategies – Deep breathing and muscle relaxation exercises.
- Cognitive restructuring – learning new ways to reframe thinking patterns, challenging negative thoughts
- Behavioral strategies – focusing on situations that cause anxiety and practicing new coping behaviors, desensitization to anxiety-provoking situations or events.

Defense Mechanism

- Coping: term that describes how an individual deals with problems and issues. (Adaptive –good), Maladaptive (not good)
- Nurses' role – Identify coping strategies, promote healthy ones.
- Stress causes anxiety. Defense Mechanisms are strategies that assist client to protect their own ego and reduce anxiety.
- Dysfunctional behavior may occur when a defense mechanism is used as a response to anxiety.

- Do not take the defense mechanism away until client has established more appropriate coping strategies to effectively deal with stressors.
- Assess if defense mechanism is causing additional stress.
- Don't argue or criticize clients for their use of DM
- Healthy DM: Altruism and sublimation
- Immature DM: projection, displacement, splitting, denial

DEFENSE MECHANISM	DESCRIPTION	EXAMPLE
Altruism	› Dealing with anxiety by reaching out to others	› A nurse who lost a family member in a fire is a volunteer firefighter.
Sublimation	› Dealing with unacceptable feelings or impulses by unconsciously substituting acceptable forms of expression	› A person who has feelings of anger and hostility toward his work supervisor sublimates those feelings by working out vigorously at the gym during his lunch period.
Suppression	› Voluntarily denying unpleasant thoughts and feelings	› A person who has lost his job states he will worry about paying his bills next week.
Repression	› Putting unacceptable ideas, thoughts, and emotions out of conscious awareness	› A person who has a fear of the dentist's drill continually "forgets" his dental appointments.

DEFENSE MECHANISM	DESCRIPTION	EXAMPLE
Displacement	› Shifting feelings related to an object, person, or situation to another less threatening object, person, or situation	› A person who is angry about losing his job destroys his child's favorite toy.
Reaction formation	› Overcompensating or demonstrating the opposite behavior of what is felt	› A person who dislikes her sister's daughter offers to babysit so that her sister can go out of town.
Undoing	› Performing an act to make up for prior behavior	› An adolescent completes his chores without being prompted after having an argument with his parent.
Rationalization	› Creating reasonable and acceptable explanations for unacceptable behavior	› A young adult explains he had to drive home from a party after drinking alcohol because he had to feed his dog.

Dissociation	· Temporarily blocking memories and perceptions from consciousness	· An adolescent witnesses a shooting and is unable to recall any details of the event.
Splitting	· Demonstrating an inability to reconcile negative and positive attributes of self or others	· A client tells a nurse that she is the only one who cares about her, yet the following day, the same client refuses to talk to the nurse.
Projection	· Blaming others for unacceptable thoughts and feelings	· A young adult blames his substance use disorder on his parents' refusal to buy him a new car.
Denial	· Pretending the truth is not reality to manage the anxiety of acknowledging what is real	· A parent who is informed that his son was killed in combat tells everyone he is coming home for the holidays.
Regression	· Demonstrating behavior from an earlier developmental level · Often exhibited as childlike or immature behavior	· A school-age child begins wetting the bed and sucking his thumb after learning that his parents are separating. Source: ATI nursing education

Mental Health Disorders

Anxiety

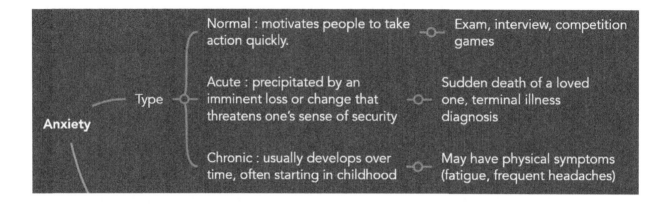

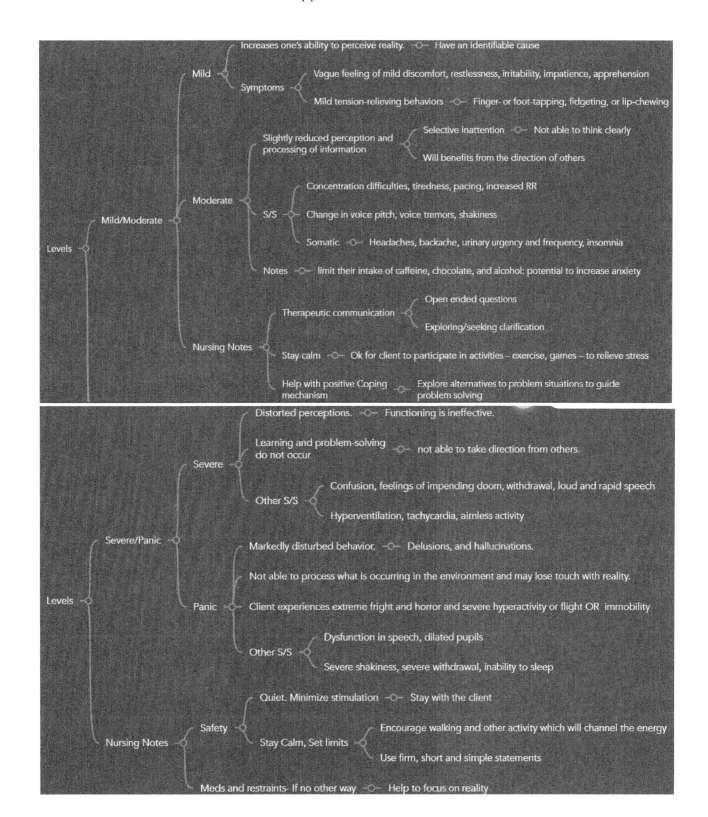

Levels

Mild/Moderate

Mild
- Increases one's ability to perceive reality. — Have an identifiable cause
- Symptoms
  - Vague feeling of mild discomfort, restlessness, irritability, impatience, apprehension
  - Mild tension-relieving behaviors — Finger- or foot-tapping, fidgeting, or lip-chewing

Moderate
- Slightly reduced perception and processing of information
  - Selective inattention — Not able to think clearly
  - Will benefits from the direction of others
- S/S
  - Concentration difficulties, tiredness, pacing, increased RR
  - Change in voice pitch, voice tremors, shakiness
  - Somatic — Headaches, backache, urinary urgency and frequency, insomnia
- Notes — limit their intake of caffeine, chocolate, and alcohol: potential to increase anxiety

Nursing Notes
- Therapeutic communication
  - Open ended questions
  - Exploring/seeking clarification
- Stay calm — Ok for client to participate in activities – exercise, games – to relieve stress
- Help with positive Coping mechanism — Explore alternatives to problem situations to guide problem solving

Levels

Severe/Panic

Severe
- Distorted perceptions. — Functioning is ineffective.
- Learning and problem-solving do not occur — not able to take direction from others.
- Other S/S
  - Confusion, feelings of impending doom, withdrawal, loud and rapid speech
  - Hyperventilation, tachycardia, aimless activity

Panic
- Markedly disturbed behavior. — Delusions, and hallucinations.
- Not able to process what is occurring in the environment and may lose touch with reality.
- Client experiences extreme fright and horror and severe hyperactivity or flight OR immobility
- Other S/S
  - Dysfunction in speech, dilated pupils
  - Severe shakiness, severe withdrawal, inability to sleep

Nursing Notes
- Safety
  - Quiet. Minimize stimulation — Stay with the client
  - Stay Calm, Set limits
    - Encourage walking and other activity which will channel the energy
    - Use firm, short and simple statements
- Meds and restraints- If no other way — Help to focus on reality

Medications for Anxiety

Sedative Hypnotic Anxiolytic – Benzodiazepine

- alprazolam (Xanax), Diazepam (Valium), Lorazepam (Ativan), Oxazepam
- Chlordiazepoxide (Librium), Clorazepate, Clonazepam (Klonopin)
- Relief from anxiety occurs rapidly following administration
- Diazepam is contraindicated in clients who have sleep apnea, respiratory depression and/or glaucoma (close angle)
- Benzodiazepines are generally used short term –dependence
- Avoid abrupt discontinuation – Taper the dose
- Give with food to reduce GI discomfort
- Benzodiazepine toxicity – Assessment, IV, Gastric Lavage, administering flumazenil (to reverse the effect)
- Nonbarbiturate Anxiolytic - Buspirone (BuSpar)
    - Dependency is much less likely. No sedation
    - S/E: Dizziness, nausea, headache, lightheadedness, agitation
    - Might take up to 3 to 6 weeks for the full benefit
    - Buspirone is not recommended for women who are breastfeeding
    - Buspirone is contraindicated for concurrent use with MAOI antidepressants or for 14 days after MAOIs are discontinued. Hypertensive crisis may result.

Selective Serotonin Reuptake Inhibitors (SSRI - Antidepressants)

- Sertraline, Paroxetine, Escitalopram, Citalopram, Fluoxetine, Fluvoxamine (SPEC FF)
- SNRI- selective serotonin and norepinephrine reuptake inhibitors (SNRIs) – Venlafaxine
- May take up to 4 weeks for therapeutic effect
- Medications may be taken with food. Avoid alcohol.
- Sleep disturbances are minimized by taking medication in the morning.
- Early adverse effects (first few days/weeks):

- nausea, diaphoresis, tremor, fatigue, drowsiness: Instruct clients to take the medication as prescribed, advise clients that these effects should soon subside.

SSRI - Other Side Effects

- Later adverse effects (after 5 to 6 weeks of therapy): sexual dysfunction, weight gain, GI bleeding, Hyponatremia
- Bruxism: grinding and clenching of teeth, usually during sleep
- Paroxetine is contraindicated in clients taking some antidepressants like MAOIs or a TCA.
- Withdrawal syndrome: Taper the dose
- Nausea, sensory disturbances, anxiety, tremor, malaise, unease:

Serotonin syndrome: HATRED FACT

- Hallucinations, Agitation, Tremors, Reflex - hyper, easily distracted (difficulty concentrating), Diaphoresis, Fever, Anxiety, Confusion (disorientation), Tachycardia
- Usually begins 2 to 72 hr after initiation of treatment. Resolves when the medication is discontinued
- Watch for and advise clients to report any of these manifestations, which could indicate a lethal problem.
- SSRI side effects (major)
- S – Sleep problems,
- S – Sexual Dysfunction
- S - Stomach upset
- S – Serotonin Syndrome
- S – Scale (weight gain – long term)

Obsessive-Compulsive Disorder (OCD)

- Obsessions: Preoccupation with persistent intrusive thoughts and ideas
- Compulsions: Performance of rituals or repetitive behaviors designed to prevent some event, divert unacceptable thoughts, and decrease anxiety.

- If the ritual is interrupted, the client will experience increased anxiety.
- Interventions
  - Ensure basic needs are met
  - Identify situations that precipitate the compulsive behavior
  - Encourage client to express feelings
  - Do not interrupt the compulsive behavior; set limits and protect client from harm
  - Establish written contract that will assist client to decrease frequency of behaviors

Post-Traumatic Stress Disorder

- After experiencing a psychologically traumatic event, the individual re-experiences the event and has recurrent and intense dreams and flashbacks
- Stressors: Natural disaster/Terrorist attack /Combat experience/Accidents/ Victims of rape, crime, or violence
- Assessment
  - Sleep disturbances and nightmares, Flashbacks of event
  - Poor concentration, avoidance of activities that trigger recollection of event
  - Emotional numbness, detachment, depression

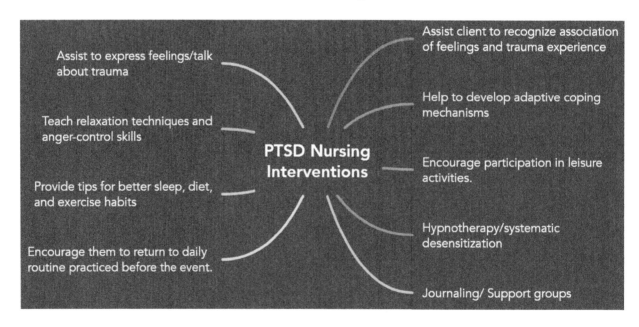

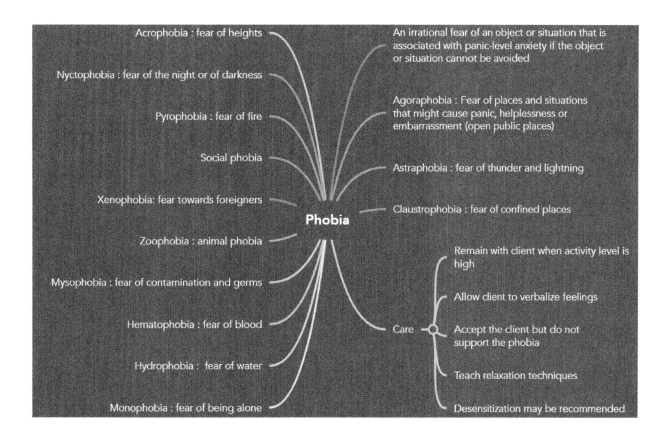

Generalized Anxiety Disorder

- Unrealistic anxiety about everyday worries that persists over time and is not associated with a mental health or medical disorder
- Assessment
  - Restlessness, Chronic muscular tension, Inability to concentrate
  - Chronic fatigue and sleep problems
- Interventions
  - Address physical discomforts
  - Assist client to identify thoughts that aroused anxiety (stressors/triggers)
  - Assist client to change unrealistic thoughts to more realistic ones
  - Recognize that some level of anxiety is normal in daily life.

How to help family when there is a critical incident (NCLEX points)

- Acknowledge the severity of the event. It's overwhelming for family.
- Assis the family in identifying their feelings.
  - Shock, denial, anger, helplessness, numbness, disbelief, and confusion are common.
- Give the family an opportunity to ventilate: This reduces immediate emotional stress.
- Reduce the immediate emotional impact of disruptive crisis on family.
  - Provide psychological support
- Check for physical symptoms and offer supportive care
  - Hyperventilation, abdominal pain, and dizziness are common

Delusions and Hallucinations

- Delusion: Alterations in thought which are false fixed beliefs that cannot be corrected by reasoning.
- Hallucinations: Alterations in perception/senses
- Auditory – hearing voices or sounds. (Command – the voice instructs the client to perform an action, such as to hurt self or others)
- Visual – seeing persons or things.
- Olfactory – smelling odors.
- Gustatory – experiencing tastes.
- Tactile – feeling bodily sensations.

DELUSIONS	EXAMPLES
Ideas of reference	› Misconstrues trivial events and attaches personal significance to them, such as believing that others, who are discussing the next meal, are talking about him.
Persecution	› Feels singled out for harm by others (e.g., being hunted down by the FBI).
Grandeur	› Believes that she is all powerful and important, like a god.
Somatic delusions	› Believes that his body is changing in an unusual way, such as growing a third arm.
Jealousy	› May feel that her spouse is sexually involved with another individual.
Being controlled	› Believes that a force outside his body is controlling him.
Thought broadcasting	› Believes that her thoughts are heard by others.
Thought insertion	› Believes that others' thoughts are being inserted into his mind.
Thought withdrawal	› Believes that her thoughts have been removed from her mind by an outside agency.
Religiosity	› Is obsessed with religious beliefs.

Source: ATI nursing education

Communication – Delusion and Hallucination

- Ask the client directly about hallucinations. The nurse should not argue or agree with the client's view of the situation but may offer a comment: "I don't hear anything, but you seem to be feeling frightened."
- Do not argue with a client's delusions but focus on the client's feelings and possibly offer reasonable explanations: "I can't imagine that the president of the United States would have a reason to kill a citizen, but it must be frightening for you to believe that."
- Assess the client for paranoid delusions, which can increase the risk for violence against others.
- Provide for safety if the client is experiencing command hallucinations due to the increased risk for harm to self or others.
- Attempt to focus conversations on reality-based subjects.

- Identify symptom triggers, such as loud noises (may trigger auditory hallucinations in certain clients) and situations that seem to trigger conversations about the client's delusions.
- Be genuine and empathetic in all dealings with the client.
- Symptom management techniques:
  - Using music to distract from "voices,"
  - Attending activities, walking, talking to a trusted person when hallucinations are most bothersome,
  - Interacting with an auditory or visual hallucination by telling it to stop or go away.

Depression

Major Depression (WONT WISH LIFE)

- Withdrawal/ worthlessness
- Overwhelming Mood (agitation/retardation)
- No concentration or Thinking

- Weight change (loss /gain)
- Insomnia
- Suicidal ideation
- Hopelessness

- Loss of interest in life
- Interest Deficit (Diminished interest in pleasure)
- Fatigue or loss of energy everyday
- Energy loss

- Treatment
- Cognitive-behavioral therapy (CBT): assists the client to identify and change negative behavior and thought patterns.

Electroconvulsive therapy (ECT)

- ECT is effective for clients who have bipolar disorder and suicidal ideation.
- Temporary memory loss is possible
- Nursing care – same for surgery patient with sedation.

- Protect airway, Monitor vital signs, safety
- ECT – when meds don't work. 6-12 treatments- 2-5 days. NPO, concent
- In general, medications that raise seizure threshold or impede seizure propagation (interfere with induction or spread of a robust seizure) should be avoided if possible, or the dose decreased (e.g., anticonvulsants and benzodiazepines).
- Cardiac medications, antihypertensives, and GI medications can typically be continued.

Nursing care – Depression

- Assist with activities of daily living and attend to physiological needs (e.g., nutrition, rest, sleep)
- Avoid presenting complex decision-making situations to client
- Provide structured environment and activities in which client can achieve success
- Safety of Nurse: Remove objects or barriers to prevent injury
- Decrease environmental stimuli

Measures to help the client sleep (Nonpharmacological)

- Avoid naps throughout the day
- Physical activity: Should be completed at least 5 hours before bedtime
- Adequate sunlight (at least 20 minutes during daytime)
- Avoid alcohol/coffee/smoking/heavy meals/large amount of fluids before bedtime (a cup of warm milk is ok)
- Relaxing activity before bedtime: warm bath, reading, listening to music
- Dark, cool, and quiet bedroom

Antidepressants

- Do not discontinue medication suddenly.
- Therapeutic effects are not immediate, and it may take several weeks or more to reach full therapeutic benefits.

- Avoid hazardous activities, such as driving or operating heavy equipment/machinery, due to the potential adverse effect of sedation.
- Notify the provider of any thoughts of suicide.
- Avoid alcohol while taking an antidepressant.
- St. John's wort- herbal med

Suicidal ideation

- Assess for suicidal ideation and provide safety
- Danger more prominent when client begins to regain strength and hope, especially beginning of antidepressant meds
- Assess frequently – ask questions about any plans for suicide, Sign "No self-harm" contract.
- Assess carefully for verbal and nonverbal clues. It is essential to ask the client if he is thinking of suicide. This will not give the client the idea to commit suicide.
- Overt sign – sudden happiness, giving away possessions, inability to see future of self, refuse meds or therapy, making comments.

SAD PERSONS (risk for suicide)

- S: **S**ex (men kill themselves more often than women; women make more attempts)
- A: **A**ge (teenagers/young adults, age >45)
- D: **D**epression (and hopelessness)
- P: **P**rior history of suicide attempt
- E: **E**thanol and/or drug abuse
- R: **R**ational thinking loss (hearing voices to harm self)
- S: **S**upport system loss (living alone)
- O: **O**rganized plan; having a method in mind (with lethality and availability)
- N: **N**o significant other
- S: **S**ickness (terminal illness)

Tricyclic Antidepressant Overdose

- Effects:
    - Cardiac Arrest: Life threatening arrythmia (Vtac/Vfib) due to QT prolongation; tachycardia, orthostatic hypotension
    - CNS Effects: LOC changes, Seizures, respiratory depression
    - Anticholinergic: Urinary retention, blurred vision, dilated pupils, dry mouth, flushing, hyperthermia, dry skin
- Intervention
    - IV fluids, Sodium bicarbonate IV (to neutralize toxic levels of TCA), 12 lead ECG, Urinary catheter

Opioid Overdose

- Effects
    - CNS Effects: LOC changes, respiratory depression, pupillary constriction (miosis/pinpointed)
    - Bradycardia, hypothermia, hypoactive bowel sounds
    - Methadone overdose? – QT prolongation (need ECG)
- Intervention
    - Labs: ABG, Blood sugar, ECG
    - Naloxone – antidot
    - Airway management/ventilation
    - Telemetry

Suicide precautions

- Initiate one-on-one constant supervision around the clock, always having the client in sight and close.
- Document the client's location, mood, quoted statements, and behavior every 15 min or per facility protocol.
- Remove all glass, metal silverware, electrical cords, vases, belts, shoelaces, metal nail files, matches, razors, perfume, shampoo, and plastic bags from the client's room and vicinity.

- Allow the client to use only plastic eating utensils.
- Check the environment for possible hazards (such as windows that open)
- Do not assign to a private room if possible and keep door open at all times.
- Ensure that the client swallows all medications.
- Restrict the visitors from bringing possibly harmful items to the client.

Bipolar Disorder: Manic Depressive Disorder

- Periods of normal functioning alternate with periods of illness,
- Some clients are not able to maintain full occupational and social functioning.
- Also called Manic- Depressive disorder
- A client in a truly manic state usually will not stop moving, and does not eat, drink, or sleep. This can become a medical emergency.

BIPOLAR DISORDER CLINICAL MANIFESTATIONS	
Manic characteristics	
› Labile mood with euphoria	› Demanding and manipulative behavior
› Agitation and irritability	› Distractibility and decreased attention span
› Restlessness	› Poor judgment
› Dislike of interference and intolerance of criticism	› Attention-seeking behavior – flashy dress and makeup, inappropriate behavior
› Increase in talking and activity	› Impairment in social and occupational functioning
› Flight of ideas – rapid, continuous speech with sudden and frequent topic change	› Decreased sleep
› Grandiose view of self and abilities (grandiosity)	› Neglect of ADLs, including nutrition and hydration
› Impulsivity – spending money, giving away money or possessions	› Possible presence of delusions and hallucinations
	› Denial of illness

Source: ATI nursing education

Depressive characteristics	
› Flat, blunted, labile affect	› Difficulty concentrating, focusing, problem-solving
› Tearfulness, crying	› Self-destructive behavior, including suicidal ideation
› Lack of energy	› Decrease in personal hygiene
› Anhedonia – loss of pleasure and lack of interest in activities, hobbies, sexual activity	› Loss or increase in appetite and/or sleep, disturbed sleep
› Physical reports of discomfort/pain	› Psychomotor retardation or agitation

Source: ATI nursing education

Acute Manic Episode care

- Provide a safe environment during the acute phase.
- Priority for staff: Manage escalating agitation (client may get violent and pose a threat to everyone)
- Assess the client regularly for suicidal thoughts, intentions, and escalating behavior.
- Decrease stimulation without isolating the client if possible.
- Be aware of noise, music, television, and other clients, all of which may lead to an escalation of the client's behavior.
- In certain cases, seclusion may be the only way to safely decrease stimulation for the client
- Provide high-calorie finger foods, fluids
- Provide outlets for physical activity (dancing, walking)
- Implement frequent rest periods.
- Do not involve the client in activities that last a long time or that require a high level of concentration and/or detailed instructions. Group therapy may have to wait until acute mania subsides. One-to-one interactions are better.
- Avoid competitive games.
- Ok to watch TV – so mind is not preoccupied with bad thoughts
- Supervise self-administration of medication

- Protect client from poor judgment and impulsive behavior, such as giving money away and sexual comments and triggers.
- Communications- Use a calm, matter of fact, specific approach.
- Do not react personally to the client's comments
- A private room is preferred.

Medications and treatment

- Mood stabilizers
    - Lithium carbonate
    - Anticonvulsants that act as mood stabilizers, including valproic acid, clonazepam
- Benzodiazepines, such as lorazepam (Ativan), used on a short-term basis for a client experiencing sleep impairment related to mania
- Antidepressants, such as the SSRI fluoxetine (Prozac), used to manage a major depressive episode
- Therapeutic Procedures – ECT (not helpful in prevention of bipolar, not used for initial therapy- medications are used as initial therapy)

Lithium

- Therapeutic drug level – 1.2 mEq/l (Toxicity starts by 1.5)
- Mild side effects: Drowsiness, weight gain, dry mouth, GI upset
- Take with food. Maintain adequate fluids and salt
- Lithium toxicity: Increased risk with dehydration- hyponatremia, decreased renal function, and drug-drug interactions (e.g., nonsteroidal anti-inflammatory drugs, thiazide diuretics).
- Educate and monitor for above conditions to avoid lithium toxicity
- Toxicity S/S: Start with N/V/D…progress to neurological symptoms (ataxia, LOC changes, agitation, tremors)
- May affect thyroid functions

Autism Spectrum disorder (ASD)

- Genetic component: Common in siblings

- Children exhibit sensory processing problems: Hyper- or hypo-sensitive to sounds, lights, movement, touch, taste, and smells
- Follow a structured routine in the hospital consistent with client's usual patterns at home as much as possible to decrease anxiety and stimulation
- A calming environment with minimal stimulation: Nursing Action: -
- Use a quiet or monotone voice when speaking to the child
- Use eye contact and gestures carefully, Move slowly
- Limit visual clutter, Maintain minimal lighting
- Provide the child with a single object to focus on
- Private rooms away from busy areas are the best room assignment.

Aspergers and Retts syndrome

- Aspergers- deficiencies in social and communication skills. A form of autism
- Retts: Neurodevelopmental disorder: More in girls (linked to X chromosome)
    - Characterized by psychomotor regression with loss of purposeful hand use and spoken language, the development of repetitive hand stereotypies, and gait impairment.
    - Children with Rett syndrome often exhibit autistic-like behaviors in the early stages
- Care: Situation basis: Supportive Care: Follow general instructions for ASD

Intermittent Explosive Disorder (IED)

- Recurrent episodes of aggression involving violence or destruction of property out of proportion to provocation or precipitating stressors.
- Impulsive (happen rapidly) outbursts – not planned
- IED clients may attack others and their possessions, causing bodily injury and property damage. (Animals may be harmed).
- Temper tantrums, domestic violence, and road rage can also be part of IED.
- IED predisposes clients to depression, anxiety, and substance abuse disorders.

- Treatment: Psychotherapy, CBT, Meds (SSRI, Antidepressants, mood stabilizers, Anticonvulsants, Antianxiety)

Schizophrenia

- Characterized by psychotic features (hallucinations and delusions), disordered thought processes, and disrupted interpersonal relationships

Assessment

- Neglecting physical needs (Nutrition/rest/sleep)
- Inappropriate or bizarre motor activity: catatonic posture- waxy flexibility (Set Limits/ daily routines)
- May view the world as threatening or unsafe (Safety)
- Compulsive rituals (OCD management)
- Inappropriate affect
- Impaired thought processes (Re-orient, use simple commands)
- Hallucinations, delusions (long lasting/ difficult to treat)
- Language and communication disturbances
- Responding to internal stimuli (laughing for no reason/self-talk)

ALTERATIONS IN SPEECH	
Flight of ideas	› Associative looseness › The client may say sentence after sentence, but each sentence may relate to another topic, and the listener is unable to follow the client's thoughts.
Neologisms	› Made-up words that have meaning only to the client, such as, "I tranged and flittled."
Echolalia	› The client repeats the words spoken to him.
Clang association	› Meaningless rhyming of words, often forceful, such as, "Oh fox, box, and lox."
Word salad	› Words jumbled together with little meaning or significance to the listener, such as, "Hip hooray, the flip is cast and wide-sprinting in the forest." Source: ATI nursing education

Types of schizophrenia

- Paranoid: Others are out to harm him, auditory hallucinations (suspicious)
- Disorganized: Disorganized speech, behavior, flat affect
- Catatonic: Stupor (change - consciousness), inappropriate posture, echolalia (waxy flexibility)
- Undifferentiated: Delusions and hallucinations present
- Residual: No prominent symptom, social withdrawal present.

Medications – Antipsychotics

- Antipsychotics- to treat positive and negative symptoms
- Positive symptoms – The manifestation of things that are not normally present. These are the most easily identified symptoms
    - Example- Delusions, Hallucinations, Bizarre behavior, such as walking backward constantly, disorganized speech
- Negative symptoms – The absence of things that are normally present. These symptoms are more difficult to treat successfully than positive symptoms.
    - Example: Affect –flat (facial expression never changes)
- Alogia- poverty of speech-reduced volume, lack of spontaneous comments, brief responses), Anergia – lack of energy,
- Avolition – lack of motivation in activities and hygiene.
- Catatonia

Personality Disorders

- Maladaptive behavior (Antisocial, paranoid, OCD, Dependent)
- Self-assessment is vital for nurses.
- Maintain safety
- A firm, yet supportive approach and consistent care, realistic choices
- Encourage client to discuss feelings rather than act on them - expectations and consequences of behaviors
- Assist client to deal directly with mood changes (e.g., anger). Set and maintain limits to decrease manipulative behavior

- Provide praise for positive behaviors
- Clients who have schizoid personality disorders tend to isolate themselves, and the nurse should respect this need.
- Codependent personality
    - They will plan their entire life around pleasing the other person
    - Codependent person will first fulfill all the needs of the addict
    - (Codependent person (enabler) will keep the addiction as a secret, will be ok with suffering abuse from addict, make excuses for addict's habits, will try to portray the addict as an ok person.
    - Enablers continually try to fix the problem, or they ignore it and pretend it doesn't exist.
- Avoidant personality disorder - They fear abandonment
- Narcissistic personality: Arrogant, self-importance, want consistent admiration, lack of empathy, don't accept criticism, fragile self-esteem
- Munchausen syndrome (factitious disorder): A person repeatedly and deliberately acts as if they have a physical or mental illness when they are not really sick
- Munchausen syndrome by proxy – a caregiver makes up or causes an illness or injury in a person under his or her care, such as a child, an elderly adult, or a person who has a disability

Somatoform Disorders

Persistent worry or complaints regarding physical illness without supporting physical findings. Might be benefiting from secondary gains of "being sick" (attention from others, freedom from responsibilities)

- Discourage verbalization about physical symptoms (Redirect the conversation to neutral, unrelated topics)
- Allow specific time period to discuss physical complaints
- Address triggers (stress) and encourage appropriate coping mechanism (relaxation techniques, diversional activities)
- Convey understanding that physical symptoms are real to client (be nonjudgmental)

Substance Abuse

- Common: Alcohol, sedatives (pain meds), stimulants (cocaine)
- Self-assessment of own feelings by nurse
- Safety is the primary focus of nursing care during acute intoxication or withdrawal.
- Prevent falls; implement seizure precautions, Create a low-stimulation environment.
- Orient the client to time, place, and person.
- Maintain adequate nutrition and fluid balance.
- Alcoholism: Thiamine (vit B1) replacement to prevent Wernicke encephalopathy (occurs due to thiamine deficiency in alcoholics) and Korsakoff psychosis (neurological morbidity)
- Administer medications, folic acid, magnesium, glucose (thiamine is given before glucose- as glucose will get oxidized by available thiamine in client's body, leading to more deficiency of thiamine and WE if given without enough supplementation)
- Teaching – client and family

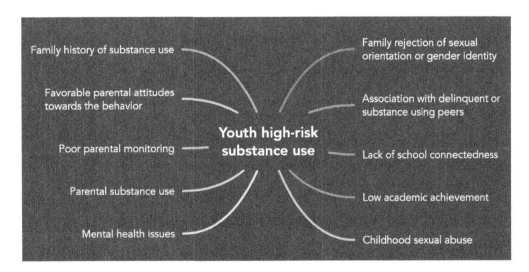

Opioid withdrawal

- Fentanyl, oxycodone, hydrocodone, codeine, morphine

- Signs: Generalized myalgias, abdominal cramps, diarrhea, piloerection (goose bumps), Tachycardia, insomnia, anxiety, and pupillary dilation
- Other common features include nausea, vomiting, frequent yawning, restlessness, rhinorrhea, and increased lacrimation.
- Patients with addictive disease and pain have the right to be treated with dignity, respect and manage their pain.
- Severe pain (post op) should be treated with opioids (might need higher dose)
- OK to use non opioids and non-pharmacological methods to support.
- Analgesic should be given around the clock at scheduled times – to maintain therapeutic levels
- PCA is a good option to use.

CAGE (Alcoholism Screening Questions)

- Have you ever felt you should cut down on your drinking?
- Have people annoyed you by criticizing your drinking?
- Have you ever felt bad or guilty about your drinking?
- Have you ever had a drink first thing in the morning to steady your nerves or get rid of a hangover (eye-opener).

Alcohol - Resources and self-help groups

- Alcoholics Anonymous (AA) – provides help and support to individuals who want to stop drinking. AA uses a 12-step approach that provides guidelines on attaining and maintaining sobriety.
- Adult Children of Alcoholics (ACOA) – provides assistance to adults who grew up in homes that were dysfunctional due to alcoholism.
- Al-Anon – provides help for spouses, significant others, family, and friends of alcoholics to share their personal experiences and coping strategies.
- Alateen – part of Al-Anon; provides support to adolescent children of alcoholics

- National Association for Children of Alcoholics (NACOA) – raises public awareness of alcoholism and its effects through leadership in public policy, advocacy for prevention services, and online resources.

Disulfiram (Antabuse)

- Aversion therapy: For abstinence from alcohol
- Effect can last for 2 weeks even after stopping Disulfiram
- Client may experience N/V, headache, confusion, dyspnea, tachycardia, sweating: if alcohol is taken after having disulfiram
- Teach: Avoid alcohol of any forms (cold and cough meds, aftershave/ mouthwashes, sauces/vinegar/flavors)

Eating Disorders

Anorexia nervosa

- Clients are preoccupied with food and the rituals of eating, along with a voluntary refusal to eat.
- Clients exhibit a morbid fear of obesity and a refusal to maintain a minimally normal body weight (body weight is less than 85% of expected normal weight for the individual) in the absence of a physical cause.
- Most often in females from adolescence to young adulthood.
- May try to hide weight loss by wearing oversized bulky clothing
- Two types:
    - Restricting type – The individual drastically restricts food intake and does not binge or purge.
    - Binge-eating/purging type – The individual engages in binge eating or purging behaviors.

Bulimia nervosa

- Clients recurrently eat large quantities of food over a short period of time (binge eating), which may be followed by inappropriate compensatory

behaviors, such as self-induced vomiting (purging), to rid the body of the excess calories.
- Most clients maintain a weight within a normal range or slightly higher.
- The average age of onset in females is 15 to 18 years of age.
- Two types:
    - Purging type, in which the client uses self-induced vomiting, laxatives, diuretics, and/or enemas to lose or maintain weight
    - Non-purging type, in which the client may also compensate for binge eating through other means, such as excessive exercise and the misuse of laxatives, diuretics, and/or enemas

Eating disorder Signs

- Russell's Sign - calluses- due to constant touch with teeth
- Tooth decay and cavities
- Enlarged salivary gland – due to nutritional deficiency
- Others: Severe weight loss may lead to decreasing metabolism (hypotension, bradycardia, hypothermia, cold intolerance, dry skin with lanugo)
- Fluid and electrolyte imbalance, Cardiac dysrhythmia

Nursing Care

- Self-assessment by nurse
- Highly structured milieu
- Trusting nurse/client relationship
- Positive approach and support - self-esteem and positive self-image.
- Encourage client participation in decision making - sense of control.
- Realistic goals for weight loss or gain (2-3 lb/week)
- Promote cognitive-behavioral therapies:
- Relaxation techniques, Journal writing, Desensitization exercises
- Monitor the client's vital signs, intake and output, and daily weight (same time every day)
- Use behavioral contracts to modify client behaviors.

- Reward the client for positive behaviors, such as completing meals or consuming a set number of calories.
- Closely monitor the client during and after meals to prevent purging, which may necessitate accompanying the client to the bathroom.
- Teach and encourage self-care activities, exercise
- Work with a dietitian: correcting misinformation regarding food, meal planning, and food selection.
  - Consider the client's preferences.
  - High in fiber (constipation), low sodium (fluid retention)
  - Supplements (vitamins, Minerals)
  - A structured and inflexible eating schedule
  - Provide small, frequent meals, which are better tolerated.
  - No stimulants (caffein)
  - Enteral feeding is given for severe malnourishment/have not responded to oral nutritional therapy

Complications - Refeeding syndrome

- Refeeding syndrome is the potentially fatal complication that can occur when fluids, electrolytes, and carbohydrates are introduced to a severely malnourished client, resulting in rapid insulin release, which move potassium, magnesium, phosphorus into the cells, making it low levels in blood.
- Electrolyte Imbalance: Hypokalemia, hypomagnesemia, hypophosphatemia
- Dilutional hyponatremia can occur due to excessive fluid retention.
- Metabolic acidosis may develop in the early days of refeeding due to tissue resistance to glucose after period of starvation.

Nursing actions: Refeeding syndrome

- Before refeeding, administer 100 mg of thiamine, or supplement of B vitamins (vitamin deficiency complicated refeeding syndrome)
- Care for the client in a hospital setting.

- Consult with the provider and dietitian to develop a controlled rate of nutritional support during initial treatment.
- Monitor serum electrolytes and administer fluid replacement as prescribed.
- Monitor for Cardiac dysrhythmias, severe bradycardia, and hypotension
- Place the client on continuous cardiac monitoring.
- Monitor patient's condition, body mass, edemas, fluid balance, electrolyte concentration daily for the first week
- Monitor the client's vital signs frequently.
- Report changes in the client's status to the provider.

Miscellaneous Topics

Change Behavior Theory

Stages	What it is	Example
Precontemplation	Unmotivated people who see no need to find a solution to a problem because they usually do not believe that one exists. Client in denial/resistant/defensive	"My friends think I am eating too much fat food" (but the client does not see any issues). "I don't see a problem with what I'm doing, so there's no reason to change anything."
Contemplation	Awareness and acknowledgment of the problem; serious consideration to change; but uncertain if it is worthy of correcting. Ambivalence/ indecisiveness	"I know I have a problem, and I think I should do something about it." "I understand that eating healthy is good for my heart"
Preparation	Acknowledge that a behavior is problematic and can make a commitment to correcting it. Gathers information from various sources/ Establish goals	"Smoking is such a bad habit. I've been reading about different ways to quit, and even though I haven't totally quit yet, I am smoking less than I did before."
Action	Change happens. People gain confidence as they believe they have the willpower to continue the journey of change.	"I have enrolled in a smoking cessation program" "I go for a walk instead of lighting a cigarette"
Maintenance	Continuing the new behavior change	"I haven't smoked a cigarette in four months."

Assertiveness: Nurses should be Assertive

- Assertiveness is expressing thoughts and feelings without denying the rights of others.
- Do self-assessment – to identify your feelings/needs/wants
- Be direct - deliver your message directly to the person it is intended for
- Maintain eye contact
- Use "I" statements. Avoid statement that begin with "why" and "you"
- Ask for feedbacks from others – will help clarify any misinterpretation of what you meant
- Be confident, use neutral tone and stop apologizing un-necessarily
- Feel free to say "No" /I don't understand/I don't know
- Be willing to compromise after evaluating your expectations

Care of Nurses Who are Grieving

- Caring long term for clients can create personal attachments for nurses.

- Nurses can use coping strategies:
- Going to the client's funeral.
- Communicating in writing to the family.
- Attending debriefing sessions with colleagues.
- Using stress management techniques.
- Talking with a professional counselor.

End of life care

- End-of-life care attempts to meet the client's physical, spiritual, emotional, and psychosocial needs.
- End-of-life issues
  - Decision-making in a highly stressful time during which the nurse must consider the desires of the client and the family.
  - Decisions are shared with other health care personnel for a smooth transition during this time of stress, grief, and bereavement.

Palliative Care

- The nurse serves as an advocate for the client's sense of dignity and self-esteem by providing palliative care at the end of life.
- It improves the quality of life of clients and their families facing end-of-life issues.
- Primarily used for dying patients and family members who are grieving.
- Palliative care interventions focus on the relief of physical manifestations such as pain as well as addressing spiritual, emotional, and psychosocial aspects of the client's life.
- Palliative care may be provided by an inter professional team
  - Physicians, nurses, social workers, physical therapists, massage therapists, occupational therapists, music/art therapists, touch/energy therapists, and chaplains.

Hospice care

- A comprehensive care delivery system implemented when a client is not expected to live longer than 6 months.
- Further medical care aimed toward a cure is stopped, and the focus becomes enhancing quality of life and supporting the client toward a peaceful and dignified death.

Nursing care:

- Promote continuity of care and communication by limiting assigned staff changes.
- Assist the client and family to set priorities for end-of-life care.
- Physical Care
    - Give priority to controlling clinical findings.
    - Administer medications that manage pain, air hunger, and anxiety.
    - Perform ongoing assessment to determine the effectiveness of treatment and the need for modifications of the treatment plan, such as lower or higher doses of medications.
    - Manage adverse effects of medications. Reposition the client to maintain airway patency and comfort.
    - Maintain the integrity of skin and mucous membranes.

Signs of nearing death

- Coolness and paleness or mottling of the extremities
- A slack, relaxed jaw, and open mouth from loss of facial muscle tone
- Difficulty in maintaining body posture or positions
- Eyelids half-open
- Cheyne-Stokes or uneven respirations with periods of apnea
- Urine output usually decreases and darkens (concentrated) from dehydration as the client nears death.

Nursing Responsibility

- Therapeutic communication. Respect culture and religion
- Provide an environment that promotes dignity and self-esteem.
- Use of relaxation techniques- breathing, music
- Promote decision-making in food selection, activities, and health care to give the client as much control as possible.
- Allow patient to control own ADL as much as possible
- Support family in grieving process.

Cognitive Disorder

- Cognitive disorders are a group of conditions characterized by the disruption of thinking, memory, processing, and problem solving.
- Two types: Delirium and Neurocognitive Disorder (includes Alzheimer's disease)
- Cause Delirium: secondary to another medical condition, such as infection, substance use
- Cognitive deficits are not related to another mental health disorder.
- But can be related to Alzheimer's disease, Traumatic brain injury, Parkinson's disease and other disorders affecting the neurological system

Defense Mechanisms Used in Cognitive Disorders

- Denial: Both the client and family members may refuse to believe that changes, such as loss of memory, are taking place, even when those changes are obvious to others.
- Confabulation: The client may make up stories when questioned about events or activities that she does not remember. This may seem like lying, but it is actually an unconscious attempt to save self-esteem and prevent admitting that she does not remember the occasion.
- Perseveration: The client avoids answering questions by repeating phrases or behavior. This is another unconscious attempt to maintain self-esteem when memory has failed.

Nursing Care

- Assign the client to a room close to the nurse's station for close observation.
- Provide a room with a low level of visual and auditory stimuli.
- Provide for a well-lit environment, minimizing contrasts and shadows.
- Have the client sit in a room with windows to help with time orientation.
- Have the client wear an identification bracelet; use monitors and bed alarm devices as needed.
- Use restraints only as an intervention of last resort.
- Monitor client's level of comfort and assess for non-verbal indications of discomfort.
- Use caution when administering medications PRN for agitation or anxiety.
- Assess client's risk for injury and ensure safety in the physical environment, such as a lowered bed and removal of scatter rugs to prevent falls.
- Provide compensatory memory aids, such as clocks, calendars, photographs, memorabilia, seasonal decorations, and familiar objects. Reorient, as necessary.
- Provide eyeglasses and assistive hearing devices as needed.
- Keep a consistent daily routine. Maintain consistent caregivers.
- Ensure adequate food and fluid intake. Allow for safe pacing and wandering.
- Cover or remove mirrors to decrease fear and agitation.

Communication in Cognitive disorders

- Communicate in a calm, reassuring tone.
- Speak in positive rather than negatively worded phrases. Do not argue or question hallucinations or delusions.
- Reinforce reality. Reinforce orientation to time, place, and person.
- Introduce self to client with each new contact.
- Establish eye contact and use short, simple sentences when speaking to the client. Focus on one item of information at a time.
- Encourage reminiscence about happy times; talk about familiar things.
- Break instructions and activities into short timeframes.
- Limit the number of choices when dressing or eating.

- Minimize the need for decision making and abstract thinking to avoid frustration.
- Avoid confrontation. Encourage family visitation as appropriate.

Medications

- Donepezil, rivastigmine, and galantamine
- Avoid NSAIDs with these meds (GI Bleed)
- Nausea and diarrhea, which occur in approximately 10% of clients
- Monitor for gastrointestinal adverse effects and for fluid volume deficits.
- Promote adequate fluid intake.
- Bradycardia: Teach the family to monitor pulse rate for the client who lives at home
- Screen for underlying heart disease
- Memantine (Namenda): the only medication approved for moderate to severe stages of Alzheimer's disease.
    - S/E: dizziness, headache, confusion, and constipation.
- Other Points
    - Home safety measures - same as Alzheimer's disease

Grief and Care

- Clients experience loss in many aspects of their lives:
- Actual and Perceived loss: Grief is the inner emotional response to loss and is exhibited in as many ways as there are individuals.
- Theories of Grief
    - Denial – The client has difficulty believing a terminal diagnosis or loss.
    - Anger – The client lashes out at other people or things.
    - Bargaining – The client negotiates for more time or a cure.
    - Depression – The client is overwhelmingly saddened over the inability to change the situation.
    - Acceptance – The client acknowledges what is happening and plans for the future.

- Stages may not be experienced in order, and the length of each stage varies from person to person.
- Nursing Interventions: Facilitate Mourning
  - Grant time for the grieving process.
  - Identify expected grieving behaviors, such as crying, somatic manifestations, and anxiety. Use therapeutic communication.
  - Name the emotion the client is feeling. For example, the nurse can say, "You sound as though you are angry. Anger is a normal feeling for someone who has lost a loved one. Tell me about how you are feeling."
- Communication Tips
  - Avoid communication that inhibits the open expression of feelings:
  - Avoid offering false reassurance, do not give advice
  - Do not change the subject. Avoid taking the focus away from the grieving individual.
- Assist the grieving individual to accept the reality of the loss and take forwards steps.
- Provide continuing support; encourage the support of family and friends.
- Assess for evidence of ineffective coping, such as refusing to leave the home months after the client's spouse died.
- Resources: Share information, support groups, Spiritual Advisor

Victim Abuse and Nursing Care

- Age-Specific Assessments
- Infants
  - Shaken baby syndrome – Shaking may cause intracranial hemorrhage.
  - Assess for respiratory distress, bulging fontanelles, and an increase in head circumference.
  - Retinal hemorrhage may be present.
  - Any bruising on an infant before age 6 months is suspicious.
- Preschoolers to adolescents
  - Assess for unusual bruising, such as on abdomen, back, or buttocks.
  - Bruising is common on arms and legs in these age groups.

- Assess the mechanism of injury, which may not be congruent with the physical appearance of the injury.
- Numerous bruises at different stages of healing may indicate ongoing beatings.
- Be suspicious of bruises or welts that resemble the shape of a belt buckle or other object.
- Assess for burns. Burns covering "glove" or "stocking" areas of the hands or feet may indicate forced immersion into boiling water.
- Small, round burns may be from lit cigarettes.
- Assess for fractures with unusual features, such as forearm spiral fractures, which could be a result of twisting the extremity forcefully.
- The presence of multiple fractures is suspicious. Assess for human bite marks.
- Assess for head injuries – level of consciousness, equal and reactive pupils, and nausea or vomiting
- Older and other vulnerable adults
  - Assess for any bruises, lacerations, abrasions, or fractures in which the physical appearance does not match the history or mechanism of injury.
- Patient-Centered Care
  - Priority must be placed on ascertaining whether the person is in any immediate danger.
  - Mandatory reporting of suspected or actual cases of child or vulnerable adult abuse. Complete and accurate documentation of subjective and objective data obtained during assessment.
- Self-Check by Nurses:
  - The nurse must work through personal fears and prejudices in order to be an advocate and to effectively identify and interact therapeutically with victims of physical violence.
- Nursing Care Abused clients
  - Conduct a nursing history. Provide privacy when conducting interviews about family abuse.

- Be direct, honest, and professional. Use language the client understands. Be understanding and attentive.
- Use therapeutic techniques that demonstrate understanding.
- Use open-ended questions to elicit descriptive responses.

Psychosocial - Medications

Name	Action	Side Effect	Nursing Role
	Selective Serotonin Reuptake Inhibitors (SSRI Antidepressants)		
Paroxetine (Paxil), Sertraline (Zoloft), Escitalopram (Lexapro), Fluoxetine (Prozac), Fluvoxamine (Luvox)	Paroxetine is contraindicated in clients taking MAOIs or a TCA	Early adverse effects (first few days/weeks):nausea, diaphoresis, tremor, fatigue, drowsiness	Instruct clients to report adverse effects to the provider. Instruct clients to take the medication as prescribed. Advise clients that these effects should soon subside.
	Use paroxetine cautiously in clients who have liver and renal dysfunction, seizure disorders, or a history of GI bleeding.	**Serotonin syndrome.** Agitation, confusion, disorientation, difficulty concentrating, anxiety, hallucinations,hyperreflexia, incoordination, tremors, fever, diaphoresis	Watch for and advise clients to report any of these manifestations, which could indicate a lethal problem. Usually begins 2 to 72 hr after initiation of treatment. Resolves when the medication is discontinued
	Later adverse effects (after 5 to 6 weeks of therapy): sexual dysfunction, Weight gain, GI bleeding, Hyponatremia	Bruxism: grinding and clenching of teeth (sleep). Withdrawal syndrome	Use a mouth guard during sleep.Switch the client to another class of medication. Sleep disturbances are minimized by taking med in morning. Do not discontinue use abruptly
	Atypical Antidepressants		
bupropion HCL (Wellbutrin)	treat Depression, Aid to quit smoking	Headache, dry mouth, GI distress, constipation, increased heart rate, nausea, restlessness, and insomnia,Seizures	Advise clients to observe for effects and to notify the dr., Treat headache with mild analgesic,sip on fluids to treat dry mouth,increase dietary fiber to prevent constipation.Monitor clients for seizures, and treat accordingly
	Other Atypical Antidepressants		
Venlafaxine (Effexor), duloxetine (Cymbalta)		headache, nausea, agitation, anxiety,sleep disturbances, hyponatremia	Monitor sodium level, Monitor for increase in diastolic pressure.
Mirtazapine (Remeron)		sleepiness, weight gain, high cholesterol	
Reboxetine (Edronax)		dry mouth, decreased blood pressure, constipation, sexual dysfunction, and urinary hesitancy or retention, Sedation	Donot use with MAOI.

Name	Action	Side Effect	Nursing Role
Tricyclic Antidepressants (TCAs)			
Amitriptyline (Elavil), Imipramine (Tofranil) Doxepin (Sinequan) Nortriptyline (Aventyl) Amoxapine (Asendin) Trimipramine (Surmontil)	Use cautiously in clients who have coronary artery disease; diabetes; liver, kidney, and respiratory disorders; urinary retention and obstruction; angle-closure glaucoma; benign prostatic hyperplasia; and hyperthyroidism.	Orthostatic hypotension, Sedation	Instruct clients about the effects of postural hypotension, (lightheadedness, dizziness). If these occur, advise the client to sit or lie down. Orthostatic hypotension is minimized by changing positions slowly. Monitor blood pressure and heart rate for clients in the hospital for orthostatic changes before administration and 1 hr after. If a significant decrease in blood pressure and/or increase in heart rate is noted, do not administer the medication, and notify the provider
	contraindicated in clients who have seizure disorders.	Anticholinergic effects, »Dry mouth »Blurred vision »Photophobia »Urinary hesitancy or retention »Constipation »Tachycardia	Instruct clients on ways to minimize anticholinergic effects. Chewing sugarless gum »»Sipping on water »»Wearing sunglasses when outdoors »»Eating foods high in fiber »»Participating in regular exercise »»Increasing fluid intake to at least 2 to 3 L a day from beverages and food sources »»Voiding just before taking medication »» Advise the client to notify the provider if effects persist.
Monoamine Oxidase Inhibitors (MAOIs)	These medications block MAO in the brain, thereby increasing the amount of norepinephrine, dopamine, and serotonin available for transmission of impulses. An increased amount of these neurotransmitters at nerve endings intensifies responses and relieves depression.	Toxicity (restlessness, anxiety, insomnia, Dizziness, hypertension, dysrhythmias, mental confusion, and agitation, followed by seizures, coma, and possible death)	Obtain clients' baseline ECG.Monitor vital signs frequently. »Monitor clients for signs of toxicity. »» Notify the provider if signs of toxicity occur.
phenelzine (Nardil), Isocarboxazid (Marplan), Tranylcypromine (Parnate), Selegiline (Emsam) – transdermal MAOI	These medications are contraindicated in clients taking SSRIs and in those who have pheochromocytoma, heart failure, cardiovascular and cerebral vascular disease, and severe renal insufficiency	CNS stimulation (anxiety, agitation, mania, or hypomania), Orthostatic hypotension	Advise clients to observe for effects and notify the provider if they occur.

Name	Action	Side Effect	Nursing Role
	Assist with medication regimen adherence by informing clients that it can take 1 to 3 weeks to begin experiencing therapeutic effects. Full therapeutic effects may take 2 to 3 months.	Hypertensive crisis resulting from intake of dietary tyramine » Severe hypertension occurs as a result of intensive vasoconstriction and stimulation of the heart. » Clients will most likely experience headache, nausea, and increased heart rate and blood pressure.	Administer phentolamine (Regitine) IV, a rapid-acting alpha-adrenergic blocker or nifedipine (Procardia) SL. » Provide continuous cardiac monitoring and respiratory support as indicated.
		Local rash may occur with transdermal preparation.	Choose a clean, dry area for each application. » Apply a topical glucocorticoid on the affected area.

Name	Action	Side Effect	Nursing Role
	Mood Stabilizer		
lithium carbonate	Can be used in Bipolar, Alcohol use disorder, Bulimia nervosa, Psychotic disorders	Gastrointestinal (GI) distress (nausea, diarrhea, abdominal pain)	Advise clients that effects are usually transient. » Administer medication with meals or milk.
Monitor plasma lithium levels while undergoing treatment.	**Lithium toxicity:**Early indications: Less than 1.5 mEq/L : Diarrhea, nausea, vomiting, thirst, polyuria, muscle weakness, fine hand tremor, slurred speech	Fine hand tremors that can interfere with purposeful motor skills and can be exacerbated by factors such as stress and caffeine	» Administer beta-adrenergic blocking agents such as propranolol (Inderal). » Adjust to lowest possible dosage, give in divided doses, or use long-acting formulations. » Advise clients to report an increase in tremors.
	Advanced indications: 1.5 to 2.0 mEq/L, Ongoing gastrointestinal distress, including nausea, vomiting, and diarrhea; mental confusion; poor coordination; coarse tremors: - Advise clients to withhold medication and notify the provider	Polyuria, mild thirst	Use a potassium-sparing diuretic, such as spironolactone (Aldactone). » Instruct clients to maintain adequate fluid intake by consuming at least 2,000 to 3,000 mL of fluid from beverages and food sources.
	Severe toxicity : 2.0 to 2.5 mEq/L. Extreme polyuria of dilute urine, tinnitus, blurred vision, ataxia, seizures, severe hypotension leading to coma and possibly death from respiratory complications. Gastric lavage or administer urea, mannitol, or aminophylline to increase the rate of excretion.	Renal toxicity	Monitor the client's I&O. » Adjust dosage, and keep dose low. » Assess baseline kidney function, and monitor kidney function periodically.
	Greater than 2.5 mEq/L, Rapid progression of symptoms leading to coma and death, Need Hemodialysis	Goiter and hypothyroidism with long-term treatment	Monitor thyroid function

Name	Action	Side Effect	Nursing Role
	Mood-Stabilizing Antiepileptic Drugs (AEDs)		
Carbamazepine (Tegretol, Equetro)	Advise clients to avoid use in pregnancy. Carbamazepine is contraindicated in clients who have bone marrow suppression or bleeding disorders.	nystagmus, double vision, vertigo, staggering gait, headache	Administer low doses initially, then gradually increase dosage. » Advise clients that CNS effects should subside within a few weeks. » Administer dose at bedtime.
	Monitor serum sodium. »Monitor the client for edema, decrease in urine output, and hypertension.	Blood dyscrasias (leukopenia, anemia, thrombocytopenia)	Obtain the client's baseline CBC and platelets, and perform ongoing monitoring. »Observe the client for indications of bruising and bleeding of gums. »Monitor the client for sore throat, fatigue, or other indications of infection.
	Grapefruit juice inhibits metabolism, thus increasing carbamazepine levels.	Skin disorders (dermatitis, rash, Stevens-Johnson syndrome)	Treat mild reactions with anti-inflammatory or antihistamine medications. » Advise clients to wear sunscreen. » Instruct clients to notify the provider if Stevens-Johnson syndrome rash occurs and to withhold medication.
Lamotrigine (Lamictal)		double or blurred vision, dizziness, headache, nausea, and vomiting.Serious skin rashes including Stevens-Johnson syndrome	Caution clients about performing activities requiring concentration.Instruct client to withhold medication and notify provider if rash occurs.
Valproic acid (Depakote),	Valproic acid is contraindicated in clients who have liver disorders.	GI effects (nausea, vomiting, indigestion)	» Advise clients that manifestations are usually self-limiting. » Advise clients to take medication with food or switch to enteric-coated pills.
	Advise the client to avoid use in pregnancy.	Hepatotoxicity as evidenced by anorexia, nausea, vomiting, fatigue abdominal pain, jaundice	» Assess baseline liver function, and monitor liver function regularly. » Advise clients to observe for indications and to notify the provider if they occur. » Avoid using in children younger than 2 years old. » Administer lowest effective dose.

Name	Action	Side Effect	Nursing Role
		Pancreatitis as evidenced by nausea, vomiting, and abdominal pain	» Advise clients to observe for indications and to notify the provider immediately if they occur. »Monitor amylase levels. » Discontinue medication if pancreatitis develops.
		Thrombocytopenia	» Advise clients to observe for manifestations, such as bruising, and to notify the provider if these occur. »Monitor the client's platelet counts.

Name	Action	Side Effect	Nursing Role
Antipsychotics			
chlorpromazine, Haloperidol (Haldol), Fluphenazine, Perphenazine,Thiothixene	Treatment of acute and chronic psychotic disorders, Schizophrenia spectrum disorders, Bipolar disorders (primarily the manic phase), Tourette's disorder	**Extrapyramidal side effects (EPSs):** - Acute dystonia (severe spasms of tongue, neck, face, or back), Parkinsonism, Akathisia (continuosly pacing and agitated), Tardive dyskinesia (involuntary movements)	Continuos monitoring, Administer the lowest dosage possible, treat each condition in EPS with respective meds. Administer anticholinergics, beta-blockers, and benzodiazepines to control early EPS. Advise clients that some therapeutic effects may be noticeable within a few days, but significant improvement may take 2 to 4 weeks, and possibly several months for full effects.
	gynecomastia, Seizures, skin effets (photosensitivity), Sexual dysfunction, Agranulocytosis, dysrhythmias	**Neuroleptic malignant syndrome** (high-grade fever, blood pressure fluctuations, dysrhythmias, muscle rigidity, and LOC changes)	Stop antipsychotic medication, Monitor vital signs. »Apply cooling blankets.Administer antipyretics (aspirin, acetaminophen). Increase fluid intake. » Administer diazepam (Valium) to control anxiety. Wait 2 weeks before resuming therapy.
		Anticholinergic effects (Dry mouth » Blurred vision » Photophobia » Urinary hesitancy/retention » Constipation » Tachycardia)	»Chewing sugarless gum, Sipping water »»Avoid hazardous activities »»Wearing sunglasses when outdoors »»Eat foods high in fiber, Participating in regular exercise »»Maintaining fluid intake of 2 to 3 L of water each day from food and beverage sources »»Voiding just before taking medication
risperidone (Risperdal), Olanzapine (Zyprexa) ⃝⃝ Quetiapine (Seroquel) ⃝⃝ Aripiprazole (Abilify) ⃝⃝ Ziprasidone (Geodon) ⃝⃝ Clozapine (Clozaril) ⃝⃝ Asenapine (Saphris) ⃝⃝ Lurasidone (Latuda) ⃝⃝ Paliperidone (Invega) ⃝⃝ Iloperidone (Fanapt)		New onset of diabetes mellitus or loss of glucose control in clients who have diabetes, Weight gain, Hypercholesterolemia, Orthostatic hypotension, Anticholinergic effects such as urinary hesitancy or retention, dry mouth, Mild EPS, such as tremor, Agitation, dizziness, sedation, and sleep disruption	Obtain baseline fasting blood glucose and monitor throughout treatment. » Instruct client to report indications (increased thirst, urination, and appetite. Monitor cholesterol, triglycerides.

Pharmacology Concepts

Medication Calculation

- Standard conversion factors
- 1 mg = 1,000 mcg
- 1 g = 1,000 mg
- 1 kg = 1,000 g
- 1 oz = 30 mL
- 1 L = 1,000 mL
- 1 tsp = 5 mL
- 1 tbsp = 15 mL
- 1 tbsp = 3 tsp
- 1 kg = 2.2 lb (pounds)
- 1 gr = 60 mg
- 1 million = 1,000,000 (10 lacs)

General Rounding Guidelines

- Rounding up: If the number to the right is equal to or greater than 5, round up by adding 1 to the number on the left. Example: 5.6 = 6
- Rounding down: If the number to the right is less than 5, round down by dropping the number, leaving the number to the left as is. Example: 5.4 = 5
- For dosages less than 1.0, round to the nearest hundredth.
  - For example (rounding up): 0.746 mL = 0.75 mL.
  - (Rounding down): - 0.743 mL = 0.74 mL
- For dosages greater than 1.0, round to the nearest tenth.
  - 1.38 = 1.4
  - 1.34 mL = 1.3 mL.

Medication Calculation

- What is the dose needed?
- Dose needed = Desired $\dfrac{\text{Desired} \times \text{Quantity}}{\text{Have}} = X$

- What is the dose available?
- Dose available = Have.
- What is the quantity of the dose available?
- Quantity
- Do conversions if needed(gm/mg/cap/lb/kg)
- Use Equation.
- **IV Flow rate Calculations**: Using an IV pump.

$$\frac{\text{Volume (mL)}}{\text{Time (hr)}} = X$$

- Look for need of conversion (mt to hr, hr today)
- **Drop factor (Manual)**: the number of drops that fall into the drip chamber over the period of 1 min.
- IV flow rates

$$\frac{\text{Volume (mL)}}{\text{Time (min)}} \times \text{Drop factor (gtt/mL)} = X$$

Pharmacology Notes

- Have a complete order.
- Check allergies (including Latex, food, contrast media)
- Assessment first- implementation later
- Notify Physician and clarify if there is a questionable order

Oral	Transdermal	Drops (eyes/ears)	NG/GT	IV/IM/SubQ
Don't give with vomiting, no gag reflex, swallowing difficulty, decreased LOC	Wash skin with soap and water, dry completely	Surgical aseptic techniques	Check tube placement	Vastus lateralis- 2 yrs and younger
Position – upright/fowlers	Place patch on hairless area	Eyes- conjunctival sac, look up ceiling	Med flow by gravity	Ventral gluteal after 2 yrs
With food/without food.	Remove previous patch	Ear- Pinna up and back for adults. Down and back for kids	Use liquid forms	Needle size/syringe
Not in large amounts. Crush/cut/dilute?	Use gloves.	Ear- side lying position	Check compatibility. Don't mix with feedings	Rotate injection site. No site with edema, inflamed, birthmarks, moles.
Better empty stomach (1 hr before /2 hr after meal)		Nose- breath through mouth. No blowing for 5 mts	Med one at a time, Flush with saline (15 ml) before and after	Discard all sharps, Monitor for side effects immediately

- 6 R's – calculate dose accurately
- Right Patient, Dose, Medicine, Time, Route, Documentation

- Do not use unlabeled medicine
- Discard any partially used single dose containers. Label the multi dose vials with date, time, initial and expiration date.
- Patient education!!!

Standing or routine: Administered until the dosage is changed or another medication is prescribed	prn: Given when the patient requires it
Single (one-time): Given one time only for a specific reason	STAT: Given immediately in an emergency
Now: When a medication is needed right away, but not STAT	Prescriptions: Medication to be taken outside of the hospital

Therapeutic effect: Expected or predicted physiological response	Side effect: Predictable, Unavoidable secondary effect
Adverse effect: Unintended, undesirable, often unpredictable	Toxic effect: Accumulation of medication in the bloodstream
Idiosyncratic reaction: Over-reaction or under-reaction or different reaction from normal	Allergic reaction: Unpredictable response to a medication

- Tips: Dialysis – Hold blood pressure meds
- Pediatric liquid medications are often dispensed with a measuring device designed to administer the exact dose prescribed (Avoid using spoons)
- Therapeutic level is expected range- might be more than normal (warfarin – INR) – beware of herbal meds

- Check apical pulse before giving digoxin. Hold for bradycardia
- Peak and Trough (Vancomycin: therapeutic range =10-20 mg/L)
- Hyperkalemia- Might get IV insulin. (Without the insulin, the potassium cannot enter the cells and more of the potassium is allowed to float around in the blood)

Ophthalmic Medication Administration

- Guidelines administering eye medications
- Wash hands and don gloves
- If both eye drops, and eye ointment are scheduled administer the drops first
- Separate instillation by 3 to 5 minutes if two medications are scheduled
- Place medication in lower conjunctival sac
- Apply gentle pressure to nasolacrimal duct for 30
- seconds to 1 minute following administration of drops
- If possible, administer ointment at bedtime

Suppository for kids

- Age-appropriate explanations and/or distractions should be implemented to reduce distress.
- Toddlers and infants may benefit from distraction with a toy; preschoolers and older children can be instructed to take deep breaths or count during the procedure.
- Basic steps for suppository administration include the following
- Apply clean gloves and position the client appropriately based on age and size (e.g., infant supine with knees and feet raised, older child side-lying with knees bent)
- Lubricate the tip of the suppository with water-soluble jelly. Petroleum-based products can reduce absorption.
- Insert the suppository past the internal sphincter using the fifth finger if the child is under 3 years.
- Use of the index finger may cause injury to the colon or sphincters in children younger than age 3 years.

- Angle suppository and guide it along the rectal wall.
- The suppository should remain in contact with the rectal mucosa (and not be buried inside stool) to ensure systemic absorption.
- Hold the buttocks together for several minutes, or until the urge to defecate has passed, to prevent immediate expulsion.
- If a bowel movement occurs within 10-30 minutes, observe for the presence of the suppository.

Topical Medications

- Skin: Use gloves. Use sterile technique if the patient has an open wound.
- Clean skin first. Follow directions for each type of medication.
- Transdermal patches:
    - Remove old patch before applying new ones.
    - Document the location of the new patch.
    - Ask about patches during the medication history.
    - Apply a label to the patch if it is difficult to see.
    - Document removal of the patch as well.

Patient-controlled analgesia (PCA)

- PCA delivers a set amount of IV analgesic each time the client presses the administration button.
- With many PCA pumps, a continuous IV solution (e.g., normal saline) is required to keep the vein open and flush the PCA medication through the line so that the boluses reach the client.
- Two nurses need to witness when initiating PCA, changing Medication/ syringe, and when discontinuing PCA.

Herbal Medications

- Garlic, ginkgo biloba, and vitamin E may interfere with platelet aggregation and increase the risk for bleeding in clients who are taking warfarin, which is an anticoagulant medication.
- St John's wort – use for depression and insomnia- Risk for Hypertensive crisis
- Licorice –to treat Stomach ulcers – Risk for Hypertension, Hypokalemia
- Echinacea-Treatment & prevention of cold & flu- Risk for Anaphylaxis (more likely in asthmatics)
- The ones with bleeding Risk: GGGGF (garlic, Ginger, Ginkgo, Ginseng, Feverfew)
- Those affect blood sugar: Aloe, Ginseng, Ginkgo
- Those with S/E of Hypertension: Licoroot, St. John's Wort
- Those taken for mental issues: Valerian, St. John's Wort, Kava, Ginseng
- Those taken for immunity: Echinacea
- Those which affect Liver: Kava, Echinacea

Points to remember _ central venous catheters

- Patency is maintained by flushing with diluted heparin solution or normal saline, depending on type of catheter and agency policy.
- Upper body central lines are preferred- less chance of contamination (urine, stool)
- Sterile technique – dressing change, removal

Discontinuing a central venous catheter

- Instruct the client to lie in a supine position.
- This will increase the central venous pressure and decrease the possibility of air getting into the vessel.
- Instruct the client to bear down or exhale.
- The client should never inhale during removal of the line; inhalation will suck more air into the blood vessel via negative suction pressure.

- Apply an air-occlusive dressing (usually gauze with a Tegaderm dressing) to help prevent a delayed air embolism. If possible, the nurse should attempt to cover the site with the occlusive dressing while pulling out the line.
- Pull the line cautiously and never pull harder if there is resistance.
- Doing so could cause the catheter to break or become dislodged in the client's vessel

Z track Injection

- Using the non-dominant hand to move and to hold the skin and subcutaneous tissue.
- Dart the syringe rapidly into the displaced skin at a 90-degree angle.
- Aspirate on the syringe to be sure that a blood vessel has not been penetrated. Inject the medication slowly into the muscle.
- Continue holding the displaced skin and tissue until after the needle is removed.
- Upon withdrawal of the syringe, immediately release the skin and subcutaneous tissue.
- Do not message the site.
- Do not let patient wear any tight-fitting cloths at the injection site.

Special Topics

Cultural Aspects

Arab American culture

- Females avoid eye contact with males.
- Touch is accepted if done by same-sex healthcare providers.
- Physical exposure should be minimized.
- Nurses should respect the women's privacy and maintain the Hijab throughout hospitalization
- Most decisions are made by males.
- Muslims (Sunni), refuse organ donation
- Most Arabs do not eat pork; they avoid icy drinks when sick or hot/cold drinks together.
- Colostrum is considered harmful to the newborn

Asian American

- They avoid direct eye contact.
- Feet are considered dirty (the feet should be touched last during assessment).
- Males make most of the decisions.
- They usually refuse organ donation.
- They generally do not prefer cold drinks.

Native American

- They sustain eye contact.
- Blood and organ donation is generally refused.
- They might refuse circumcision.
- Might prefer care from the tribal shaman rather than using western medicine.

Mexican American

- They might avoid direct eye contact with authorities.

- They might refuse organ donation.
- Most are very emotional during bereavement; believe in the "hot-cold" theory of illness
- ailments are thought to develop as a result of an imbalance between these: hot and cold.

"Mal de ojo"

- In Latin American culture, an illness called "mal de ojo" ("evil eye") is believed to be caused when a stranger or someone perceived as powerful admires or compliments a child.
- The "illness," or "curse," is usually manifested by vomiting, fever, and crying. The mal de ojo curse can be broken if the admirer touches the child while speaking to the child or immediately afterward
- Mexican American mothers may worry when strangers compliment their babies without touching them.
- To protect against mal de ojo, the child may wear charms or beaded bracelets.
- If a child is believed to be afflicted with mal de ojo, the parents may consult a traditional healer, or curandero, who may perform rituals meant to cure the child of the curse.

Religious beliefs

- Jehovah's Witness—No blood products should be used.
- Hindu—No beef or items containing gelatin
- (Gelatin is made from animal bones and collagen, the most common source being pig skin)
- Jewish—Special dietary restrictions, use of kosher foods: Halal meat – minimal pain to animal.
- bulls, cows, sheep, lambs, goats, veal, and springbok OK to eat.
- Milk and meat products may not be mixed together.

- Traditional Orthodox Jews believe that the body of the deceased should not be desecrated and is to be treated with respect. Therefore, autopsies are generally not permitted
- An autopsy is performed only when required by law, if the client provided consent before death, or if the client had a hereditary disease and an autopsy would help save others.
- Orthodox Jews believe that the body belongs to God and that a complete burial is required to enter heaven. In the event that an autopsy is required, all fluids and body parts are to be returned to the body before burial.

Fluid and electrolytes

Intravenous Fluids

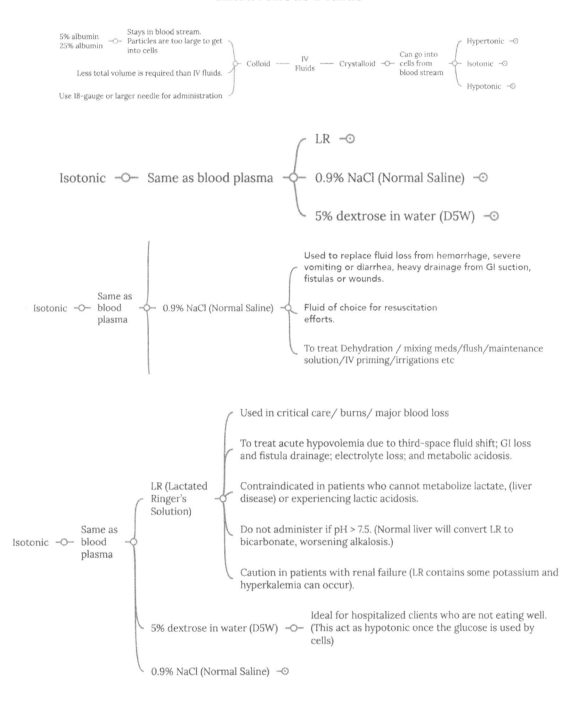

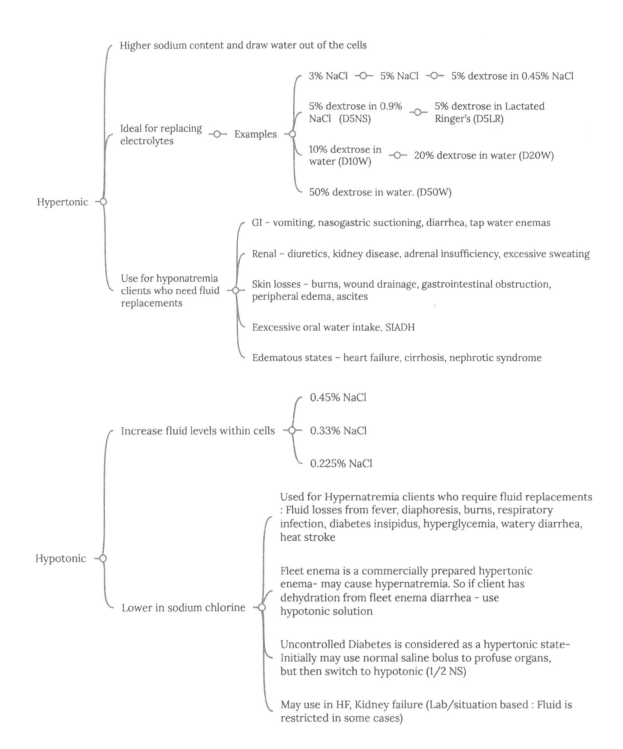

Hypertonic

- Higher sodium content and draw water out of the cells
- Ideal for replacing electrolytes — Examples
  - 3% NaCl — 5% NaCl — 5% dextrose in 0.45% NaCl
  - 5% dextrose in 0.9% NaCl (D5NS) — 5% dextrose in Lactated Ringer's (D5LR)
  - 10% dextrose in water (D10W) — 20% dextrose in water (D20W)
  - 50% dextrose in water. (D50W)
- Use for hyponatremia clients who need fluid replacements
  - GI – vomiting, nasogastric suctioning, diarrhea, tap water enemas
  - Renal – diuretics, kidney disease, adrenal insufficiency, excessive sweating
  - Skin losses – burns, wound drainage, gastrointestinal obstruction, peripheral edema, ascites
  - Eexcessive oral water intake, SIADH
  - Edematous states – heart failure, cirrhosis, nephrotic syndrome

Hypotonic

- Increase fluid levels within cells
  - 0.45% NaCl
  - 0.33% NaCl
  - 0.225% NaCl
- Lower in sodium chlorine
  - Used for Hypernatremia clients who require fluid replacements : Fluid losses from fever, diaphoresis, burns, respiratory infection, diabetes insipidus, hyperglycemia, watery diarrhea, heat stroke
  - Fleet enema is a commercially prepared hypertonic enema- may cause hypernatremia. So if client has dehydration from fleet enema diarrhea - use hypotonic solution
  - Uncontrolled Diabetes is considered as a hypertonic state- Initially may use normal saline bolus to profuse organs, but then switch to hypotonic (1/2 NS)
  - May use in HF, Kidney failure (Lab/situation based : Fluid is restricted in some cases)

Fluid and electrolyte imbalances:

Sodium

- Sodium (Na) Normal – 135 to 145 mEq/L
- Sodium is the major electrolyte in ECF – regulated mainly by kidney, aldosterone, ADH
- Sodium is important in
  - Generation and transmission of nerve impulses, Cardiac function/ neuro function
  - Muscle contractility – sodium potassium pump, Acid-base balance
- Sodium leaves the body through urine, sweat, and feces.
- The kidneys are the primary regulator of sodium balance.
- The serum sodium level reflects the ratio of sodium to water, not necessarily the loss or gain of sodium.

Hypernatremia

- Elevated serum sodium level. More than 145
- Act like hypertonic. Lead to cell dehydration: Primary protection is thirst from hypothalamus
- Causes
  - Water Deficit: Excessive Diuresis (ADH issues – Diabetes Insipidus), dehydration
  - Excessive Sodium intake with inadequate water intake
  - Hypertonic saline administration/ sodium tablets
- Hypernatremia Manifestations
  - SALT – Seizure, Agitation, Lethargy, Thirst
- If due to water deficit: Symptoms of fluid volume deficit (HIM LOW WATER)

H : Hypotension

I : Irritability

M : Membrane dry

L : Lethargy

O : Output low (urine)

W : Weakness

W : Weight loss

A : Agitated

T : Thirst/ Tachycardia/Tachypnea

E : Elasticity gone (skin)

R : Refill slow (capillary refill)

- Nursing Diagnosis
    - Risk for injury
    - Risk for fluid volume deficit
    - Risk for electrolyte imbalance
    - Potential complication: Seizures and coma leading to irreversible brain damage
- Treat underlying cause
- Primary water deficit—replace fluid orally or IV with isotonic or hypotonic fluids
- Excess sodium—dilute with sodium-free IV fluids and promote excretion with diuretics
- Monitor carefully – quick reduction of sodium can cause a rapid shift of water back into the cells, leading to cerebral edema and neurological complications

Hyponatremia

- Serum Sodium less than 135
- Two causes: 1. Loss of sodium-containing fluids. 2. Due to water excess (dilutional)
- Common causes of hyponatremia from loss of sodium-rich body fluids
    - Profuse diaphoresis, draining wounds, excessive diarrhea or vomiting, and trauma with significant blood loss.

- Excessive diarrhea can cause fluid and sodium loss. Replacing fluid with plain water can lead to dilutional hyponatremia.
- Hyponatremia is a hypotonic state - Can result in cellular edema
- Manifestations: first – CNS
  - Confusion, irritability, headache, seizures, and coma
- Hyponatremia with water excess results from
  - Excess intake of water/forcing hypotonic fluids
  - Inability of kidneys to excrete water (renal failure)
  - Retention of water (as in heart failure or cirrhosis of the liver)
  - Excess tap water enemas
  - Excess intravenous fluids of dextrose in water
  - SIADH (syndrome of inappropriate antidiuretic hormone secretion)
- Nursing Diagnosis
  - Acute confusion
  - Risk for injury
  - Risk for electrolyte imbalance
  - Potential complication: Severe neurologic changes
- Fluid replacement with sodium-containing solution.
- But if hyponatremia is caused by water excess, fluid restriction is needed
- If Severe symptoms (seizures)
  - Give small amount of IV hypertonic saline solution (3% NaCl)
  - It must be administered with extreme caution because it may cause dangerous intravascular volume overload and pulmonary edema.

Potassium (K+)

- Major ICF electrolyte: 3.5 to 5.0 mEq/L.

K is Necessary for

- Transmission and conduction of nerve and muscle impulses
- Cellular growth – K is needed to deposit glycogen in muscle and liver
- Maintenance of cardiac rhythms
- Acid-base balance

- Neuromuscular and cardiac function are commonly affected by potassium imbalances
- Hyperkalemia increases the concentration of potassium outside of the cell, altering the normal ECF and ICF ratio, resulting in increased cellular excitability.
- Sources
  - Fruits and vegetables (BP DC NS: Banana, Potato, Dry Fruits, Citrus Fruits, Nuts, Spinach)
  - Salt substitutes
  - Potassium medications (PO, IV)
  - Stored blood (Hemolyzed blood)
- Regulated by kidneys: Kidneys eliminate about 90% of the daily potassium intake

Hyperkalemia

- Impaired renal excretion: Most common in renal failure
- Shift from inside cell to outside cell: Acidosis, Exercise, Burn, Tumor lysis, Severe infection
- Massive intake – diet and meds
- Potassium sparing diuretic (amiloride, Spironolactone)
- ACE/ARB cause hyperkalemia by reducing the kidney's ability to excrete potassium.
- Digoxin-like drugs and β-adrenergic blocking drugs (e.g., propranolol) can impair entry of potassium into cells, resulting in a higher ECF potassium concentration

Hyperkalemia signs

Manifestations: **I CAN DIE**

- Irritability
- Cramping leg pain
- Anxiety

- Numbness, weak or paralyzed skeletal muscles
- Diarrhea or Abdominal cramping
- Irregular Pulse
- ECG changes - Cardiac dysrhythmias: Decreased cardiac depolarization – Flat P, wide QRS, Quick Repolarization – Peaked T, VF can also occur
- Nursing Diagnosis
    - Risk for activity intolerance related to lower extremity muscle weakness.
    - Risk for electrolyte imbalance
    - Risk for injury related to lower extremity muscle weakness.
    - Potential complication: dysrhythmias
- Eliminate oral and parenteral K intake
- Increase elimination of K (diuretics, dialysis, Kayexalate)
- Force K into cells – give IV Insulin or sodium bicarbonate
- Give Calcium gluconate- this will counteract K effects on heart

Hypokalemia (less than 3.5)

- Due to increased loss of K+ via the kidneys or gastrointestinal tract (diarrhea, laxative abuse, vomiting, and ileostomy drainage)
- NG suctioning: Nasogastric secretions are high in potassium.
- Increased shift of K+ from ECF to ICF: Insulin therapy, stress, coronary ischemia, delirium tremens
- Dietary K+ deficiency (rare)
- Low Magnesium – trigger renin release from kidney – sodium retention- K excretion by kidney
- Metabolic alkalosis – shift K into cells

- Hypokalemia S/S: Manifestations: HOW MEN DO CPR
  - Hyperglycemia
  - Output - polyuria
  - Weakness of muscles
  - Muscle cramps (leg)
  - ECG changes: Cardiac most serious
  - Nausea and Vomiting
  - Decreased gastrointestinal motility
  - Oxygen – weak respiratory muscles
  - Cardiac – pulse irregular, weak
  - Paresthesia
  - Reflex- decreased
- Nursing Diagnosis
  - Risk for activity intolerance: related to muscle weakness and hyporeflexia.
  - Risk for electrolyte imbalance
  - Risk for injury
  - Potential complication: Dysrhythmias

Management

- KCl supplements orally or IV
- Take liquid or tablet potassium supplements with a glass or more of water or juice and/or with food to prevent gastrointestinal irritation.
- Validation of renal function must be established before the delivery of IV KCl (urine output)
- Invert IV bags containing KCl several times to ensure even distribution in the bag (Agitate). Always dilute IV KCL. Use IV pump.
- Use central line for IV. NEVER give KCL via IV push or as a bolus
- Continuous cardiac monitoring. Give slow. Should not exceed 10-20 mEq/hr: To prevent hyperkalemia and cardiac arrest

Evidence Based Practice (EBP) and Research

- Use of EBP allows nurses to structure how to make accurate, timely, and appropriate clinical decisions. Without evidence-based practice, nursing would be a practice, based solely on tradition.
- EBP is a problem-solving approach – research based
- EBP uses of best evidence in combination with a clinician's expertise and patient preferences and values in making decisions about patient care.
- Your role: be up to date on information.

Steps to Evidence-Based Practice

- Ask the clinical question: PICOT
  - P = Patient population of interest
  - I = Intervention of interest
  - C = Comparison of interest
  - O = Outcome
  - T = Time
- Collect the best evidence: Research
- Critique the evidence: Is it good enough? Resolute enough?
- Integrate the evidence: Change policy, develop new tool
- Evaluate the practice decision or change: Is it working?
- Share the outcomes of EBP changes with others: Publish results
- Nursing and the Scientific Approach: Nursing research provides a way for nursing questions and problems to be studied in a broader context.
  - Quantitative - precise measurement
  - Qualitative - difficult to quantify or categorize

Examples of EBP

- NG tube – no auscultation with air to verify tube placement. Aspirating gastric contents and testing the pH give an indication of placement (pH should be 5.5 or below).

- Bathing an MRSA patient: Clients with MRSA or other drug-resistant organisms to be bathed with pre-moistened cloths or warm water containing chlorhexidine solution. Bathing clients in this way can significantly reduce MRSA infection.
- Skin Hair removal for procedures and surgery: Use Clippers. No shaving.
- Neonatal resuscitation: Positive pressure ventilation (PPV) is started if heart rate is <100/min. Chest compressions are started only after at least 30 seconds of quality PPV, if the newborn's heart rate still remains <60/min.
- Hypotension – No more Trendelenburg – instead supine and raise legs to 45

Quality and Performance Improvement

- Quality improvement: Continuous study and improvement of the processes to meet the needs of patients and others
    - Indicators of overall quality of care - The outcomes should be objective and measurable. Ex: fall prevention, medication error, decreases in hospital-acquired infection, and pressure ulcers
- Performance improvement: organization analyzes and evaluates current performance- help with QI. Chart audits, Patient Satisfaction Survey, incident reports

Bioterrorism

- Terrorism by intentional release of biological agents (bacteria, virus, toxins)
- Biological agents can spread through air, water, food etc.
- Three categories: Category A, B and C
- Category A
    - High-priority agents include organisms that pose a risk to national security. These agents can be easily disseminated or transmitted from person to person; result in high mortality rates and have the potential for major public health impact; might cause public panic and social disruption; and require special action for public health preparedness.
- Agents/Diseases in Category A
    - Anthrax (Bacillus anthracis)
    - Botulism (Clostridium botulinum toxin): Affects nervous system

- Plague (Yersinia pestis), Smallpox (variola major)
- Viral hemorrhagic fevers (Ebola)
- Tularemia (Francisella tularensis): Tularemia is a disease that can infect animals and people. Rabbits and rodents are especially susceptible and often die in large numbers during outbreaks: Can spread to people by tick bites, contact with animals, drinking contaminated water etc.
- Category B
  - Second highest priority agents that are moderately easy to disseminate, which require specific enhancements of CDC's diagnostic capacity and enhanced disease surveillance.
  - Ex: Food safety threats (Salmonella, E. coli, Shigella), Brucellosis (infectious disease caused by bacteria; from infected animals and their milk) Cholera

- Category C
  - Third highest priority agents include emerging pathogens that could be engineered for mass dissemination in the future because of availability, ease of production and dissemination; and potential for high morbidity and mortality rates and major health impact.
  - Ex: Nipah virus and Hantavirus (spread by rodents, cause pulmonary and hemorrhagic syndrome)

Anthrax

- Anthrax is a serious infectious disease (Bacteria: Bacillus anthracis)
- Anthrax is not contagious from person to person.
- People can get sick with anthrax if they come in contact with infected animals or contaminated animal products when spores get into the body.
- This may be when people breathe in spores, eat food or drink water that is contaminated with spores, or get spores in a cut or scrape in the skin.
- In bioterrorism, microscopic spores could be put into powders, sprays, food, and water. (Letters – 2001)

- If untreated, to spread throughout the body and cause severe illness and even death.

Types of anthrax

- Cutaneous:
    - Most common form of anthrax infection, A group of small blisters or bumps that may itch.
    - Infection usually develops from 1 to 7 days after exposure.
- Inhalation:
    - Inhalation anthrax is considered to be the deadliest form of anthrax. Fever and chills, Chest Discomfort, Shortness of breath, Confusion or dizziness, Cough
- Gastrointestinal:
    - Fever, chills, dysphagia, Nausea, hematemesis, Diarrhea, Stomach pain
- Injection:
    - This type of infection has never been reported in the United States.
- Vaccination
    - The anthrax vaccine helps protect people from anthrax
    - Pre-exposure Vaccination: For adults 18 through 65 years of age who may be at risk for occupational exposure to the bacteria:
    - Three groups:
        - Certain laboratory workers who work with anthrax
        - Some people who handle animals or animal products, such as veterinarians who handle infected animals
        - Certain U.S. military personnel
- Post-exposure Vaccination
    - 60 days of antimicrobial prophylaxis + 3 subcutaneous doses of the anthrax vaccine
- Diagnosis

- Inhalation anthrax: chest X-rays or CT scans can confirm if the patient has mediastinal widening or pleural effusion, which are X-ray findings typically seen in patients with inhalation anthrax.
- The only ways to confirm an Anthrax diagnosis are:
  - To measure antibodies or toxin in blood
  - To test directly for Bacillus anthracis in a sample of blood, skin lesion swab, spinal fluid, or respiratory secretions
- Medication – Antibiotics

Botulism

- Caused by a toxin made by clostridium group bacteria that attacks the body's nerves. (Clostridium botulinum, Clostridium butyricum, Clostridium baratii)
- Botulism usually starts with weakness of the muscles that control the eyes, face, mouth, and throat. Diplopia, Blurred vision, Ptosis, Slurred speech, Dysphagia
- This weakness progress to entire body: Respiratory paralysis - death.
- Diagnostics:
  - Nerve and muscle function tests (nerve conduction study [NCS] and electromyography [EMG])
  - Blood work (toxins)/ LP/ CT scans might also be used.

Types of Botulism

- Foodborne botulism: Contaminated food: improperly canned, preserved, or fermented food. Common food: Chopped garlic in oil, Canned cheese sauce, Canned tomatoes, Carrot juice, Baked potatoes wrapped in foil
- Wound botulism: Bacteria get into a wound and make a toxin
- Infant botulism: Spores of the bacteria get into an infant's intestines (Raw agricultural products).

- Adult intestinal toxemia (also known as Adult Intestinal Colonization) - similar to infant botulism
- Iatrogenic botulism: if too much botulinum toxin is injected for cosmetic reasons, such as for wrinkles, or medical reasons, such as for migraine headaches.
- Infant with botulism
  - appear lethargic, feed poorly, be constipated, have a weak cry, have poor muscle tone (appear "floppy")
- Treatment:
  - Antitoxin (cant heal, but prevent further damage)
  - Antibiotics
  - Supportive care
  - Might need long term therapy to recover (PT/OT/Respiratory Assistance)
- Prevention
  - Proper food preservation and use: Keep food refrigerated. Throw away unused food after opening.
  - Refrigerate homemade oils infused with garlic or herbs and throw away any unused oils after 4 days.
  - Keep potatoes that have been baked while wrapped in aluminum foil hot (at temperatures above 140°F) until they are served or refrigerate them with the foil loosened.
  - Refrigerate any canned or pickled foods after opening them.
  - Proper wound care, Handwashing
  - Infants: do not feed honey till one year.
  - BabyBIG®: Botulism antitoxin for infantile botulism: If given, don't give any live vaccine for 6 months.
  - Botulism is not transmitted person-to-person (Standard precautions are enough)

Smallpox

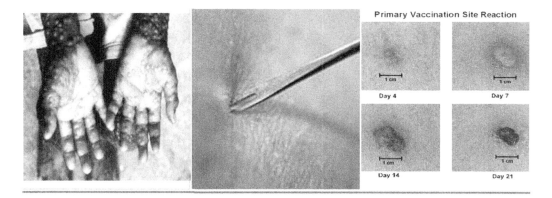

- By variola virus: spread from one person to another
- Signs and Symptoms: High fever, Head and body aches, vomiting, sores, and rash
- Smallpox patients become contagious once the first sores appear in their mouth and throat. They remain contagious until their last smallpox scab fall off.
- Virus spreads through droplets (cough or sneeze) or contaminated objects (bed/cloth)
- Meds: Antiviral (tecovirimat, cidofovir and brincidofovir)

Smallpox Vaccine

- Prevention: smallpox vaccine (3-5 yrs. protection)
- Need booster vaccinations every 3 years
- Live vaccine. Don't use alcohol as it might inactivate live virus. Vaccine does not contain smallpox virus (it is developed from vaccinia virus)
- Technique: Multiple puncture vaccination technique (Scarification) About 15 quick pokes in 5 mm diameter- over skin. Percutaneous route only. Given in deltoid.
- Use bifurcated vaccination needle.
- After care: Keep the site covered, until scab falls off (may take 4 weeks). To avoid vaccinia infection from the vaccination
- Smallpox is eradicated – so no routine vaccination. It is only for people with high risk (Lab worker/scientists)

Lab Values

CBC		ABG		ELECTROLYTE	
Platelet	150,000 to 400,000 mm3	PH	7.35 -7.45	SODIUM	135- 145
Hb	Female 12 to 16 g/dL; male 14 to 18 g/dL.	HCO3	22- 28	POTASSIUM	3.5-5.0
Hct	female 37 to 47%; male 42 to 52%.	PCO2	35-45	CALCIUM	8.6- 10.2
RBC	Female 4.2 to 5.4 million/uL; male 4.7 to 6.1 million/uL	PO2	80-100 mmHg	MAGNESIUM	1.3 -2.1
WBC	4,000 to 11,000/mm3.	SAO2	> 95%	IRON	Females: 60 to 160 mcg/dL Males: 80 to 180 mcg/dL
Platelet	150,000-400,000 u/l			CHLORIDE	98 - 106
PT	11 to 12.5 sec	**THYROID**		PHOSPHORUS	3 -4.5
PTT	1.5 to 2 times normal range of 30 to 40 seconds (desired range for anticoagulation)	TSH	0.4- 4.2 mU/L	GLUCOSE FBS	70-110
INR	INR 0.7 to 1.8.-	T3	0.6 – 3.14	Hba1c	Less than

	normal. 2 to 3 on warfarin (Coumadin) therapy		nmol/L	(Glycosylated Hb)	6.5
FIBRINOGEN	200 to 400 mg/dL	T4	4.6- 11 mcg/dl	POST PRANDIAL	Less than 140
CLOTTING TIME	4-10 mts	**LIVER FUNCTION**		**LIPIDS**	
BLEEDING TIME	2-7 mts	TOTAL BILIRUBIN	0.2 – 1.2 mg/dl	HDL	>50 mg/dl
ESR	Less than 30	DIRECT BILI	0.1 – 0.3 mg/dl	LDL	100 or less
RENAL		INDIRECT BILI	0.1- 1 mg/dl	TOTAL CHOLESTEROL	<200 mg/dl
URIC ACID	F: 2.3 – 6.6 M: 4.4 – 7.6	Alk. Phosphatase	38-126 U/L	TRIGLYCERIDE	<150 mg/dl
BUN	6-20	AST	10-30 U/L	D Dimer	0.43 to 2.33 mcg/mL 0 to 250 ng/mL
CREATININE	0.6 to 1.3 mg/dl	ALT	10-40 U/L	BNP	100 or less
AMONIA		GGT	0-30 U/L	CK	20 -200 U/L
URINE SPECIFIC GRAVITY	1.003 – 1.030	Ammonia	11 to 32 μmol/L		
GFR	90-130	**PANCREAS**			
URINE PH	4-8	AMYLASE	30-122 U/L		
URINE OSMOLARITY	300-1300	LIPASE	31- 186 U/L		

Good Luck with your Exam!

For further studies and courses please visit www.AppleRN.com or contact any of our associates at

+1 651-615-5511 (USA)

 +91 953-930-5316 (India)

(WhatsApp available on all numbers)

Other resources

https://www.youtube.com/learnnursinginternational

https://www.facebook.com/AppleRNClasses

References

- CDC.gov, Nursing journals, recently published Research articles, ncsbn.org
- Lewis's Medical-Surgical Nursing
- ATI nursing Education Resources
- Brunner & Suddath's Textbook of Medical-Surgical Nursing
- Content Mastery Series Review module, ATI nursing Education
- Wong's Essentials of Pediatric Nursing
- Saunders Comprehensive Review for NCLEX RN Examination
- Wong Maternal Child Nursing Care
- Lippincott manual of nursing practice
- Videbeck Psychiatric-Mental Health Nursing
- Mosby's Comprehensive Review of Nursing for NCLEX-RN Examination

Printed in Great Britain
by Amazon

46191461R00311